SAVE 50% OFF
THE COVER PRICE!

IT'S LIKE GETTING 6 ISSUES

FREE!

OVER 350+ PAGES PER ISSUE

THE WORLD'S MOST POPULAR MANGA

This monthly magazine contains 7 of the coolest manga available in the U.S., PLUS anime news, and info about video & card games, toys AND more!

❏ **I want 12 HUGE issues of SHONEN JUMP for only $29.95*!**

NAME

ADDRESS

CITY/STATE/ZIP

EMAIL ADDRESS   **DATE OF BIRTH**

❏ YES, send me via email information, advertising, offers, and promotions related to VIZ Media, SHONEN JUMP, and/or their business partners.

❏ **CHECK ENCLOSED** (payable to SHONEN JUMP)   ❏ **BILL ME LATER**

CREDIT CARD: ❏ **Visa** ❏ **Mastercard**

ACCOUNT NUMBER   **EXP. DATE**

SIGNATURE

D0180744

P9GNC1

RATED
FOR TEEN
ratings.viz.com

VIZ media
www.viz.com

Takeshi Obata

This is Char Aznable, a Greek tortoise. He can move swiftly, but when he gets excited he blows snot bubbles.

—Takeshi Obata

I t all began when Yumi Hotta played a pick-up game of go with her father-in-law. As she was learning how to play, Ms. Hotta thought it might be fun to create a story around the traditional board game. More confident in her storytelling abilities than her drawing skills, she submitted the beginnings of **Hikaru no Go** to **Weekly Shonen Jump**'s Story King Award. The Story King Award is an award that picks the best story, manga, character design and youth (under 15) manga submissions every year in Japan. As fate would have it, Ms. Hotta's story (originally named, "*Kokonotsu no Hoshi*"), was a runner-up in the "Story" category of the Story King Award. Many years earlier, Takeshi Obata was a runner-up for the Tezuka Award, another Japanese manga contest sponsored by **Weekly Shonen Jump** and **Monthly Shonen Jump**. An editor assigned to Mr. Obata's artwork came upon Ms. Hotta's story and paired the two for a full-fledged manga about go. The rest is modern go history.

HIKARU NO GO VOL. 16
The SHONEN JUMP Manga Edition

STORY BY YUMI HOTTA
ART BY TAKESHI OBATA
Supervised by YUKARI UMEZAWA (5 Dan)

Translation & English Adaptation/Naoko Amemiya
English Script Consultant/Janice Kim (3 Dan)
Touch-up Art & Lettering/Inori Fukuda Trant
Design/Julie Behn
Editor/Gary Leach

Editor in Chief, Books/Alvin Lu
Editor in Chief, Magazines/Marc Weidenbaum
VP, Publishing Licensing/Rika Inouye
VP, Sales & Product Marketing/Gonzalo Ferreyra
VP, Creative/Linda Espinosa
Publisher/Hyoe Narita

Printed in Canada

Published by VIZ Media, LLC
P.O. Box 77010
San Francisco, CA 94107

SHONEN JUMP Manga Edition
10 9 8 7 6 5 4 3 2 1
First printing, August 2009

www.viz.com

PARENTAL ADVISORY
HIKARU NO GO is rated A
and is suitable for readers
of all ages.
ratings.viz.com

THE WORLD'S
MOST POPULAR MANGA

www.shonenjump.com

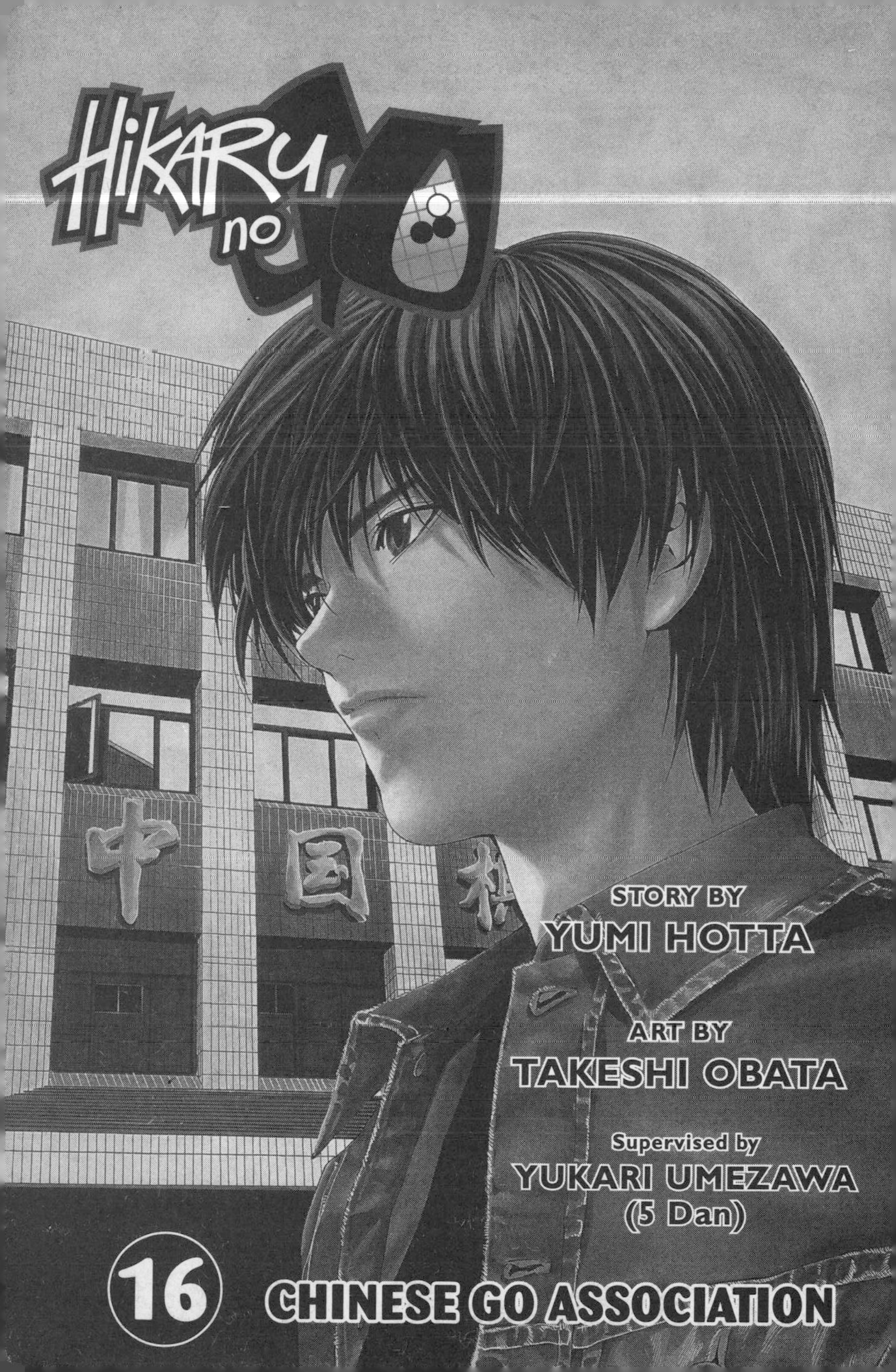

HIKARU no GO

STORY BY
YUMI HOTTA

ART BY
TAKESHI OBATA

Supervised by
YUKARI UMEZAWA
(5 Dan)

16 CHINESE GO ASSOCIATION

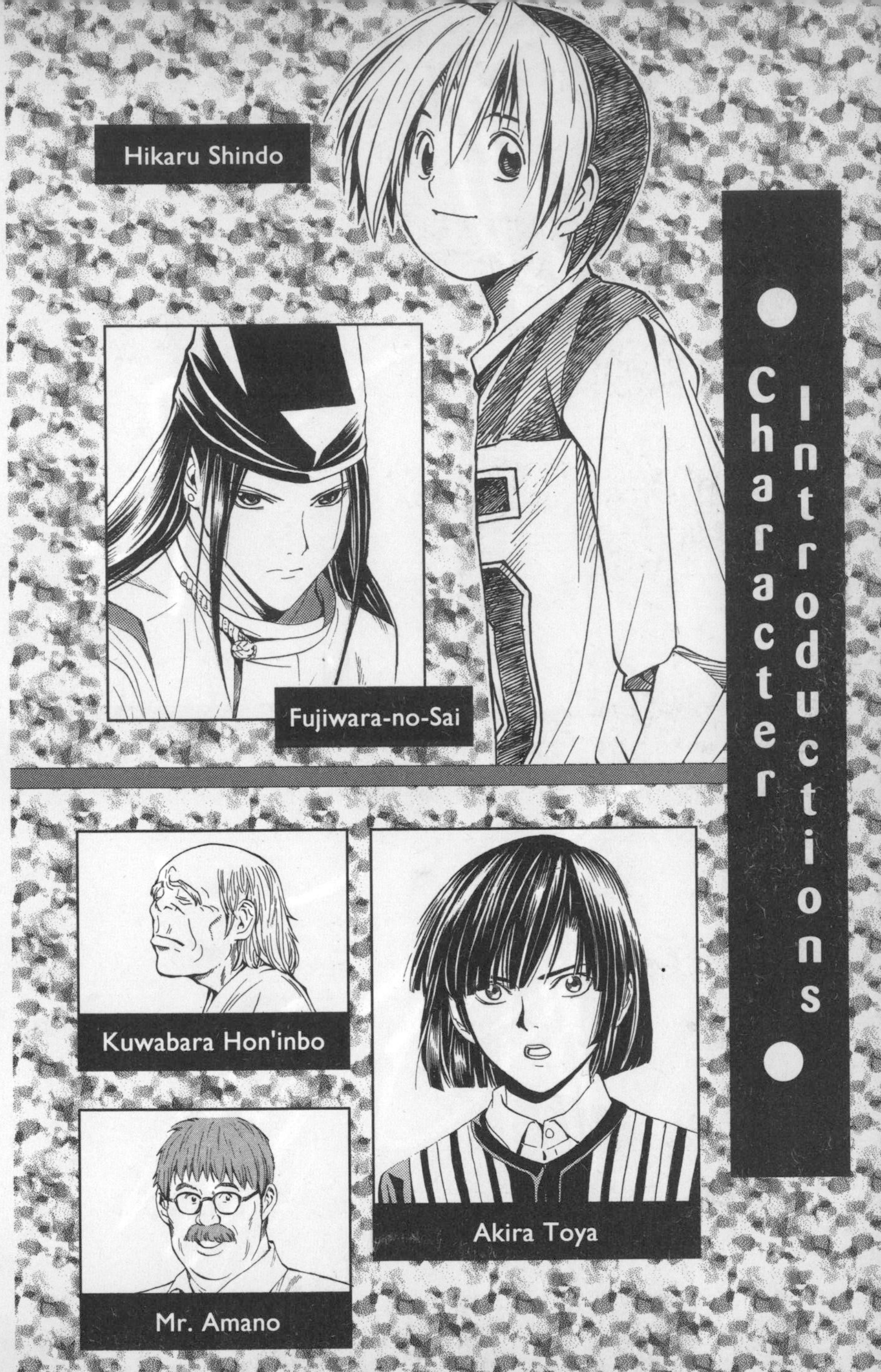
Character Introductions
Hikaru Shindo
Fujiwara-no-Sai
Akira Toya
Kuwabara Hon'inbo
Mr. Amano

Shinichiro Isumi
Kosuke Ochi
Akari Fujisaki
Yuki Mitani
Mr. Kawai
Kaneko
Yoshitaka Waya

Story Thus Far

Hikaru Shindo discovers an old go board one day up in his grandfather's attic. The moment Hikaru touches the board, the spirit of Fujiwara-no-Sai, a genius go player from Japan's Heian Era, enters his consciousness. Sai's love of go inspires Hikaru, as does a meeting with the child prodigy Akira Toya—son of go master Toya Meijin.

Worried about vanishing, Sai persistently pesters Hikaru to let him play. Hikaru does not take Sai's pleas seriously. When Hikaru goes to a go seminar to play teaching games, he allows Sai to play an intoxicated Ogata Judan. Sai wins. However, soon after returning home Sai abruptly disappears.

Hikaru refuses to accept that Sai is gone and sets out in search of him. Not finding him at the Go Association, Hikaru sets off to Innoshima, the birthplace of Shusaku, Sai's previous host. After a fruitless search Hikaru finds himself back at the Go Association in a room packed with historical archives. Looking at Shusaku's game records, Hikaru gains a renewed appreciation for Sai's genius and resolves never to play go again. When Hikaru fails to show up for his matches, his rivals start wondering what's going on. Meanwhile, Isumi, who struggled at last year's pro test, heads for some goodwill games in China.

CONTENTS

16

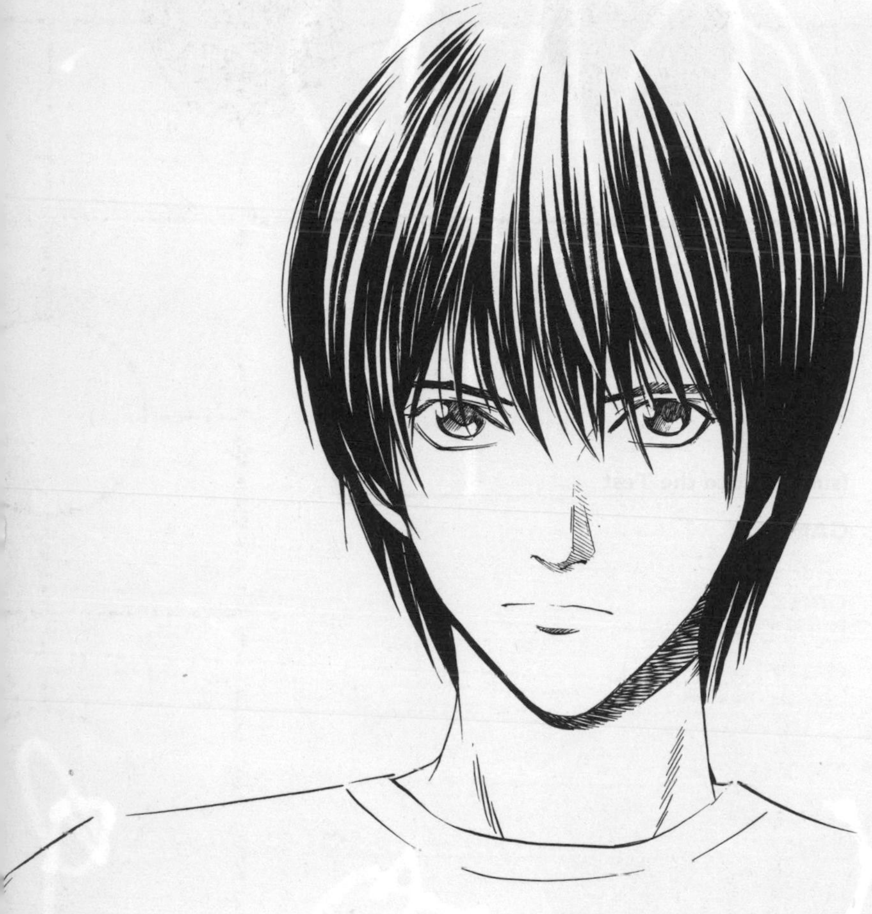

Game 131 "Chinese Go Association"

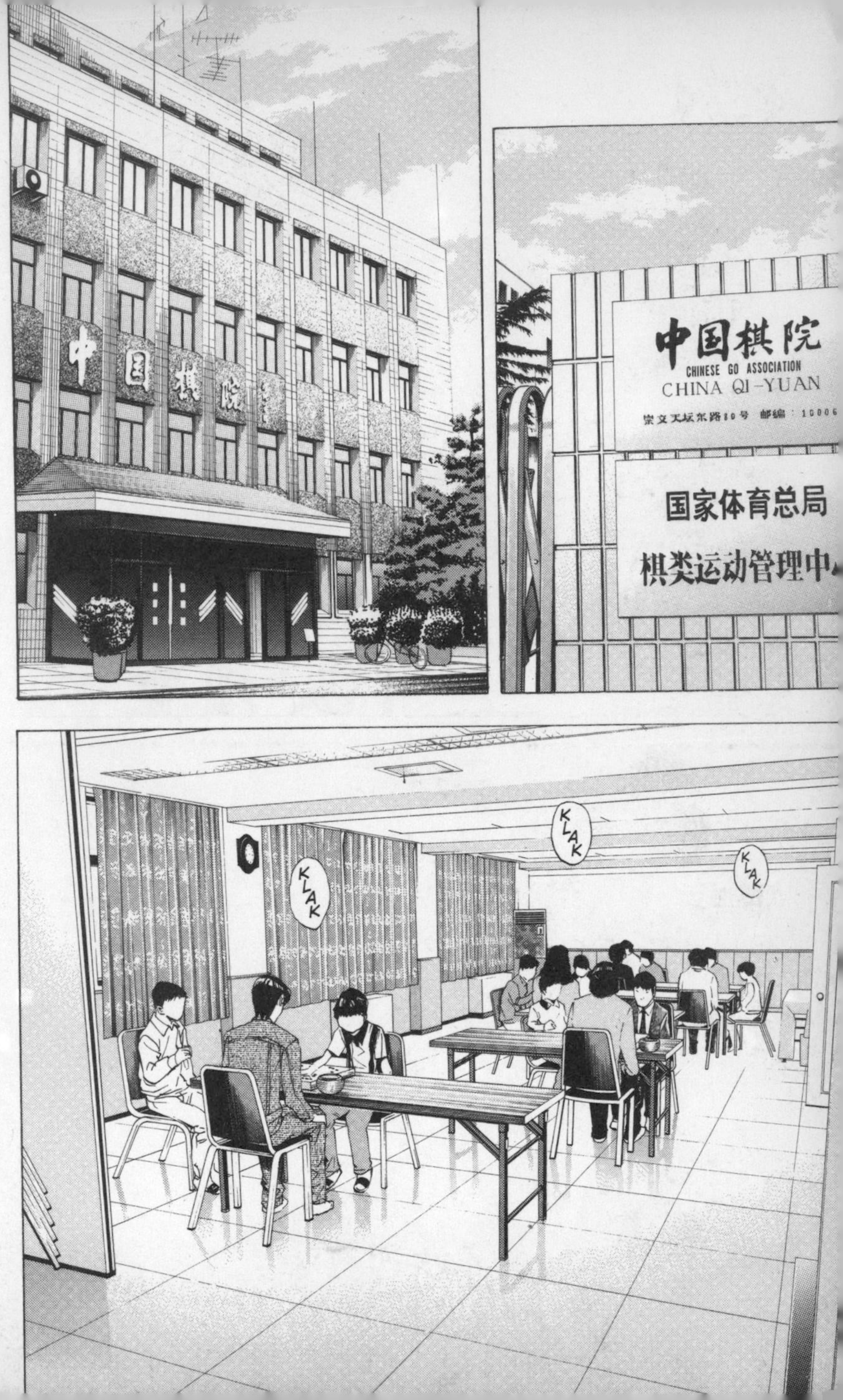
中国棋院
CHINESE GO ASSOCIATION
CHINA QI-YUAN
宗文天坛东路80号 邮编：10006
国家体育总局
棋类运动管理中
中国棋院
KLAK
KLAK
KLAK

READ THIS WAY

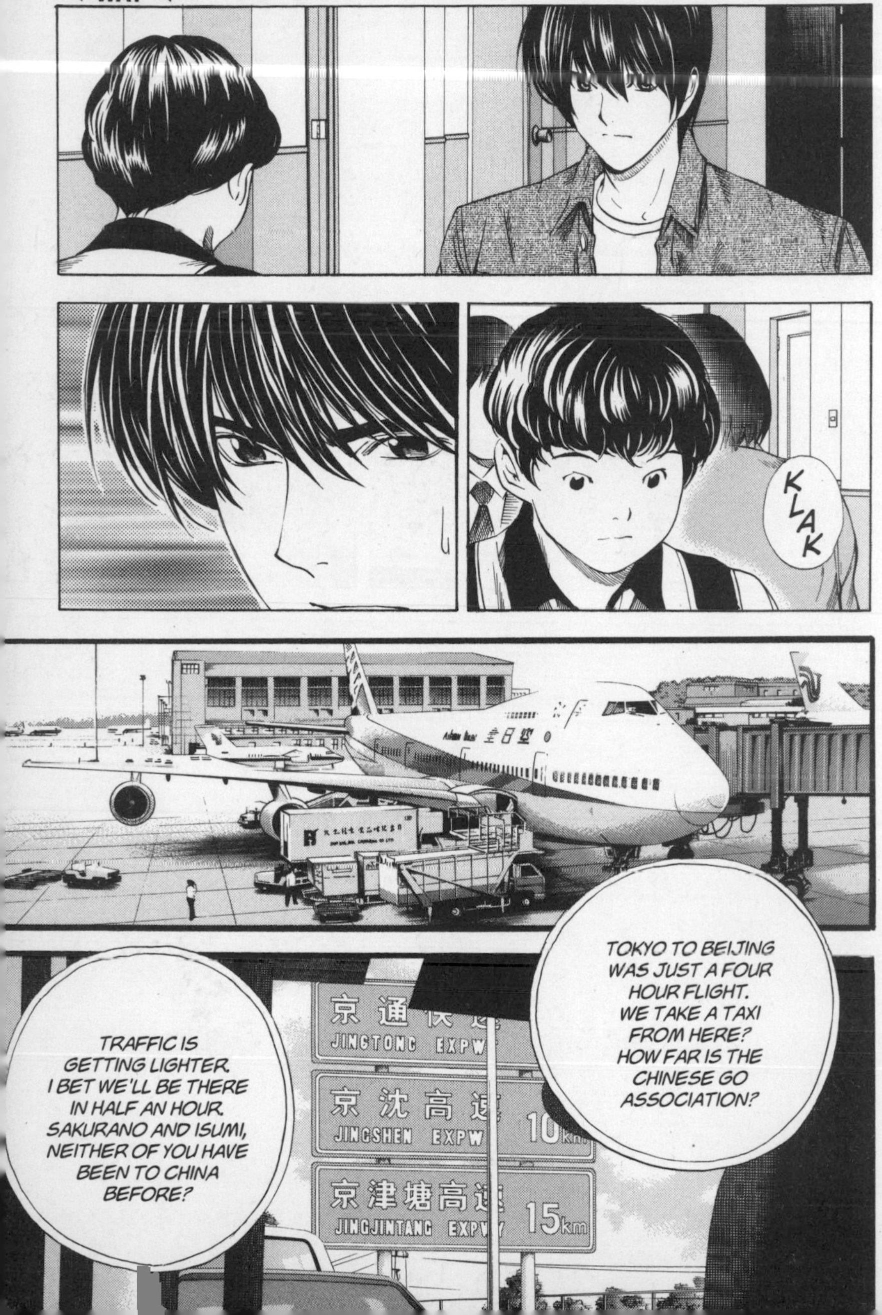
KLAK
TOKYO TO BEIJING WAS JUST A FOUR HOUR FLIGHT. WE TAKE A TAXI FROM HERE? HOW FAR IS THE CHINESE GO ASSOCIATION?
TRAFFIC IS GETTING LIGHTER. I BET WE'LL BE THERE IN HALF AN HOUR. SAKURANO AND ISUMI, NEITHER OF YOU HAVE BEEN TO CHINA BEFORE?
京沈高速
JINGSHEN
10
京津塘高速
JINGJINTANG
15km

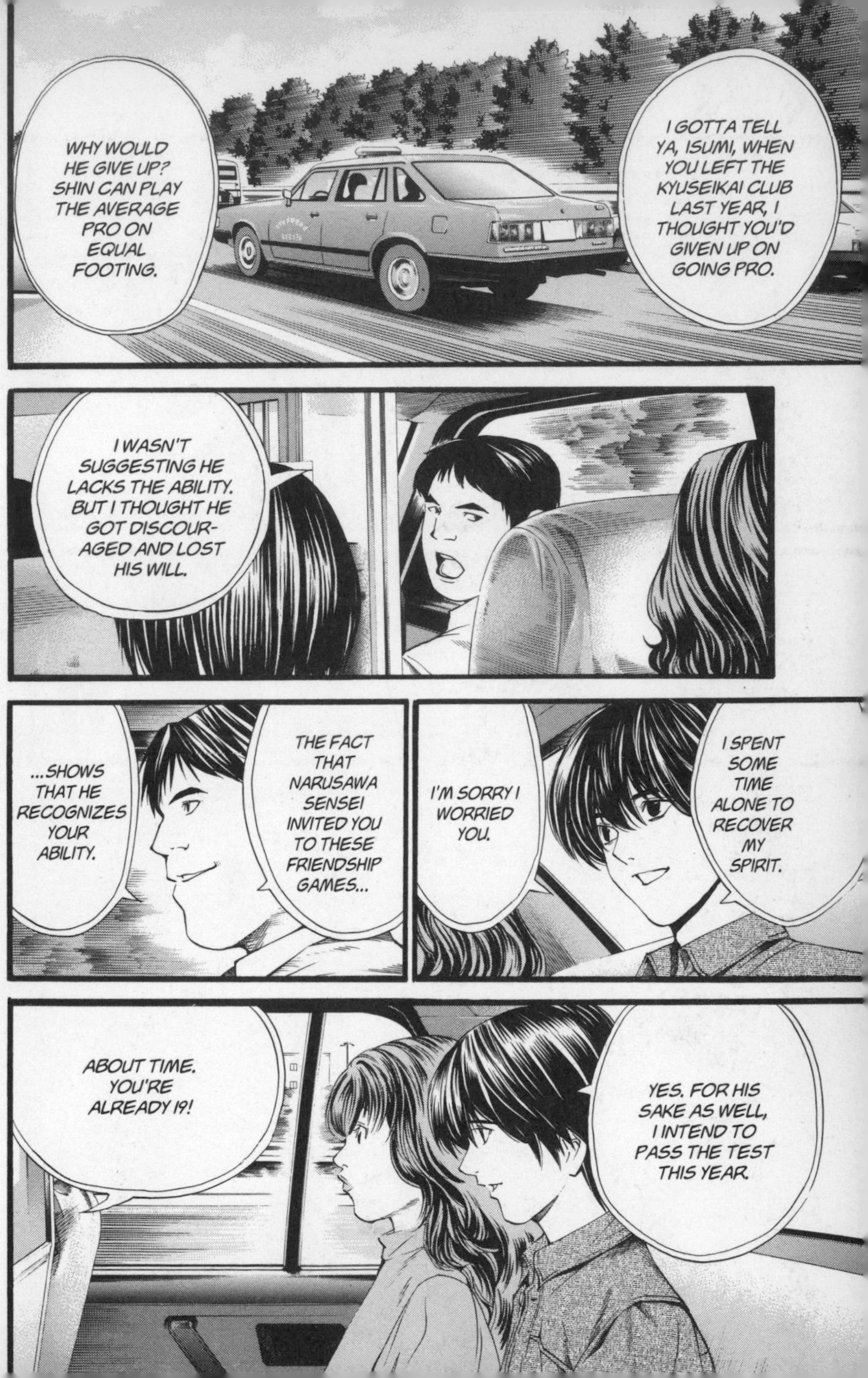
I GOTTA TELL YA, ISUMI, WHEN YOU LEFT THE KYUSEIKAI CLUB LAST YEAR, I THOUGHT YOU'D GIVEN UP ON GOING PRO.
WHY WOULD HE GIVE UP? SHIN CAN PLAY THE AVERAGE PRO ON EQUAL FOOTING.
I WASN'T SUGGESTING HE LACKS THE ABILITY. BUT I THOUGHT HE GOT DISCOURAGED AND LOST HIS WILL.
I SPENT SOME TIME ALONE TO RECOVER MY SPIRIT.
I'M SORRY I WORRIED YOU.
THE FACT THAT NARUSAWA SENSEI INVITED YOU TO THESE FRIENDSHIP GAMES...
...SHOWS THAT HE RECOGNIZES YOUR ABILITY.
YES. FOR HIS SAKE AS WELL, I INTEND TO PASS THE TEST THIS YEAR.
ABOUT TIME. YOU'RE ALREADY 19!

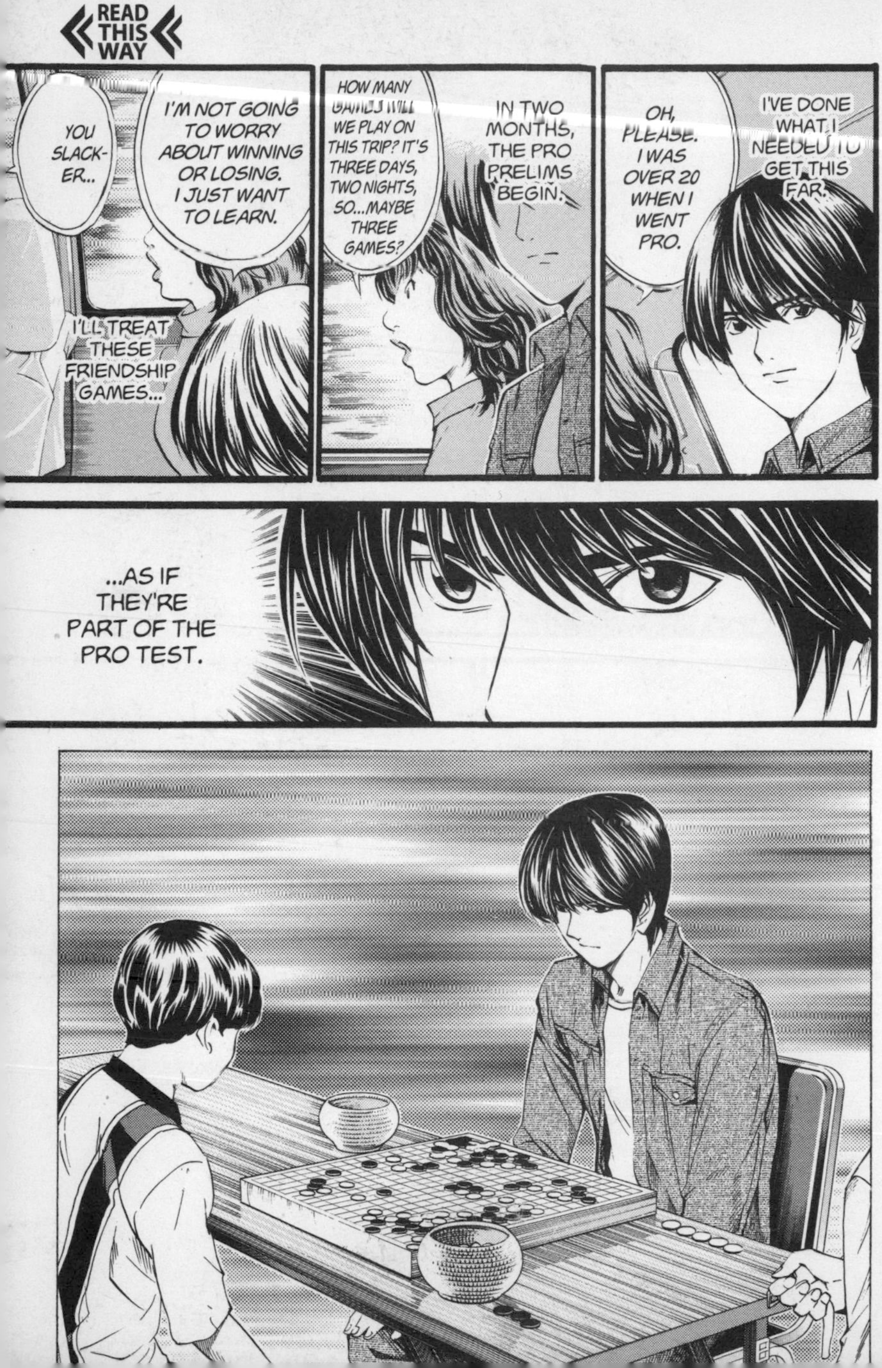
READ THIS WAY
I'VE DONE WHAT I NEEDED TO GET THIS FAR.
OH, PLEASE. I WAS OVER 20 WHEN I WENT PRO.
IN TWO MONTHS, THE PRO PRELIMS BEGIN.
HOW MANY GAMES WILL WE PLAY ON THIS TRIP? IT'S THREE DAYS, TWO NIGHTS, SO...MAYBE THREE GAMES?
I'M NOT GOING TO WORRY ABOUT WINNING OR LOSING. I JUST WANT TO LEARN.
YOU SLACKER...
I'LL TREAT THESE FRIENDSHIP GAMES...
...AS IF THEY'RE PART OF THE PRO TEST.

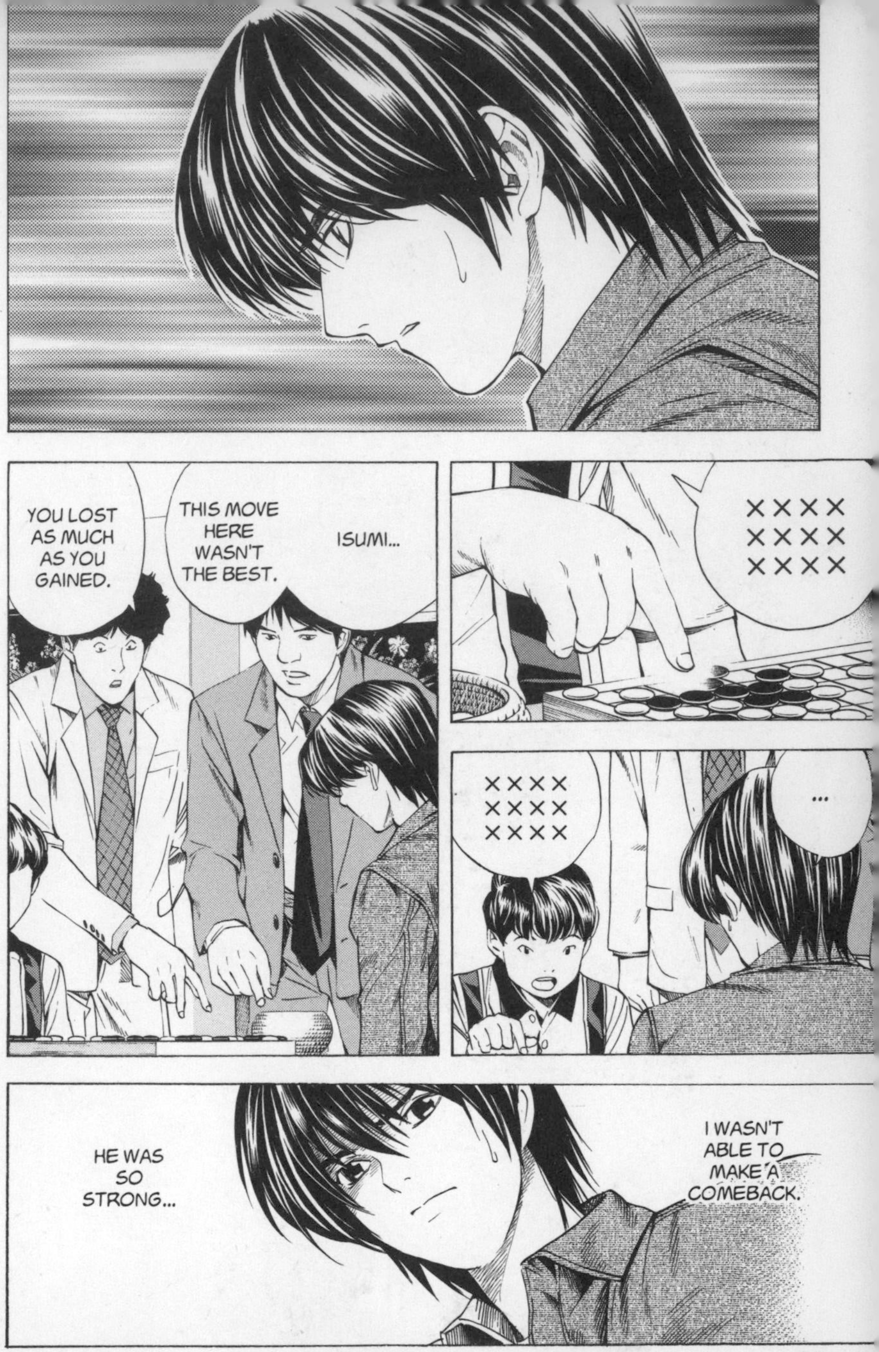
××××××××××××
...
××××××××××××
ISUMI...
THIS MOVE HERE WASN'T THE BEST.
YOU LOST AS MUCH AS YOU GAINED.
I WASN'T ABLE TO MAKE A COMEBACK.
HE WAS SO STRONG...

READ THIS WAY

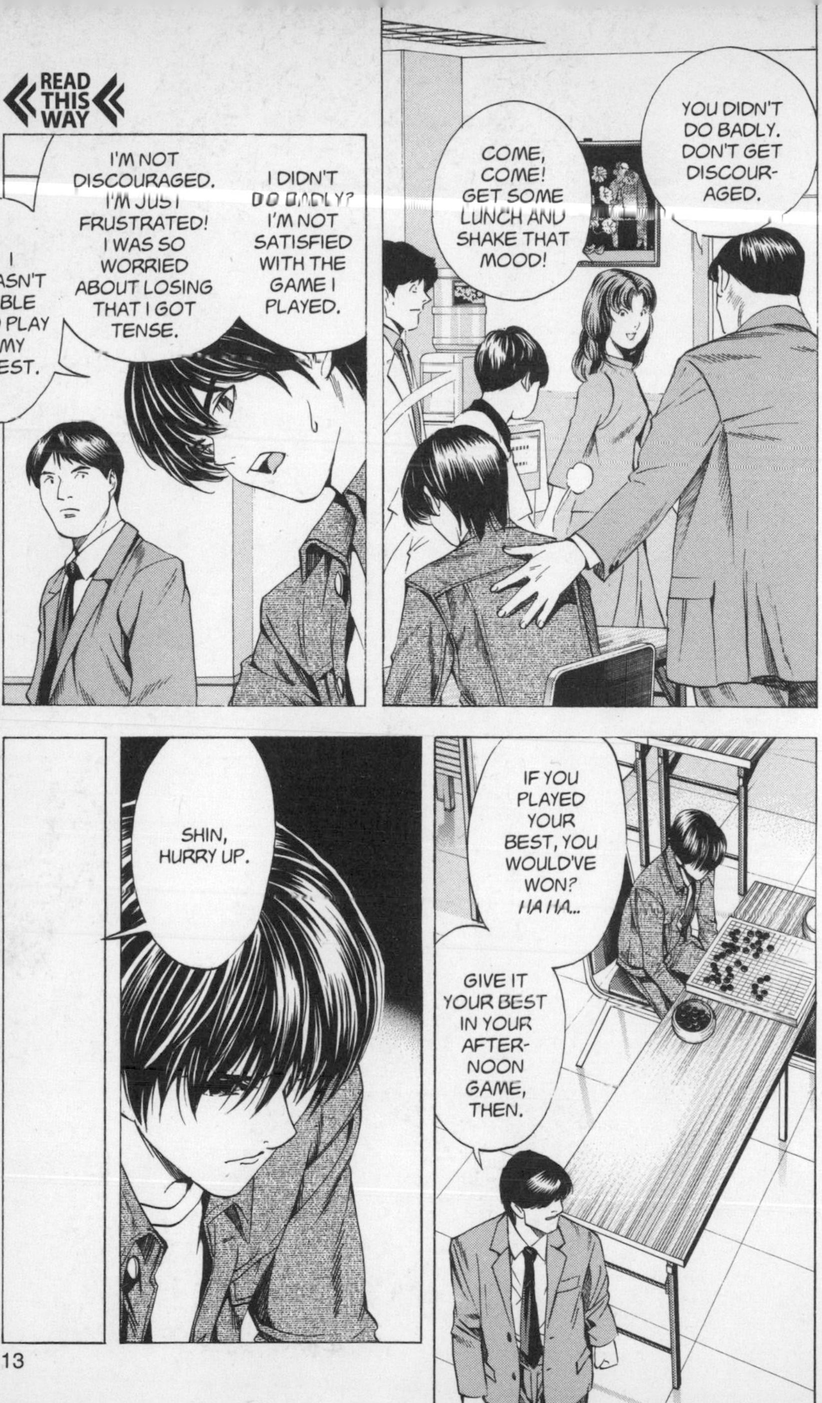

YOU DIDN'T DO BADLY. DON'T GET DISCOURAGED.
COME, COME! GET SOME LUNCH AND SHAKE THAT MOOD!
I DIDN'T DO BADLY? I'M NOT SATISFIED WITH THE GAME I PLAYED.
I'M NOT DISCOURAGED. I'M JUST FRUSTRATED! I WAS SO WORRIED ABOUT LOSING THAT I GOT TENSE.
I WASN'T ABLE TO PLAY MY BEST.
IF YOU PLAYED YOUR BEST, YOU WOULD'VE WON? HA HA...
GIVE IT YOUR BEST IN YOUR AFTERNOON GAME, THEN.
SHIN, HURRY UP.

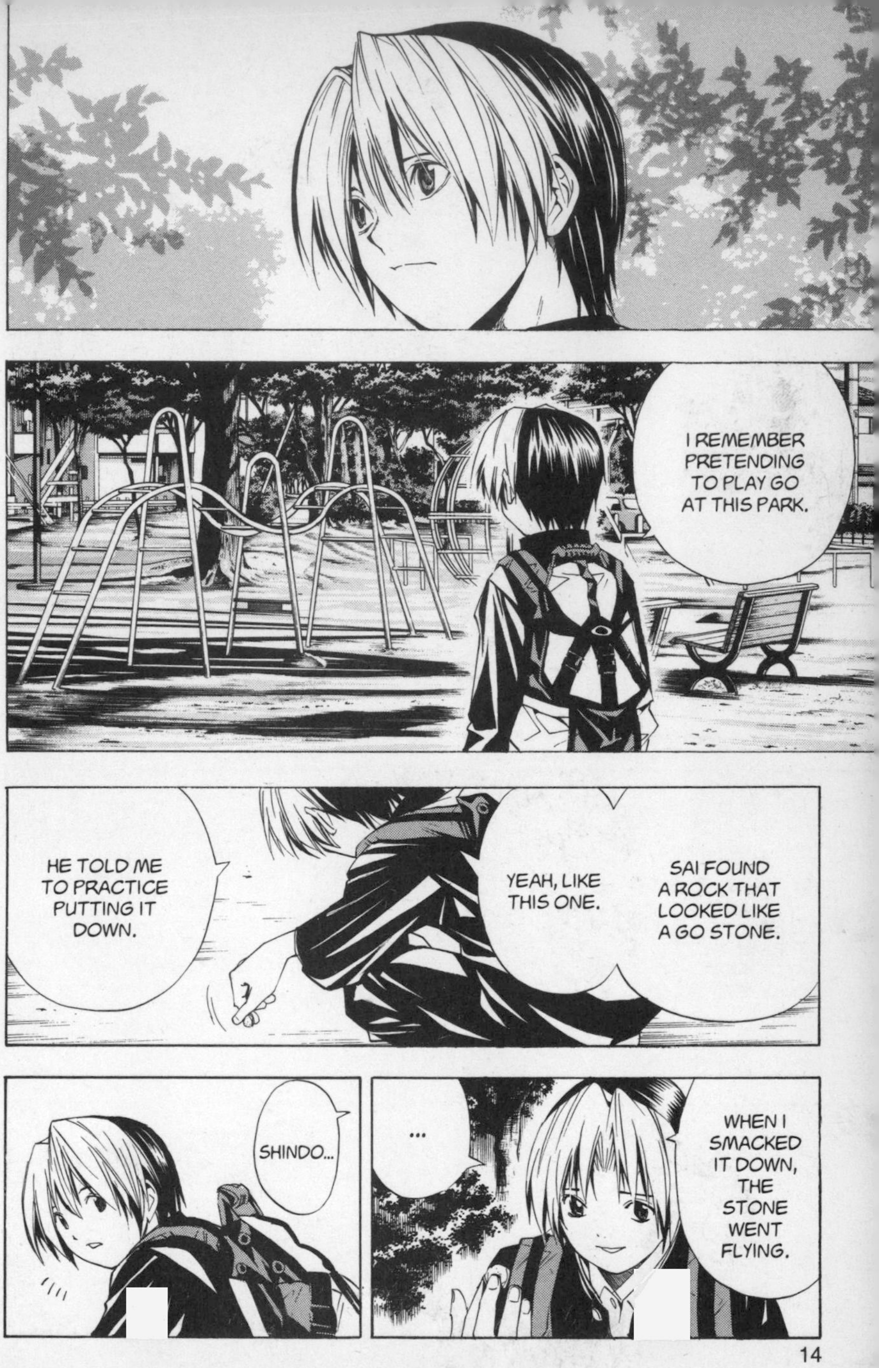
I REMEMBER PRETENDING TO PLAY GO AT THIS PARK.
SAI FOUND A ROCK THAT LOOKED LIKE A GO STONE.
YEAH, LIKE THIS ONE.
HE TOLD ME TO PRACTICE PUTTING IT DOWN.
WHEN I SMACKED IT DOWN, THE STONE WENT FLYING.
...
SHINDO...

READ THIS WAY

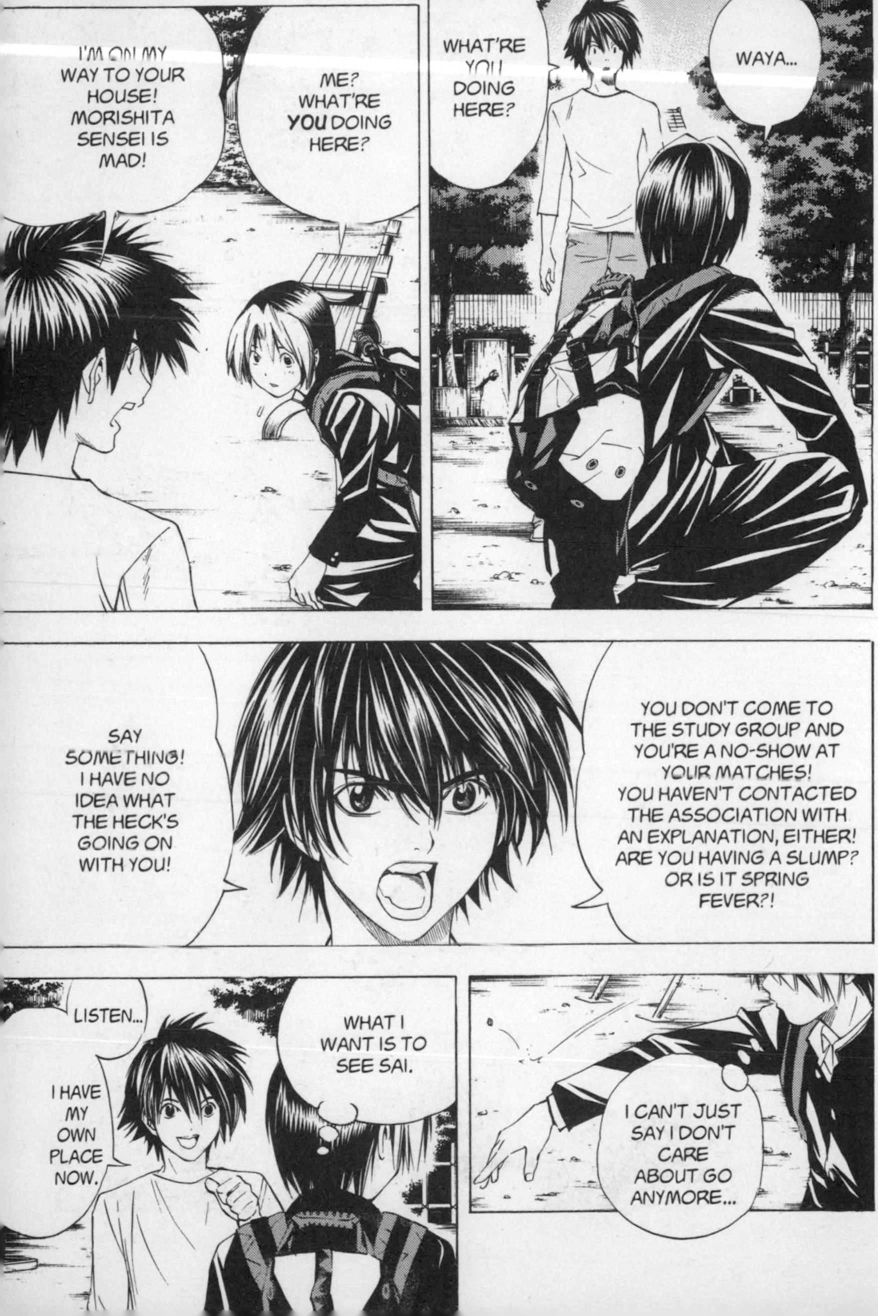
WAYA...
WHAT'RE YOU DOING HERE?
ME? WHAT'RE YOU DOING HERE?
I'M ON MY WAY TO YOUR HOUSE! MORISHITA SENSEI IS MAD!
YOU DON'T COME TO THE STUDY GROUP AND YOU'RE A NO-SHOW AT YOUR MATCHES! YOU HAVEN'T CONTACTED THE ASSOCIATION WITH AN EXPLANATION, EITHER! ARE YOU HAVING A SLUMP? OR IS IT SPRING FEVER?!
SAY SOMETHING! I HAVE NO IDEA WHAT THE HECK'S GOING ON WITH YOU!
I CAN'T JUST SAY I DON'T CARE ABOUT GO ANYMORE...
WHAT I WANT IS TO SEE SAI.
LISTEN...
I HAVE MY OWN PLACE NOW.

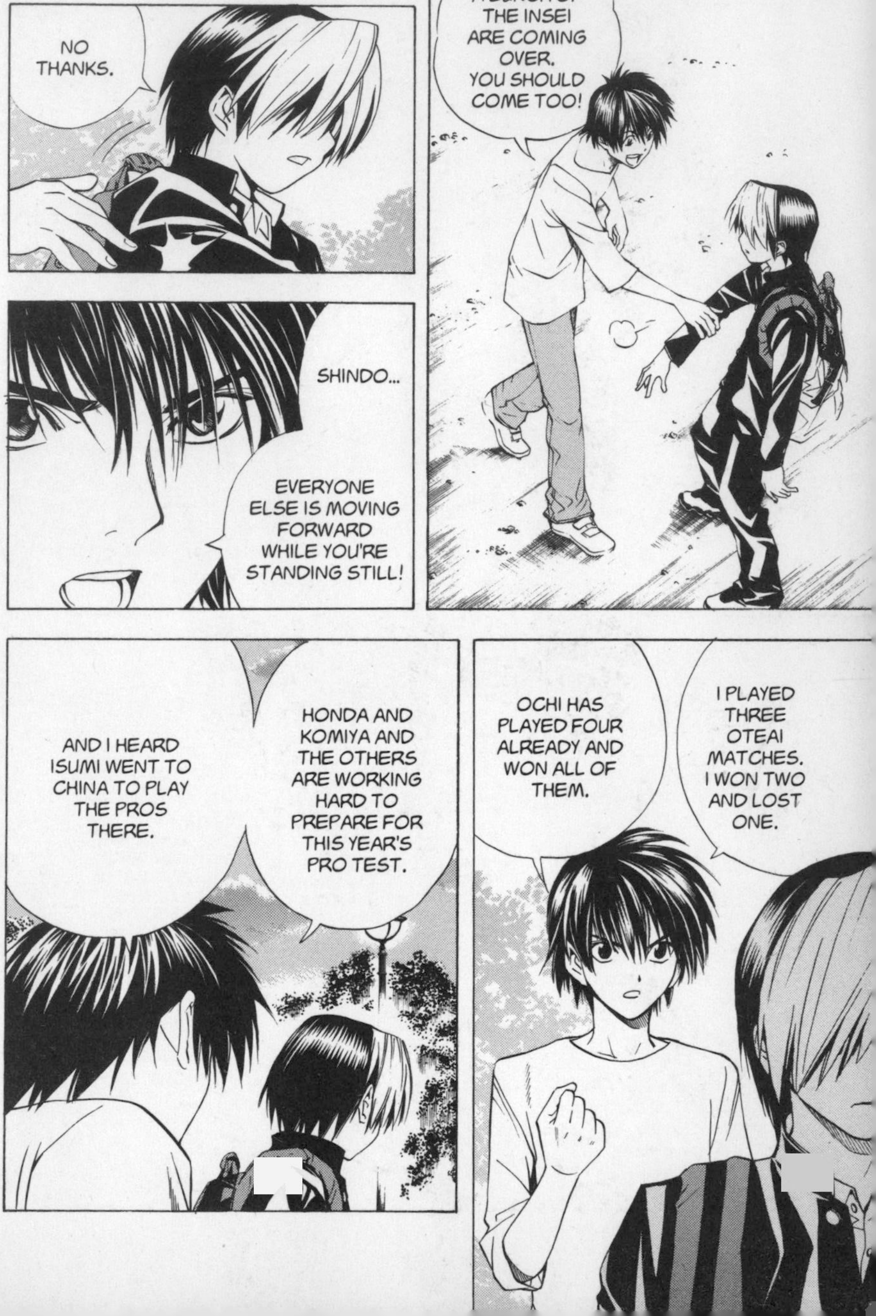
A BUNCH OF THE INSEI ARE COMING OVER. YOU SHOULD COME TOO!
NO THANKS.
SHINDO...
EVERYONE ELSE IS MOVING FORWARD WHILE YOU'RE STANDING STILL!
I PLAYED THREE OTEAI MATCHES. I WON TWO AND LOST ONE.
OCHI HAS PLAYED FOUR ALREADY AND WON ALL OF THEM.
HONDA AND KOMIYA AND THE OTHERS ARE WORKING HARD TO PREPARE FOR THIS YEAR'S PRO TEST.
AND I HEARD ISUMI WENT TO CHINA TO PLAY THE PROS THERE.

READ THIS WAY

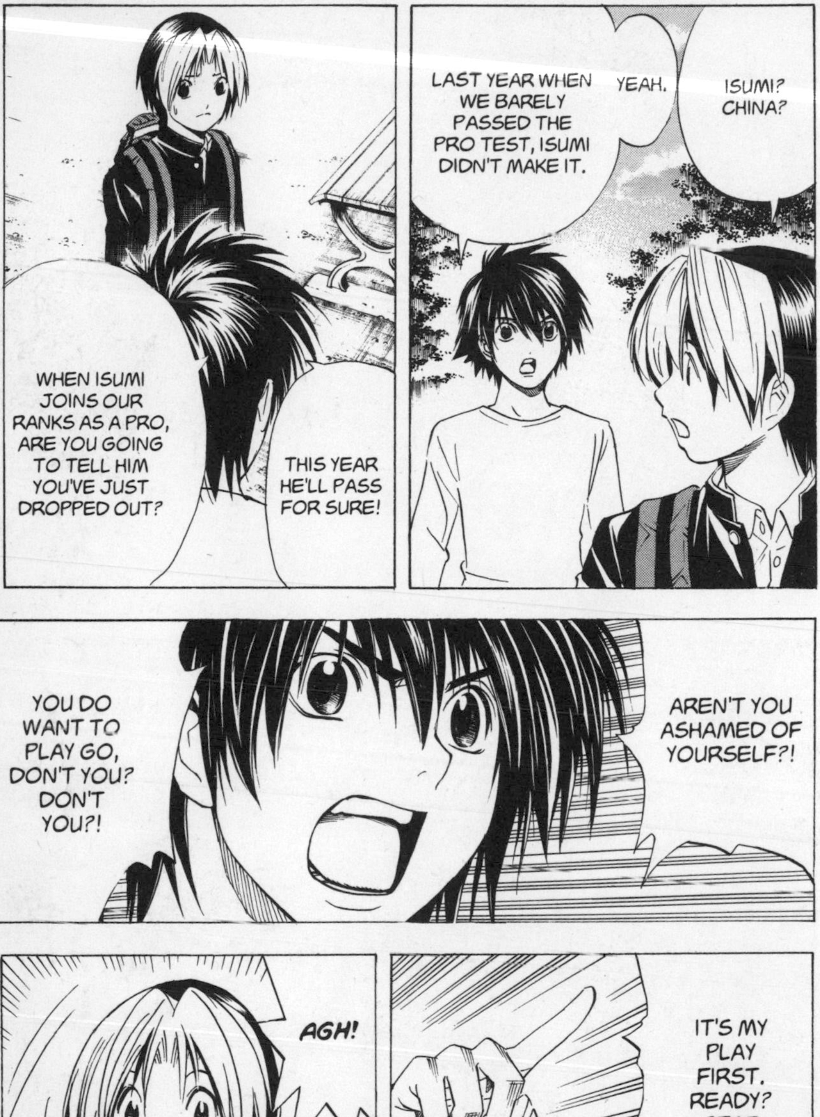
ISUMI? CHINA?
YEAH.
LAST YEAR WHEN WE BARELY PASSED THE PRO TEST, ISUMI DIDN'T MAKE IT.
THIS YEAR HE'LL PASS FOR SURE!
WHEN ISUMI JOINS OUR RANKS AS A PRO, ARE YOU GOING TO TELL HIM YOU'VE JUST DROPPED OUT?
AREN'T YOU ASHAMED OF YOURSELF?!
YOU DO WANT TO PLAY GO, DON'T YOU? DON'T YOU?!
IT'S MY PLAY FIRST. READY? STAR POINT!
AGH!

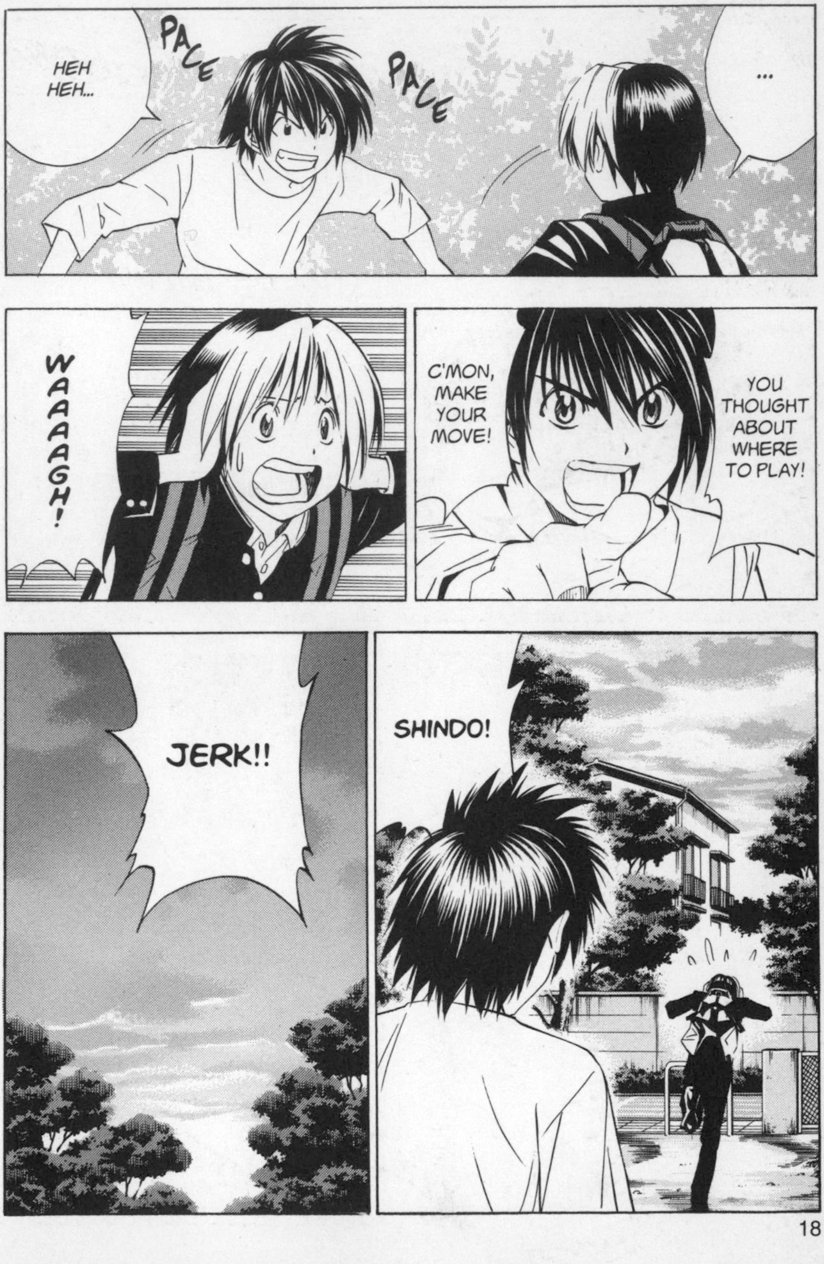
...
PACE
PACE
HEH HEH...
YOU THOUGHT ABOUT WHERE TO PLAY!
C'MON, MAKE YOUR MOVE!
WAAAAAGH!
SHINDO!
JERK!!

NOW FOR THE AFTER-NOON MATCHES...

GAME ROOM

QUIET, PLEASE. GAMES IN PROGRESS.

NARUSAWA SENSEI SENDS HIS APOLOGIES FOR BEING UNABLE TO COME THIS YEAR.

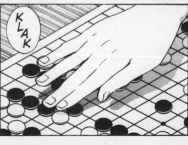

KLAK

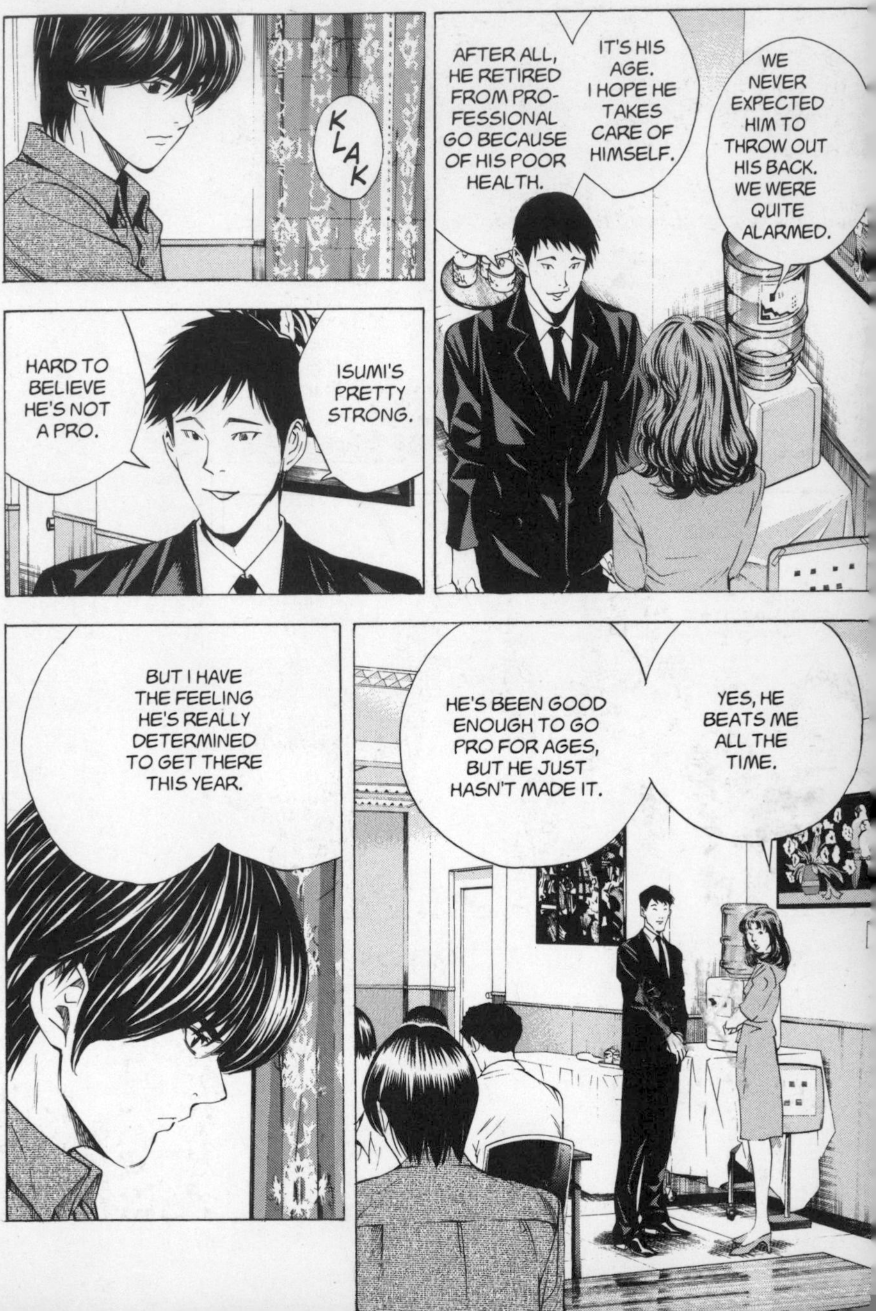
WE NEVER EXPECTED HIM TO THROW OUT HIS BACK. WE WERE QUITE ALARMED.
IT'S HIS AGE. I HOPE HE TAKES CARE OF HIMSELF.
AFTER ALL, HE RETIRED FROM PRO-FESSIONAL GO BECAUSE OF HIS POOR HEALTH.
KLAK
ISUMI'S PRETTY STRONG.
HARD TO BELIEVE HE'S NOT A PRO.
YES, HE BEATS ME ALL THE TIME.
HE'S BEEN GOOD ENOUGH TO GO PRO FOR AGES, BUT HE JUST HASN'T MADE IT.
BUT I HAVE THE FEELING HE'S REALLY DETERMINED TO GET THERE THIS YEAR.

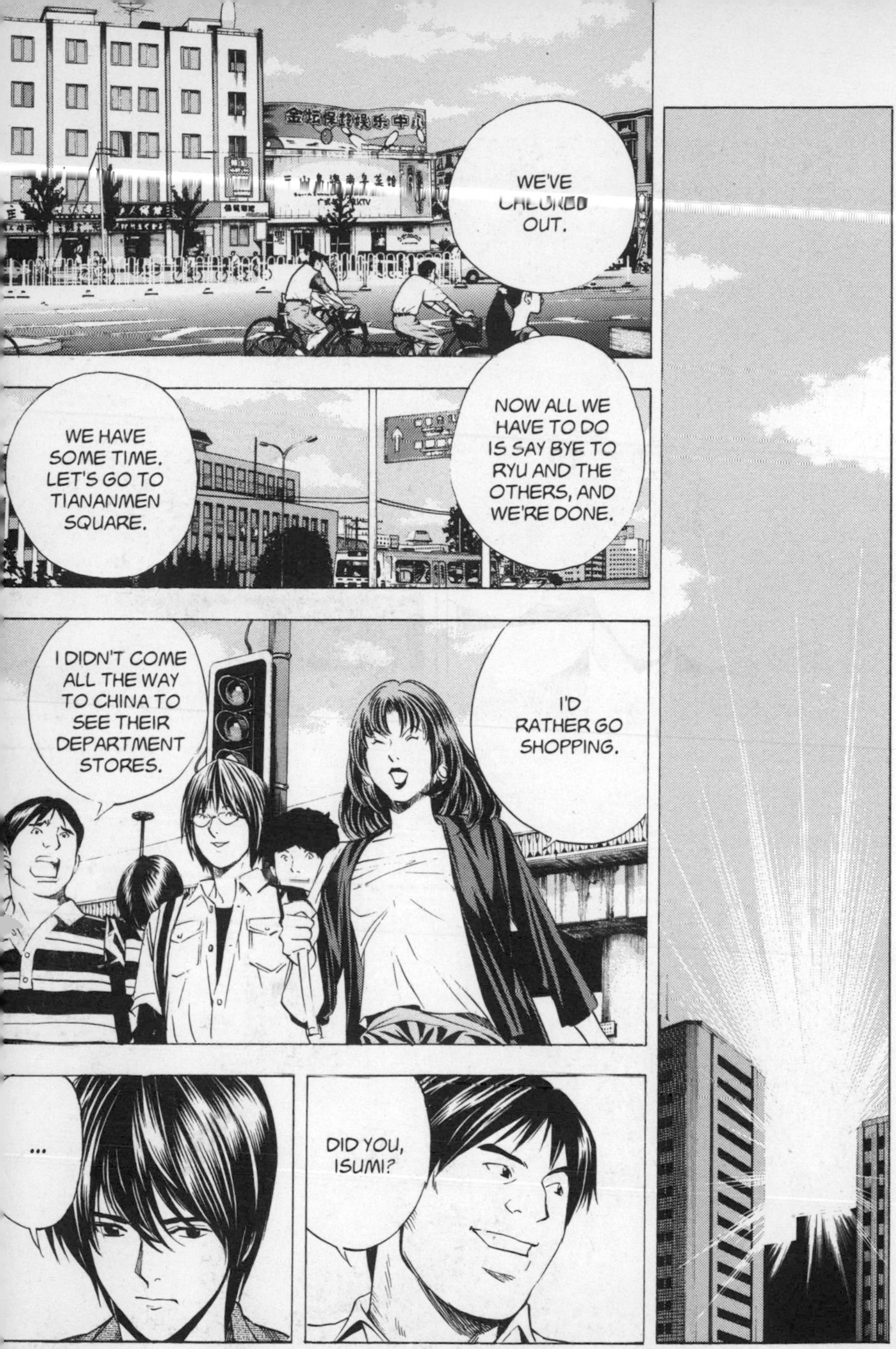
WE'VE CHECKED OUT.
NOW ALL WE HAVE TO DO IS SAY BYE TO RYU AND THE OTHERS, AND WE'RE DONE.
WE HAVE SOME TIME. LET'S GO TO TIANANMEN SQUARE.
I'D RATHER GO SHOPPING.
I DIDN'T COME ALL THE WAY TO CHINA TO SEE THEIR DEPARTMENT STORES.
DID YOU, ISUMI?
...

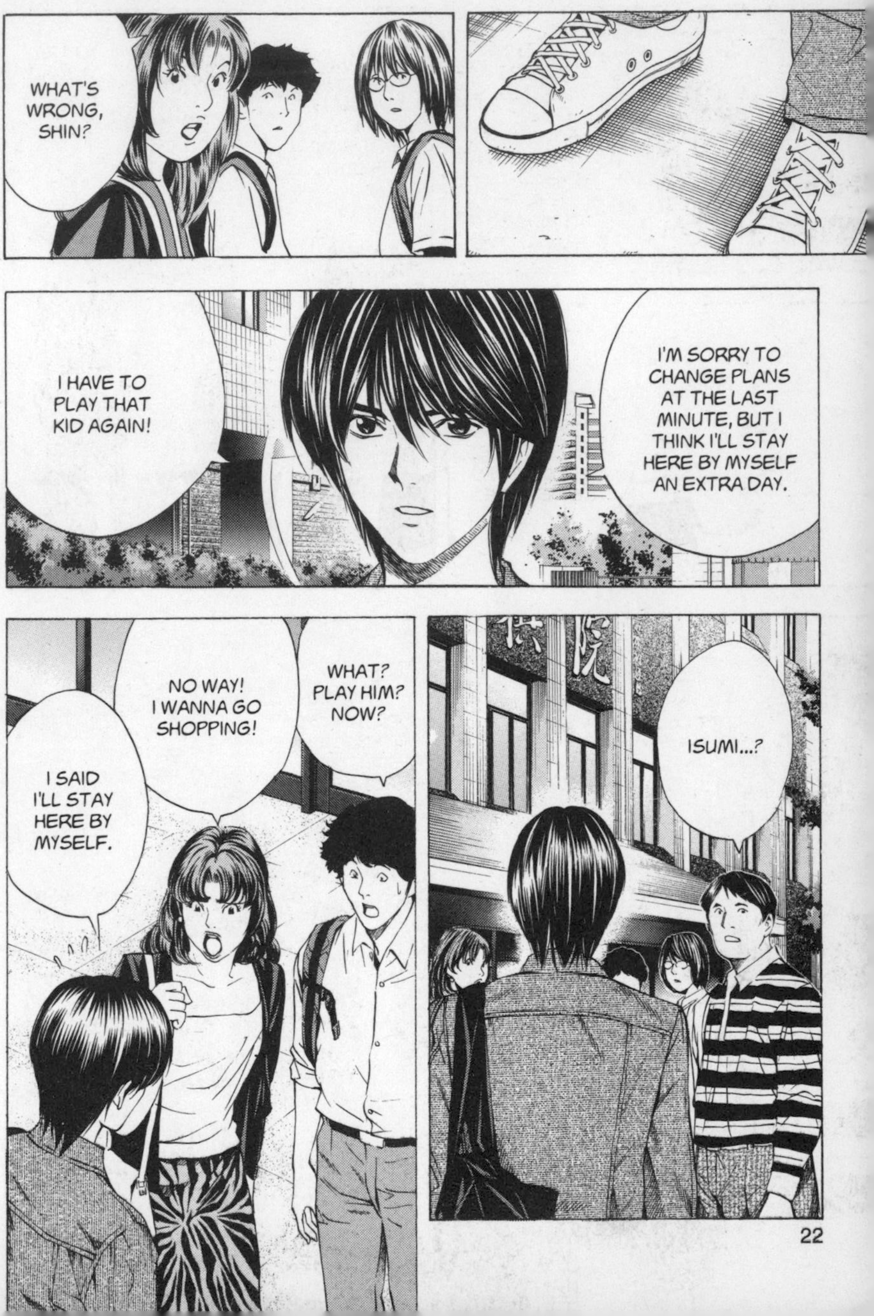
WHAT'S WRONG, SHIN?
I'M SORRY TO CHANGE PLANS AT THE LAST MINUTE, BUT I THINK I'LL STAY HERE BY MYSELF AN EXTRA DAY.
I HAVE TO PLAY THAT KID AGAIN!
ISUMI...?
WHAT? PLAY HIM? NOW?
NO WAY! I WANNA GO SHOPPING!
I SAID I'LL STAY HERE BY MYSELF.

READ THIS WAY

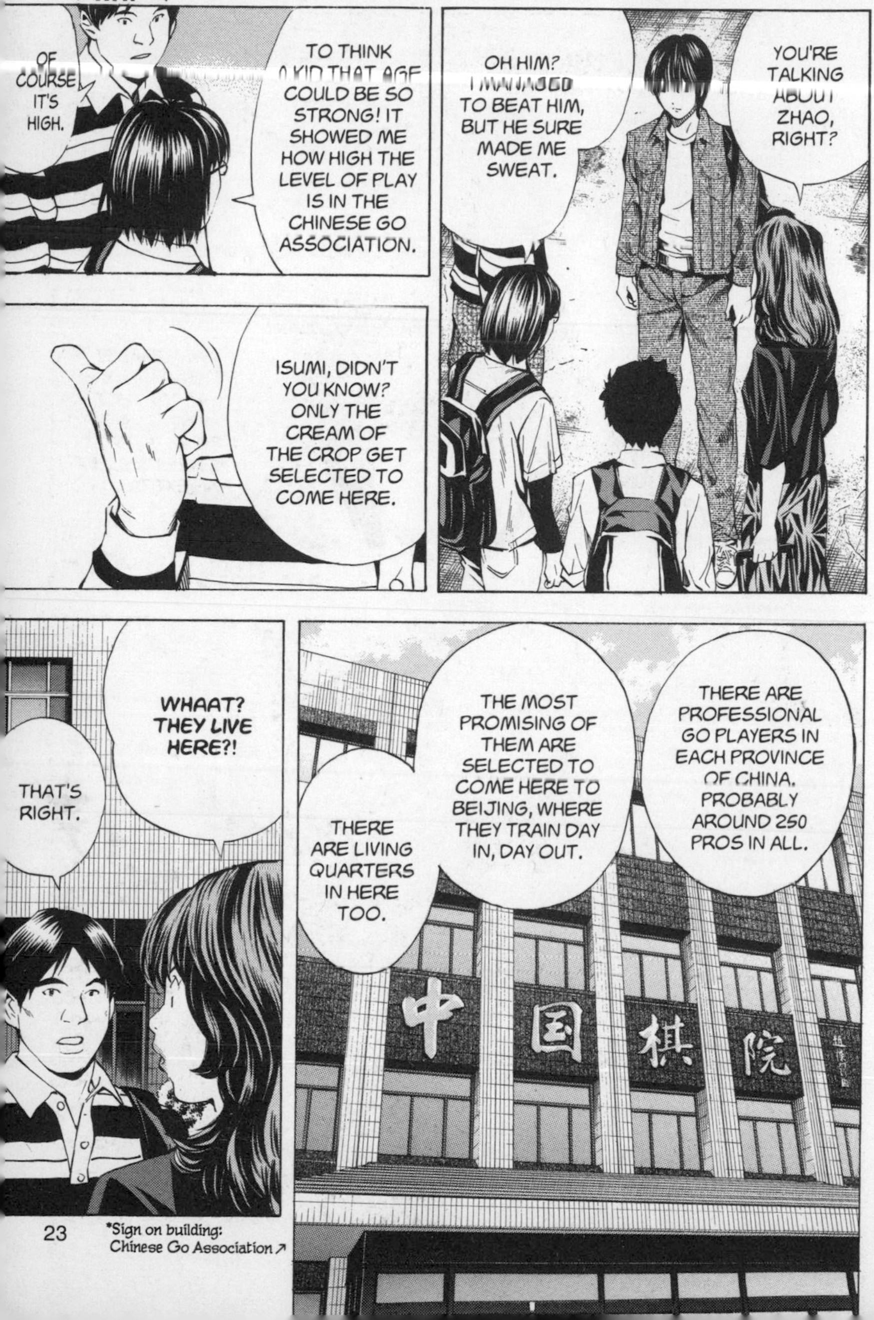
YOU'RE TALKING ABOUT ZHAO, RIGHT?
OH HIM? I MANAGED TO BEAT HIM, BUT HE SURE MADE ME SWEAT.
TO THINK A KID THAT AGE COULD BE SO STRONG! IT SHOWED ME HOW HIGH THE LEVEL OF PLAY IS IN THE CHINESE GO ASSOCIATION.
OF COURSE IT'S HIGH.
ISUMI, DIDN'T YOU KNOW? ONLY THE CREAM OF THE CROP GET SELECTED TO COME HERE.
THERE ARE PROFESSIONAL GO PLAYERS IN EACH PROVINCE OF CHINA. PROBABLY AROUND 250 PROS IN ALL.
THE MOST PROMISING OF THEM ARE SELECTED TO COME HERE TO BEIJING, WHERE THEY TRAIN DAY IN, DAY OUT.
THERE ARE LIVING QUARTERS IN HERE TOO.
中国棋院
WHAAT? THEY LIVE HERE?!
THAT'S RIGHT.

*Sign on building: Chinese Go Association ↗

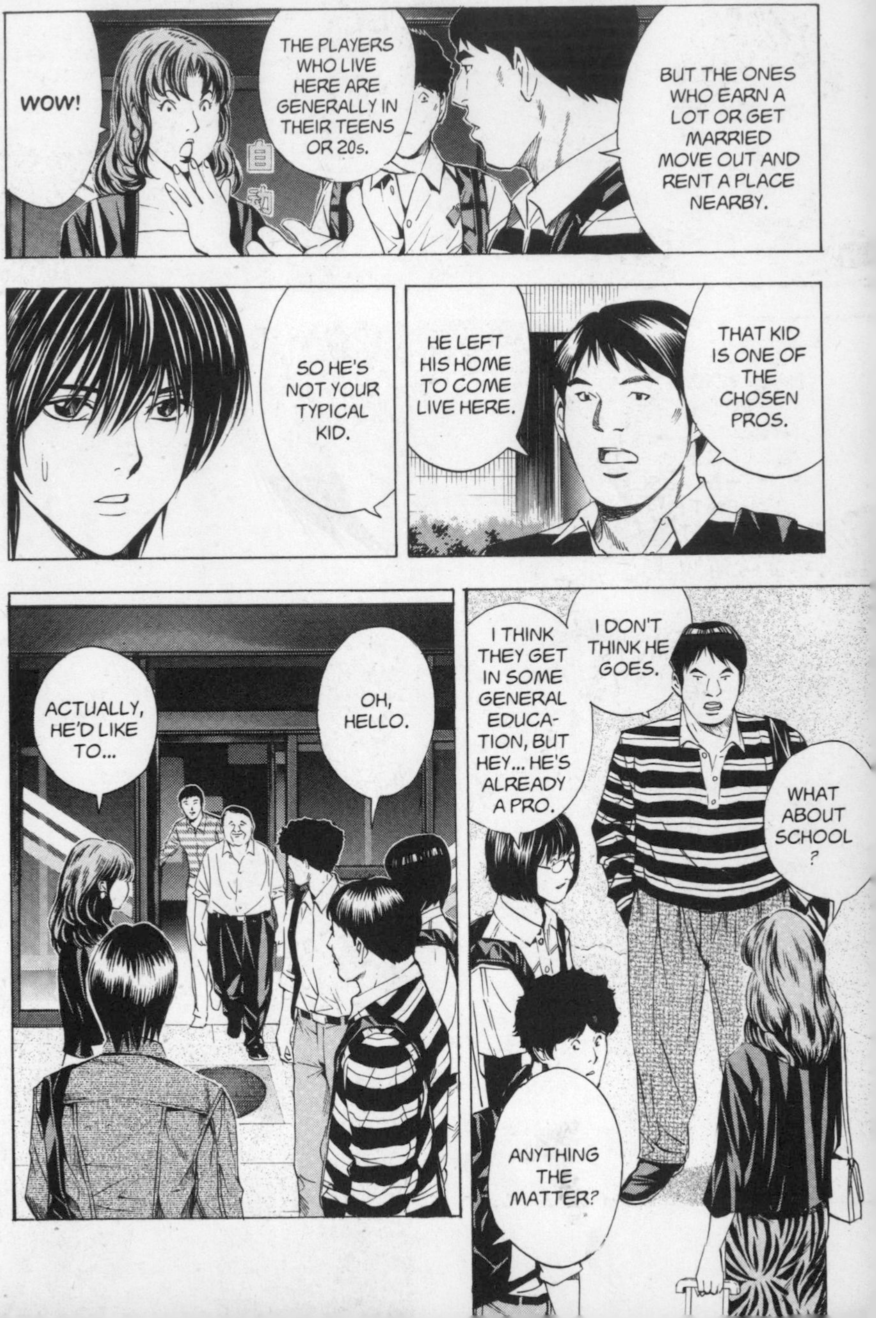
THE PLAYERS WHO LIVE HERE ARE GENERALLY IN THEIR TEENS OR 20s.
BUT THE ONES WHO EARN A LOT OR GET MARRIED MOVE OUT AND RENT A PLACE NEARBY.
WOW!
THAT KID IS ONE OF THE CHOSEN PROS.
HE LEFT HIS HOME TO COME LIVE HERE.
SO HE'S NOT YOUR TYPICAL KID.
WHAT ABOUT SCHOOL?
I DON'T THINK HE GOES.
I THINK THEY GET IN SOME GENERAL EDUCATION, BUT HEY... HE'S ALREADY A PRO.
ANYTHING THE MATTER?
OH, HELLO.
ACTUALLY, HE'D LIKE TO...

READ THIS WAY

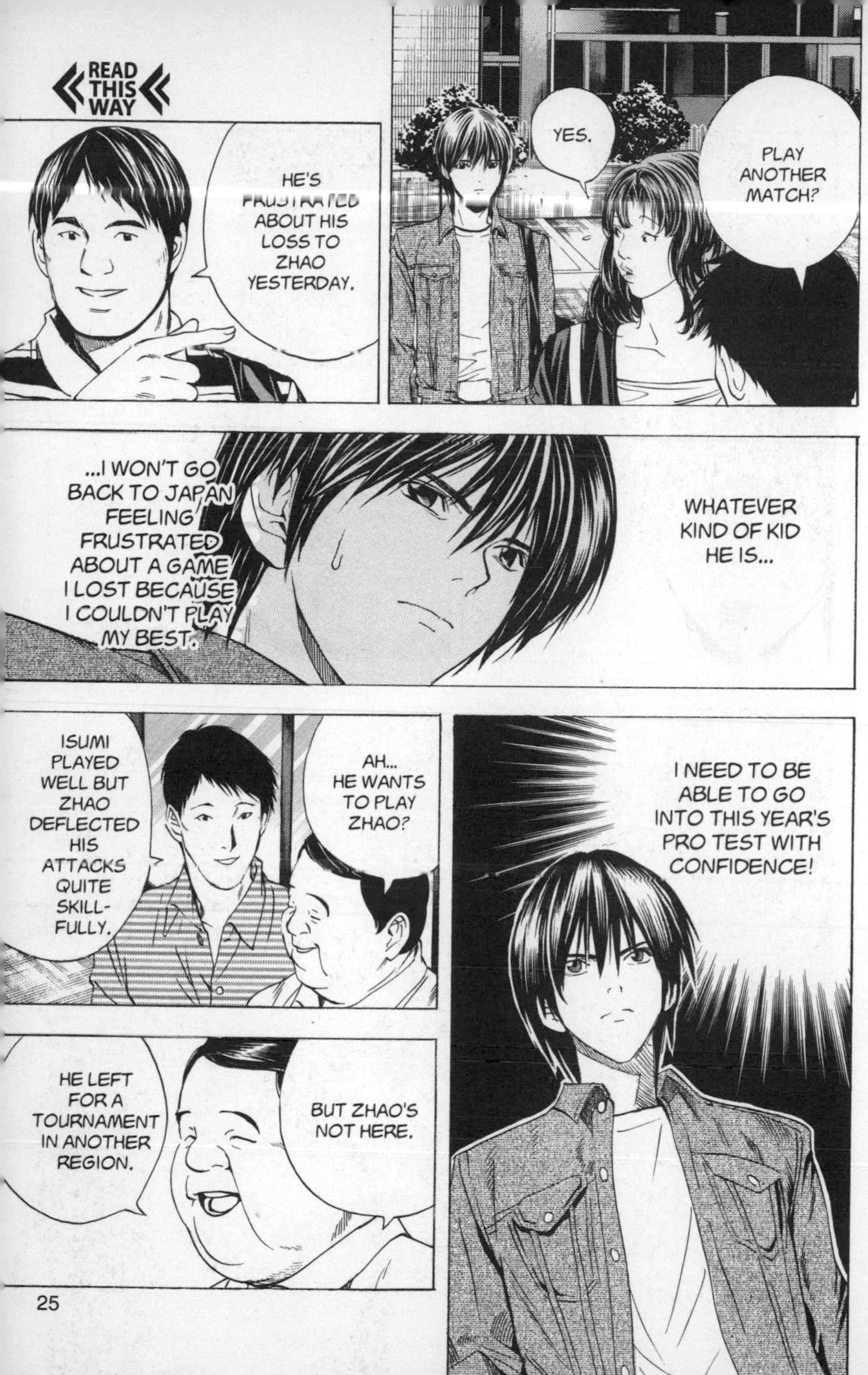
PLAY ANOTHER MATCH?
YES.
HE'S FRUSTRATED ABOUT HIS LOSS TO ZHAO YESTERDAY.
WHATEVER KIND OF KID HE IS...
...I WON'T GO BACK TO JAPAN FEELING FRUSTRATED ABOUT A GAME I LOST BECAUSE I COULDN'T PLAY MY BEST.
I NEED TO BE ABLE TO GO INTO THIS YEAR'S PRO TEST WITH CONFIDENCE!
AH... HE WANTS TO PLAY ZHAO?
ISUMI PLAYED WELL BUT ZHAO DEFLECTED HIS ATTACKS QUITE SKILL-FULLY.
BUT ZHAO'S NOT HERE.
HE LEFT FOR A TOURNAMENT IN ANOTHER REGION.

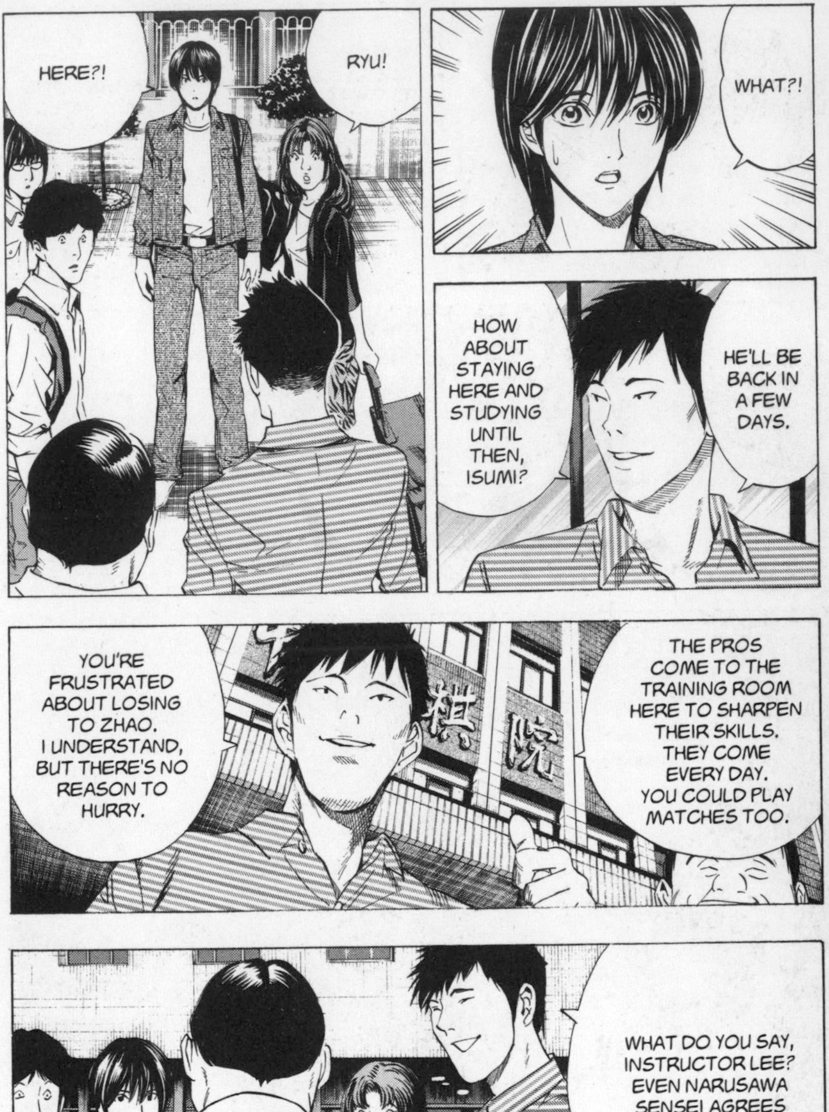
WHAT?!
HE'LL BE BACK IN A FEW DAYS.
HOW ABOUT STAYING HERE AND STUDYING UNTIL THEN, ISUMI?
RYU!
HERE?!
THE PROS COME TO THE TRAINING ROOM HERE TO SHARPEN THEIR SKILLS. THEY COME EVERY DAY. YOU COULD PLAY MATCHES TOO.
YOU'RE FRUSTRATED ABOUT LOSING TO ZHAO. I UNDERSTAND, BUT THERE'S NO REASON TO HURRY.
WHAT DO YOU SAY, INSTRUCTOR LEE? EVEN NARUSAWA SENSEI AGREES HE'S STRONG.

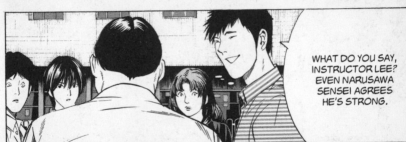

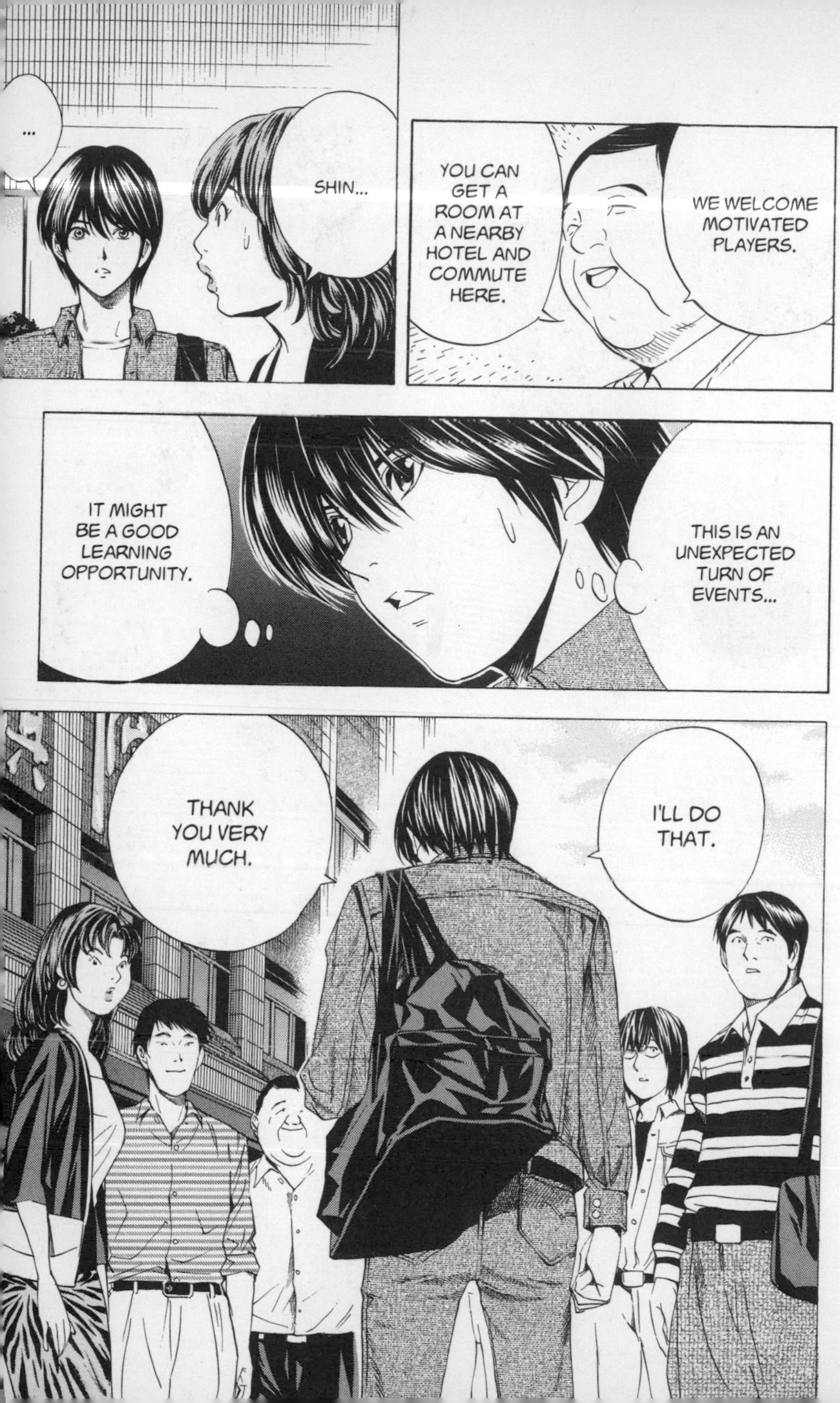
WE WELCOME MOTIVATED PLAYERS.
YOU CAN GET A ROOM AT A NEARBY HOTEL AND COMMUTE HERE.
SHIN...
...
THIS IS AN UNEXPECTED TURN OF EVENTS...
IT MIGHT BE A GOOD LEARNING OPPORTUNITY.
I'LL DO THAT.
THANK YOU VERY MUCH.

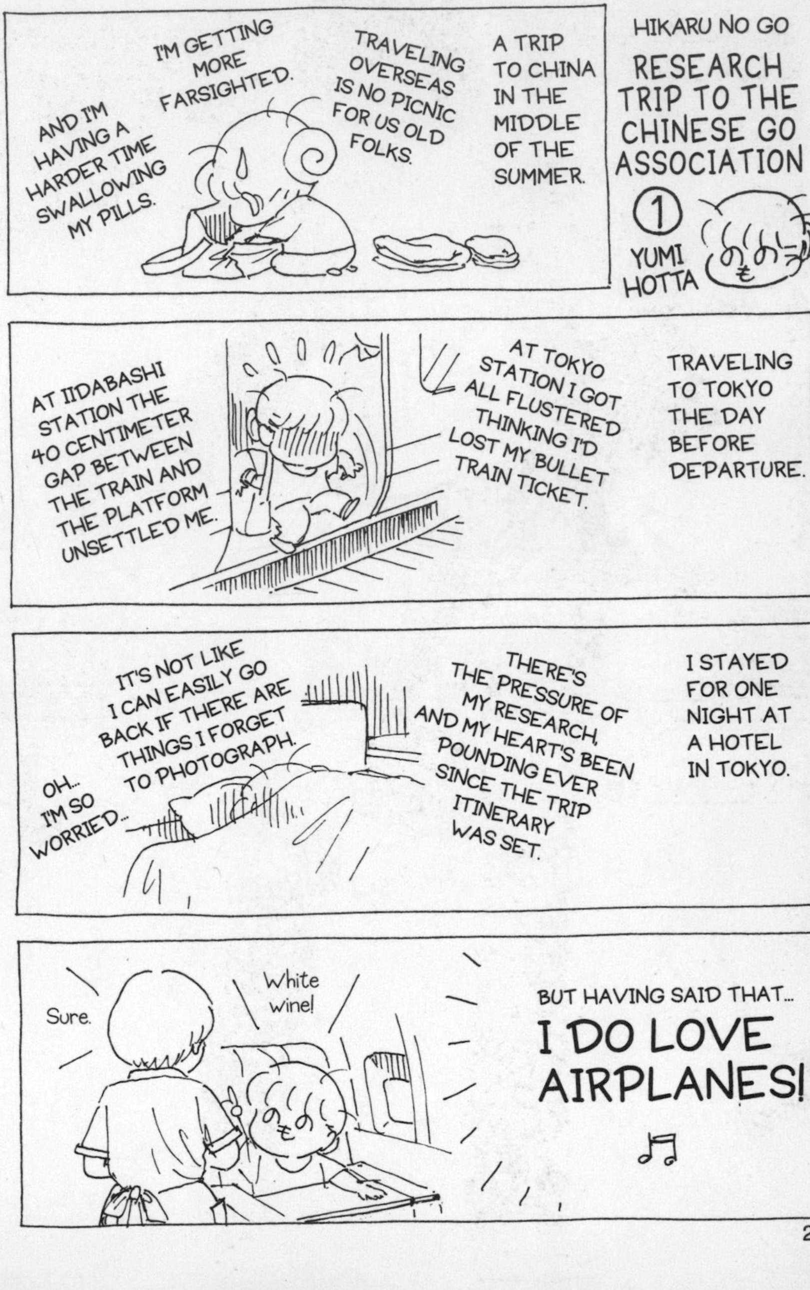
HIKARU NO GO
RESEARCH TRIP TO THE CHINESE GO ASSOCIATION
1
YUMI HOTTA
A TRIP TO CHINA IN THE MIDDLE OF THE SUMMER.
TRAVELING OVERSEAS IS NO PICNIC FOR US OLD FOLKS.
I'M GETTING MORE FARSIGHTED.
AND I'M HAVING A HARDER TIME SWALLOWING MY PILLS.
TRAVELING TO TOKYO THE DAY BEFORE DEPARTURE.
AT TOKYO STATION I GOT ALL FLUSTERED THINKING I'D LOST MY BULLET TRAIN TICKET.
AT IIDABASHI STATION THE 40 CENTIMETER GAP BETWEEN THE TRAIN AND THE PLATFORM UNSETTLED ME.
I STAYED FOR ONE NIGHT AT A HOTEL IN TOKYO.
THERE'S THE PRESSURE OF MY RESEARCH, AND MY HEART'S BEEN POUNDING EVER SINCE THE TRIP ITINERARY WAS SET.
IT'S NOT LIKE I CAN EASILY GO BACK IF THERE ARE THINGS I FORGET TO PHOTOGRAPH.
OH... I'M SO WORRIED...
BUT HAVING SAID THAT...
I DO LOVE AIRPLANES!
White wine!
Sure.

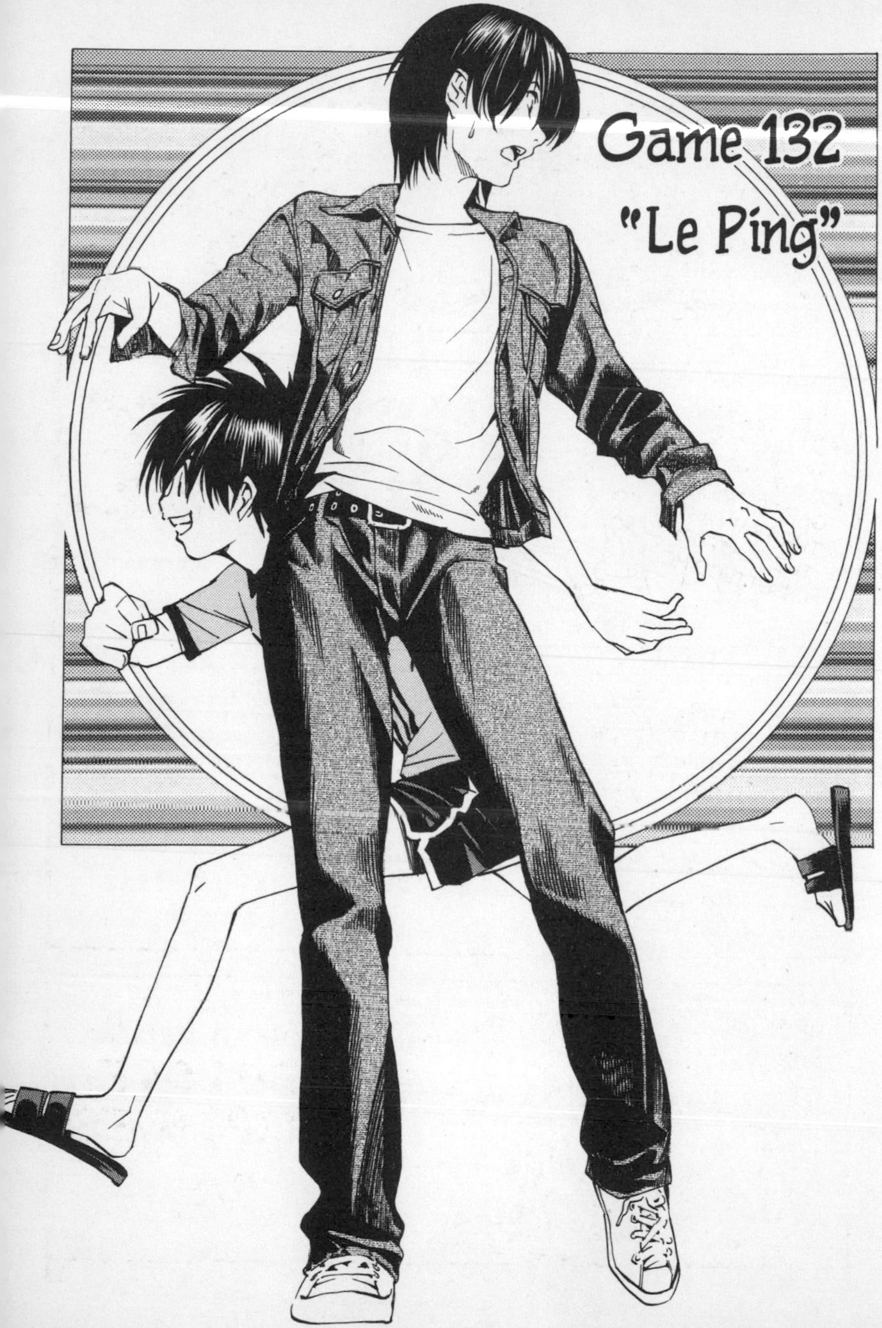Game 132
"Le Ping"

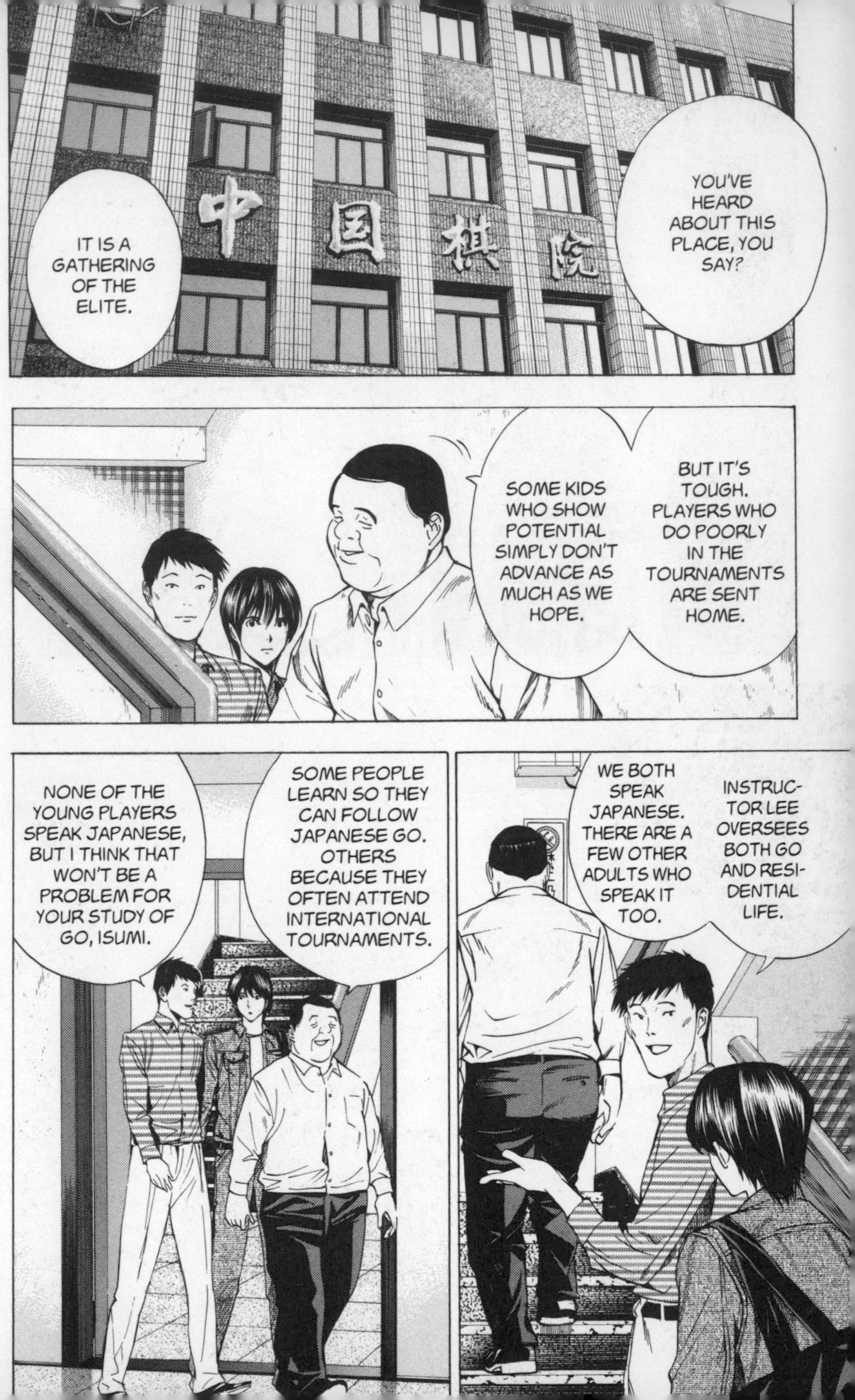

中国棋院
YOU'VE HEARD ABOUT THIS PLACE, YOU SAY?
IT IS A GATHERING OF THE ELITE.
BUT IT'S TOUGH. PLAYERS WHO DO POORLY IN THE TOURNAMENTS ARE SENT HOME.
SOME KIDS WHO SHOW POTENTIAL SIMPLY DON'T ADVANCE AS MUCH AS WE HOPE.
INSTRUCTOR LEE OVERSEES BOTH GO AND RESIDENTIAL LIFE.
WE BOTH SPEAK JAPANESE. THERE ARE A FEW OTHER ADULTS WHO SPEAK IT TOO.
SOME PEOPLE LEARN SO THEY CAN FOLLOW JAPANESE GO. OTHERS BECAUSE THEY OFTEN ATTEND INTERNATIONAL TOURNAMENTS.
NONE OF THE YOUNG PLAYERS SPEAK JAPANESE, BUT I THINK THAT WON'T BE A PROBLEM FOR YOUR STUDY OF GO, ISUMI.

READ THIS WAY

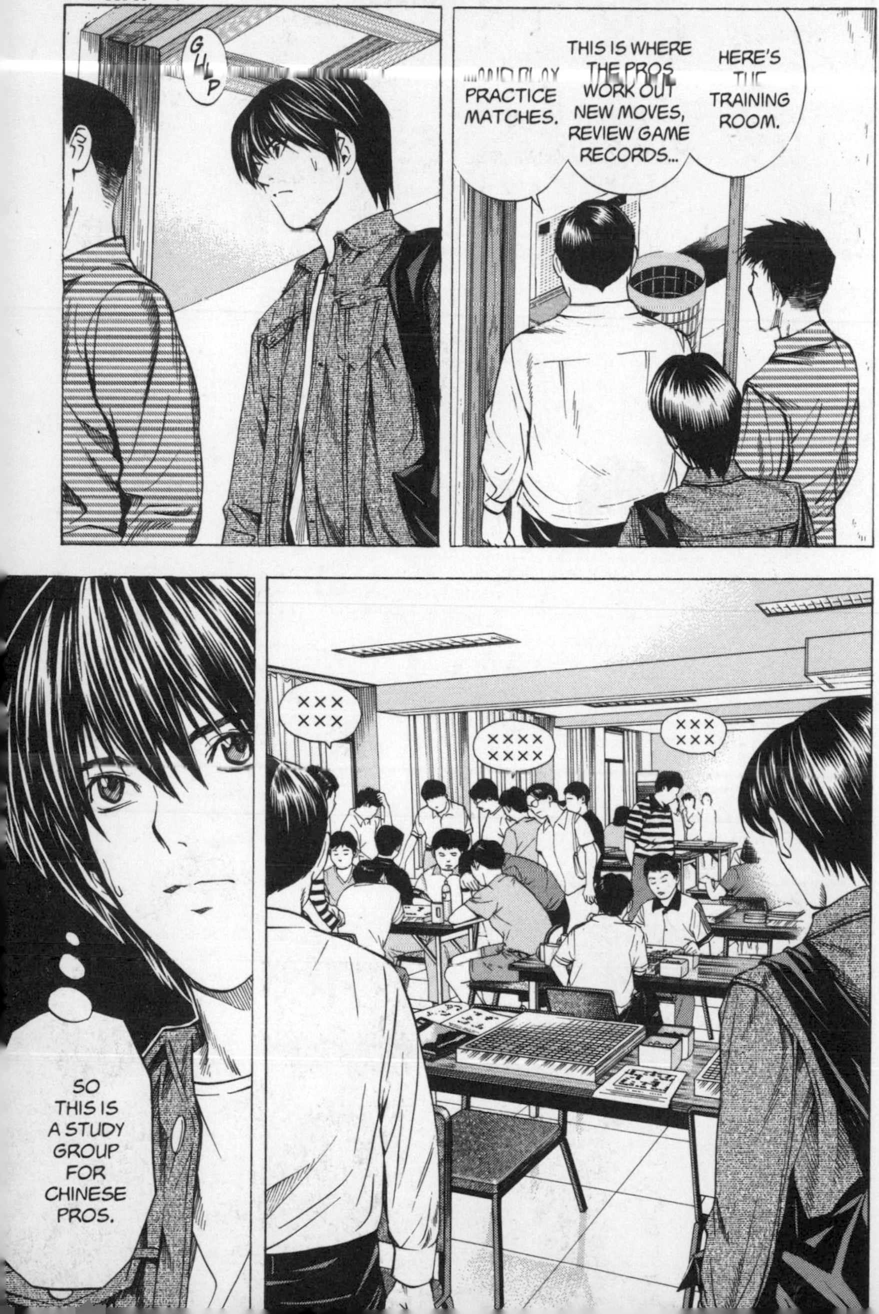
HERE'S THE TRAINING ROOM.
THIS IS WHERE THE PROS WORK OUT NEW MOVES, REVIEW GAME RECORDS...
...AND PLAY PRACTICE MATCHES.
GULP
×××
×××
××××
××××
×××
×××
SO THIS IS A STUDY GROUP FOR CHINESE PROS.

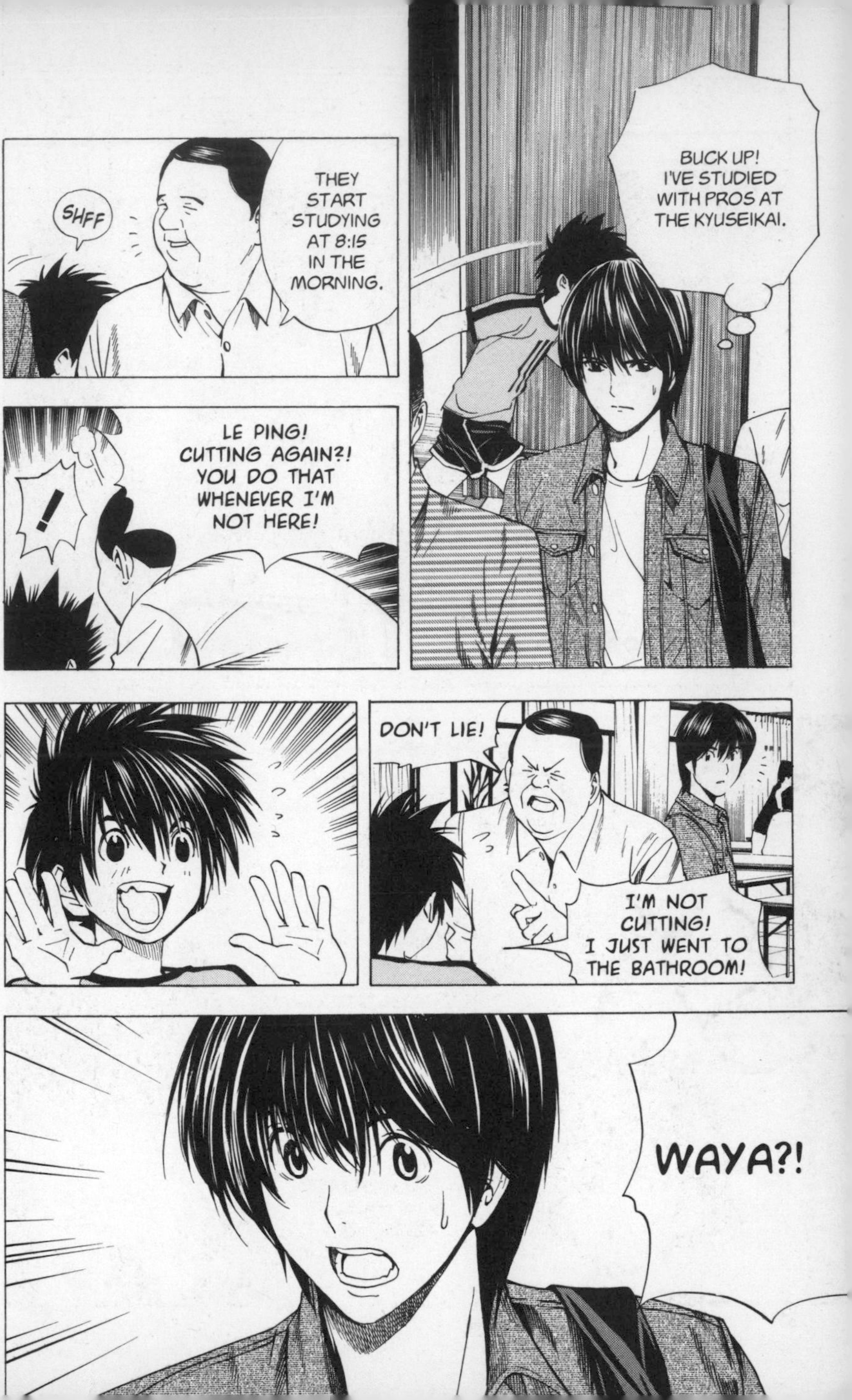
BUCK UP! I'VE STUDIED WITH PROS AT THE KYUSEIKAI.
THEY START STUDYING AT 8:15 IN THE MORNING.
SHFF
LE PING! CUTTING AGAIN?! YOU DO THAT WHENEVER I'M NOT HERE!
!
DON'T LIE!
I'M NOT CUTTING! I JUST WENT TO THE BATHROOM!
WAYA?!

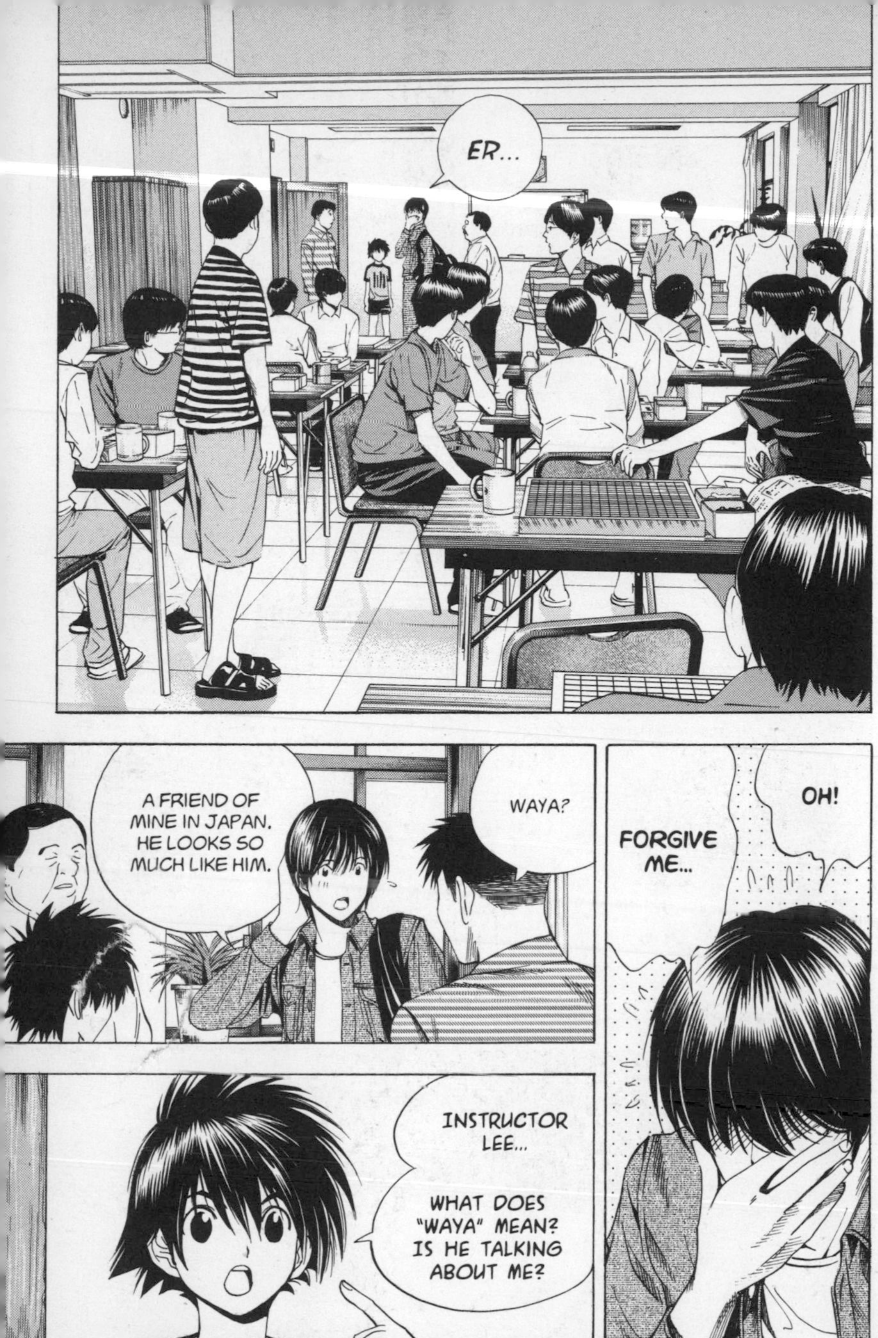
ER...
OH!
FORGIVE ME...
WAYA?
A FRIEND OF MINE IN JAPAN. HE LOOKS SO MUCH LIKE HIM.
INSTRUCTOR LEE...
WHAT DOES "WAYA" MEAN? IS HE TALKING ABOUT ME?

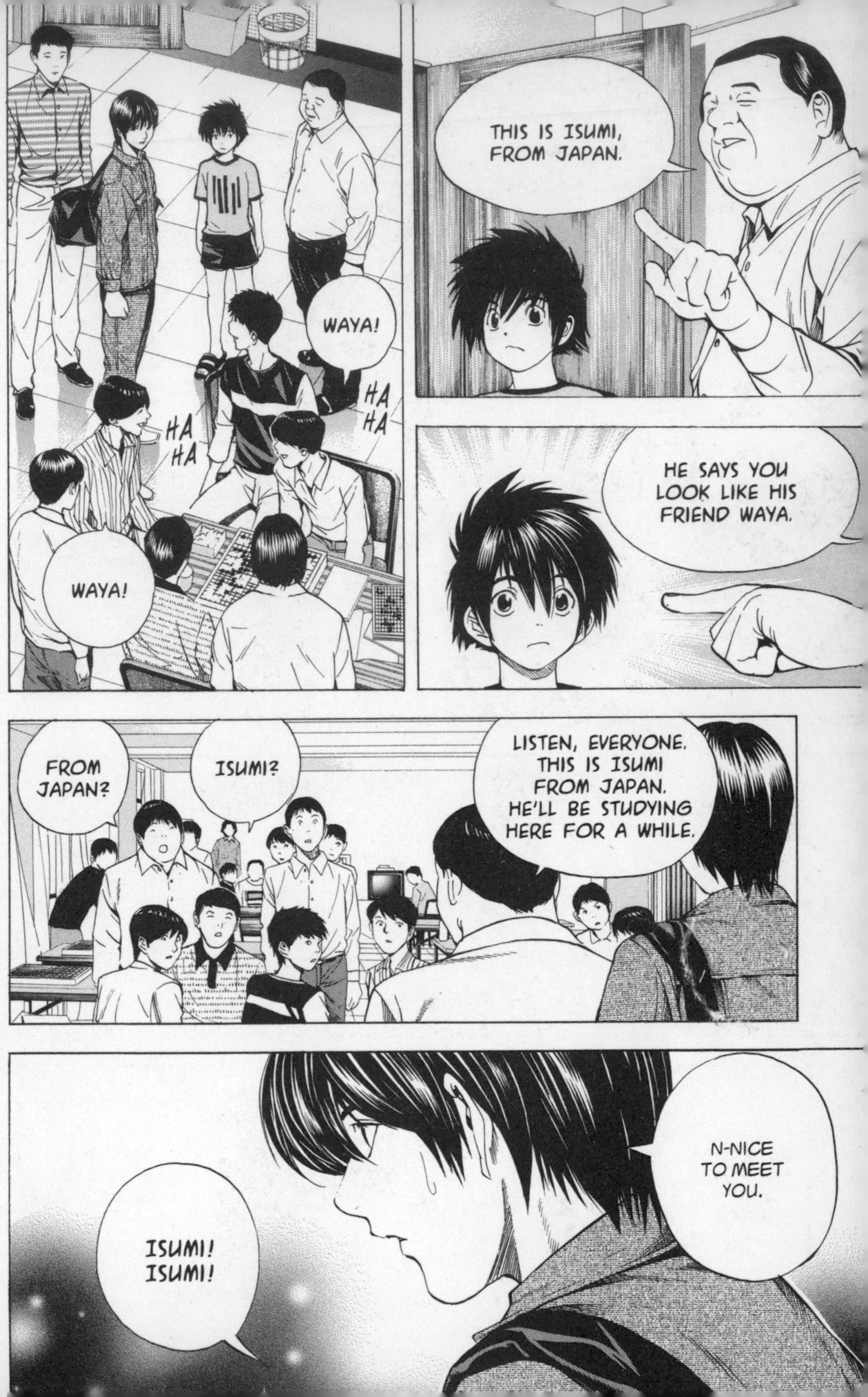

THIS IS ISUMI, FROM JAPAN.
HE SAYS YOU LOOK LIKE HIS FRIEND WAYA.
WAYA!
HA HA
HA HA
WAYA!
LISTEN, EVERYONE. THIS IS ISUMI FROM JAPAN. HE'LL BE STUDYING HERE FOR A WHILE.
ISUMI?
FROM JAPAN?
N-NICE TO MEET YOU.
ISUMI! ISUMI!

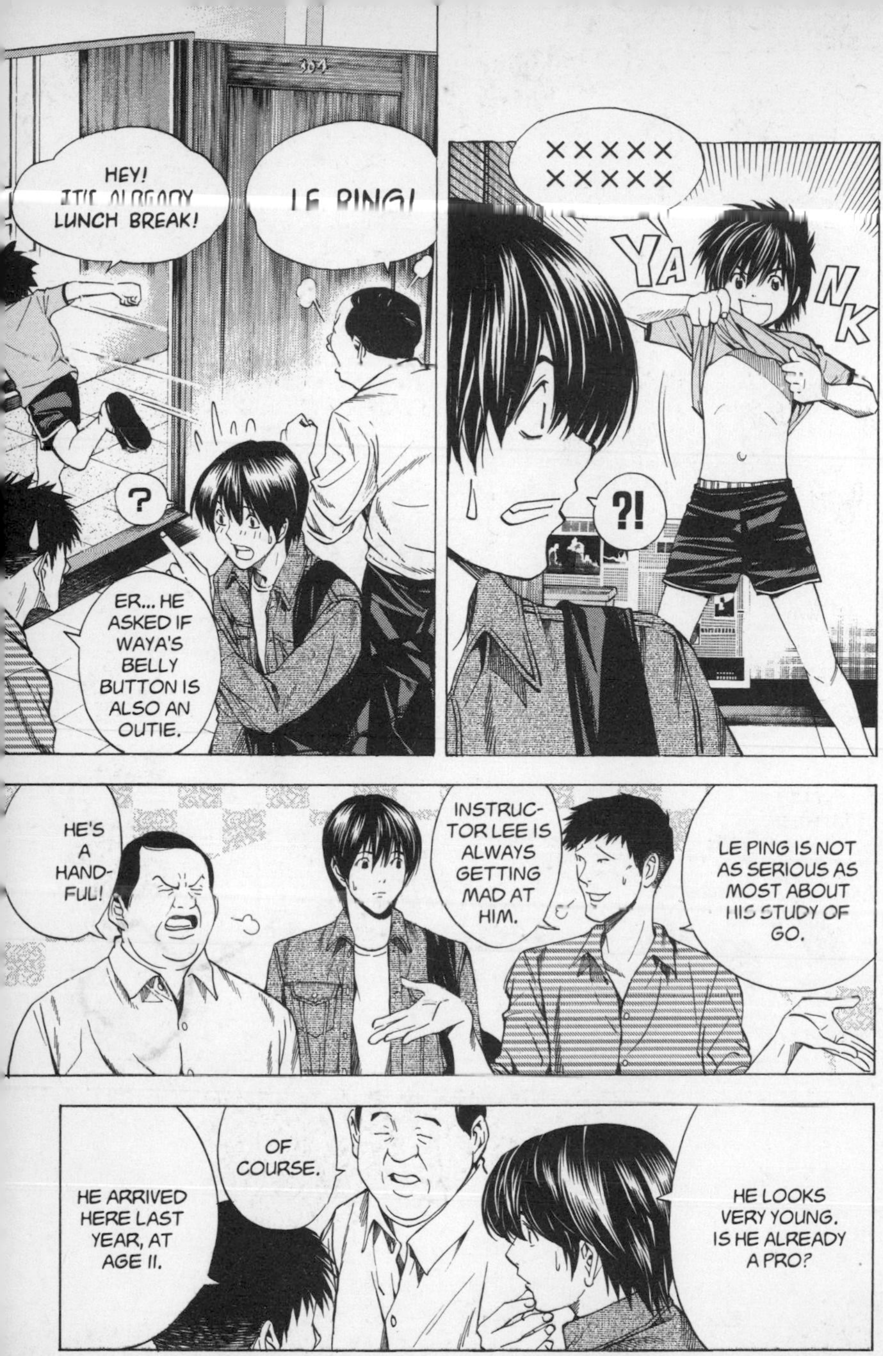
×××××
×××××
YANK
?!
LE PING!
HEY! IT'S ALREADY LUNCH BREAK!
?
ER... HE ASKED IF WAYA'S BELLY BUTTON IS ALSO AN OUTIE.
LE PING IS NOT AS SERIOUS AS MOST ABOUT HIS STUDY OF GO.
INSTRUC-TOR LEE IS ALWAYS GETTING MAD AT HIM.
HE'S A HAND-FUL!
HE LOOKS VERY YOUNG. IS HE ALREADY A PRO?
OF COURSE.
HE ARRIVED HERE LAST YEAR, AT AGE 11.

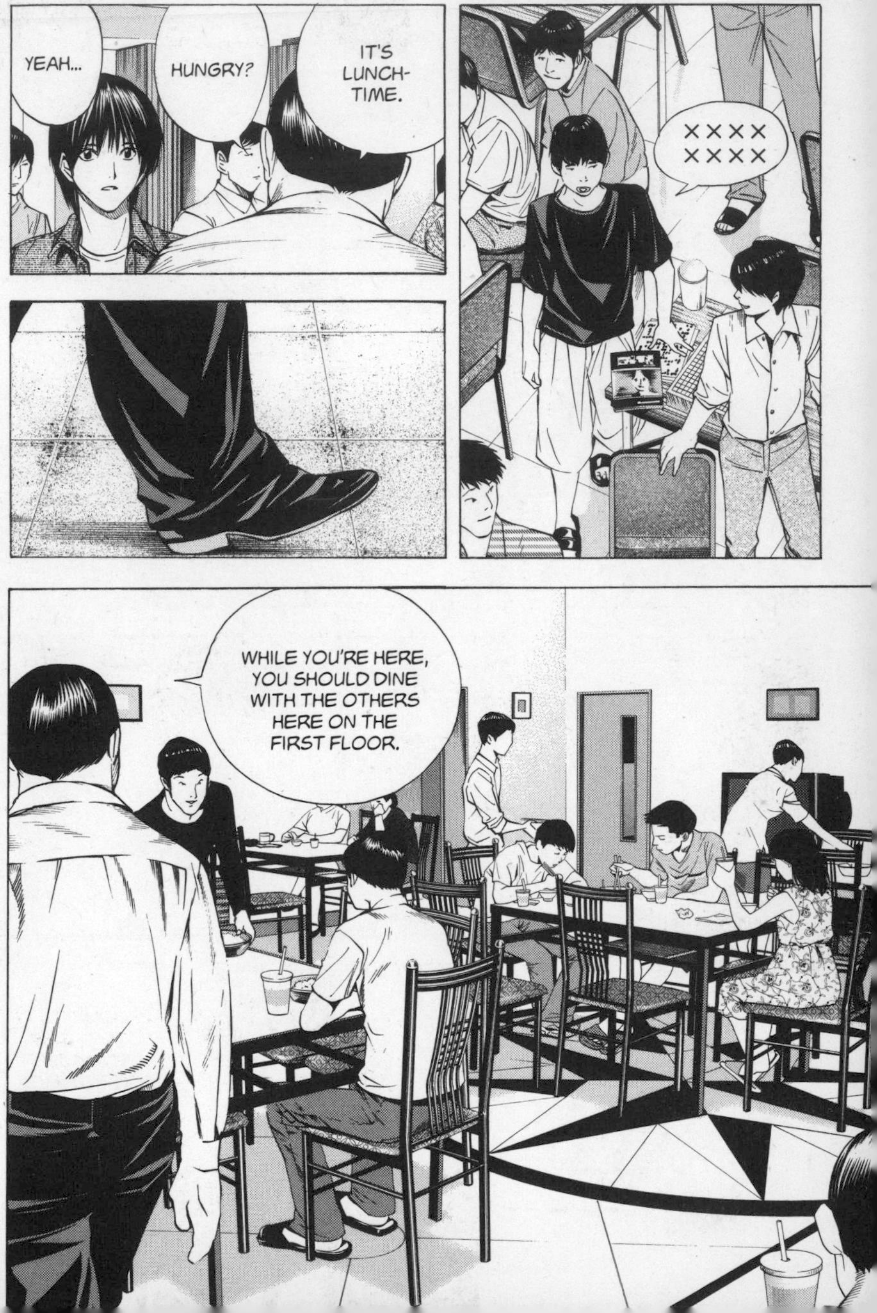
XXXX XXXX
IT'S LUNCH-TIME.
HUNGRY?
YEAH...
WHILE YOU'RE HERE, YOU SHOULD DINE WITH THE OTHERS HERE ON THE FIRST FLOOR.

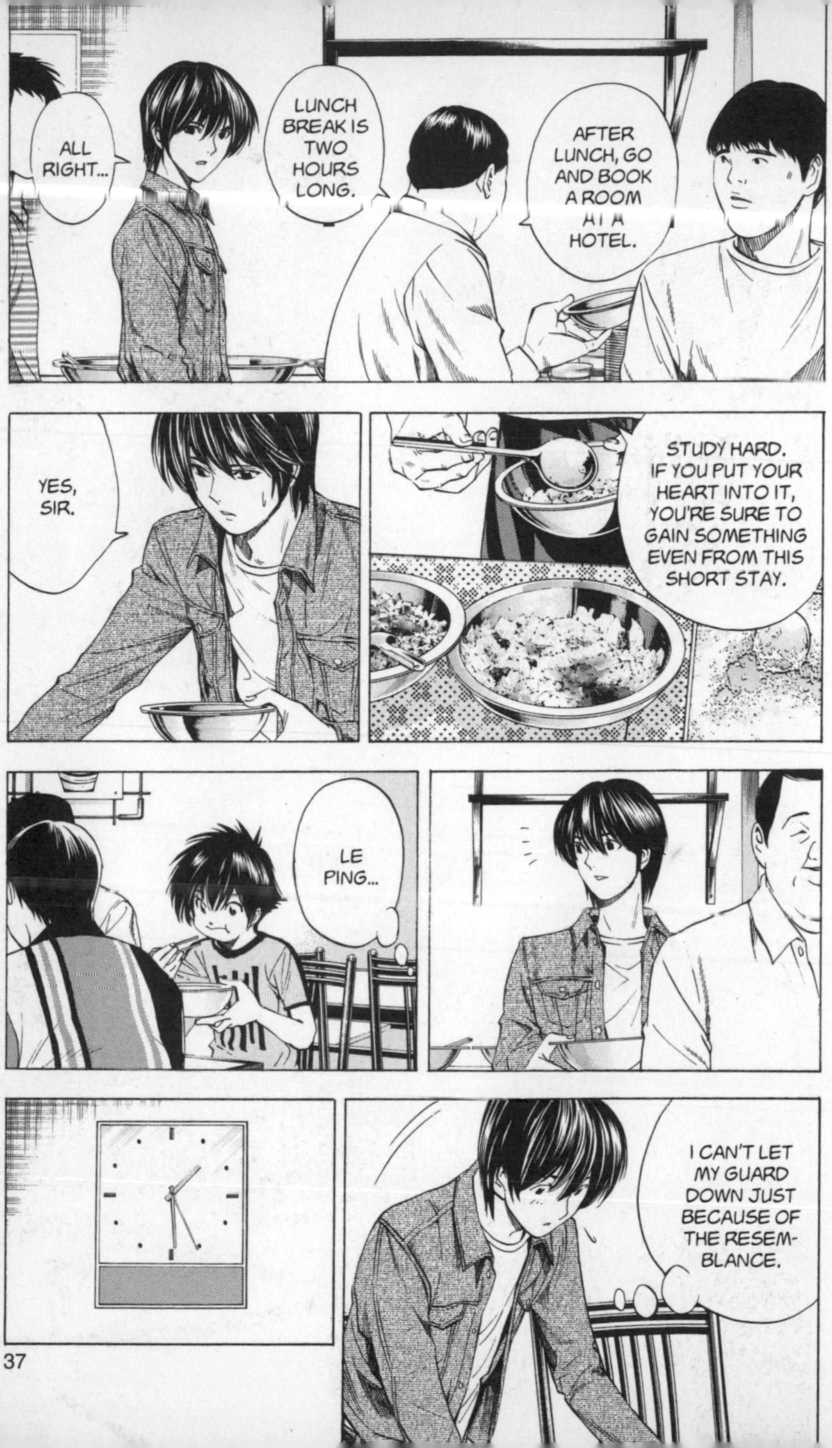
AFTER LUNCH, GO AND BOOK A ROOM AT A HOTEL.
LUNCH BREAK IS TWO HOURS LONG.
ALL RIGHT...
STUDY HARD. IF YOU PUT YOUR HEART INTO IT, YOU'RE SURE TO GAIN SOMETHING EVEN FROM THIS SHORT STAY.
YES, SIR.
LE PING...
I CAN'T LET MY GUARD DOWN JUST BECAUSE OF THE RESEM-BLANCE.

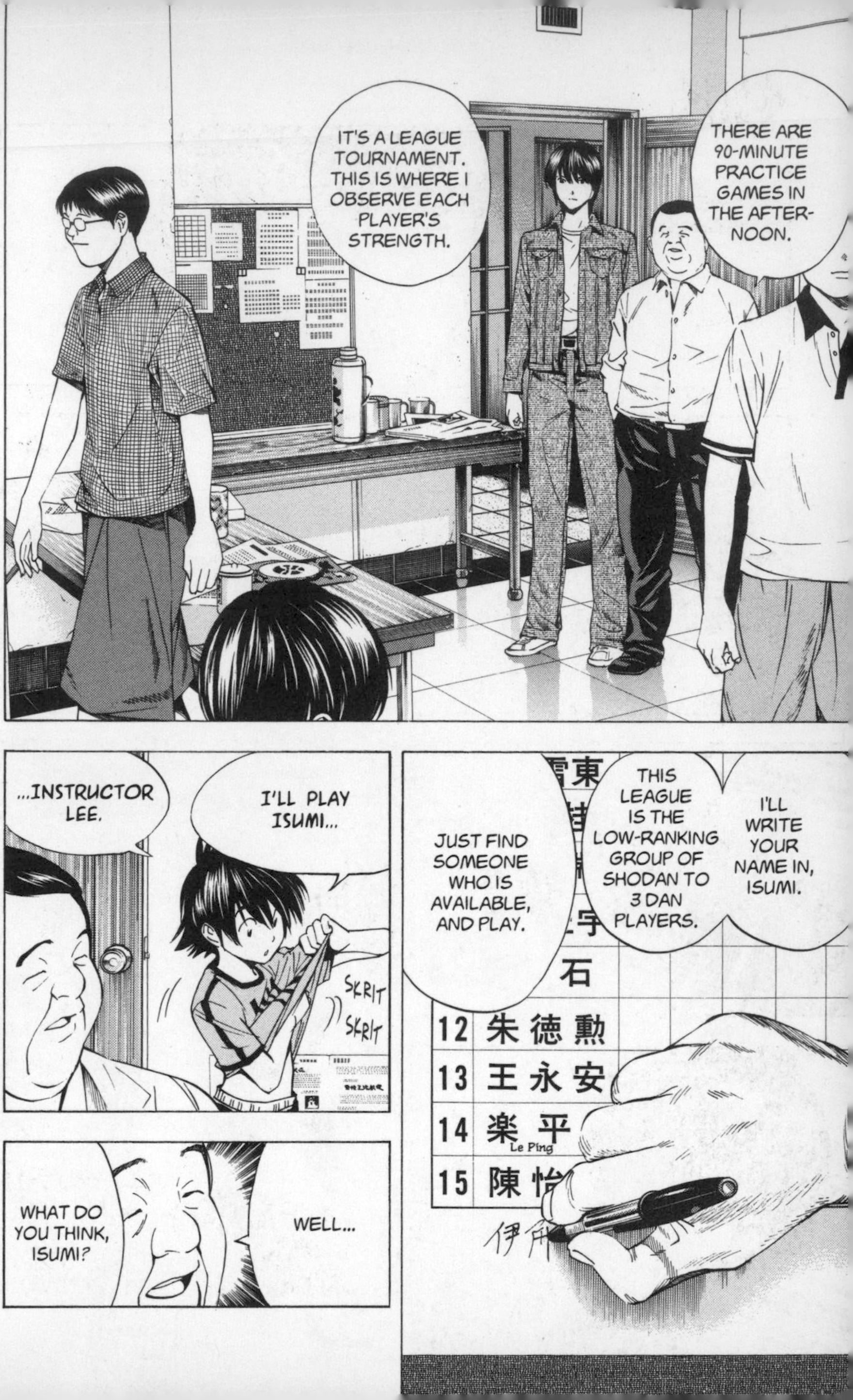
THERE ARE 90-MINUTE PRACTICE GAMES IN THE AFTER-NOON.
IT'S A LEAGUE TOURNAMENT. THIS IS WHERE I OBSERVE EACH PLAYER'S STRENGTH.
I'LL WRITE YOUR NAME IN, ISUMI.
THIS LEAGUE IS THE LOW-RANKING GROUP OF SHODAN TO 3 DAN PLAYERS.
JUST FIND SOMEONE WHO IS AVAILABLE, AND PLAY.
石
12 朱徳勲
13 王永安
14 楽平
Le Ping
15 陳
伊角
I'LL PLAY ISUMI...
...INSTRUCTOR LEE.
SKRIT
SKRIT
WELL...
WHAT DO YOU THINK, ISUMI?

READ THIS WAY

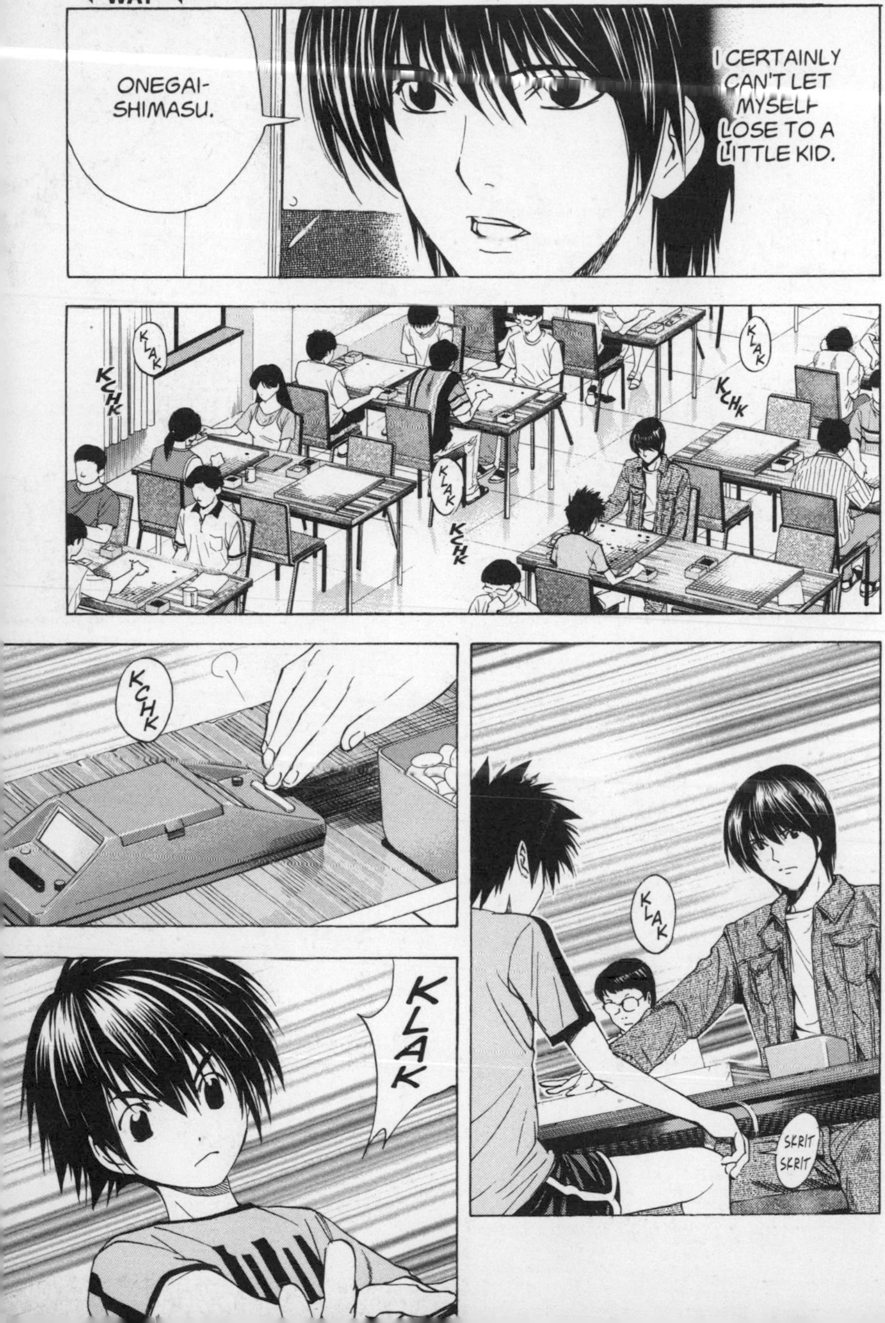
I CERTAINLY CAN'T LET MYSELF LOSE TO A LITTLE KID.
ONEGAI-SHIMASU.
KLAK
KCHK
KLAK
KCHK
KLAK
KCHK
KLAK
SKRIT SKRIT
KCHK
KLAK

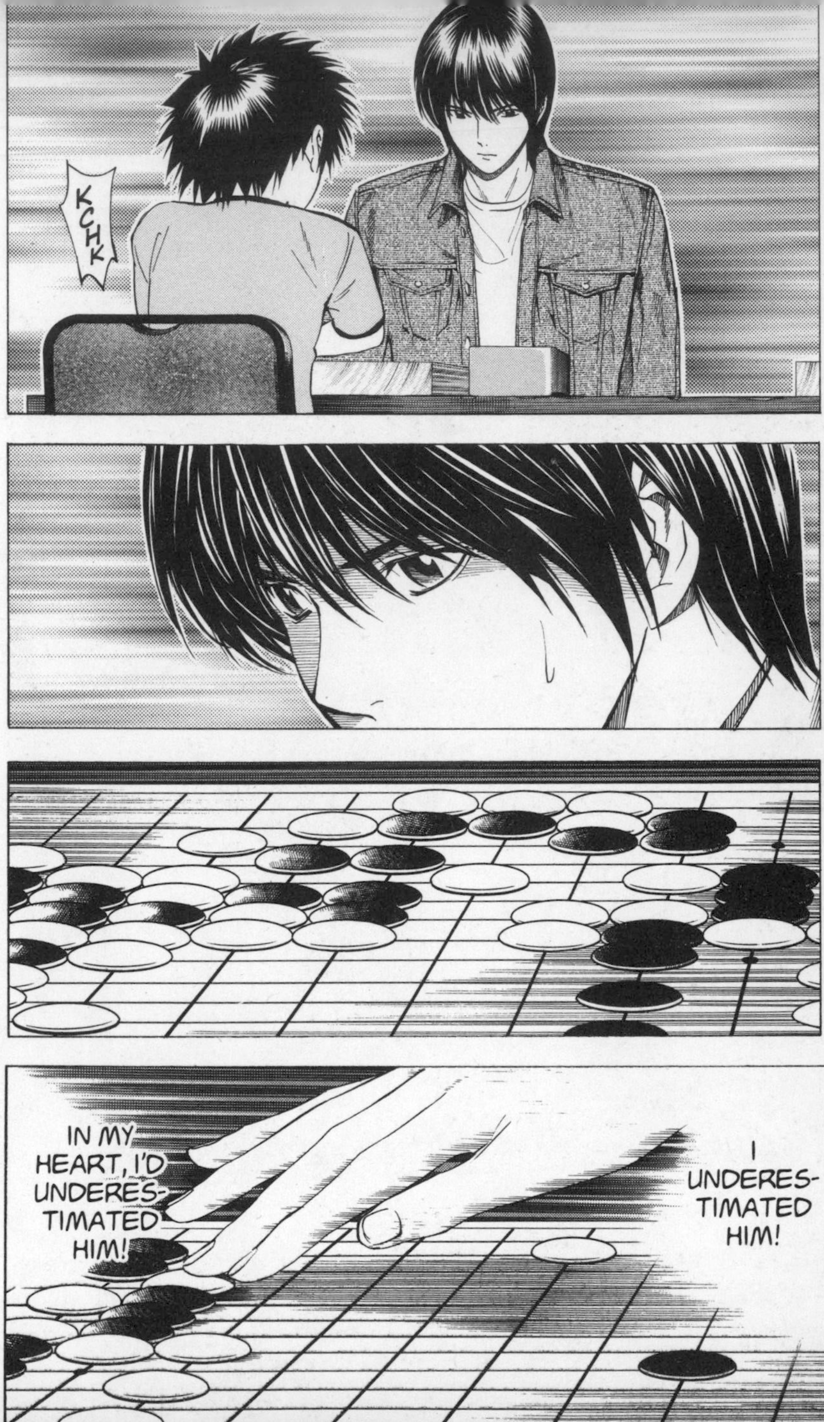
KCHK
I UNDERES-TIMATED HIM!
IN MY HEART, I'D UNDERES-TIMATED HIM!

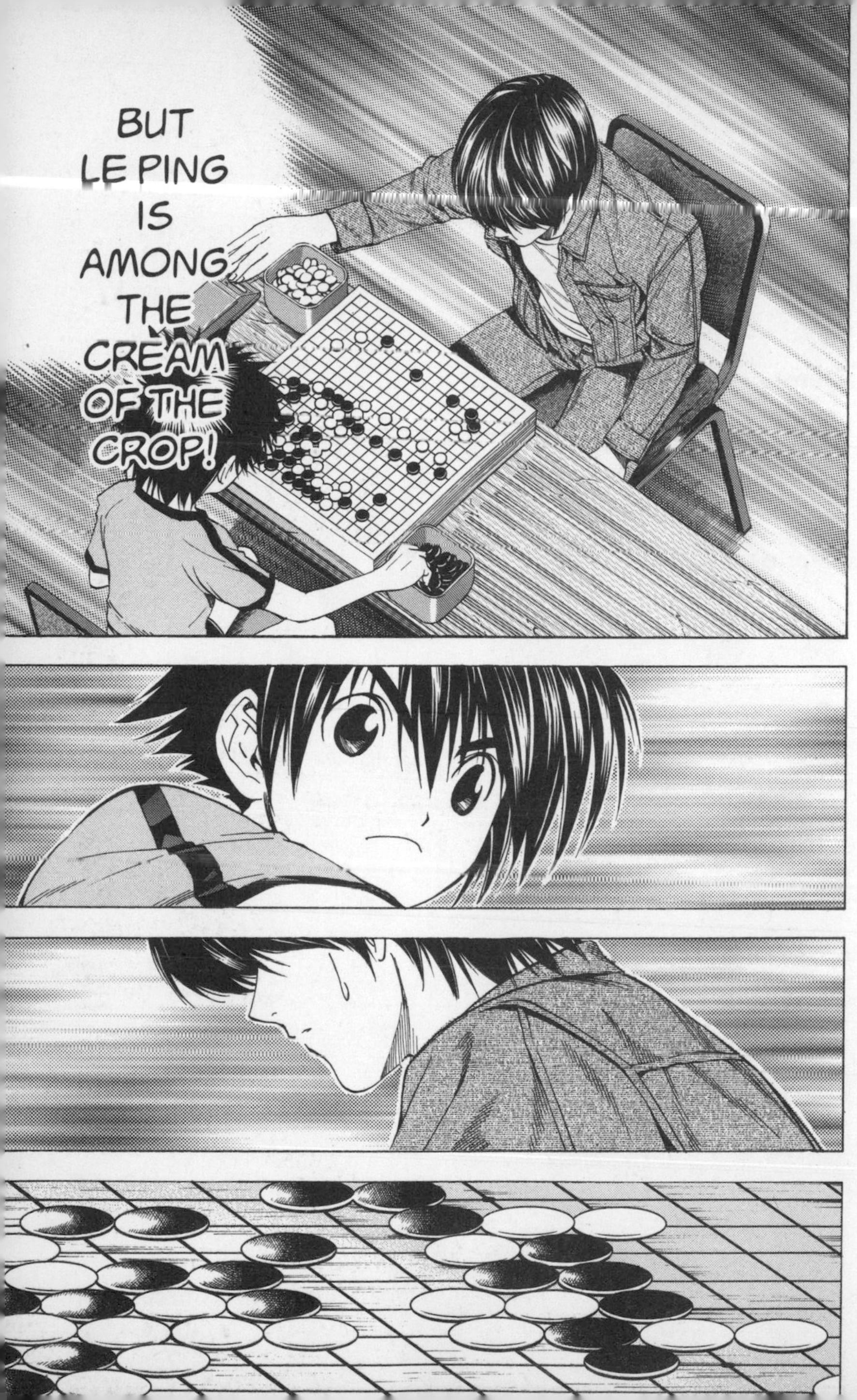
BUT LE PING IS AMONG THE CREAM OF THE CROP!

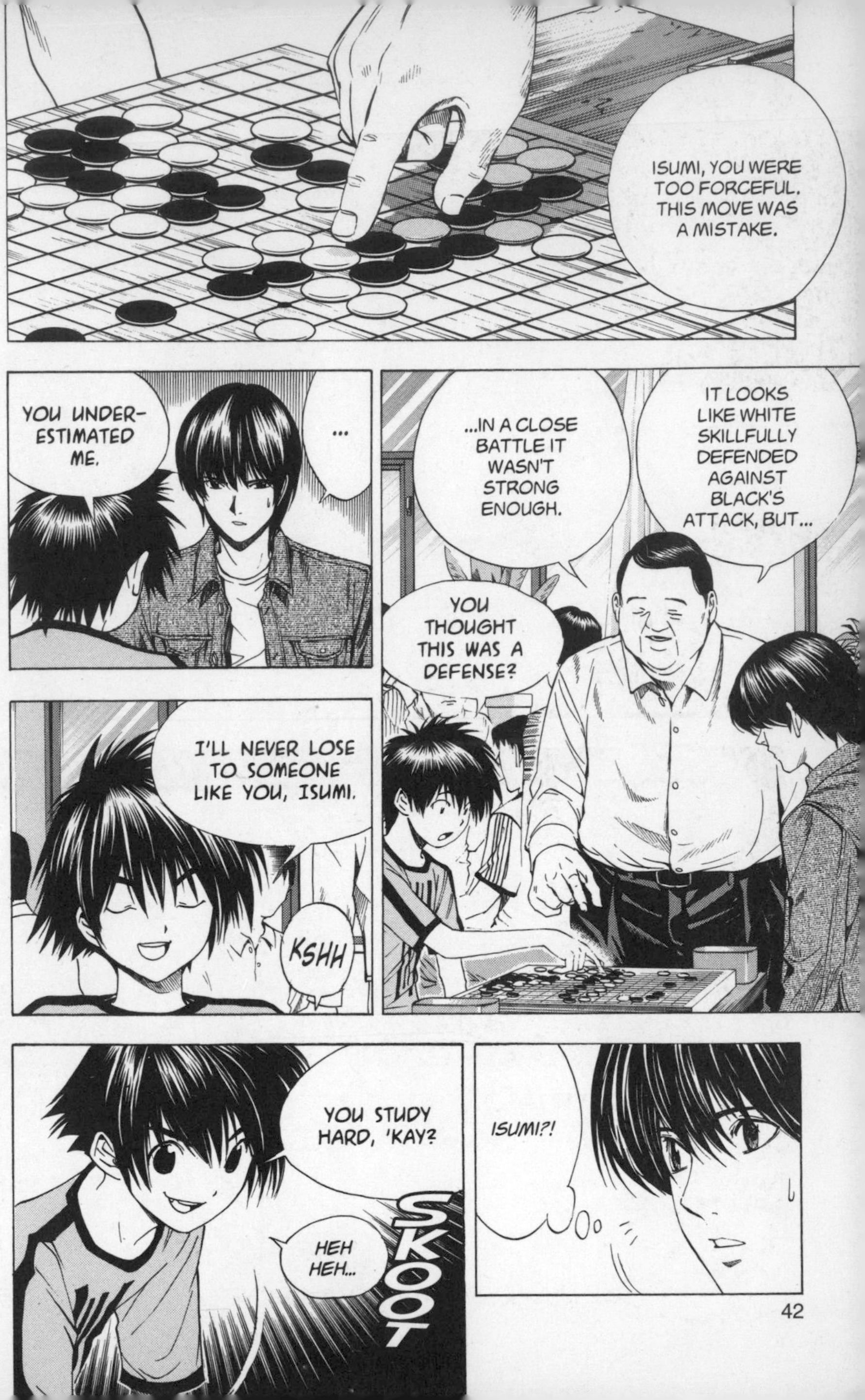
ISUMI, YOU WERE TOO FORCEFUL. THIS MOVE WAS A MISTAKE.
IT LOOKS LIKE WHITE SKILLFULLY DEFENDED AGAINST BLACK'S ATTACK, BUT...
...IN A CLOSE BATTLE IT WASN'T STRONG ENOUGH.
YOU THOUGHT THIS WAS A DEFENSE?
...
YOU UNDER-ESTIMATED ME.
I'LL NEVER LOSE TO SOMEONE LIKE YOU, ISUMI.
KSHH
ISUMI?!
YOU STUDY HARD, 'KAY?
HEH HEH...
SKOOT

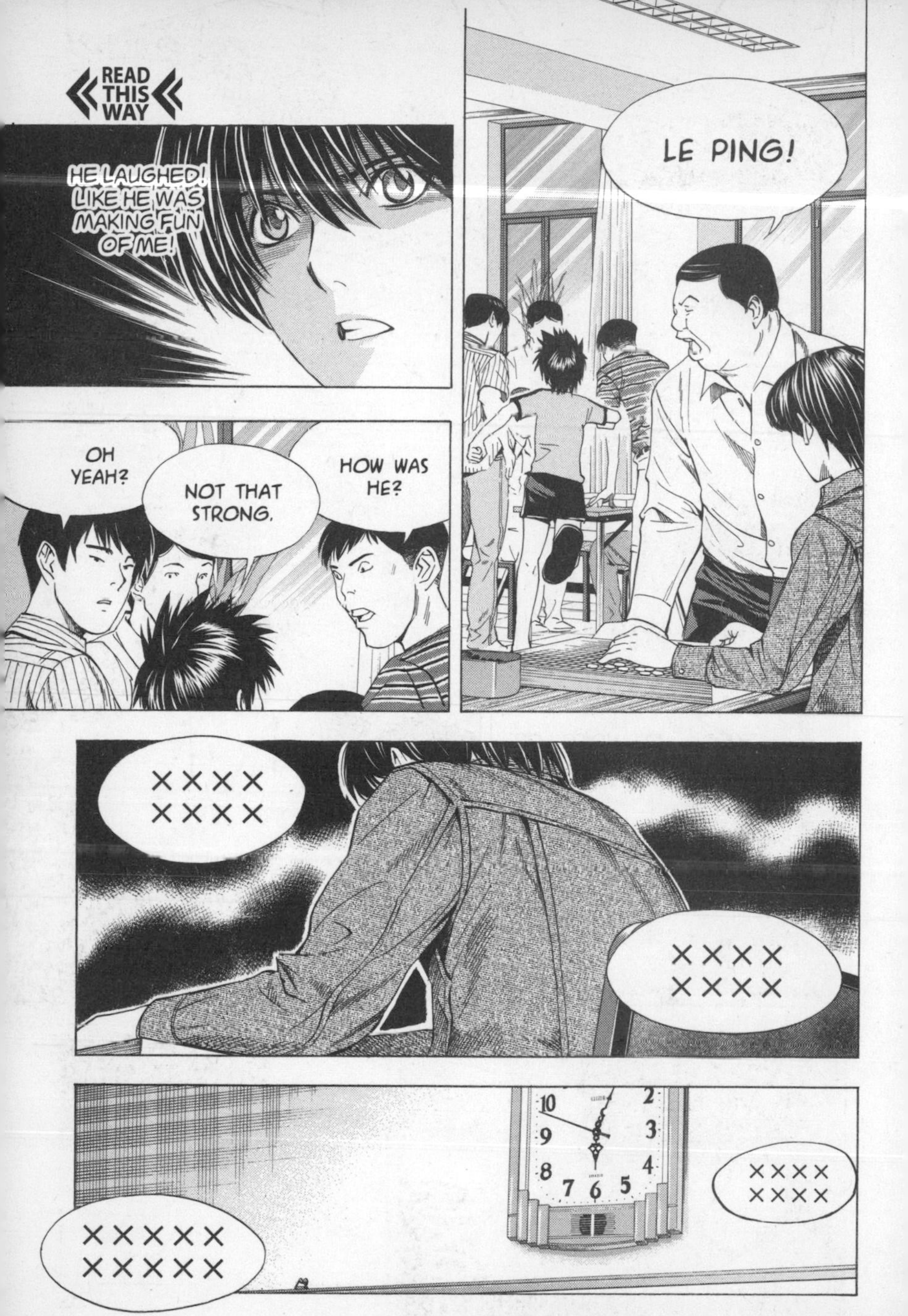
READ THIS WAY
LE PING!
HE LAUGHED! LIKE HE WAS MAKING FUN OF ME!
HOW WAS HE?
NOT THAT STRONG.
OH YEAH?
×××× ××××
×××× ××××
×××× ××××
××××× ×××××

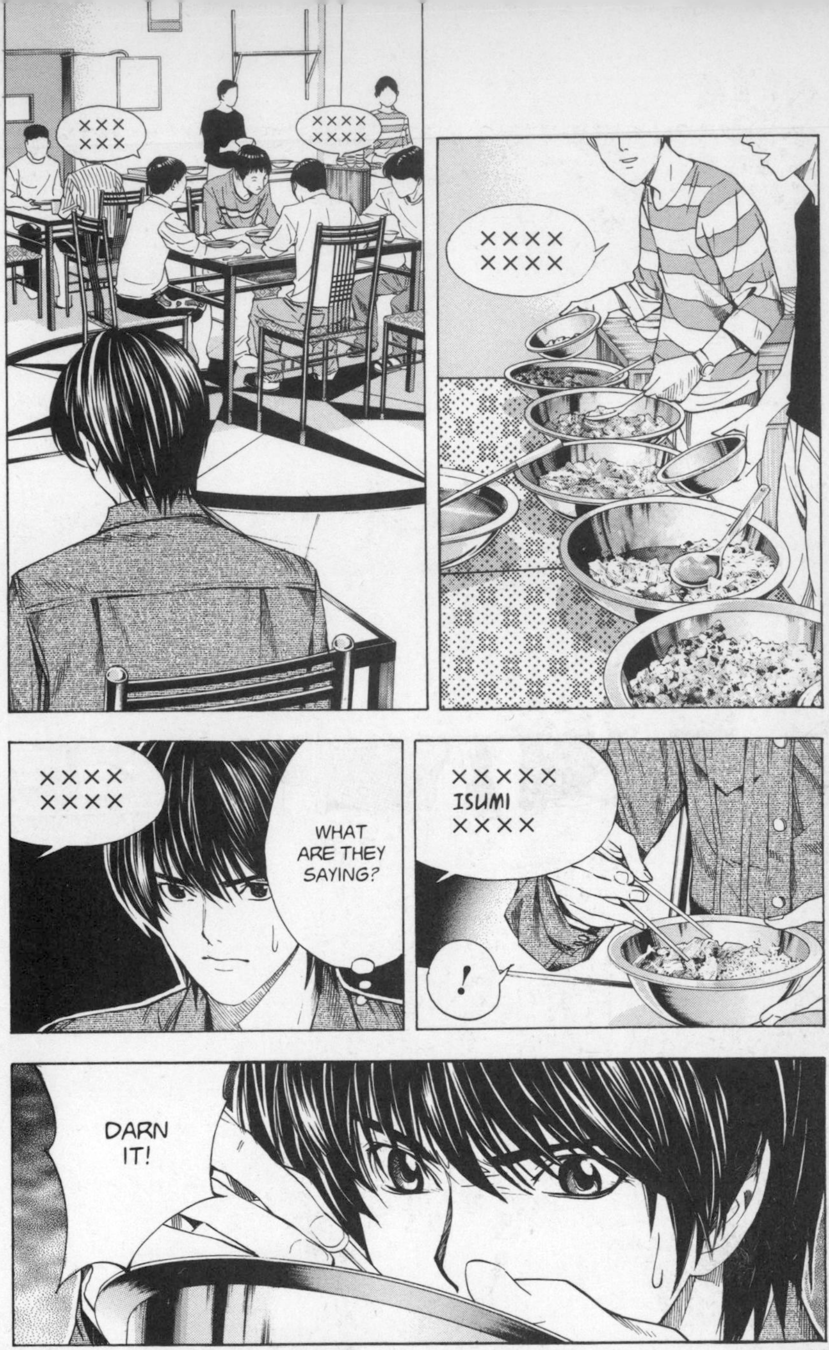
××××
××××
××××
××××
×××
×××
×××××
ISUMI
××××
!
WHAT ARE THEY SAYING?
××××
××××
DARN IT!

READ THIS WAY

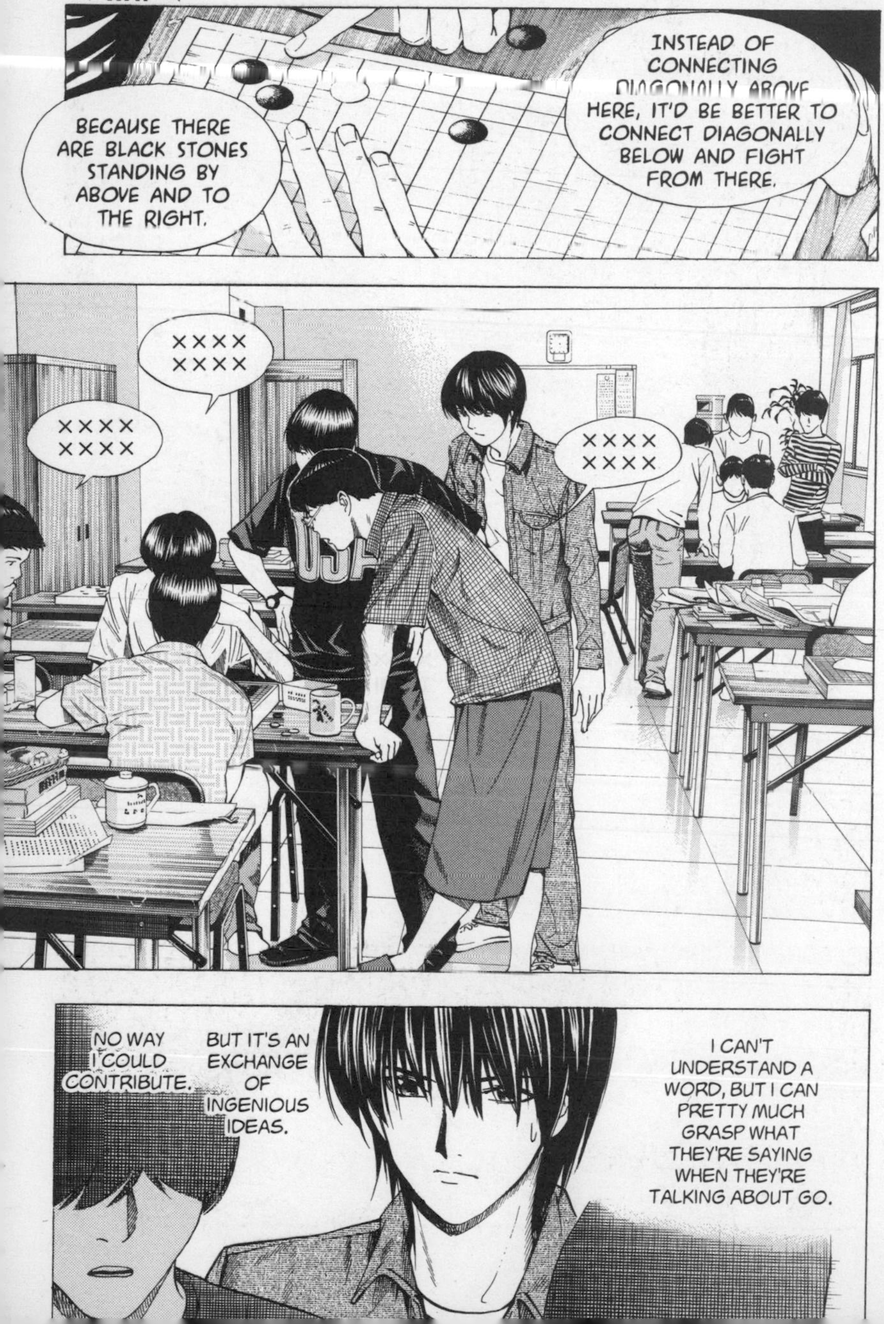
INSTEAD OF CONNECTING DIAGONALLY ABOVE HERE, IT'D BE BETTER TO CONNECT DIAGONALLY BELOW AND FIGHT FROM THERE.
BECAUSE THERE ARE BLACK STONES STANDING BY ABOVE AND TO THE RIGHT.
×××× ××××
×××× ××××
×××× ××××
I CAN'T UNDERSTAND A WORD, BUT I CAN PRETTY MUCH GRASP WHAT THEY'RE SAYING WHEN THEY'RE TALKING ABOUT GO.
BUT IT'S AN EXCHANGE OF INGENIOUS IDEAS.
NO WAY I COULD CONTRIBUTE.

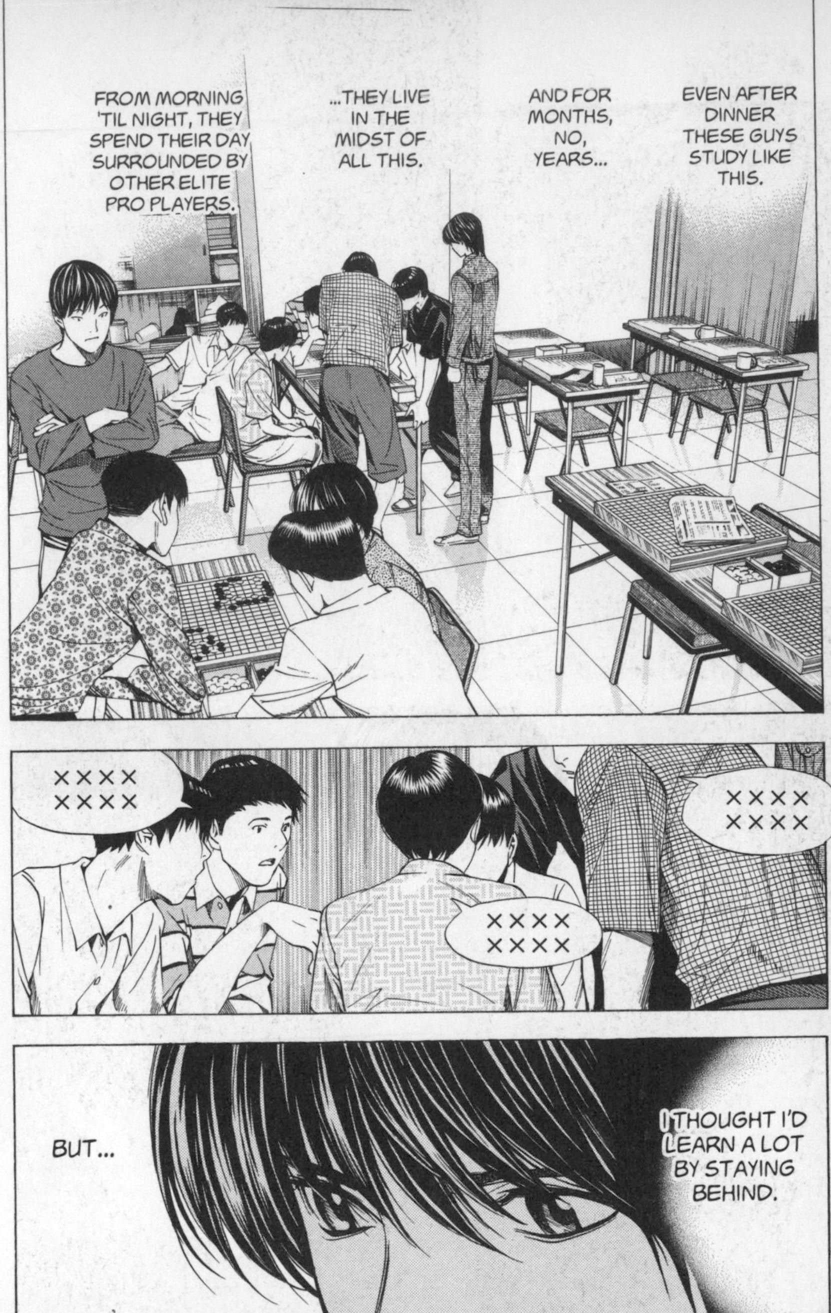
EVEN AFTER DINNER THESE GUYS STUDY LIKE THIS.
AND FOR MONTHS, NO, YEARS...
...THEY LIVE IN THE MIDST OF ALL THIS.
FROM MORNING 'TIL NIGHT, THEY SPEND THEIR DAY SURROUNDED BY OTHER ELITE PRO PLAYERS.
×××× ××××
×××× ××××
×××× ××××
I THOUGHT I'D LEARN A LOT BY STAYING BEHIND.
BUT...

READ THIS WAY

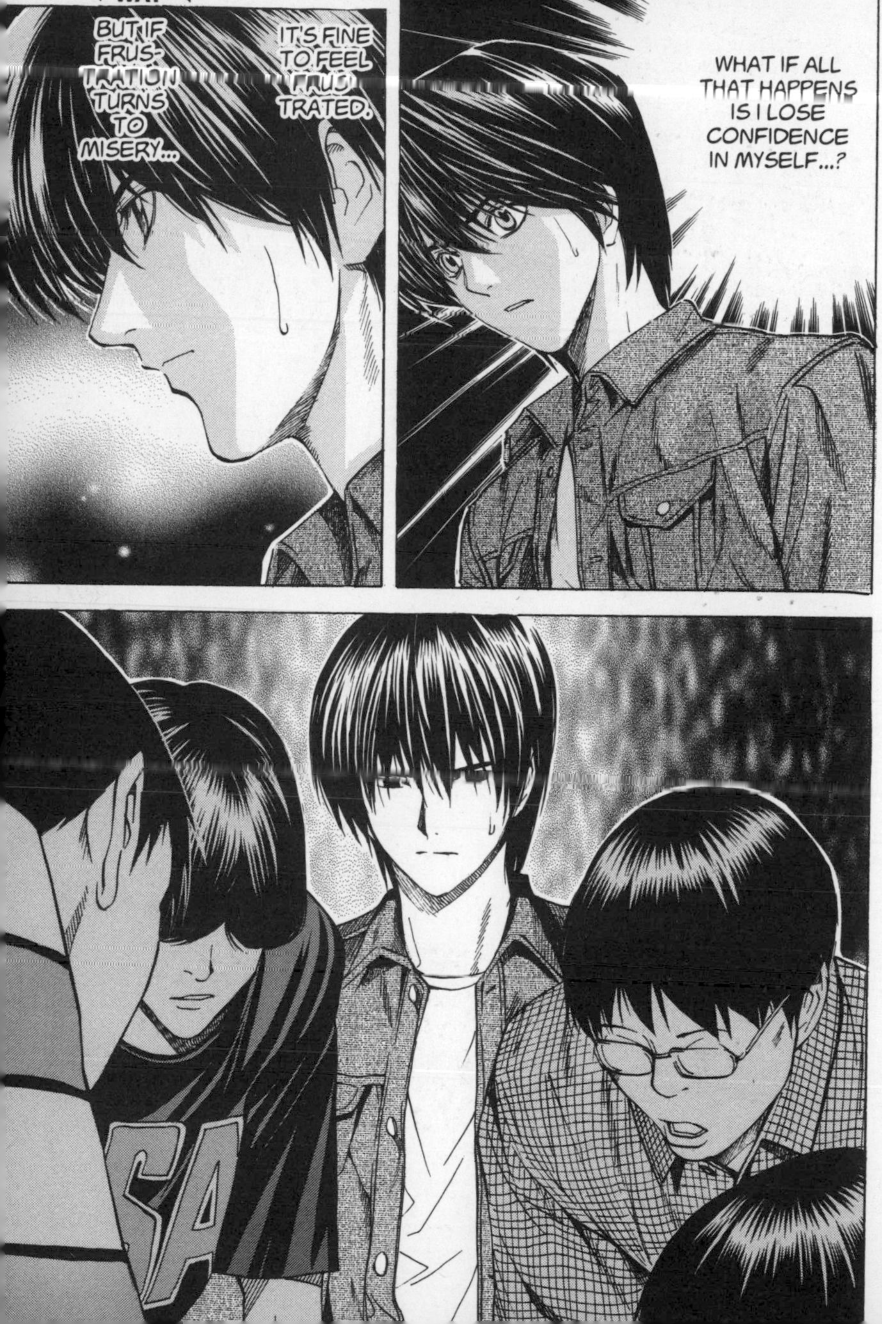
WHAT IF ALL THAT HAPPENS IS I LOSE CONFIDENCE IN MYSELF...?
IT'S FINE TO FEEL FRUSTRATED.
BUT IF FRUSTRATION TURNS TO MISERY...

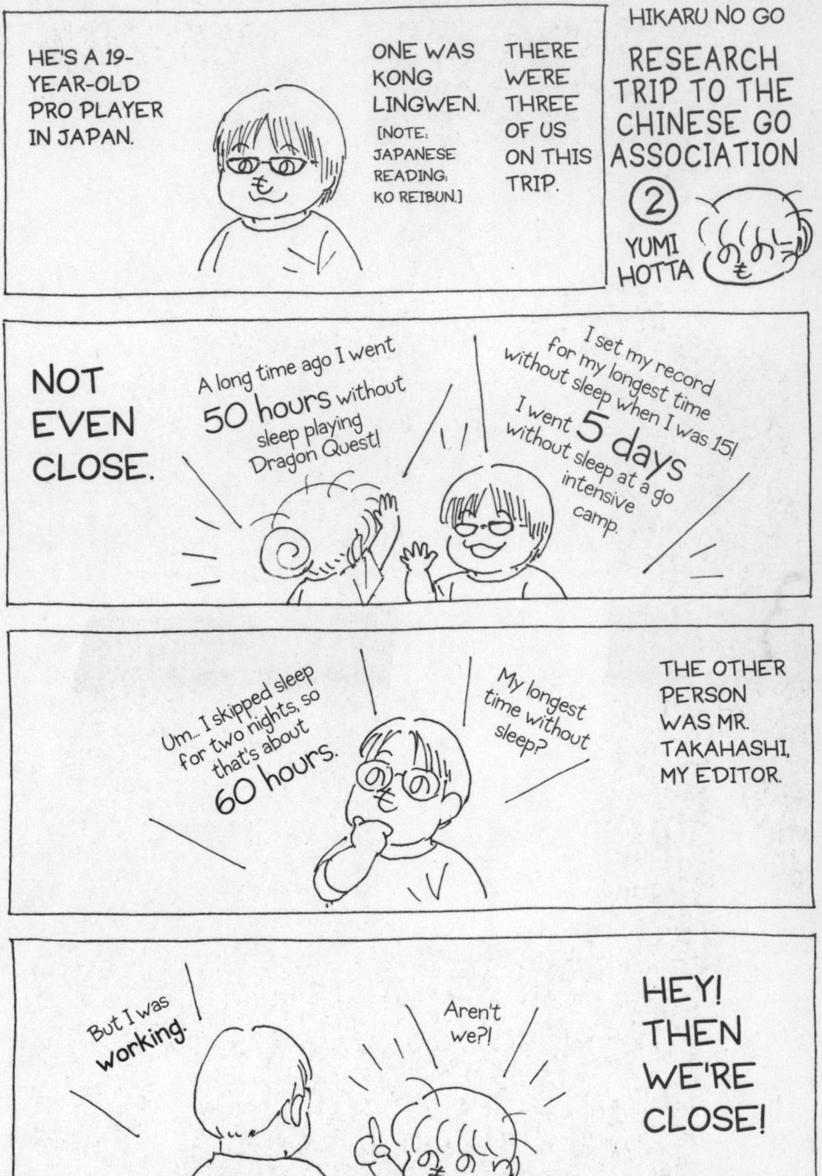
HIKARU NO GO
RESEARCH TRIP TO THE CHINESE GO ASSOCIATION
2
YUMI HOTTA
THERE WERE THREE OF US ON THIS TRIP.
ONE WAS KONG LINGWEN.
[NOTE: JAPANESE READING: KO REIBUN.]
HE'S A 19-YEAR-OLD PRO PLAYER IN JAPAN.
I set my record for my longest time without sleep when I was 15!
I went 5 days without sleep at a go intensive camp.
A long time ago I went 50 hours without sleep playing Dragon Quest!
NOT EVEN CLOSE.
THE OTHER PERSON WAS MR. TAKAHASHI, MY EDITOR.
My longest time without sleep?
Um... I skipped sleep for two nights, so that's about 60 hours.
HEY! THEN WE'RE CLOSE!
Aren't we?!
But I was working.

Game 133 "Isumi, Put to the Test"

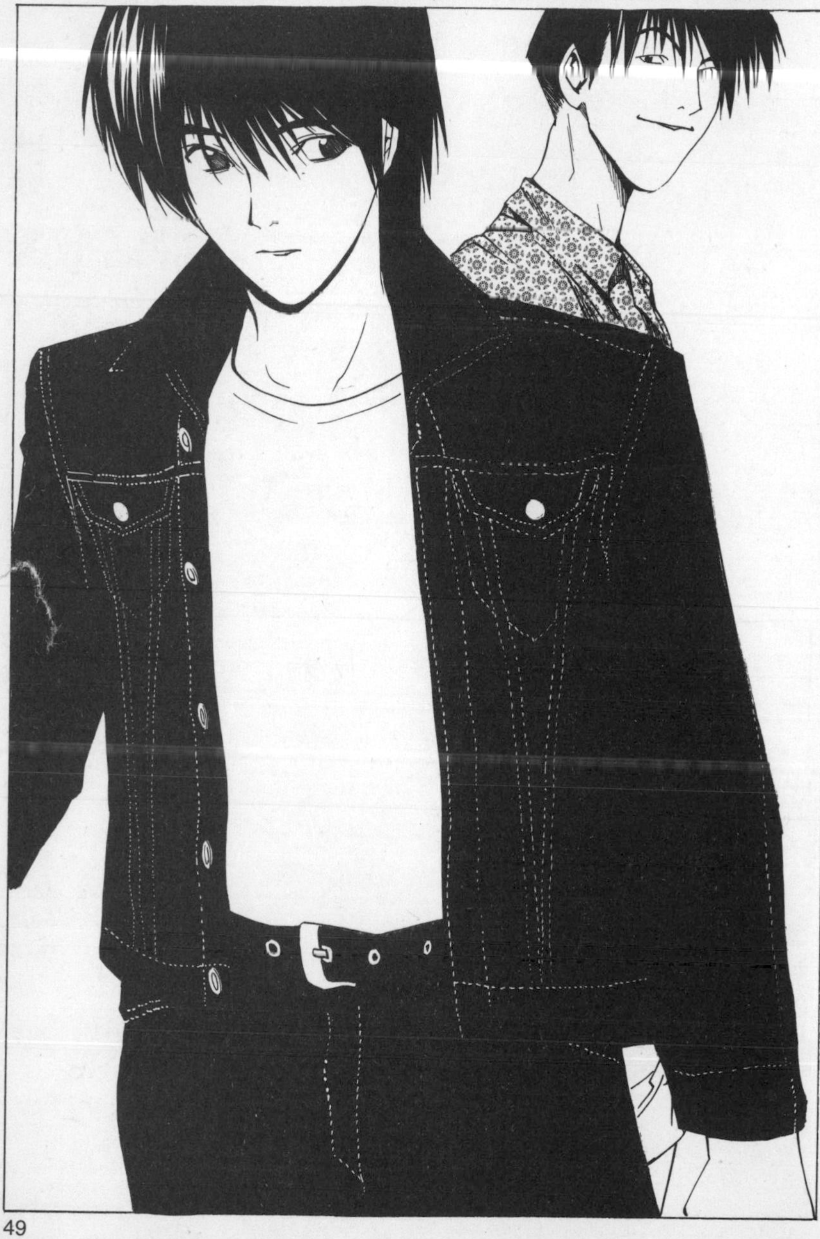

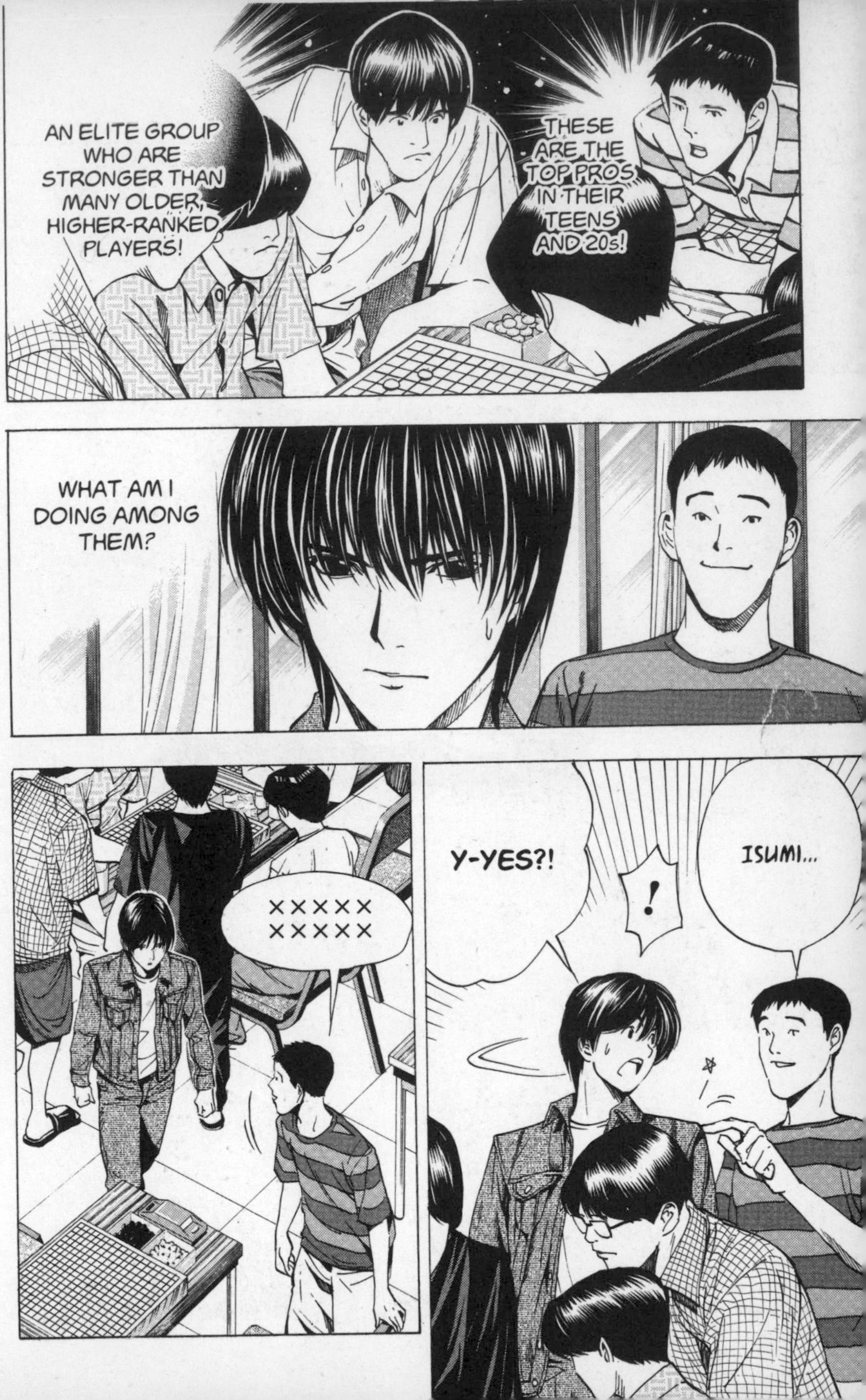
THESE ARE THE TOP PROS IN THEIR TEENS AND 20s!
AN ELITE GROUP WHO ARE STRONGER THAN MANY OLDER, HIGHER-RANKED PLAYERS!
WHAT AM I DOING AMONG THEM?
ISUMI...
!
Y-YES?!
×××××
×××××

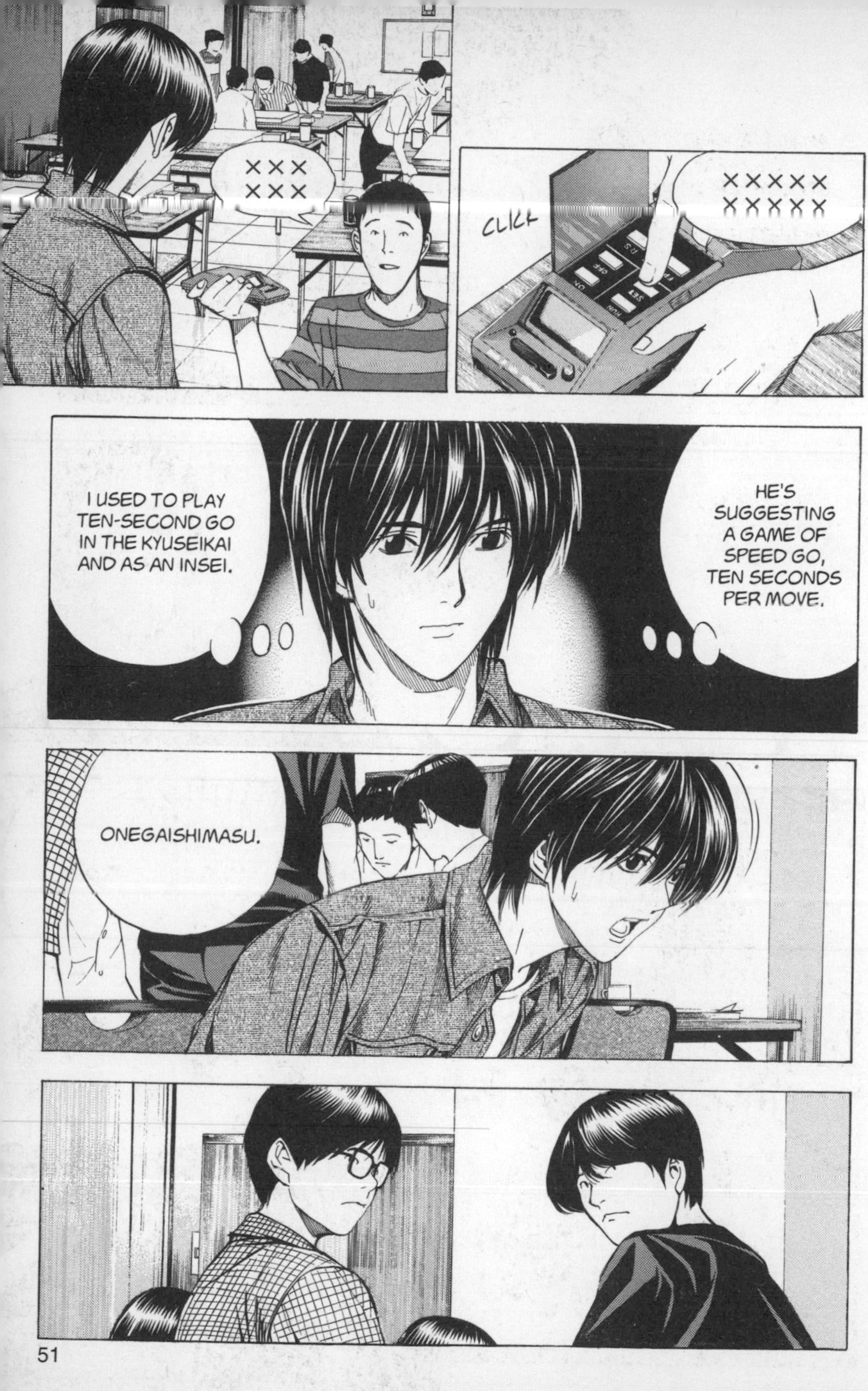
×××××
×××××
CLICK
×××
×××
HE'S SUGGESTING A GAME OF SPEED GO, TEN SECONDS PER MOVE.
I USED TO PLAY TEN-SECOND GO IN THE KYUSEIKAI AND AS AN INSEI.
ONEGAISHIMASU.

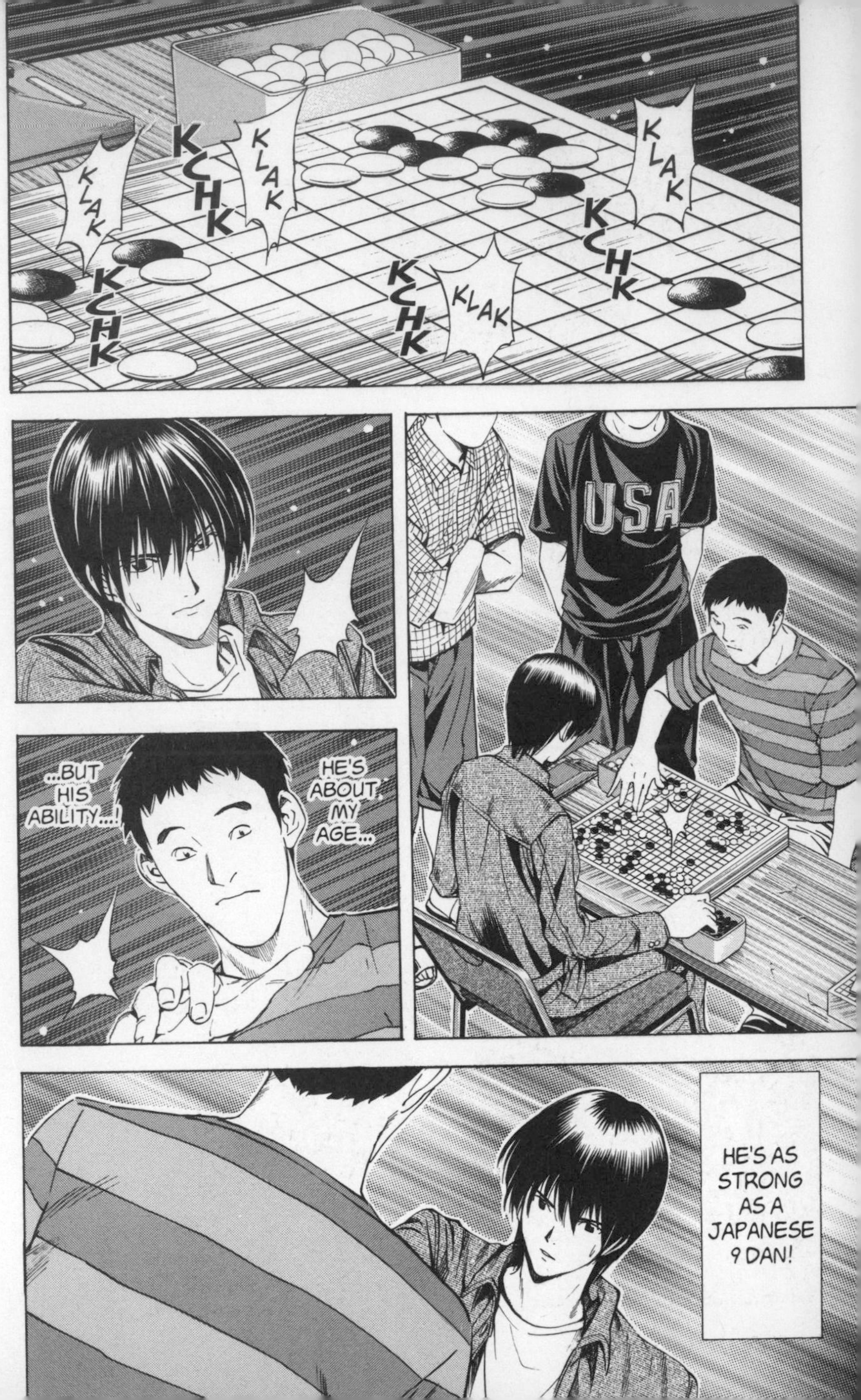
KLAK
KCHK
KLAK
KCHK
KLAK
KCHK
KLAK
KCHK
HE'S ABOUT MY AGE...
...BUT HIS ABILITY...!
HE'S AS STRONG AS A JAPANESE 9 DAN!

I...I RESIGN.

BOW

HE DOESN'T UNDERSTAND!

?!

XXXX XXXX

XXXX XXXX

XXXX XXXX

HUH?

53

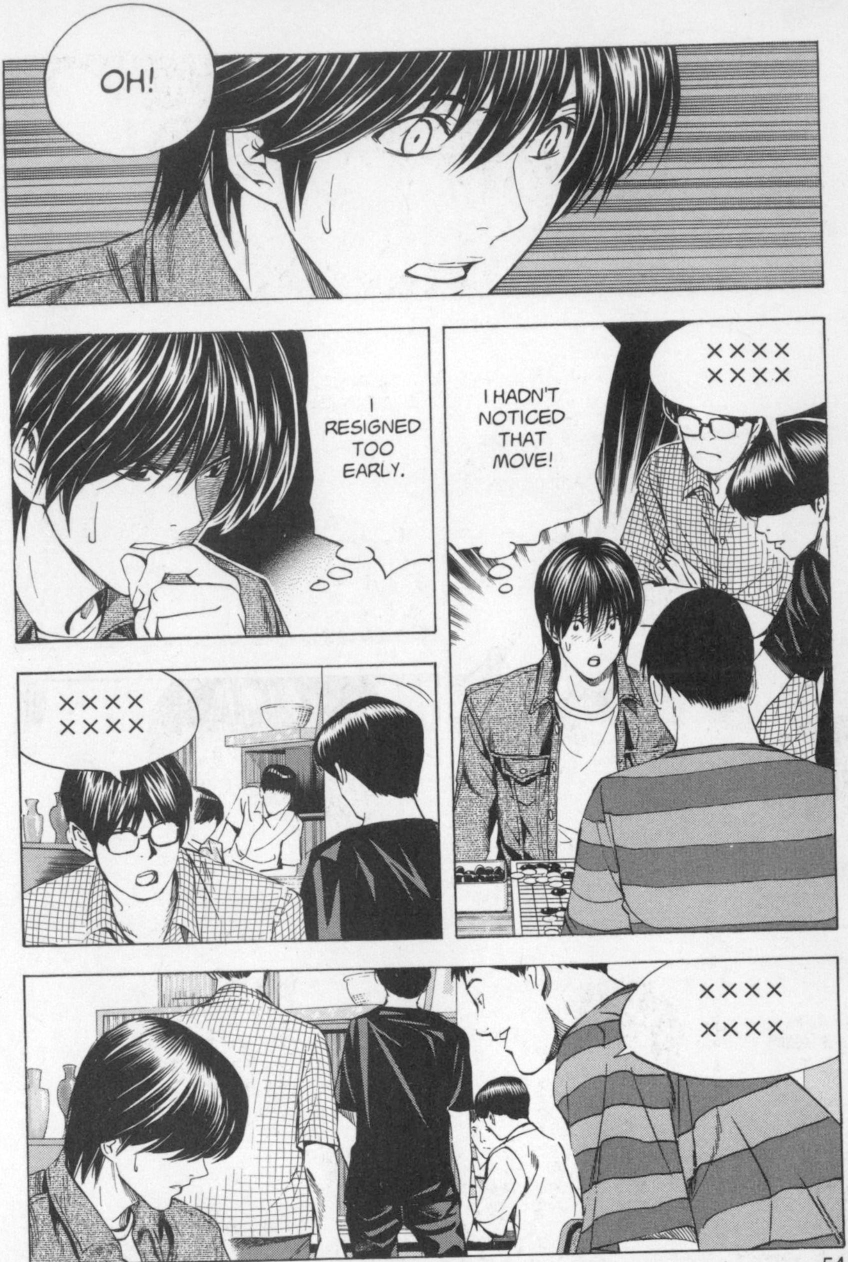
OH!
××××
××××
I HADN'T NOTICED THAT MOVE!
I RESIGNED TOO EARLY.
××××
××××
××××
××××

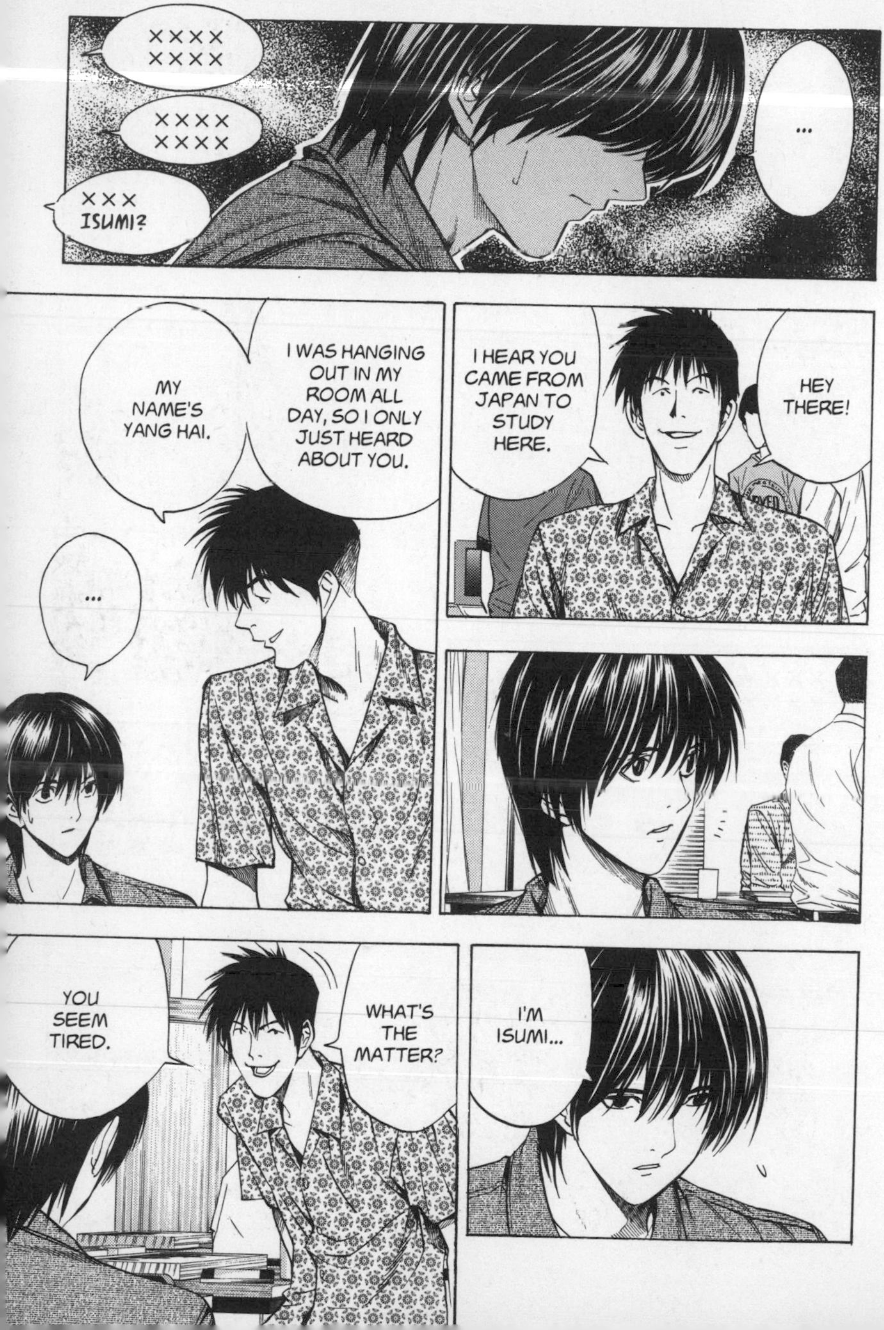

×××× ××××
×××× ××××
××× ISUMI?
...
HEY THERE!
I HEAR YOU CAME FROM JAPAN TO STUDY HERE.
I WAS HANGING OUT IN MY ROOM ALL DAY, SO I ONLY JUST HEARD ABOUT YOU.
MY NAME'S YANG HAI.
...
I'M ISUMI...
WHAT'S THE MATTER?
YOU SEEM TIRED.

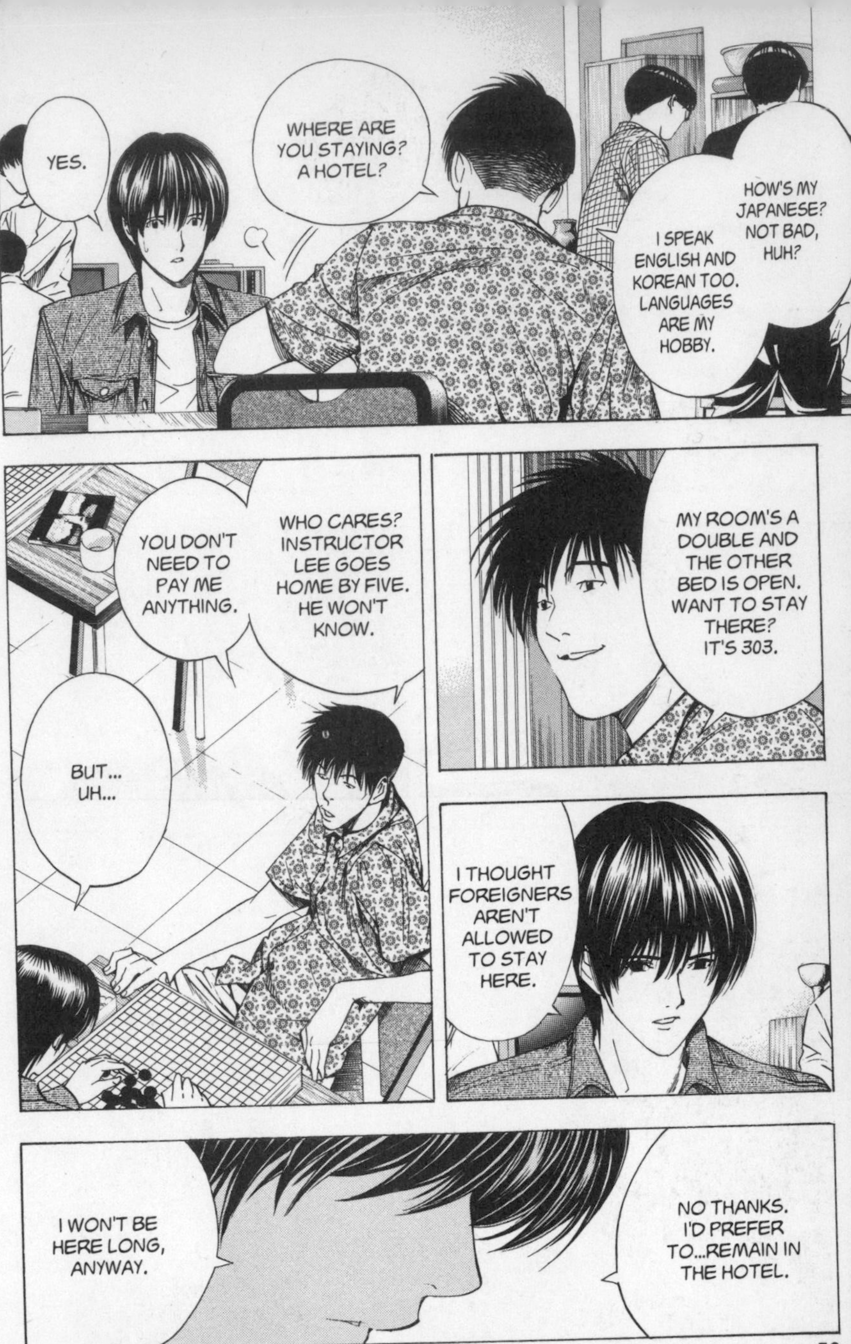
HOW'S MY JAPANESE? NOT BAD, HUH?
I SPEAK ENGLISH AND KOREAN TOO. LANGUAGES ARE MY HOBBY.
WHERE ARE YOU STAYING? A HOTEL?
YES.
MY ROOM'S A DOUBLE AND THE OTHER BED IS OPEN. WANT TO STAY THERE? IT'S 303.
I THOUGHT FOREIGNERS AREN'T ALLOWED TO STAY HERE.
WHO CARES? INSTRUCTOR LEE GOES HOME BY FIVE. HE WON'T KNOW.
YOU DON'T NEED TO PAY ME ANYTHING.
BUT... UH...
NO THANKS. I'D PREFER TO...REMAIN IN THE HOTEL.
I WON'T BE HERE LONG, ANYWAY.

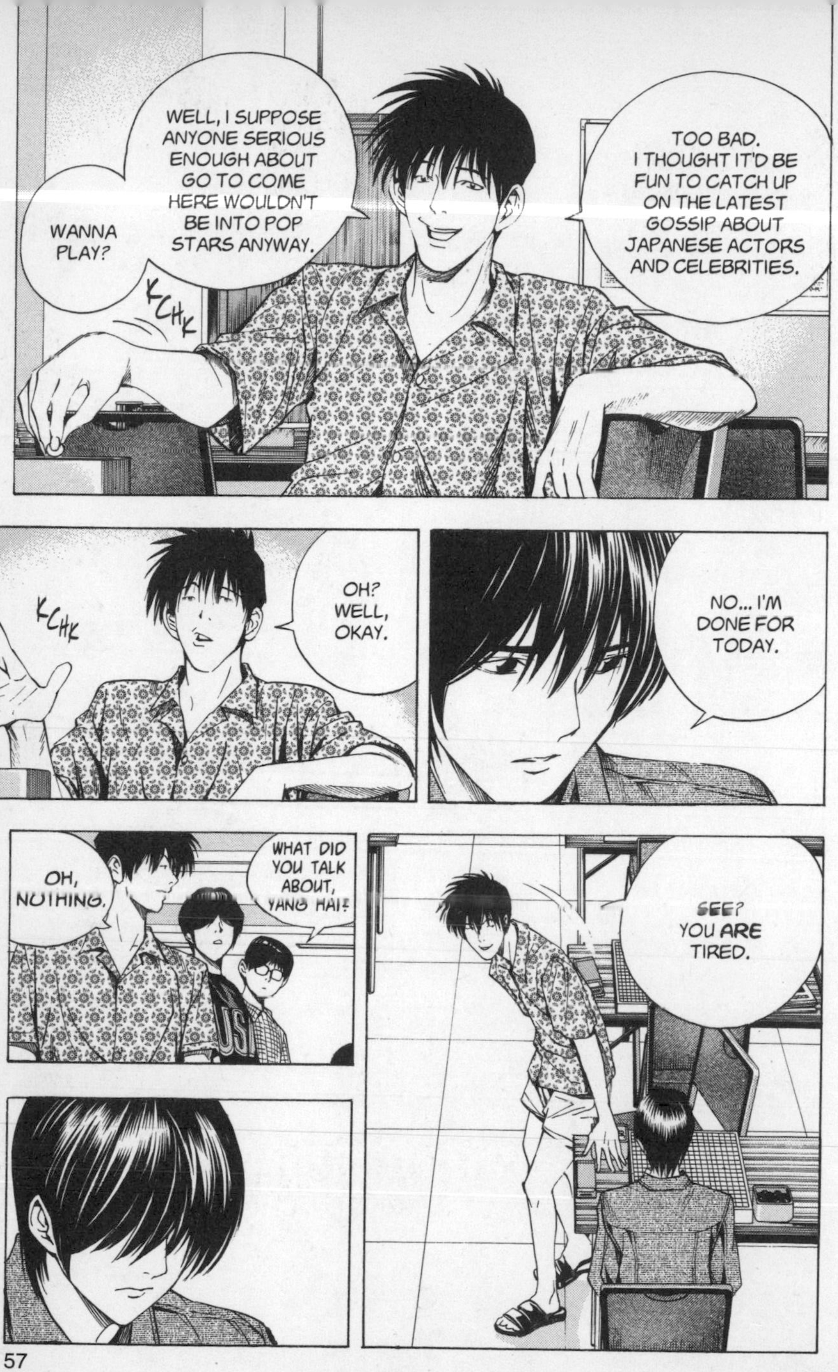
TOO BAD. I THOUGHT IT'D BE FUN TO CATCH UP ON THE LATEST GOSSIP ABOUT JAPANESE ACTORS AND CELEBRITIES.
WELL, I SUPPOSE ANYONE SERIOUS ENOUGH ABOUT GO TO COME HERE WOULDN'T BE INTO POP STARS ANYWAY.
WANNA PLAY?
KCHK
NO... I'M DONE FOR TODAY.
OH? WELL, OKAY.
KCHK
SEE? YOU ARE TIRED.
WHAT DID YOU TALK ABOUT, YANG HAI?
OH, NOTHING.

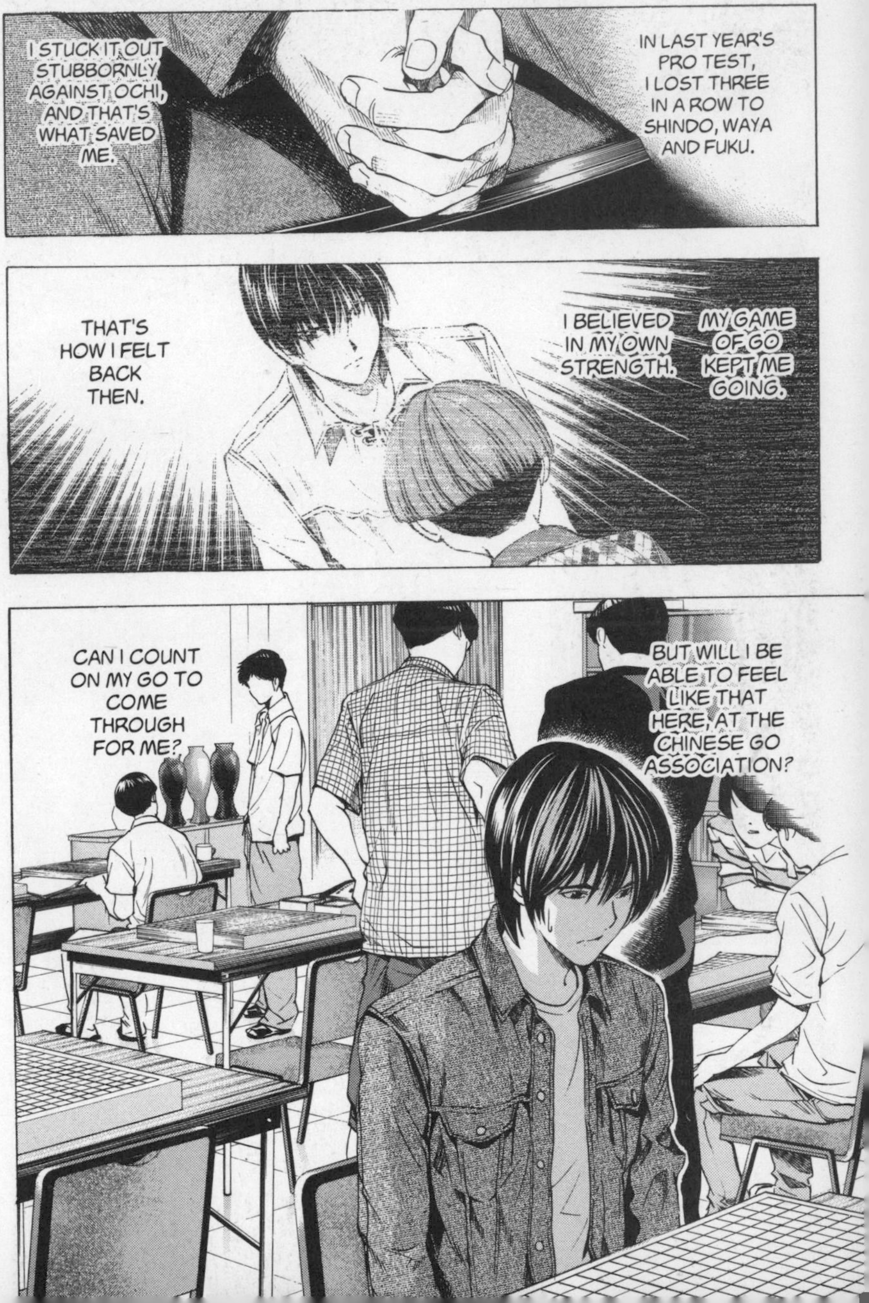
IN LAST YEAR'S PRO TEST, I LOST THREE IN A ROW TO SHINDO, WAYA AND FUKU.
I STUCK IT OUT STUBBORNLY AGAINST OCHI, AND THAT'S WHAT SAVED ME.
MY GAME OF GO KEPT ME GOING.
I BELIEVED IN MY OWN STRENGTH.
THAT'S HOW I FELT BACK THEN.
BUT WILL I BE ABLE TO FEEL LIKE THAT HERE, AT THE CHINESE GO ASSOCIATION?
CAN I COUNT ON MY GO TO COME THROUGH FOR ME?

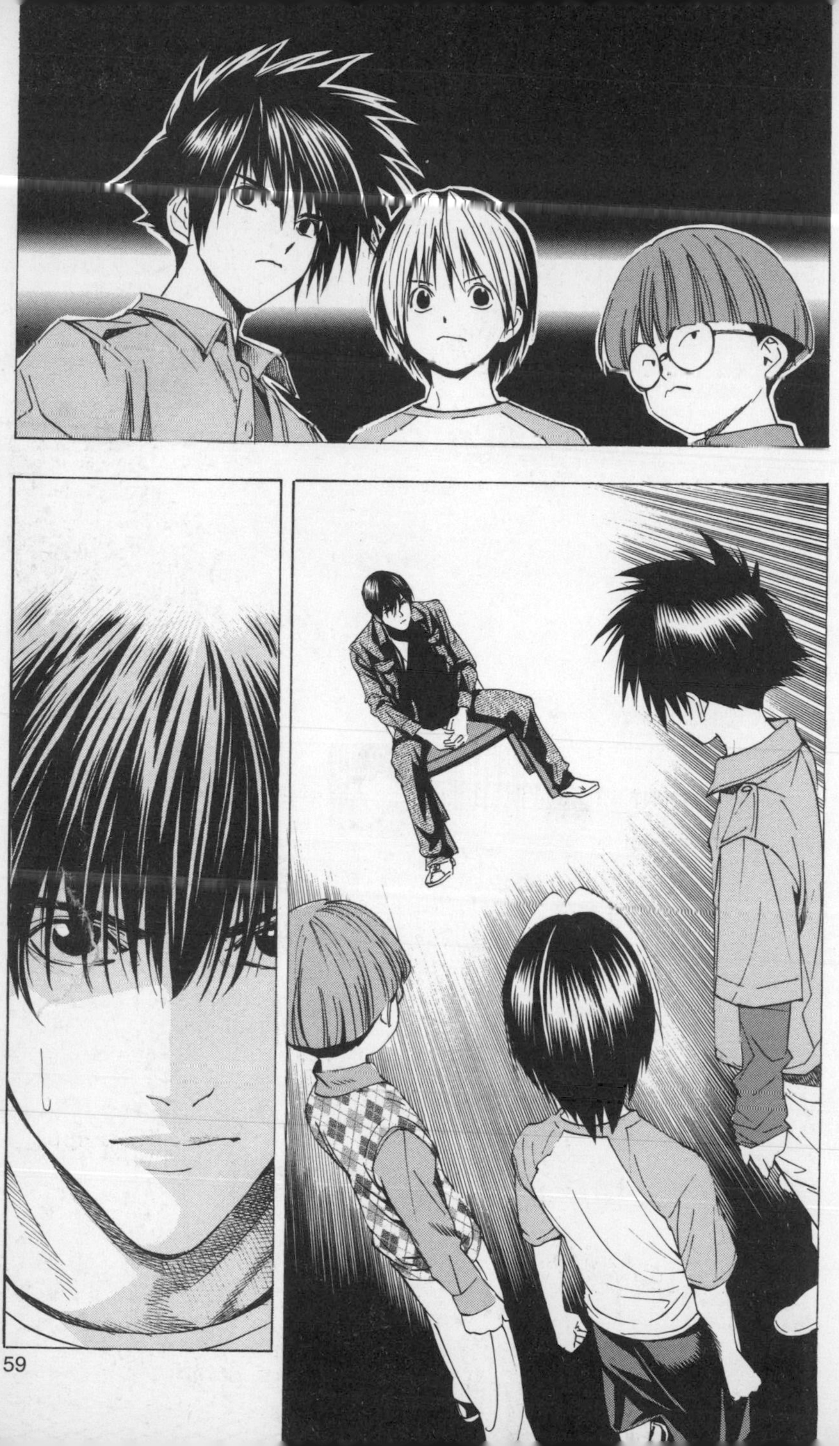

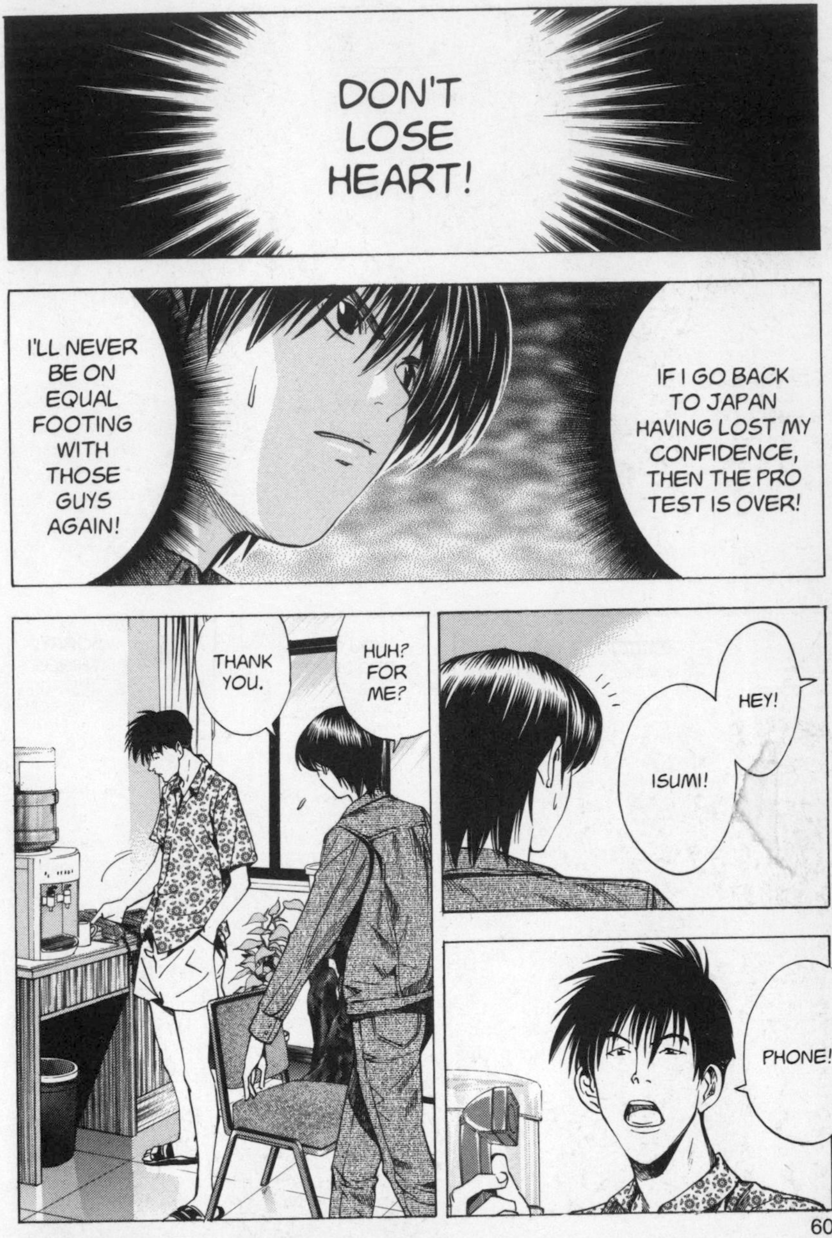
DON'T LOSE HEART!
IF I GO BACK TO JAPAN HAVING LOST MY CONFIDENCE, THEN THE PRO TEST IS OVER!
I'LL NEVER BE ON EQUAL FOOTING WITH THOSE GUYS AGAIN!
HEY! ISUMI!
PHONE!
HUH? FOR ME?
THANK YOU.

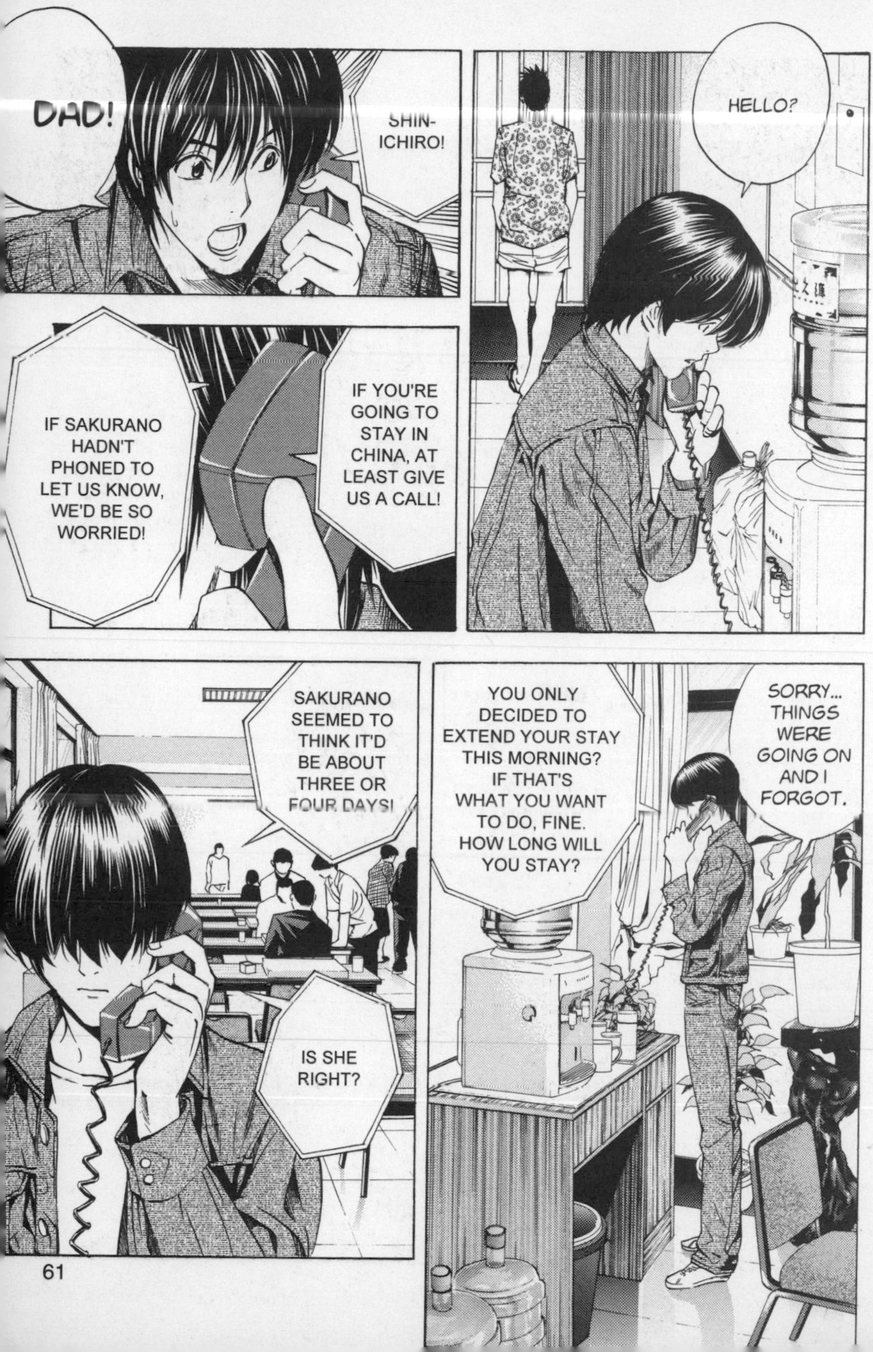
HELLO?
SHIN-ICHIRO!
DAD!
IF YOU'RE GOING TO STAY IN CHINA, AT LEAST GIVE US A CALL!
IF SAKURANO HADN'T PHONED TO LET US KNOW, WE'D BE SO WORRIED!
SORRY... THINGS WERE GOING ON AND I FORGOT.
YOU ONLY DECIDED TO EXTEND YOUR STAY THIS MORNING? IF THAT'S WHAT YOU WANT TO DO, FINE. HOW LONG WILL YOU STAY?
SAKURANO SEEMED TO THINK IT'D BE ABOUT THREE OR FOUR DAYS!
IS SHE RIGHT?

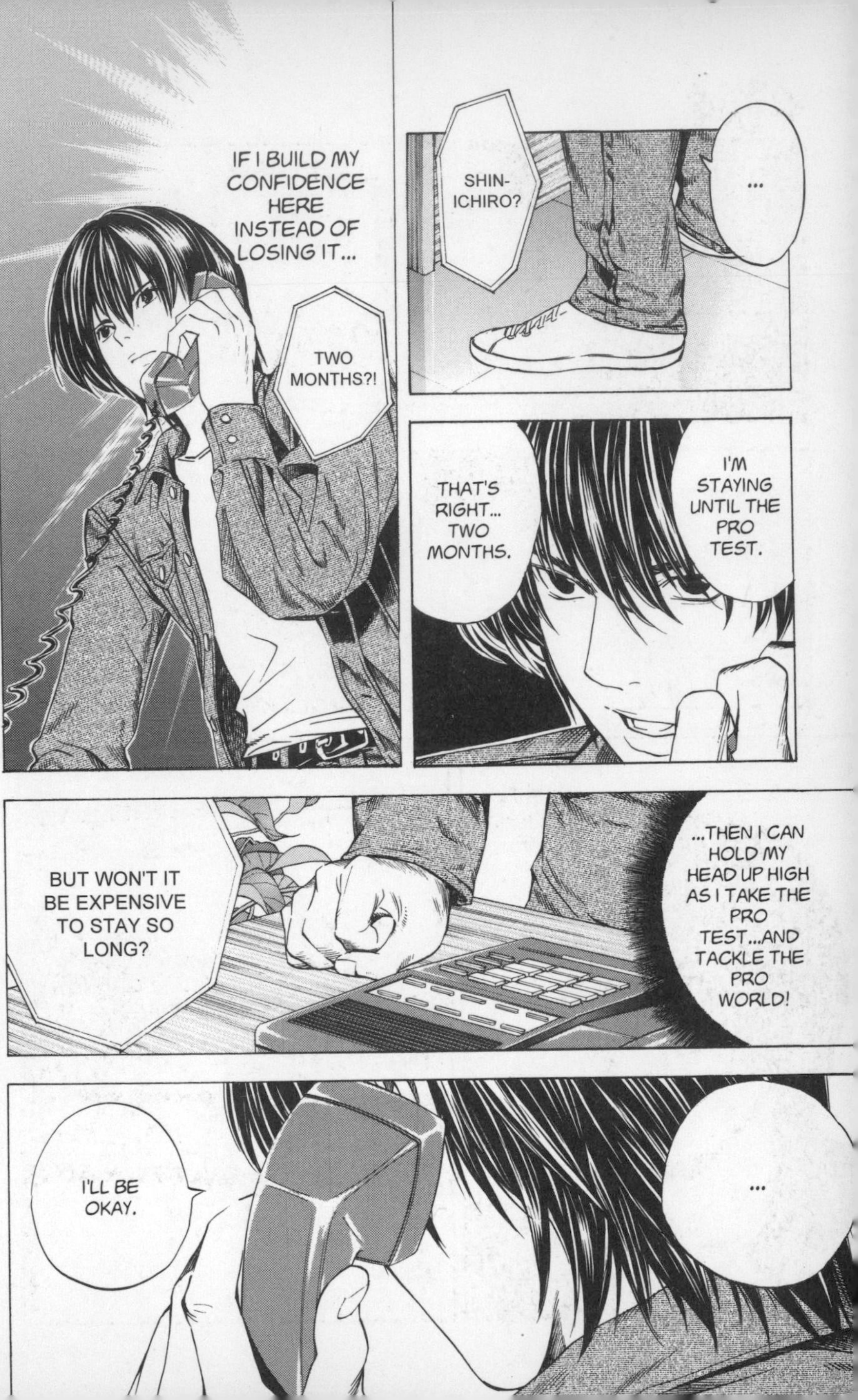
...
SHIN-ICHIRO?
I'M STAYING UNTIL THE PRO TEST.
THAT'S RIGHT... TWO MONTHS.
TWO MONTHS?!
IF I BUILD MY CONFIDENCE HERE INSTEAD OF LOSING IT...
...THEN I CAN HOLD MY HEAD UP HIGH AS I TAKE THE PRO TEST...AND TACKLE THE PRO WORLD!
BUT WON'T IT BE EXPENSIVE TO STAY SO LONG?
...
I'LL BE OKAY.

READ THIS WAY

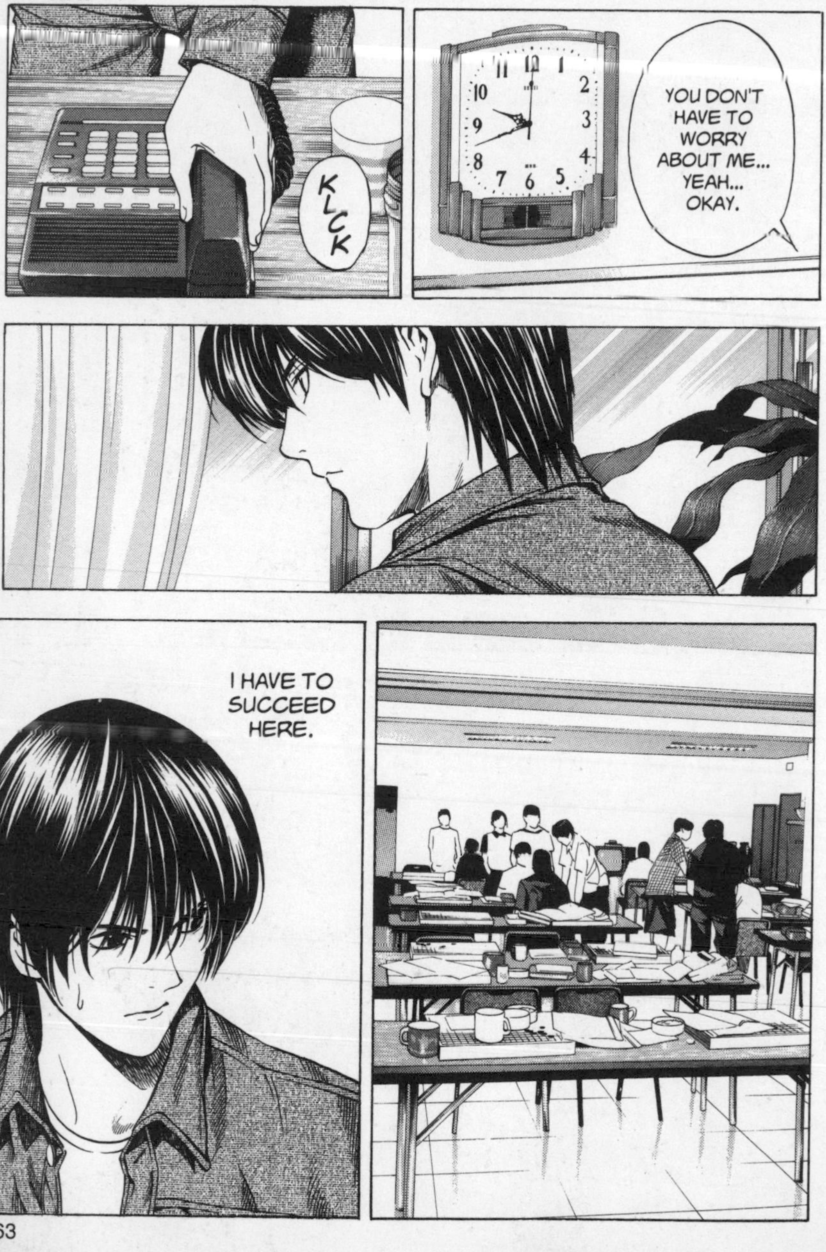
YOU DON'T HAVE TO WORRY ABOUT ME... YEAH... OKAY.
KLCK
I HAVE TO SUCCEED HERE.

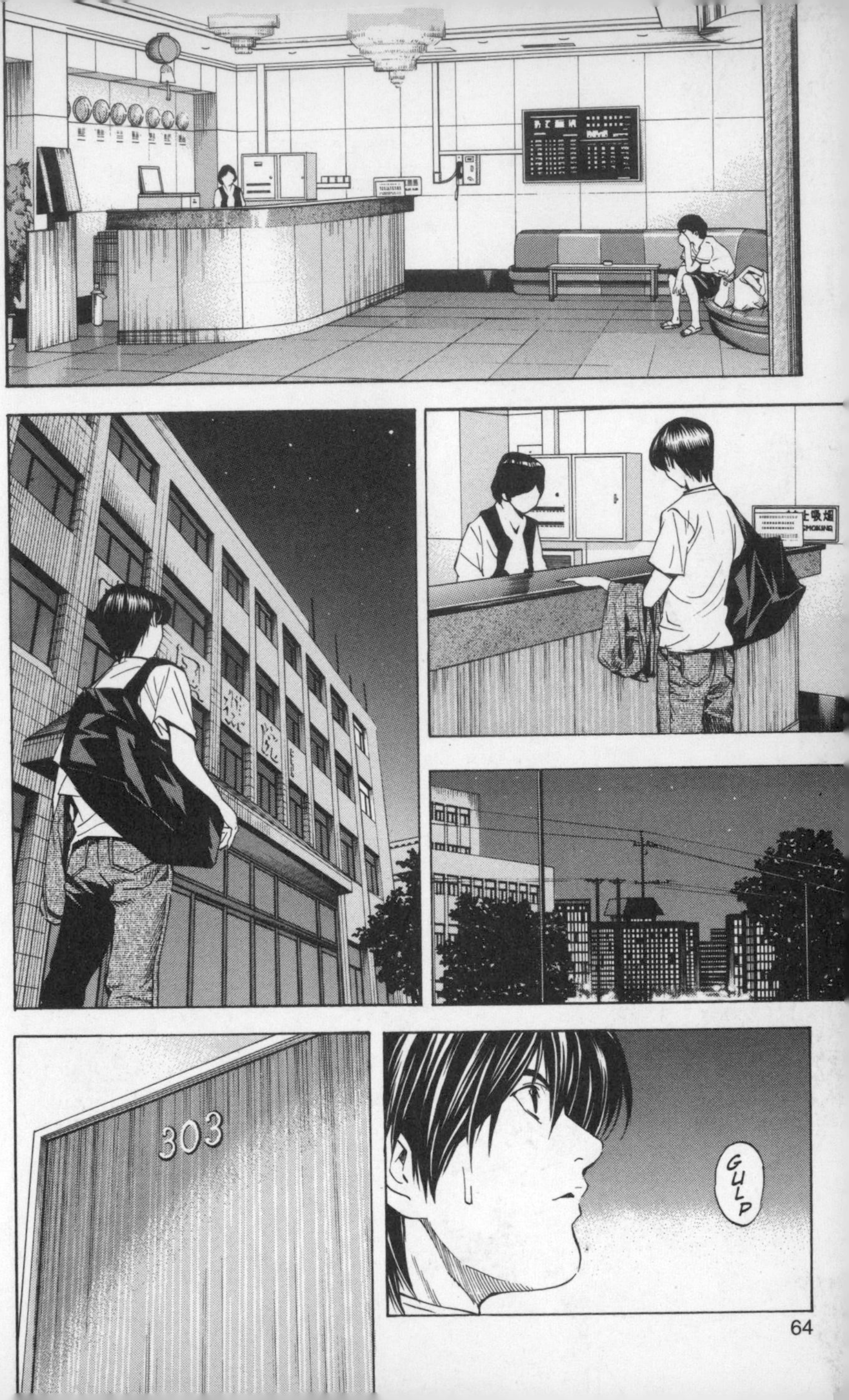
GULP
303

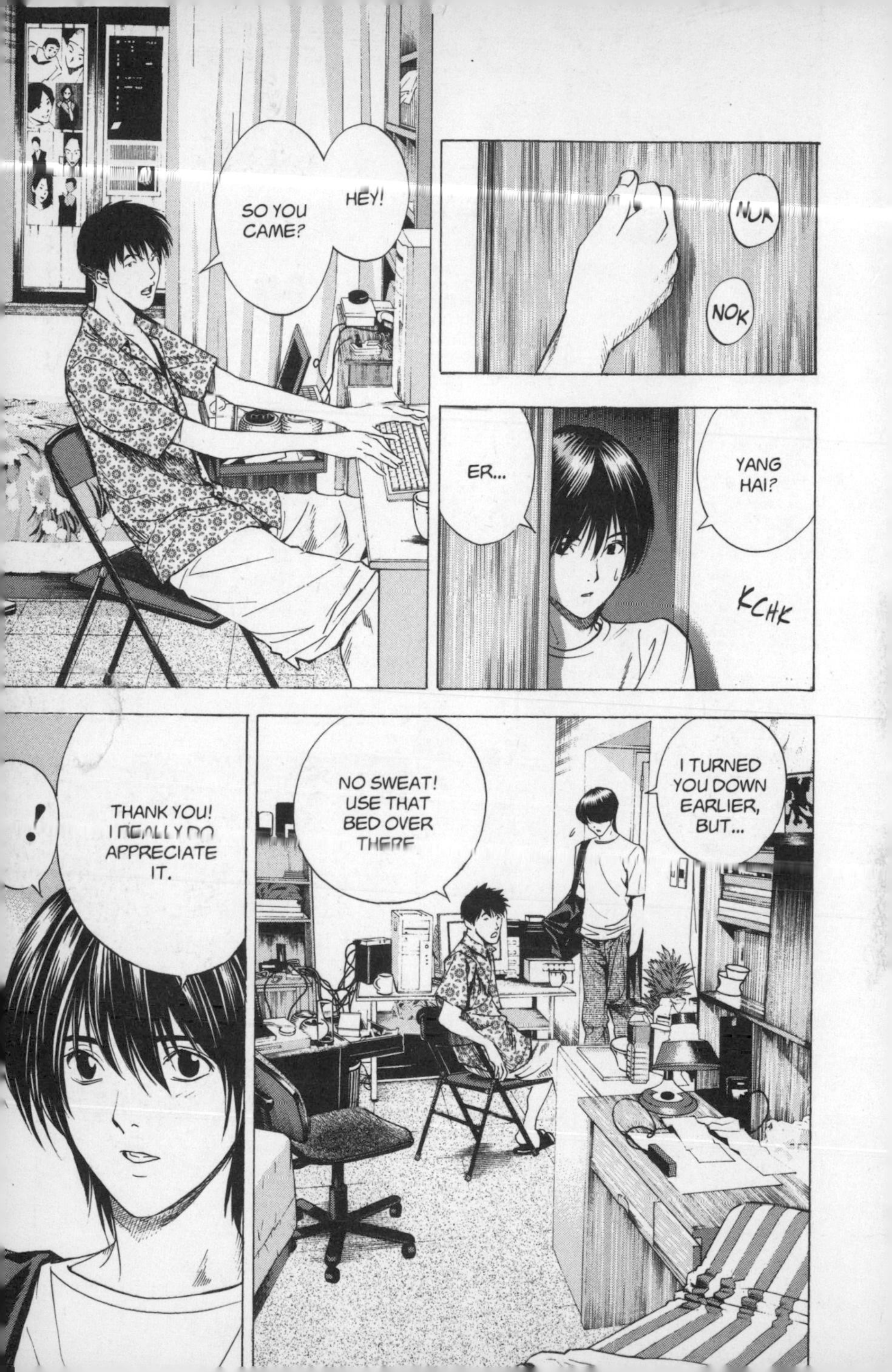
NOK
NOK
YANG HAI?
ER...
KCHK
HEY!
SO YOU CAME?
I TURNED YOU DOWN EARLIER, BUT...
NO SWEAT! USE THAT BED OVER THERE.
THANK YOU! I REALLY DO APPRECIATE IT.
!

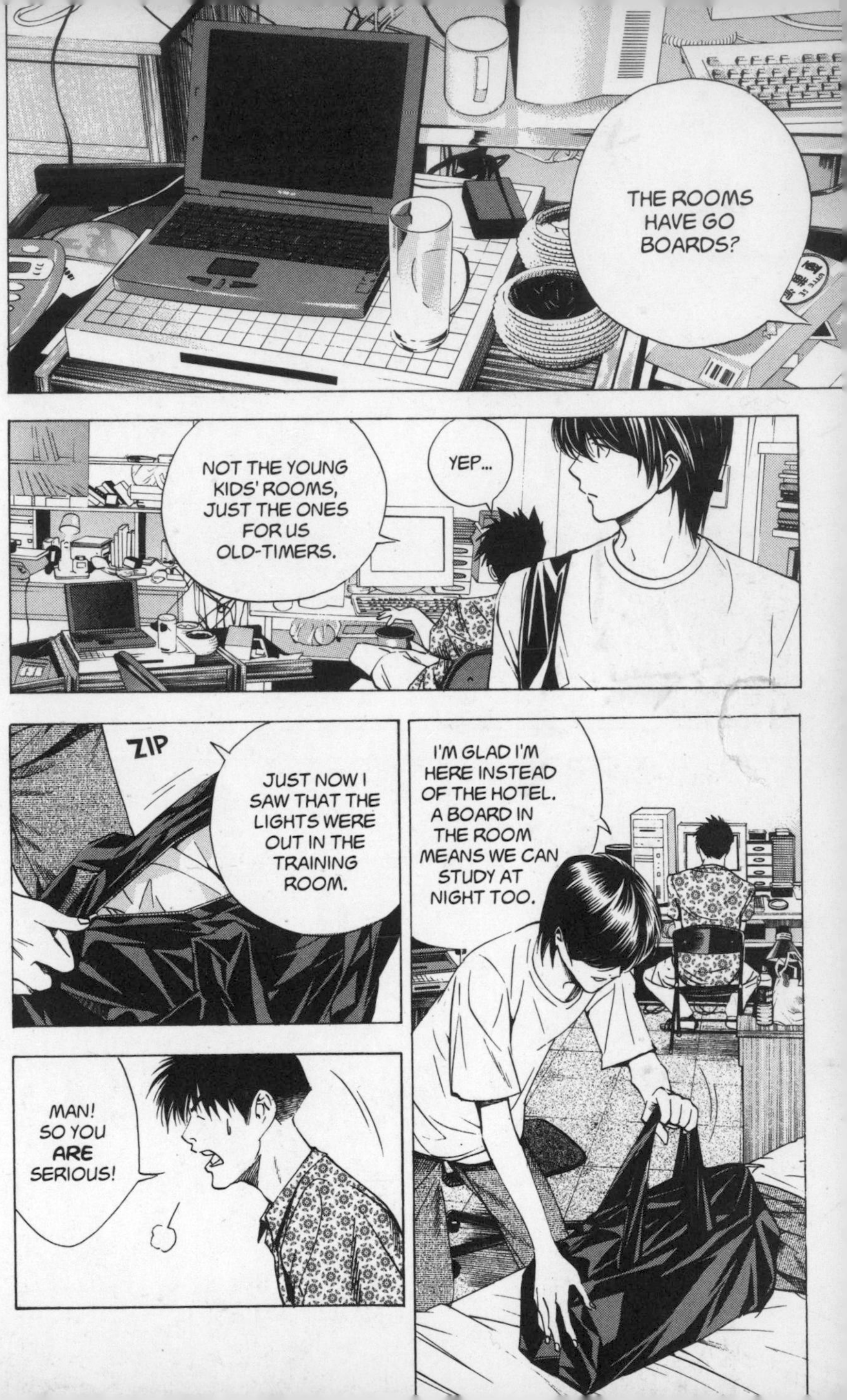
THE ROOMS HAVE GO BOARDS?
YEP...
NOT THE YOUNG KIDS' ROOMS, JUST THE ONES FOR US OLD-TIMERS.
I'M GLAD I'M HERE INSTEAD OF THE HOTEL. A BOARD IN THE ROOM MEANS WE CAN STUDY AT NIGHT TOO.
ZIP
JUST NOW I SAW THAT THE LIGHTS WERE OUT IN THE TRAINING ROOM.
MAN! SO YOU **ARE** SERIOUS!

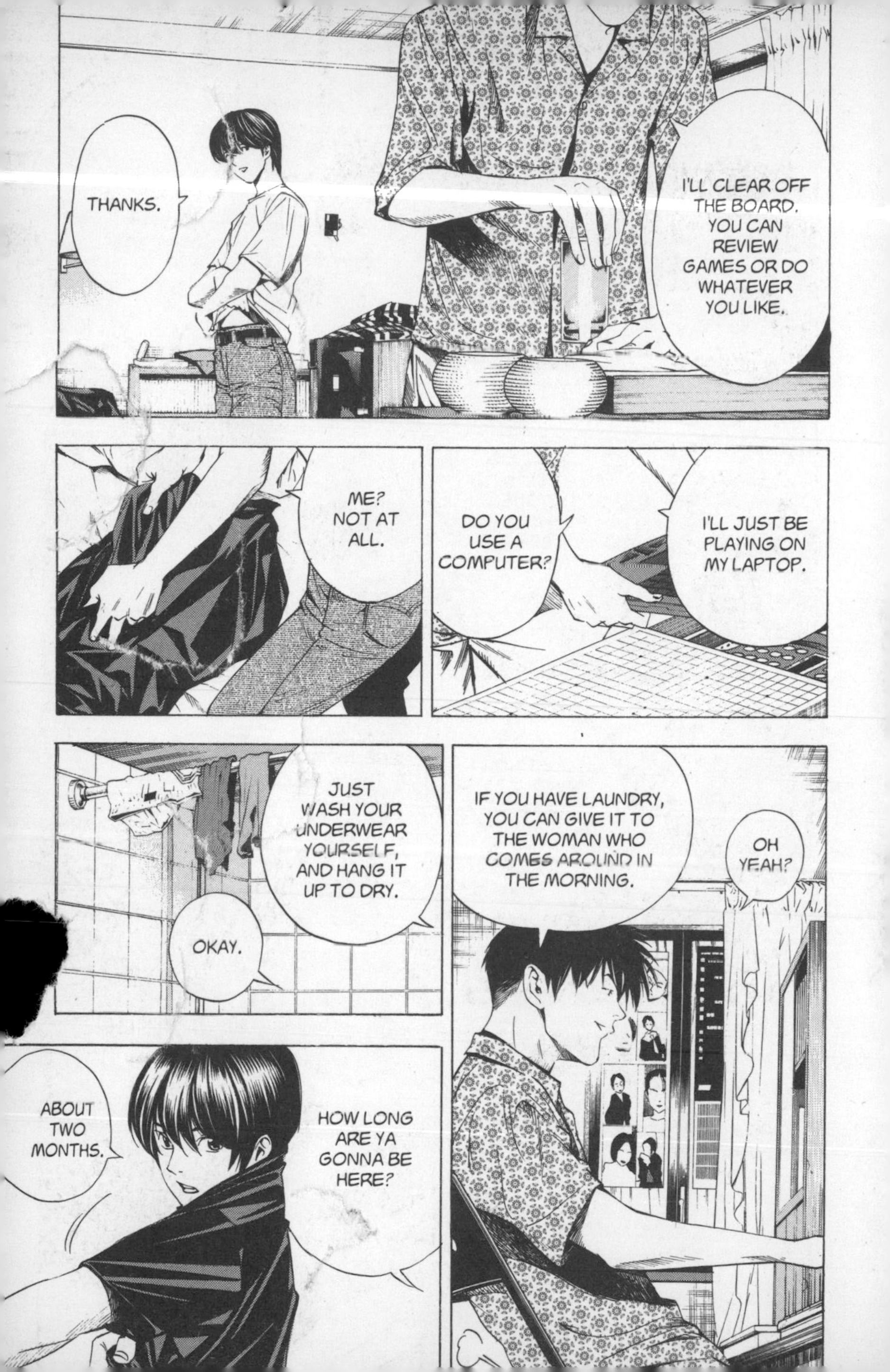
I'LL CLEAR OFF THE BOARD. YOU CAN REVIEW GAMES OR DO WHATEVER YOU LIKE.
THANKS.
I'LL JUST BE PLAYING ON MY LAPTOP.
DO YOU USE A COMPUTER?
ME? NOT AT ALL.
IF YOU HAVE LAUNDRY, YOU CAN GIVE IT TO THE WOMAN WHO COMES AROUND IN THE MORNING.
OH YEAH?
JUST WASH YOUR UNDERWEAR YOURSELF, AND HANG IT UP TO DRY.
OKAY.
HOW LONG ARE YA GONNA BE HERE?
ABOUT TWO MONTHS.

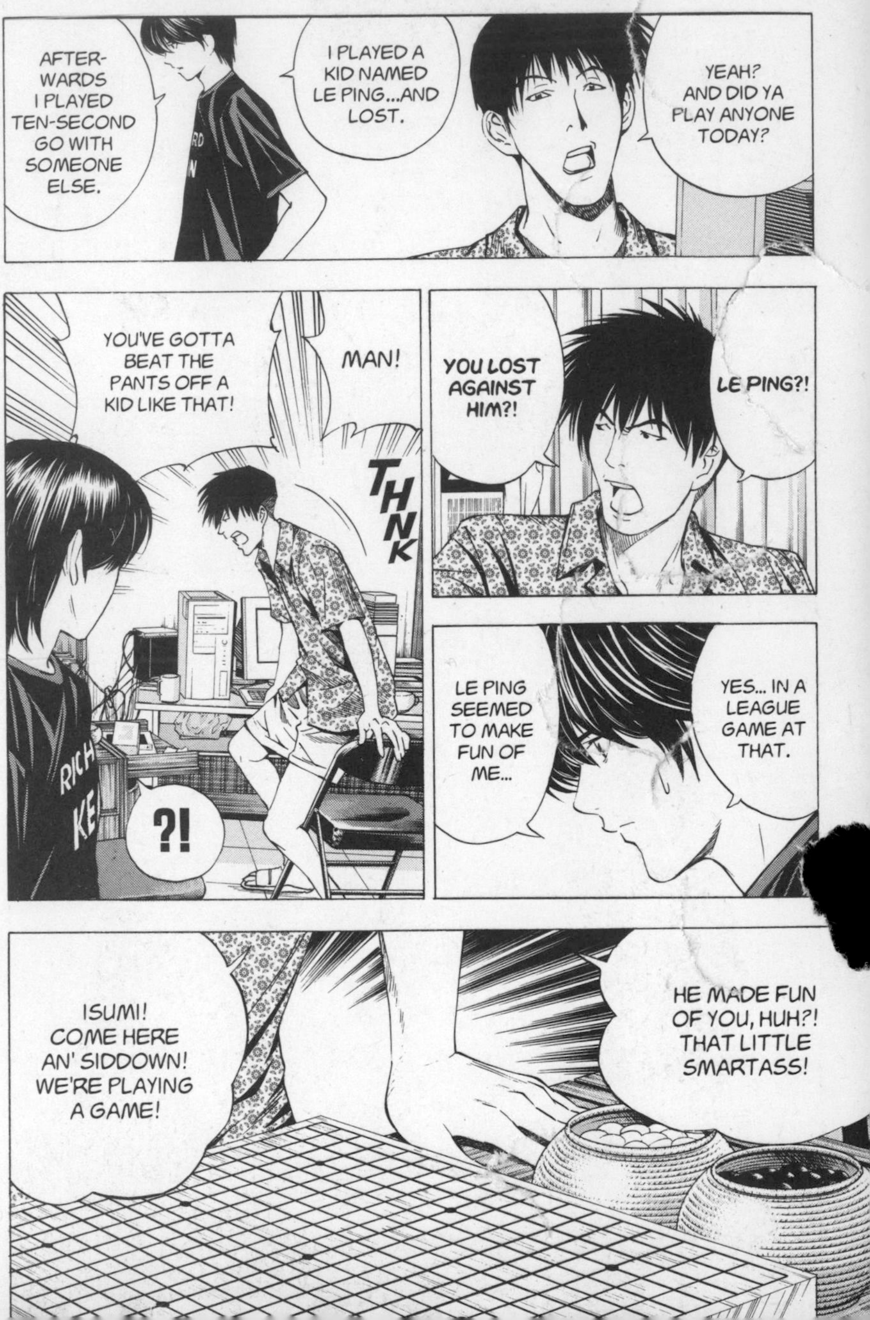
YEAH? AND DID YA PLAY ANYONE TODAY?
I PLAYED A KID NAMED LE PING...AND LOST.
AFTER-WARDS I PLAYED TEN-SECOND GO WITH SOMEONE ELSE.
LE PING?!
YOU LOST AGAINST HIM?!
YES... IN A LEAGUE GAME AT THAT.
LE PING SEEMED TO MAKE FUN OF ME...
MAN!
YOU'VE GOTTA BEAT THE PANTS OFF A KID LIKE THAT!
THNK
?!
HE MADE FUN OF YOU, HUH?! THAT LITTLE SMARTASS!
ISUMI! COME HERE AN' SIDDOWN! WE'RE PLAYING A GAME!

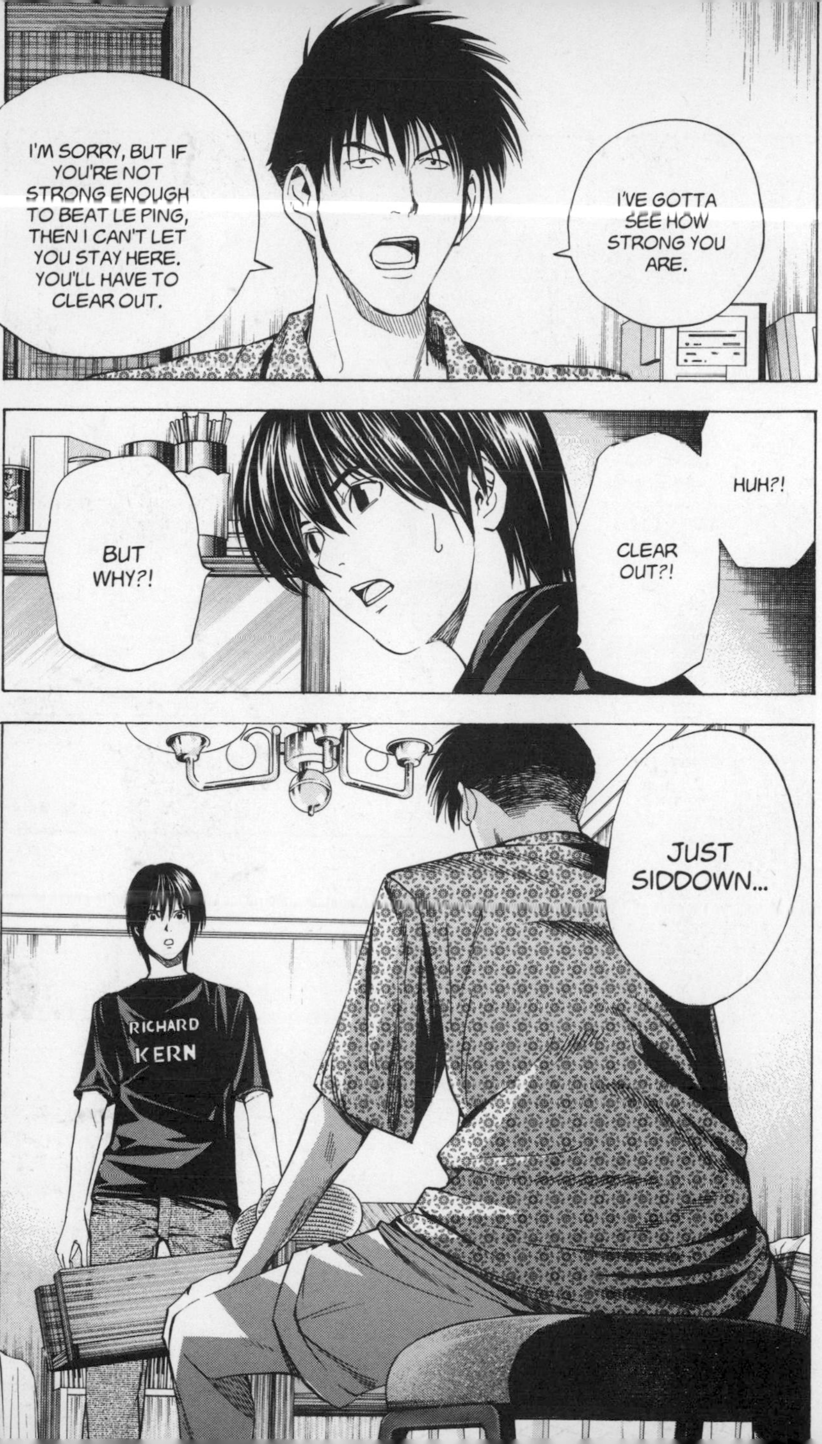
I'VE GOTTA SEE HOW STRONG YOU ARE.
I'M SORRY, BUT IF YOU'RE NOT STRONG ENOUGH TO BEAT LE PING, THEN I CAN'T LET YOU STAY HERE. YOU'LL HAVE TO CLEAR OUT.
HUH?!
CLEAR OUT?!
BUT WHY?!
JUST SIDDOWN...
RICHARD KERN

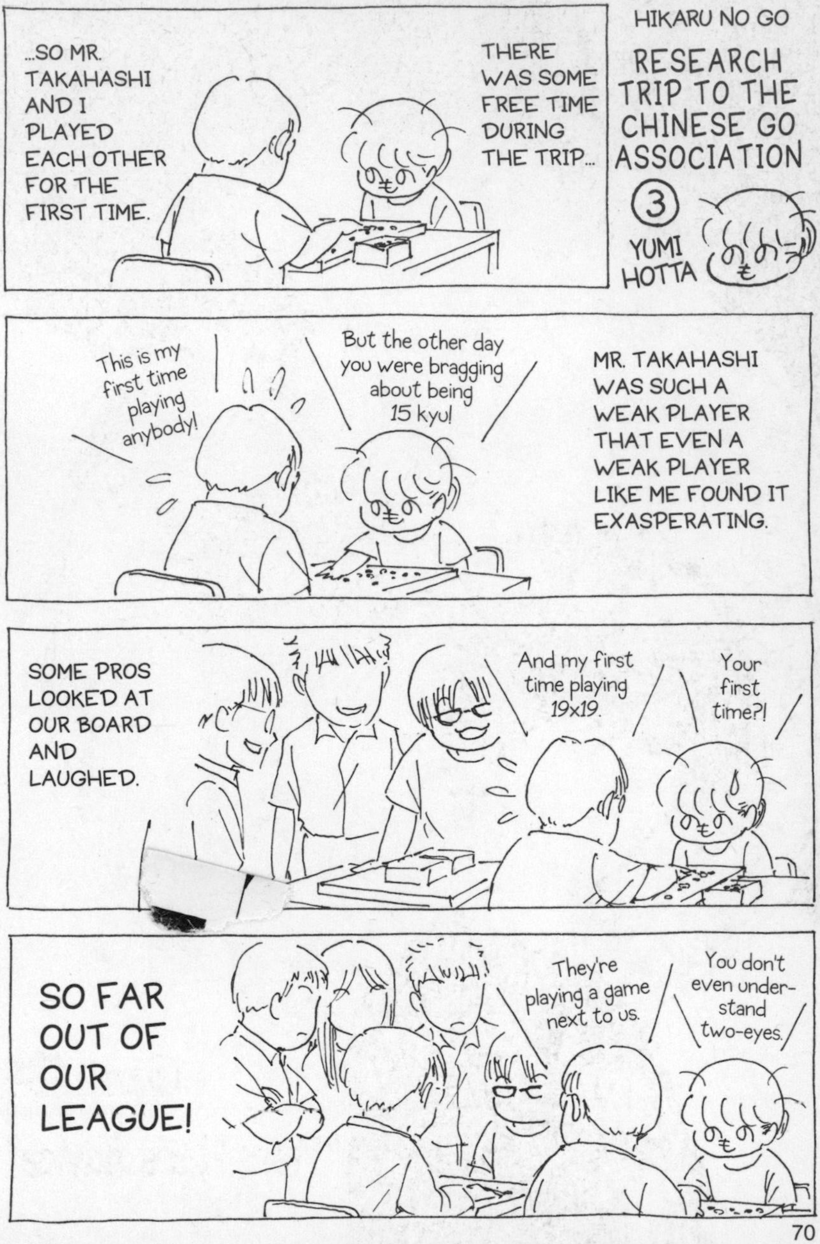
HIKARU NO GO
RESEARCH TRIP TO THE CHINESE GO ASSOCIATION
3
YUMI HOTTA
THERE WAS SOME FREE TIME DURING THE TRIP...
...SO MR. TAKAHASHI AND I PLAYED EACH OTHER FOR THE FIRST TIME.
MR. TAKAHASHI WAS SUCH A WEAK PLAYER THAT EVEN A WEAK PLAYER LIKE ME FOUND IT EXASPERATING.
But the other day you were bragging about being 15 kyu!
This is my first time playing anybody!
Your first time?!
And my first time playing 19x19.
SOME PROS LOOKED AT OUR BOARD AND LAUGHED.
You don't even understand two-eyes.
They're playing a game next to us.
SO FAR OUT OF OUR LEAGUE!

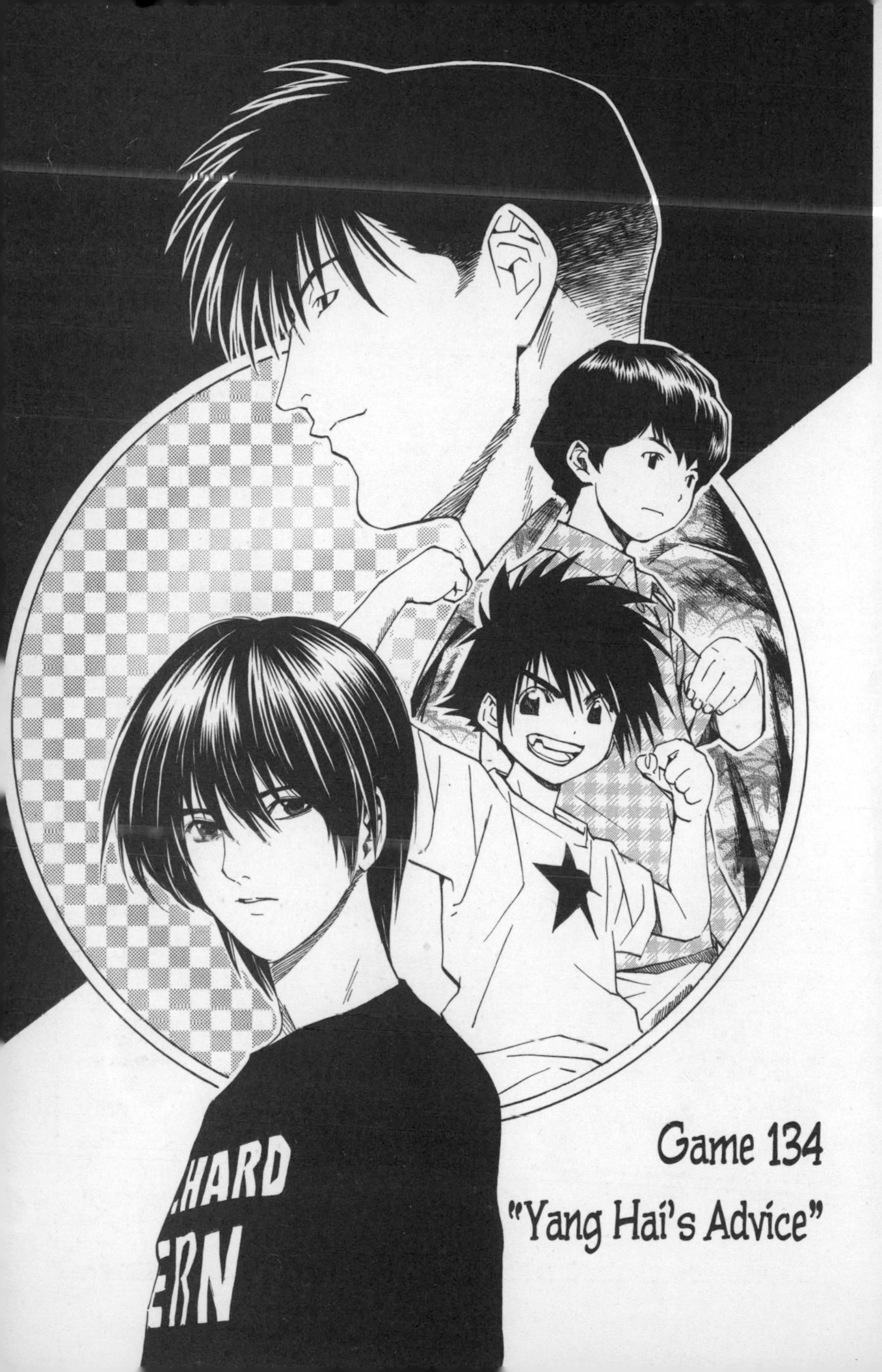
.HARD
ERN

Game 134
"Yang Hai's Advice"

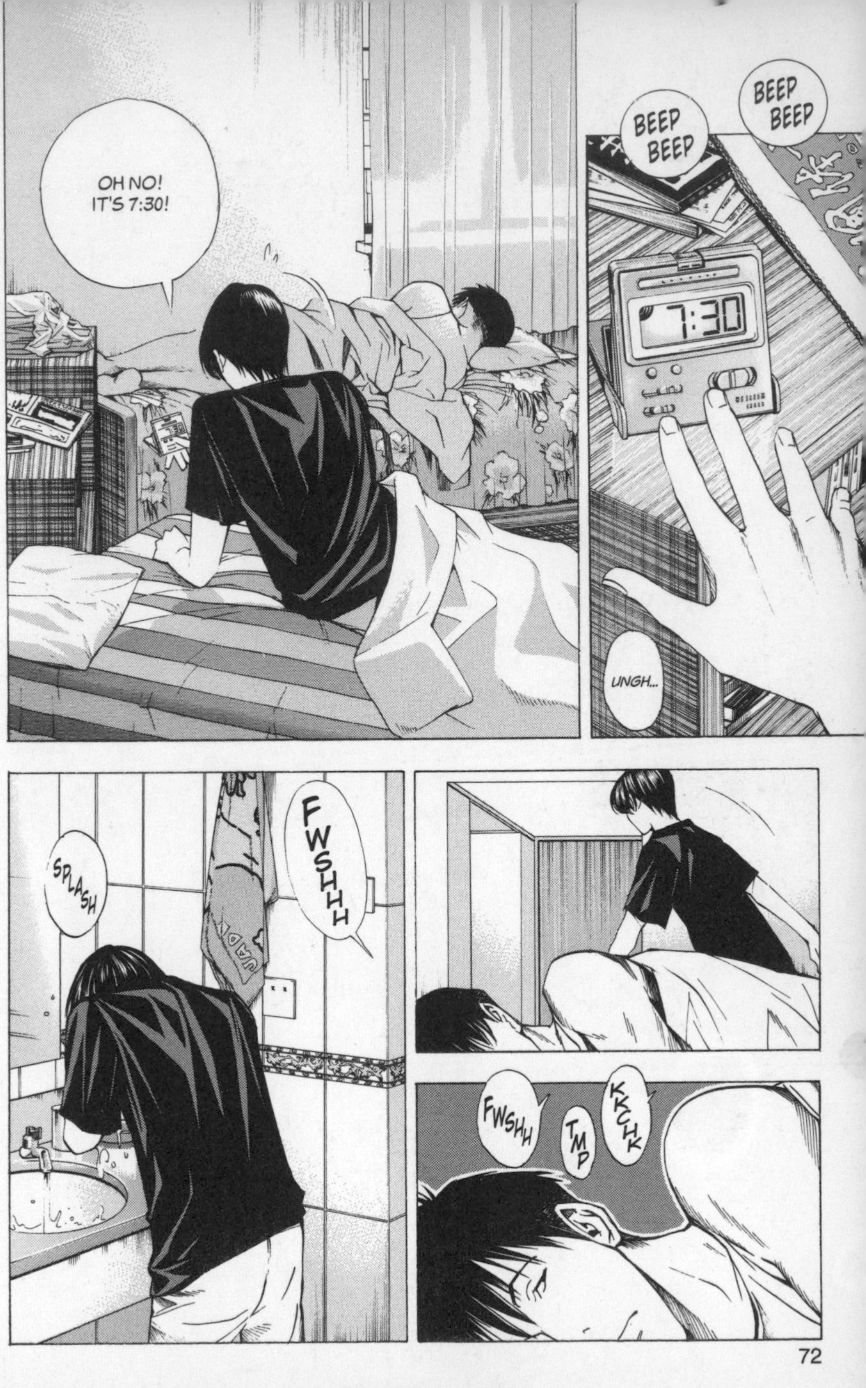
BEEP BEEP
BEEP BEEP
UNGH...
OH NO! IT'S 7:30!
KKCHK
TMP
FWSHH
FWSHHH
SPLASH

READ THIS WAY

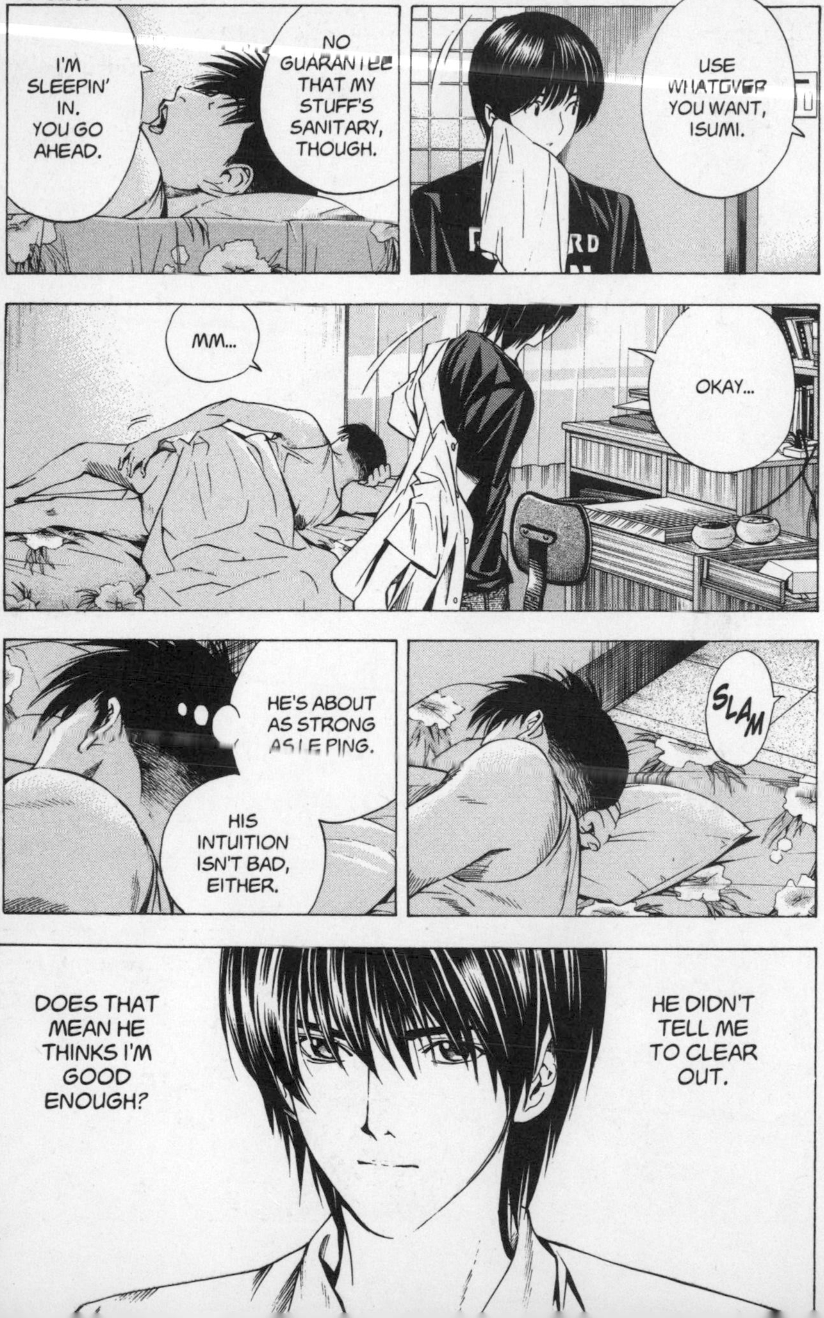
USE WHATEVER YOU WANT, ISUMI.
NO GUARANTEE THAT MY STUFF'S SANITARY, THOUGH.
I'M SLEEPIN' IN. YOU GO AHEAD.
OKAY...
MM...
SLAM
HE'S ABOUT AS STRONG AS LE PING.
HIS INTUITION ISN'T BAD, EITHER.
HE DIDN'T TELL ME TO CLEAR OUT.
DOES THAT MEAN HE THINKS I'M GOOD ENOUGH?

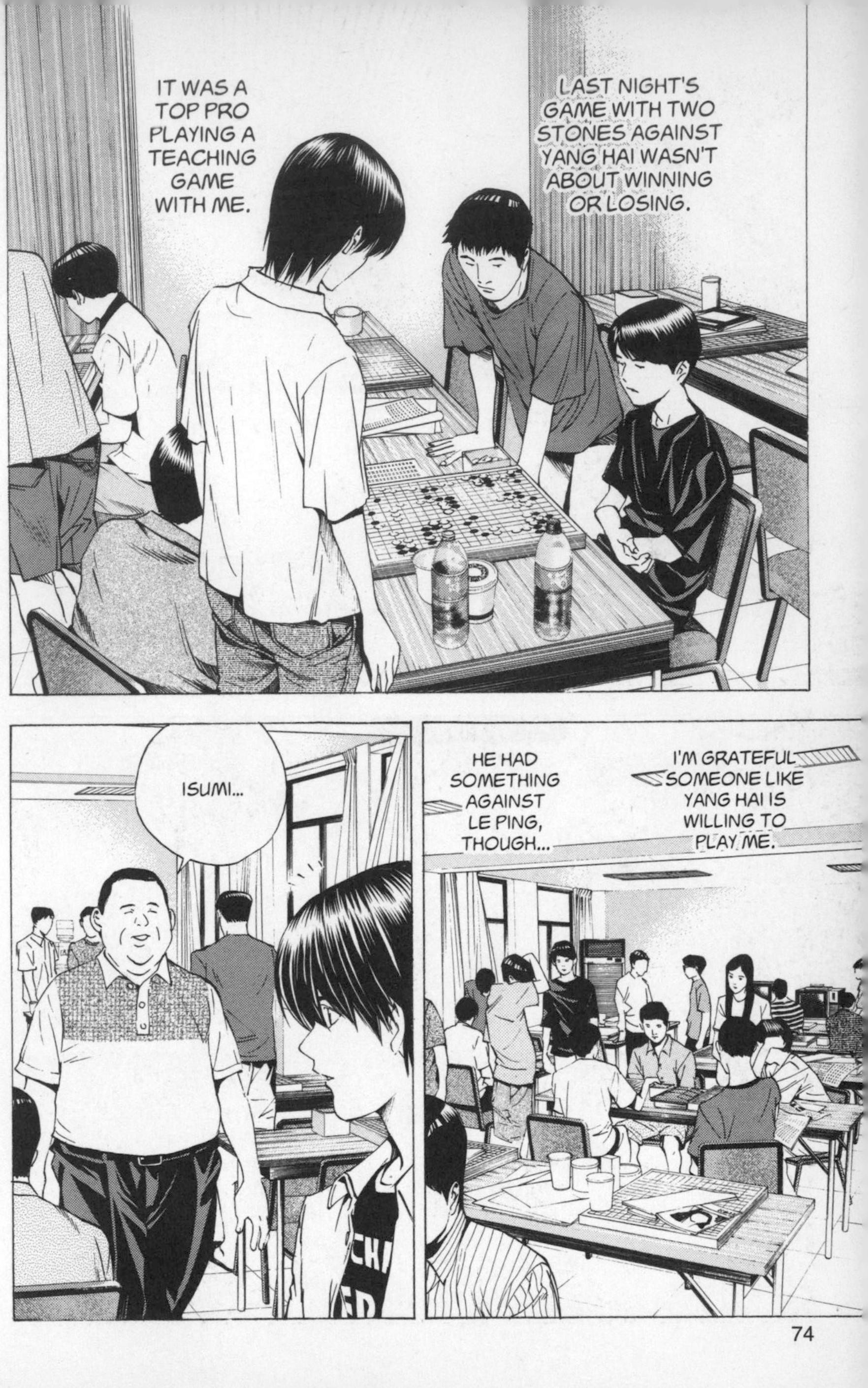
LAST NIGHT'S GAME WITH TWO STONES AGAINST YANG HAI WASN'T ABOUT WINNING OR LOSING.
IT WAS A TOP PRO PLAYING A TEACHING GAME WITH ME.
I'M GRATEFUL SOMEONE LIKE YANG HAI IS WILLING TO PLAY ME.
HE HAD SOMETHING AGAINST LE PING, THOUGH...
ISUMI...

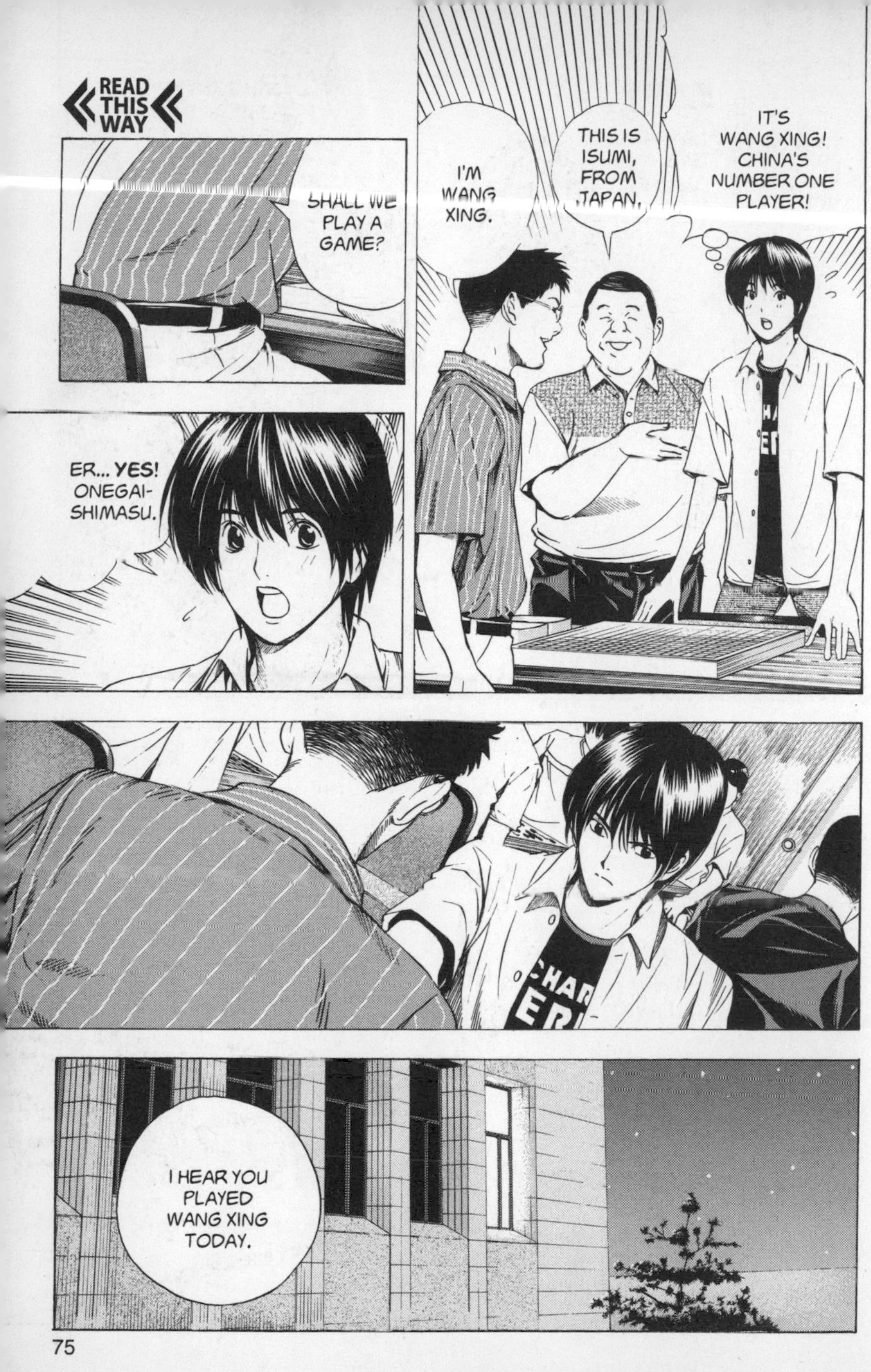
READ THIS WAY
IT'S WANG XING! CHINA'S NUMBER ONE PLAYER!
THIS IS ISUMI, FROM JAPAN.
I'M WANG XING.
SHALL WE PLAY A GAME?
ER... YES! ONEGAI-SHIMASU.
I HEAR YOU PLAYED WANG XING TODAY.

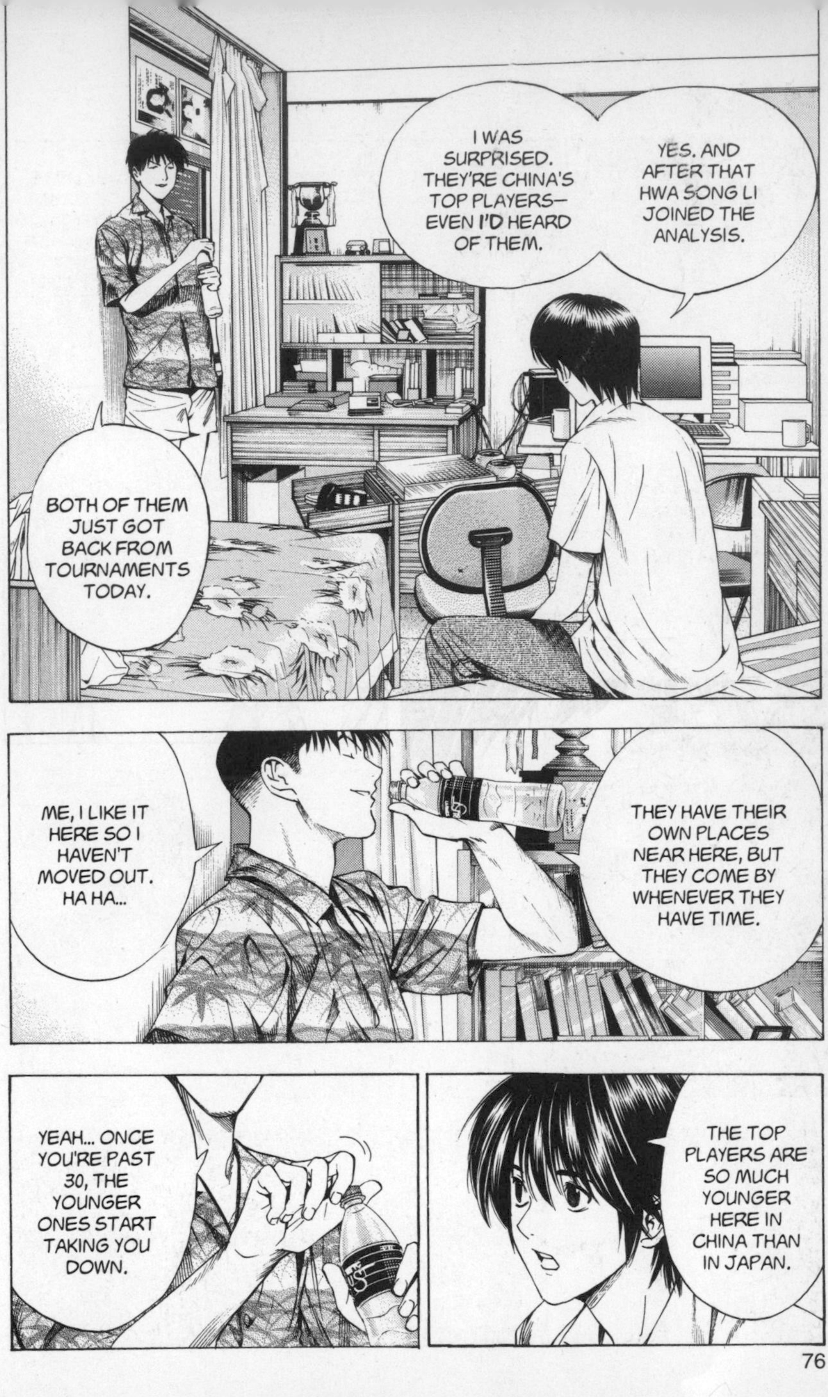

YES. AND AFTER THAT HWA SONG LI JOINED THE ANALYSIS.
I WAS SURPRISED. THEY'RE CHINA'S TOP PLAYERS—EVEN I'D HEARD OF THEM.
BOTH OF THEM JUST GOT BACK FROM TOURNAMENTS TODAY.
THEY HAVE THEIR OWN PLACES NEAR HERE, BUT THEY COME BY WHENEVER THEY HAVE TIME.
ME, I LIKE IT HERE SO I HAVEN'T MOVED OUT. HA HA...
THE TOP PLAYERS ARE SO MUCH YOUNGER HERE IN CHINA THAN IN JAPAN.
YEAH... ONCE YOU'RE PAST 30, THE YOUNGER ONES START TAKING YOU DOWN.

READ THIS WAY

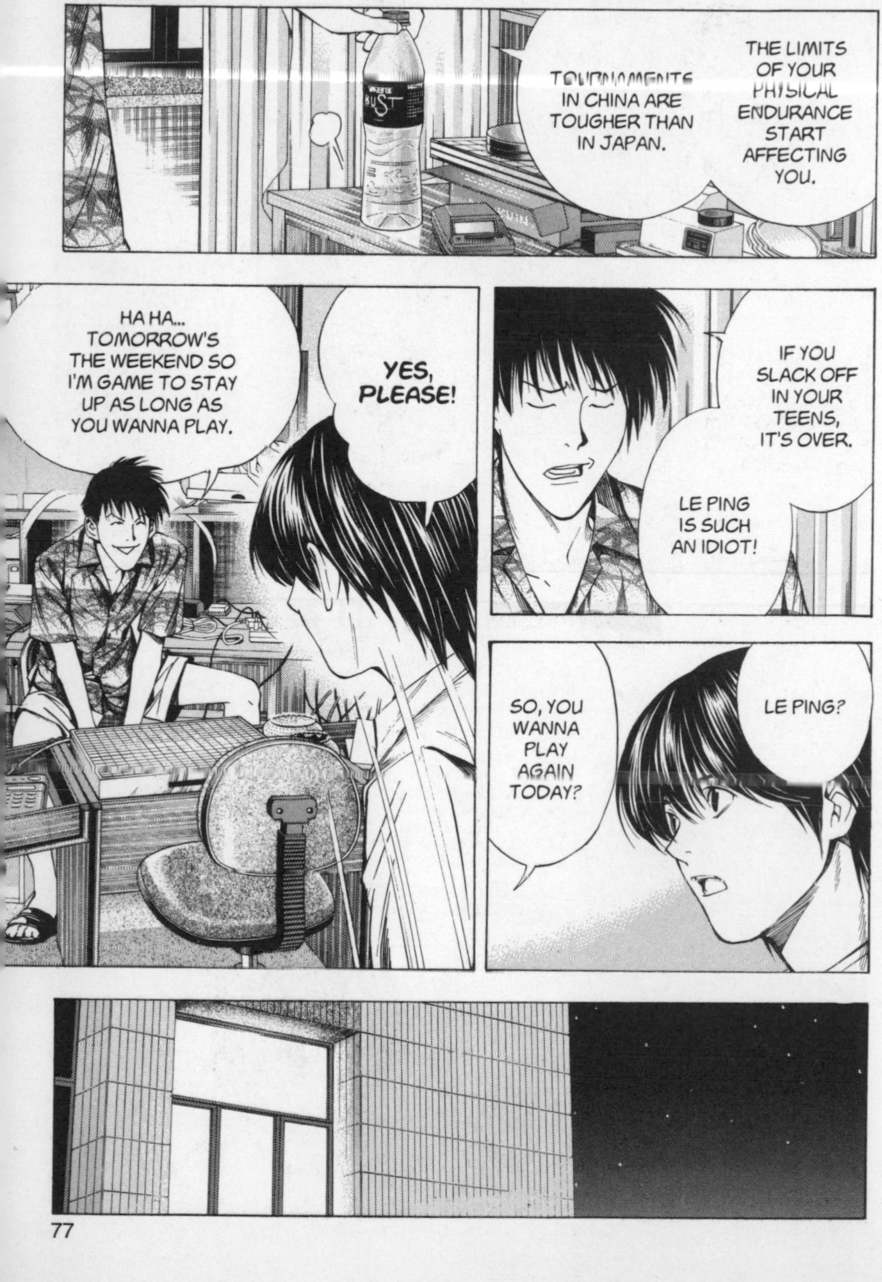

THE LIMITS OF YOUR PHYSICAL ENDURANCE START AFFECTING YOU.
TOURNAMENTS IN CHINA ARE TOUGHER THAN IN JAPAN.
IF YOU SLACK OFF IN YOUR TEENS, IT'S OVER.
LE PING IS SUCH AN IDIOT!
LE PING?
SO, YOU WANNA PLAY AGAIN TODAY?
YES, PLEASE!
HA HA... TOMORROW'S THE WEEKEND SO I'M GAME TO STAY UP AS LONG AS YOU WANNA PLAY.

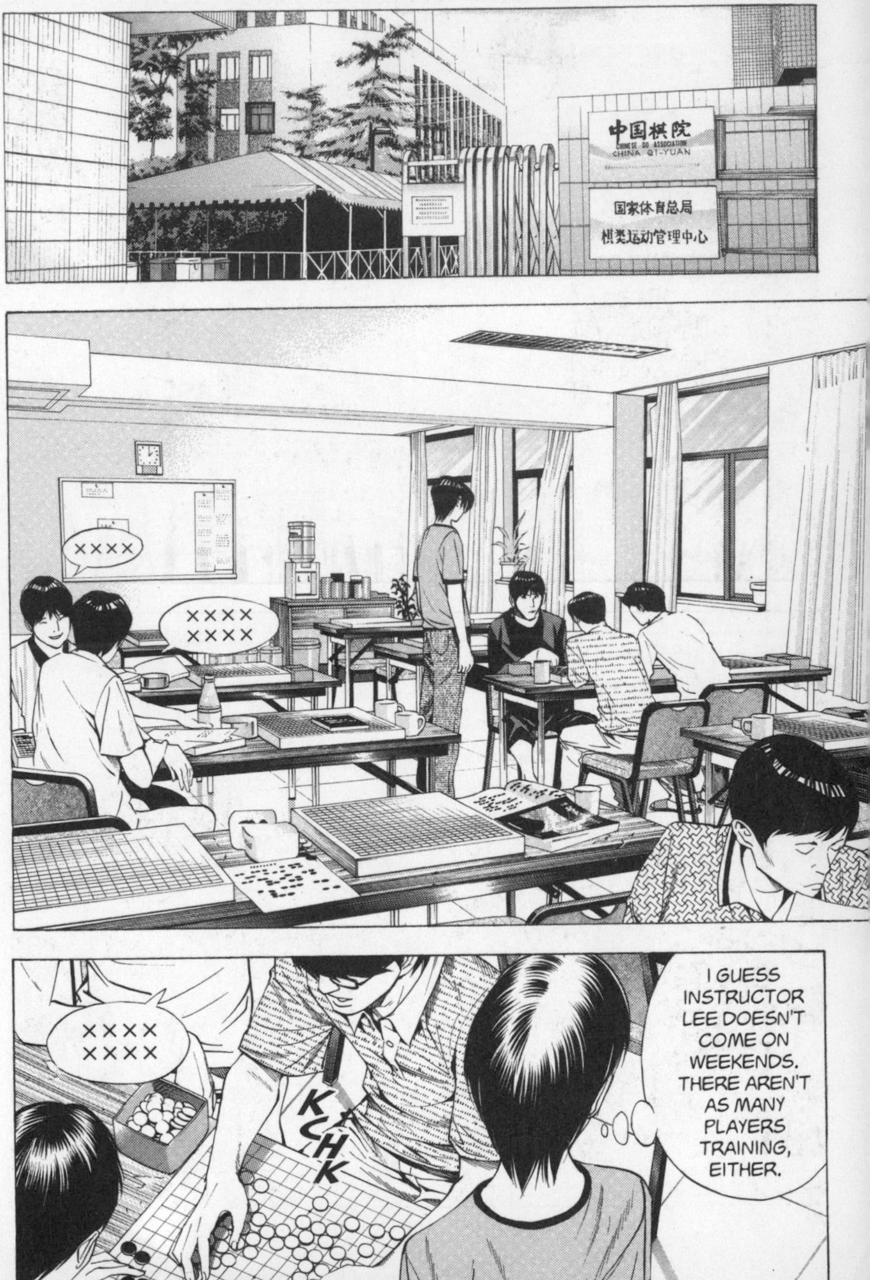
中国棋院
CHINESE GO ASSOCIATION
CHINA QI-YUAN
国家体育总局
棋类运动管理中心
××××
×××× ××××
I GUESS INSTRUCTOR LEE DOESN'T COME ON WEEKENDS. THERE AREN'T AS MANY PLAYERS TRAINING, EITHER.
KCHK
×××× ××××

READ THIS WAY

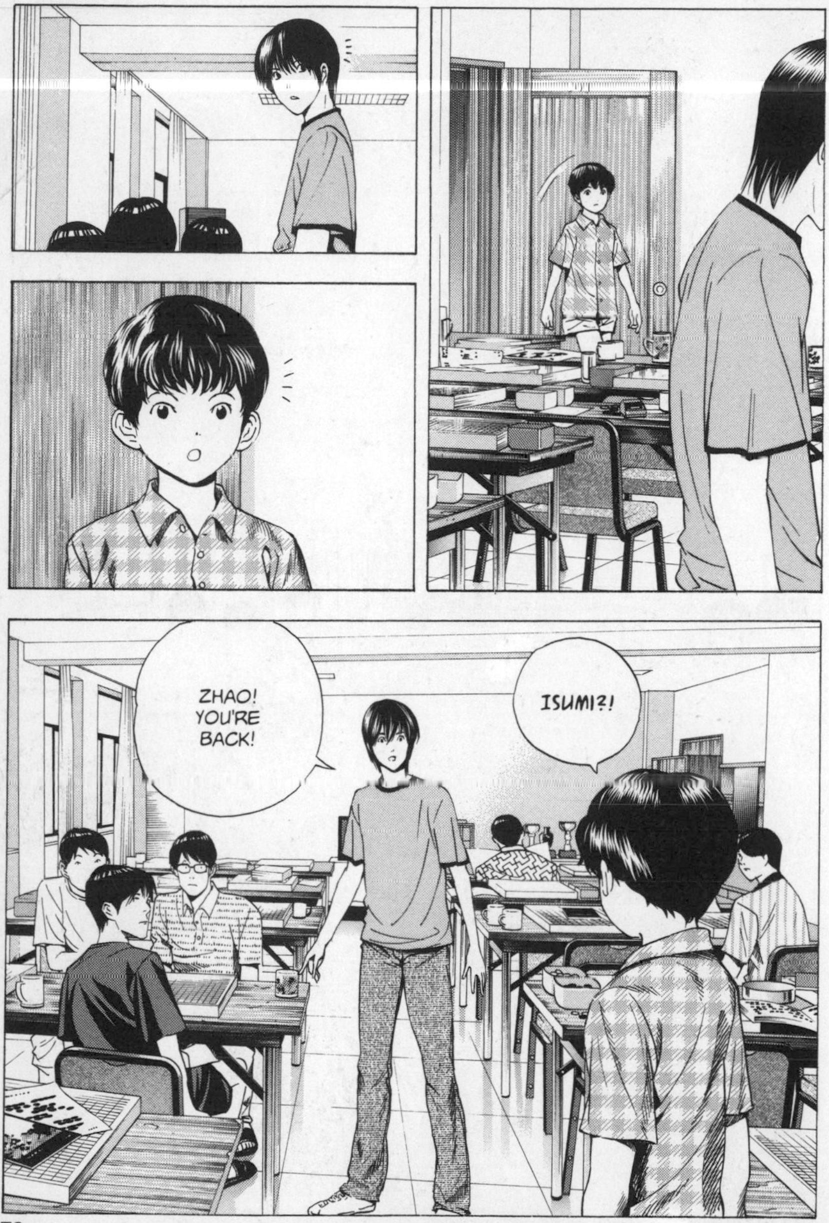
ISUMI?!
ZHAO! YOU'RE BACK!

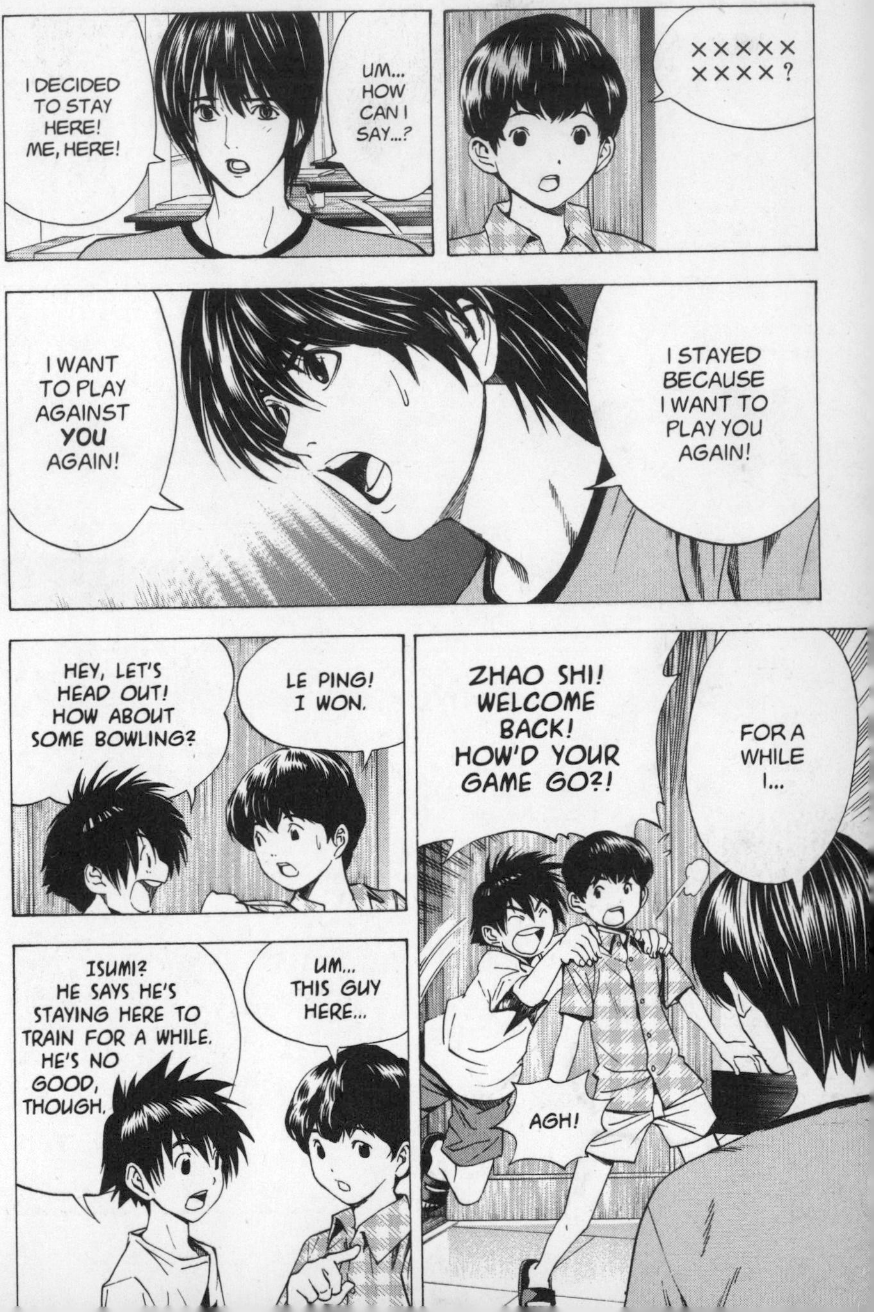
××××× ××××?
UM... HOW CAN I SAY...?
I DECIDED TO STAY HERE! ME, HERE!
I STAYED BECAUSE I WANT TO PLAY YOU AGAIN!
I WANT TO PLAY AGAINST YOU AGAIN!
FOR A WHILE I...
ZHAO SHI! WELCOME BACK! HOW'D YOUR GAME GO?!
AGH!
LE PING! I WON.
HEY, LET'S HEAD OUT! HOW ABOUT SOME BOWLING?
UM... THIS GUY HERE...
ISUMI? HE SAYS HE'S STAYING HERE TO TRAIN FOR A WHILE. HE'S NO GOOD, THOUGH.

READ THIS WAY

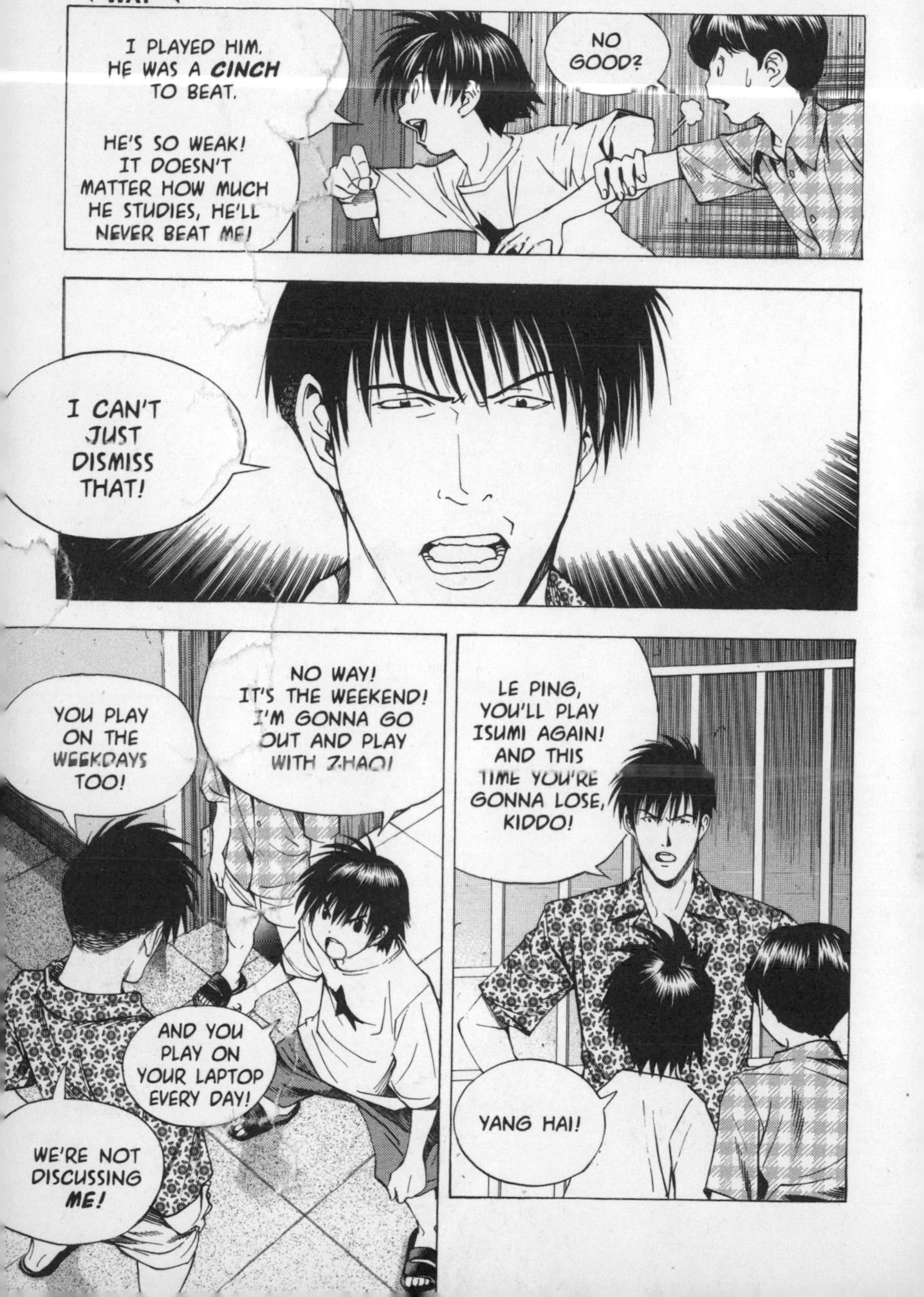

NO GOOD?
I PLAYED HIM. HE WAS A CINCH TO BEAT.
HE'S SO WEAK! IT DOESN'T MATTER HOW MUCH HE STUDIES, HE'LL NEVER BEAT ME!
I CAN'T JUST DISMISS THAT!
LE PING, YOU'LL PLAY ISUMI AGAIN! AND THIS TIME YOU'RE GONNA LOSE, KIDDO!
YANG HAI!
NO WAY! IT'S THE WEEKEND! I'M GONNA GO OUT AND PLAY WITH ZHAO!
YOU PLAY ON THE WEEKDAYS TOO!
AND YOU PLAY ON YOUR LAPTOP EVERY DAY!
WE'RE NOT DISCUSSING ME!

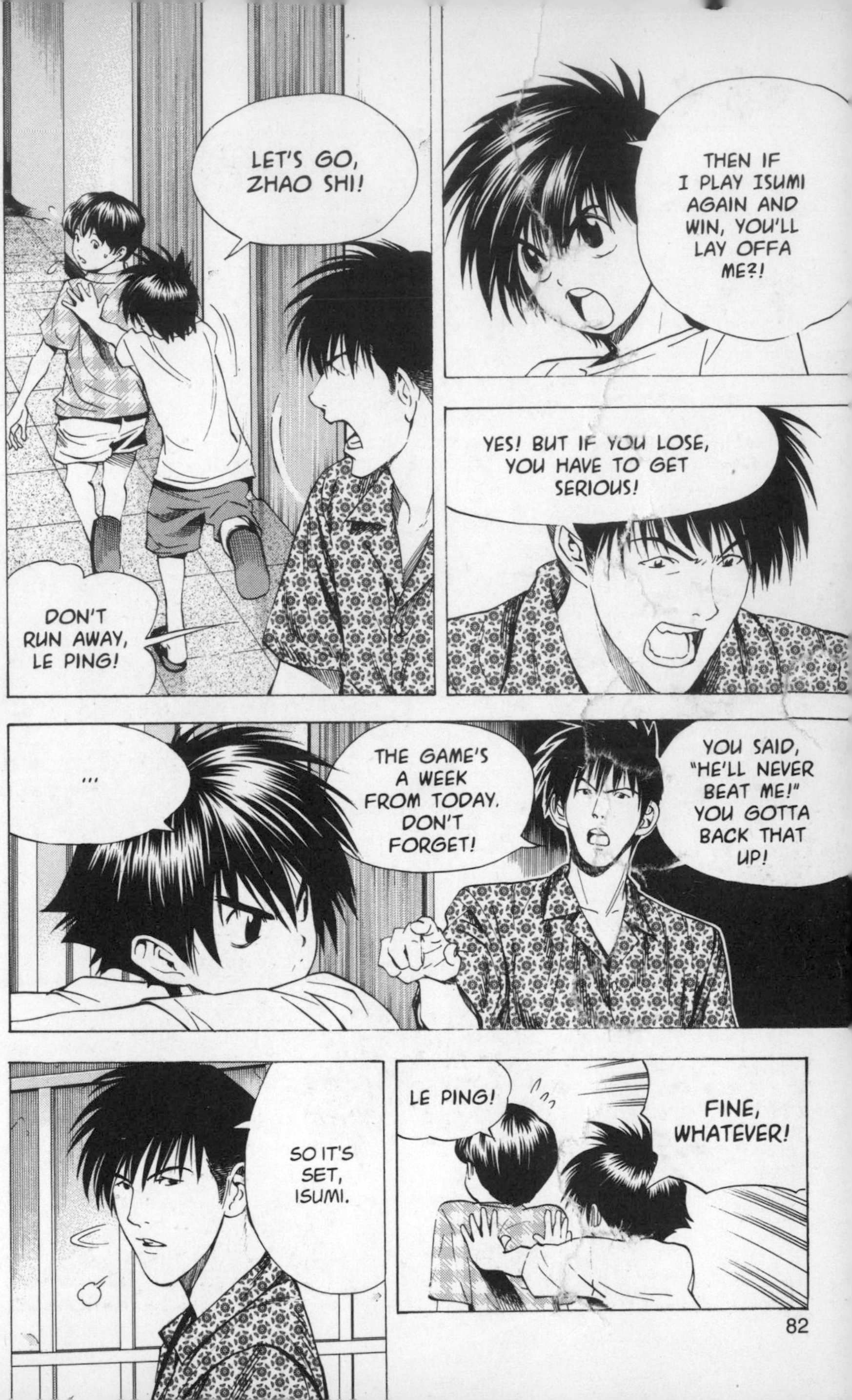
THEN IF I PLAY ISUMI AGAIN AND WIN, YOU'LL LAY OFFA ME?!
YES! BUT IF YOU LOSE, YOU HAVE TO GET SERIOUS!
LET'S GO, ZHAO SHI!
DON'T RUN AWAY, LE PING!
YOU SAID, "HE'LL NEVER BEAT ME!" YOU GOTTA BACK THAT UP!
THE GAME'S A WEEK FROM TODAY. DON'T FORGET!
...
FINE, WHATEVER!
LE PING!
SO IT'S SET, ISUMI.

READ THIS WAY

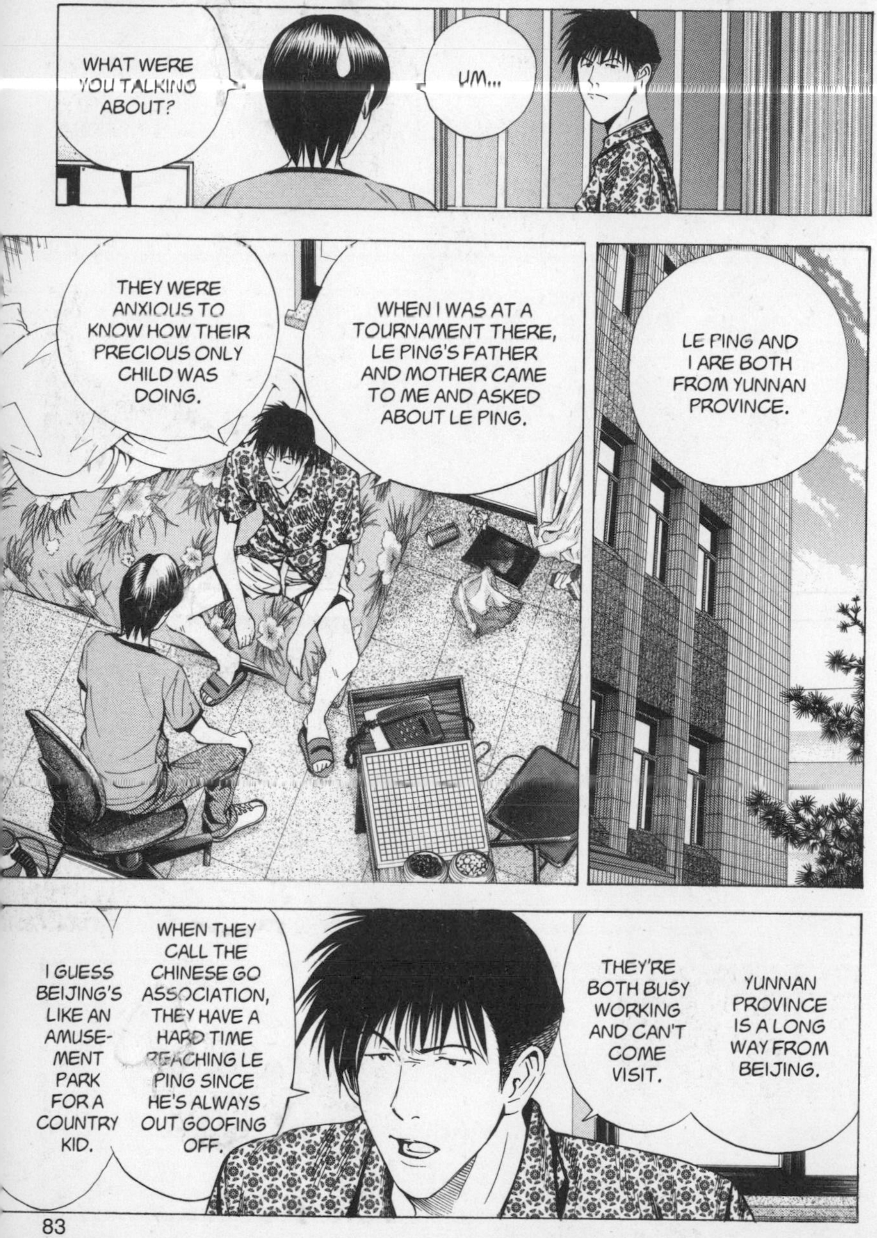

UM...
WHAT WERE YOU TALKING ABOUT?
LE PING AND I ARE BOTH FROM YUNNAN PROVINCE.
WHEN I WAS AT A TOURNAMENT THERE, LE PING'S FATHER AND MOTHER CAME TO ME AND ASKED ABOUT LE PING.
THEY WERE ANXIOUS TO KNOW HOW THEIR PRECIOUS ONLY CHILD WAS DOING.
YUNNAN PROVINCE IS A LONG WAY FROM BEIJING.
THEY'RE BOTH BUSY WORKING AND CAN'T COME VISIT.
WHEN THEY CALL THE CHINESE GO ASSOCIATION, THEY HAVE A HARD TIME REACHING LE PING SINCE HE'S ALWAYS OUT GOOFING OFF.
I GUESS BEIJING'S LIKE AN AMUSE-MENT PARK FOR A COUNTRY KID.

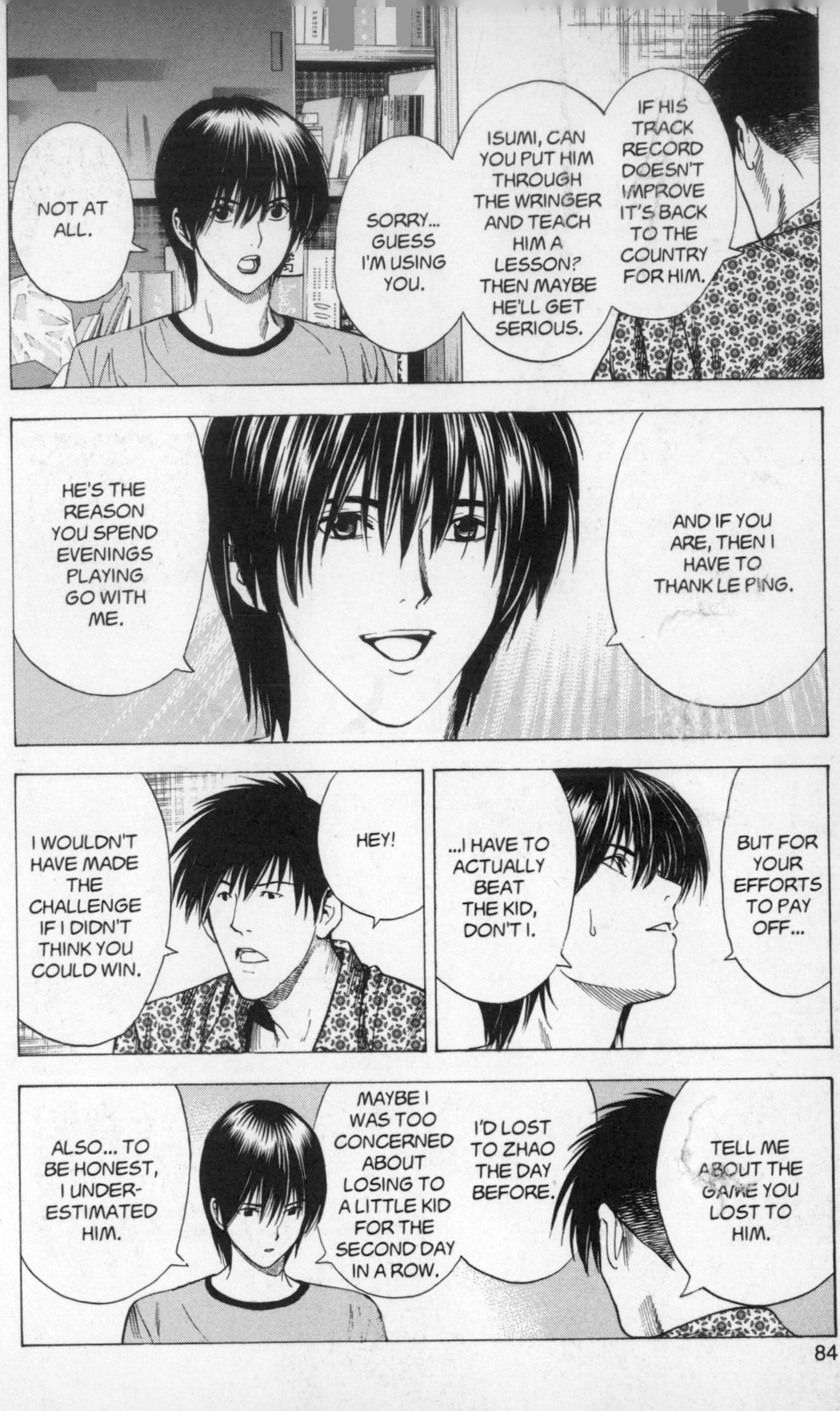
IF HIS TRACK RECORD DOESN'T IMPROVE IT'S BACK TO THE COUNTRY FOR HIM.
ISUMI, CAN YOU PUT HIM THROUGH THE WRINGER AND TEACH HIM A LESSON? THEN MAYBE HE'LL GET SERIOUS.
SORRY... GUESS I'M USING YOU.
NOT AT ALL.
AND IF YOU ARE, THEN I HAVE TO THANK LE PING.
HE'S THE REASON YOU SPEND EVENINGS PLAYING GO WITH ME.
BUT FOR YOUR EFFORTS TO PAY OFF...
...I HAVE TO ACTUALLY BEAT THE KID, DON'T I.
HEY!
I WOULDN'T HAVE MADE THE CHALLENGE IF I DIDN'T THINK YOU COULD WIN.
TELL ME ABOUT THE GAME YOU LOST TO HIM.
I'D LOST TO ZHAO THE DAY BEFORE.
MAYBE I WAS TOO CONCERNED ABOUT LOSING TO A LITTLE KID FOR THE SECOND DAY IN A ROW.
ALSO... TO BE HONEST, I UNDER-ESTIMATED HIM.

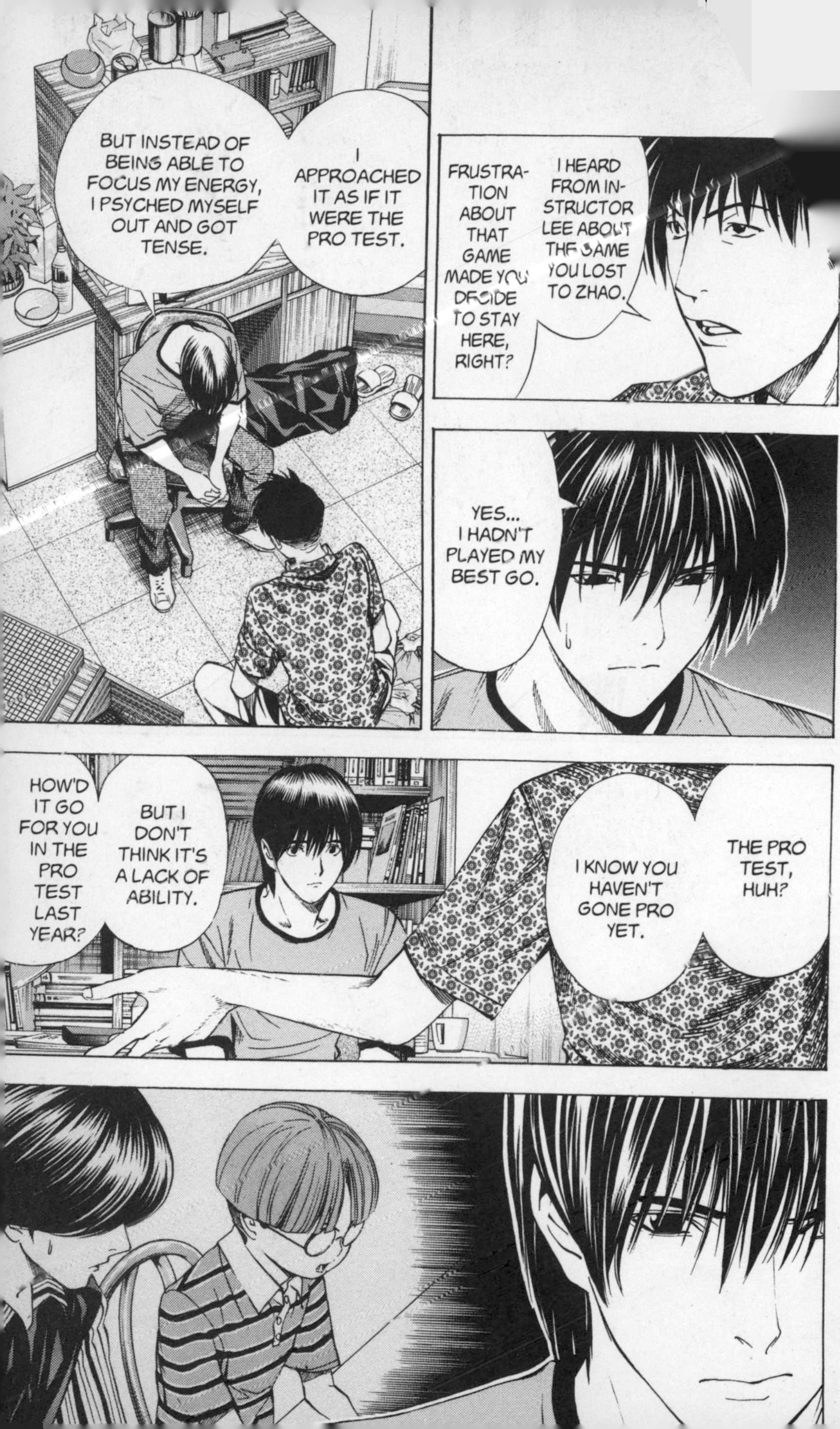
I HEARD FROM INSTRUCTOR LEE ABOUT THE GAME YOU LOST TO ZHAO.
FRUSTRATION ABOUT THAT GAME MADE YOU DECIDE TO STAY HERE, RIGHT?
YES... I HADN'T PLAYED MY BEST GO.
I APPROACHED IT AS IF IT WERE THE PRO TEST.
BUT INSTEAD OF BEING ABLE TO FOCUS MY ENERGY, I PSYCHED MYSELF OUT AND GOT TENSE.
THE PRO TEST, HUH?
I KNOW YOU HAVEN'T GONE PRO YET.
BUT I DON'T THINK IT'S A LACK OF ABILITY.
HOW'D IT GO FOR YOU IN THE PRO TEST LAST YEAR?

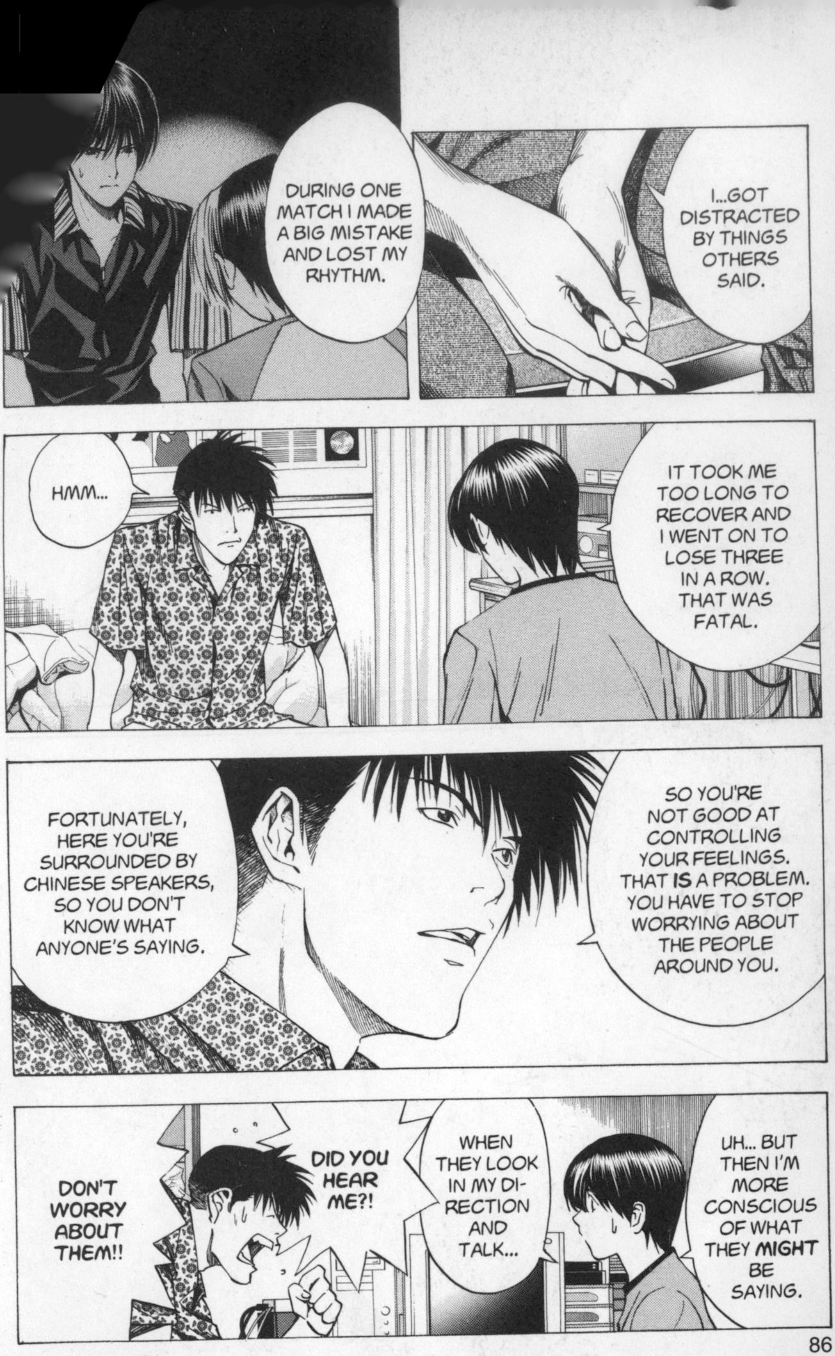
I...GOT DISTRACTED BY THINGS OTHERS SAID.
DURING ONE MATCH I MADE A BIG MISTAKE AND LOST MY RHYTHM.
IT TOOK ME TOO LONG TO RECOVER AND I WENT ON TO LOSE THREE IN A ROW. THAT WAS FATAL.
HMM...
SO YOU'RE NOT GOOD AT CONTROLLING YOUR FEELINGS. THAT **IS** A PROBLEM. YOU HAVE TO STOP WORRYING ABOUT THE PEOPLE AROUND YOU.
FORTUNATELY, HERE YOU'RE SURROUNDED BY CHINESE SPEAKERS, SO YOU DON'T KNOW WHAT ANYONE'S SAYING.
UH... BUT THEN I'M MORE CONSCIOUS OF WHAT THEY **MIGHT** BE SAYING.
WHEN THEY LOOK IN MY DI-RECTION AND TALK...
DID YOU HEAR ME?!
DON'T WORRY ABOUT THEM!!

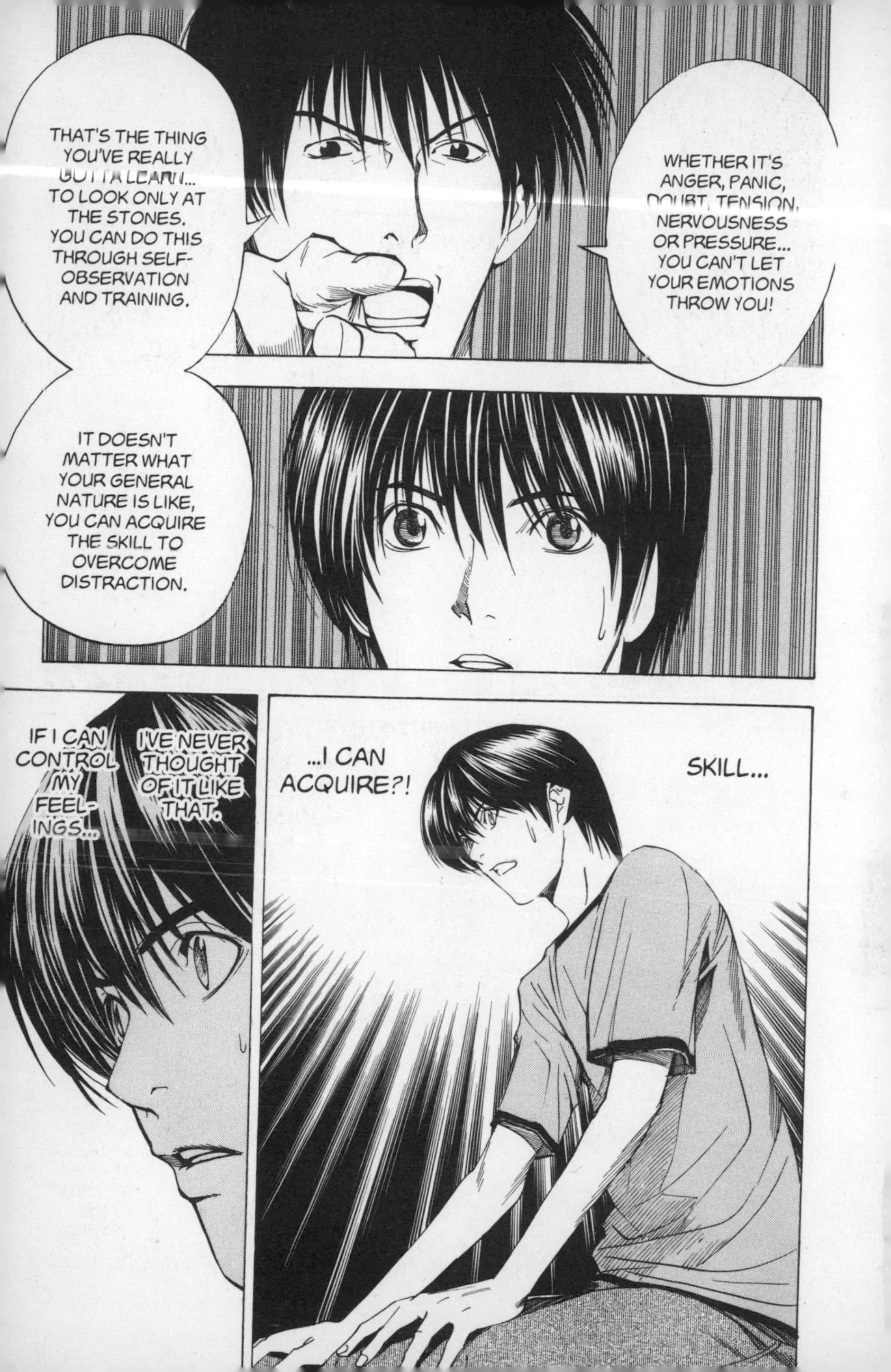
WHETHER IT'S ANGER, PANIC, DOUBT, TENSION, NERVOUSNESS OR PRESSURE... YOU CAN'T LET YOUR EMOTIONS THROW YOU!
THAT'S THE THING YOU'VE REALLY GOTTA LEARN... TO LOOK ONLY AT THE STONES. YOU CAN DO THIS THROUGH SELF-OBSERVATION AND TRAINING.
IT DOESN'T MATTER WHAT YOUR GENERAL NATURE IS LIKE, YOU CAN ACQUIRE THE SKILL TO OVERCOME DISTRACTION.
SKILL...
...I CAN ACQUIRE?!
I'VE NEVER THOUGHT OF IT LIKE THAT.
IF I CAN CONTROL MY FEEL-INGS...

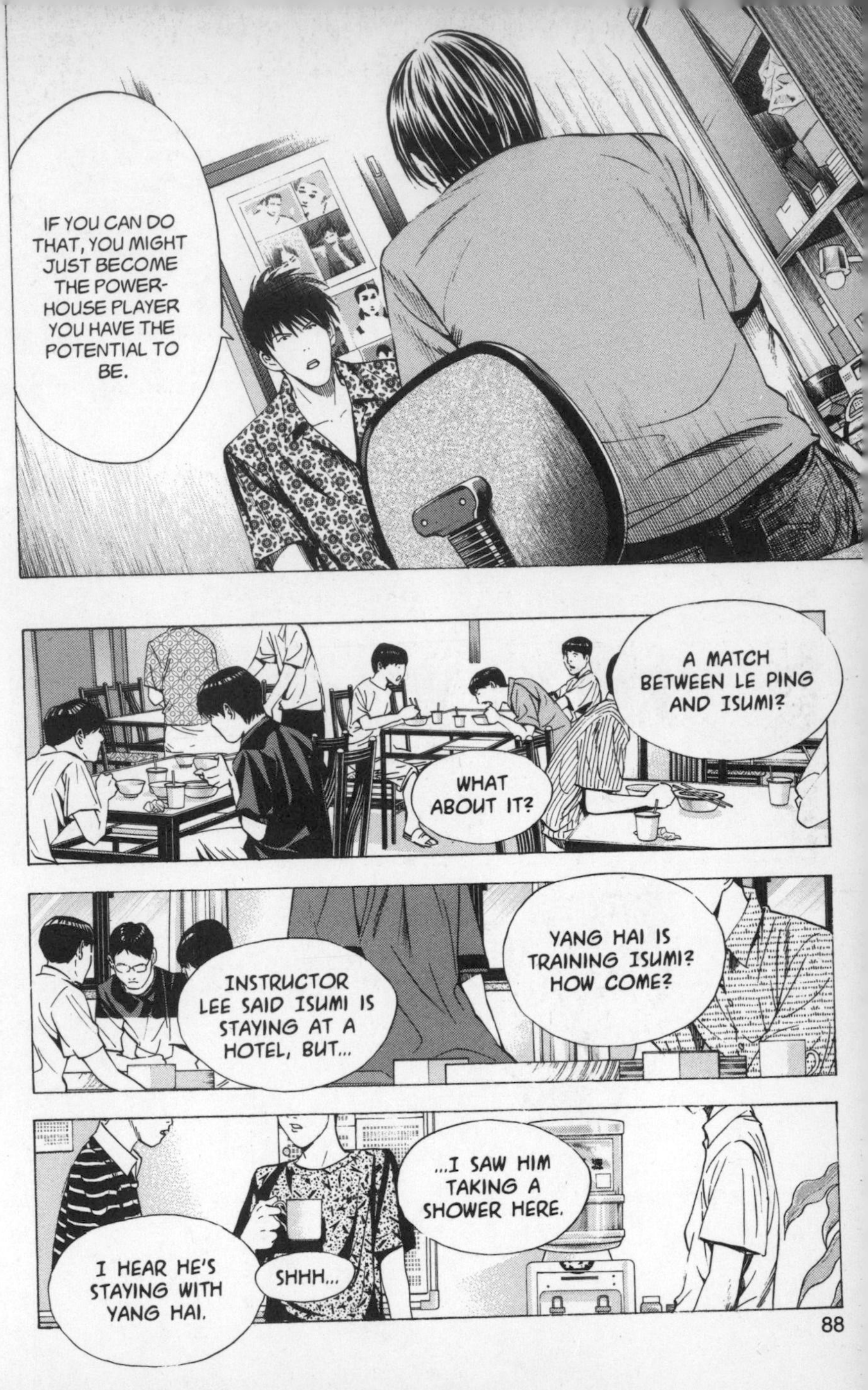
IF YOU CAN DO THAT, YOU MIGHT JUST BECOME THE POWER-HOUSE PLAYER YOU HAVE THE POTENTIAL TO BE.
A MATCH BETWEEN LE PING AND ISUMI?
WHAT ABOUT IT?
YANG HAI IS TRAINING ISUMI? HOW COME?
INSTRUCTOR LEE SAID ISUMI IS STAYING AT A HOTEL, BUT...
...I SAW HIM TAKING A SHOWER HERE.
I HEAR HE'S STAYING WITH YANG HAI.
SHHH...

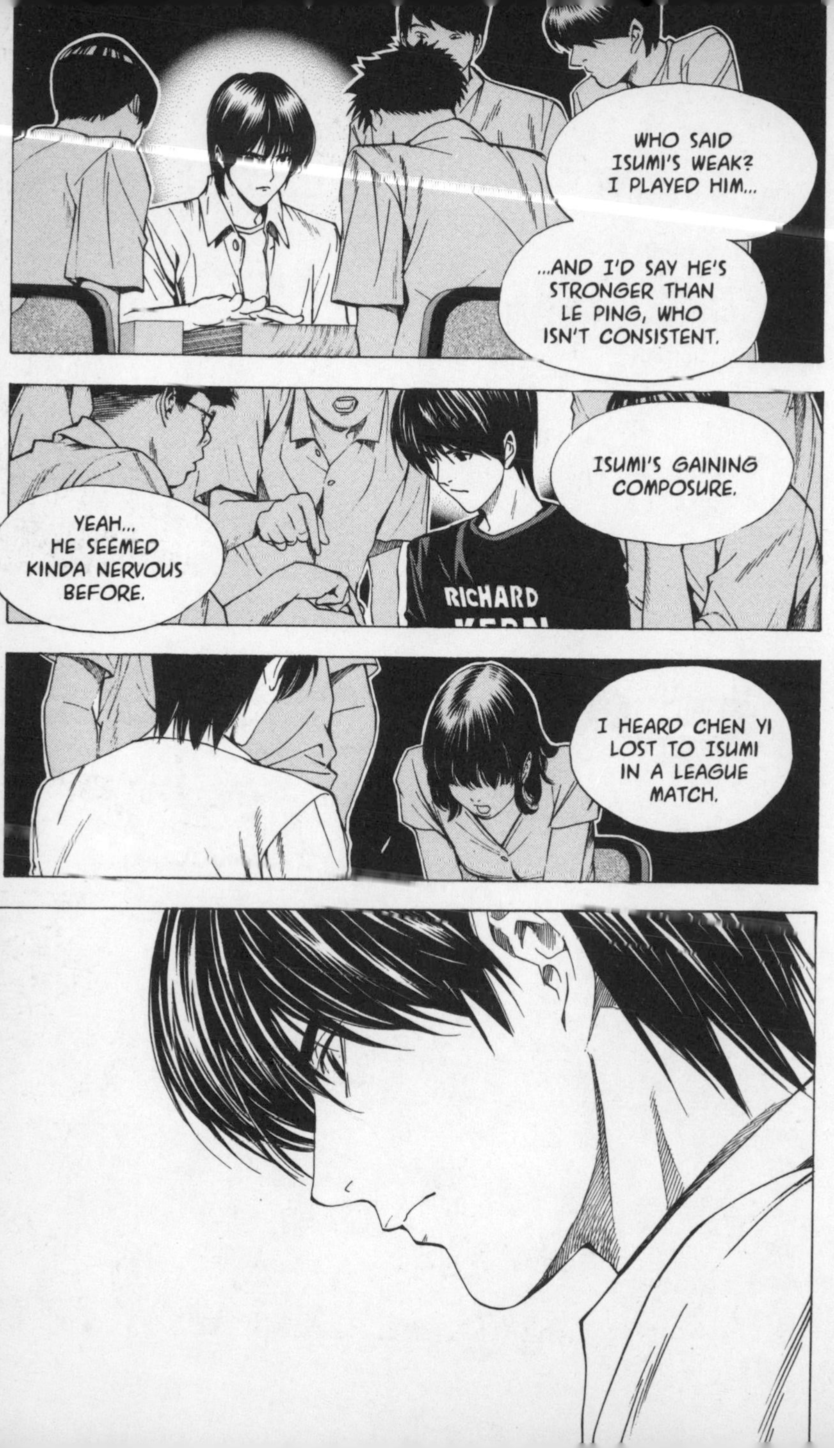
WHO SAID ISUMI'S WEAK? I PLAYED HIM...
...AND I'D SAY HE'S STRONGER THAN LE PING, WHO ISN'T CONSISTENT.
ISUMI'S GAINING COMPOSURE.
RICHARD
YEAH... HE SEEMED KINDA NERVOUS BEFORE.
I HEARD CHEN YI LOST TO ISUMI IN A LEAGUE MATCH.

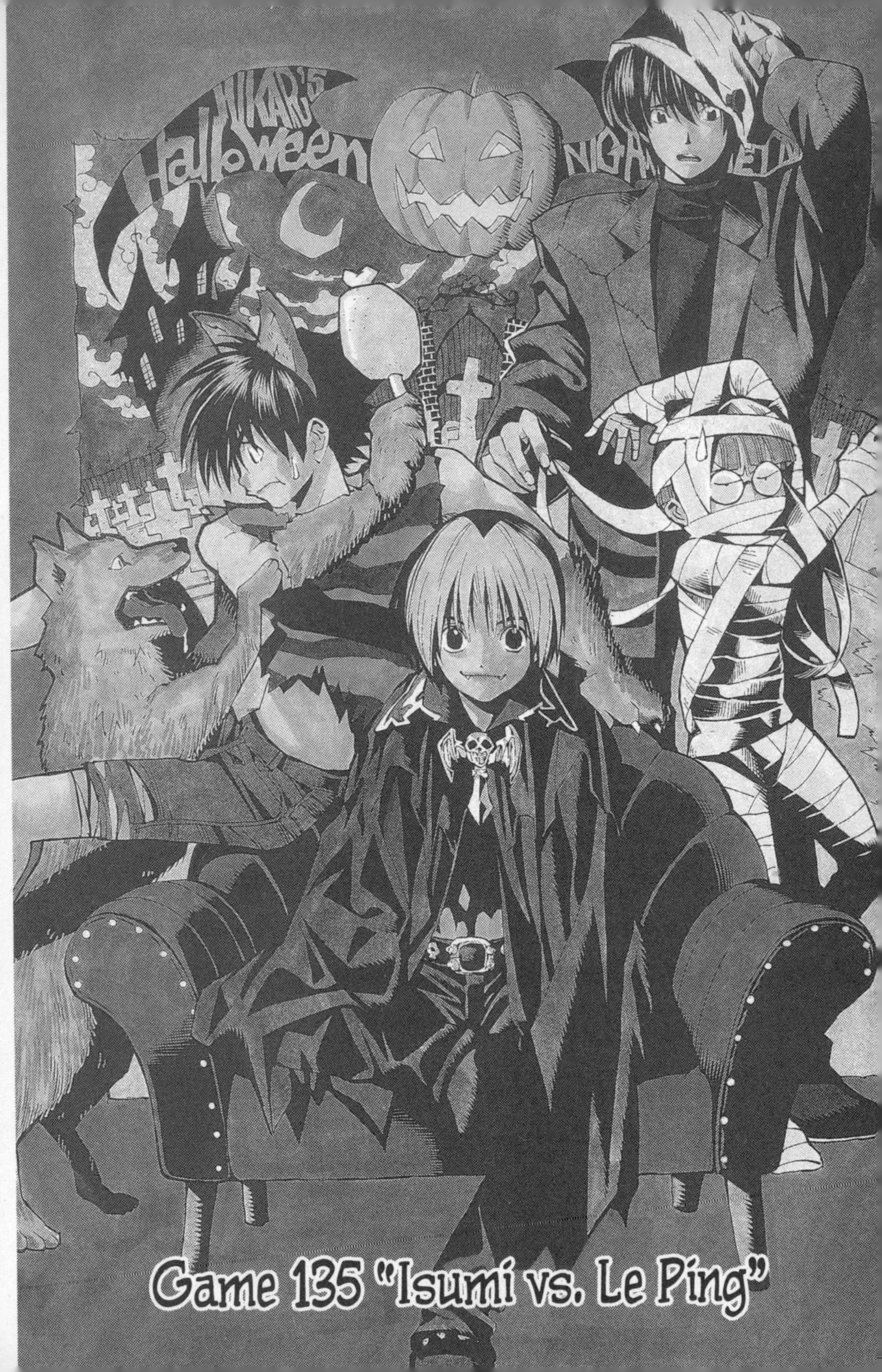
HIKARU'S
Halloween

Game 135 "Isumi vs. Le Ping"

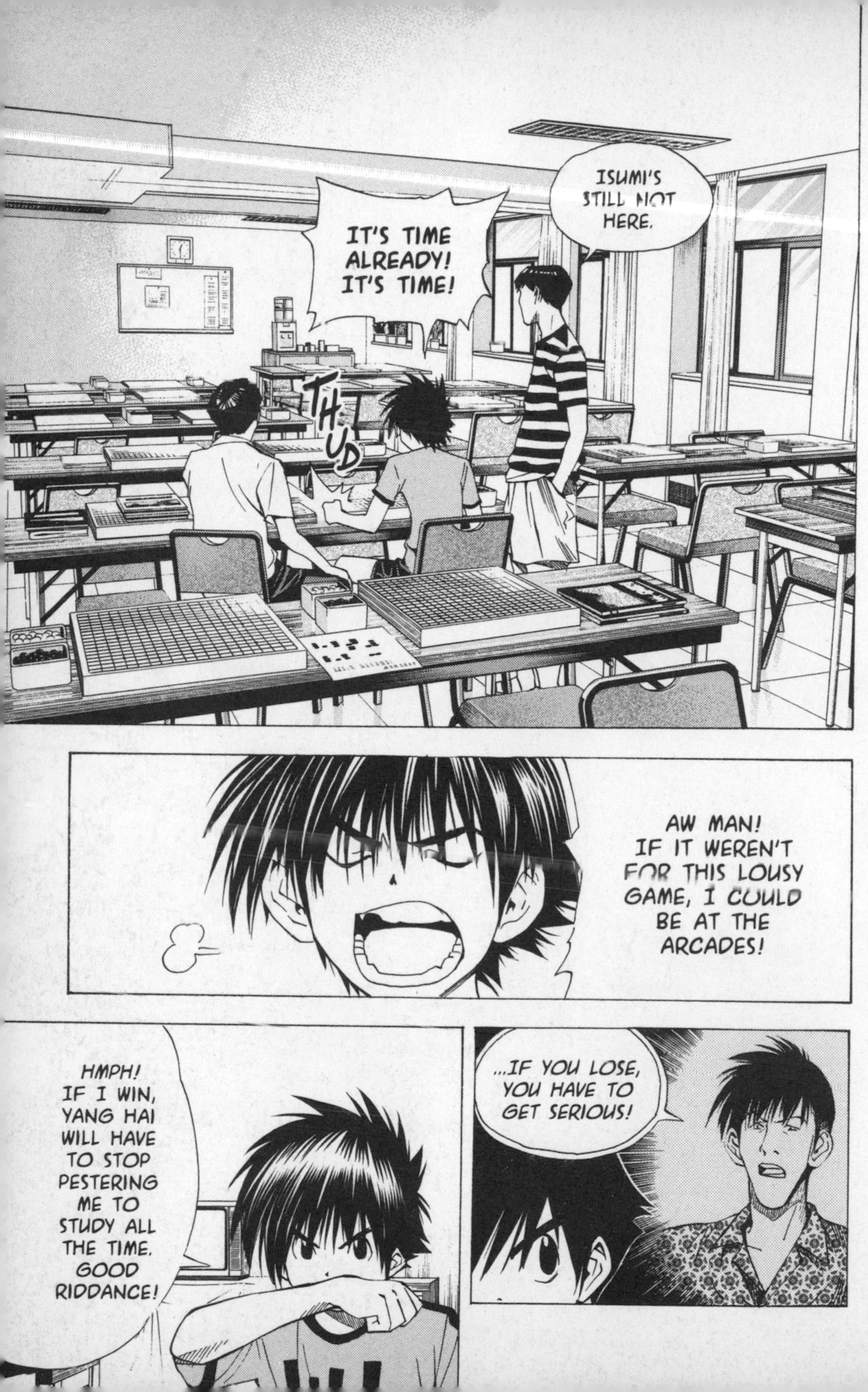
ISUMI'S STILL NOT HERE.
IT'S TIME ALREADY! IT'S TIME!
THUD
AW MAN! IF IT WEREN'T FOR THIS LOUSY GAME, I COULD BE AT THE ARCADES!
...IF YOU LOSE, YOU HAVE TO GET SERIOUS!
HMPH! IF I WIN, YANG HAI WILL HAVE TO STOP PESTERING ME TO STUDY ALL THE TIME. GOOD RIDDANCE!

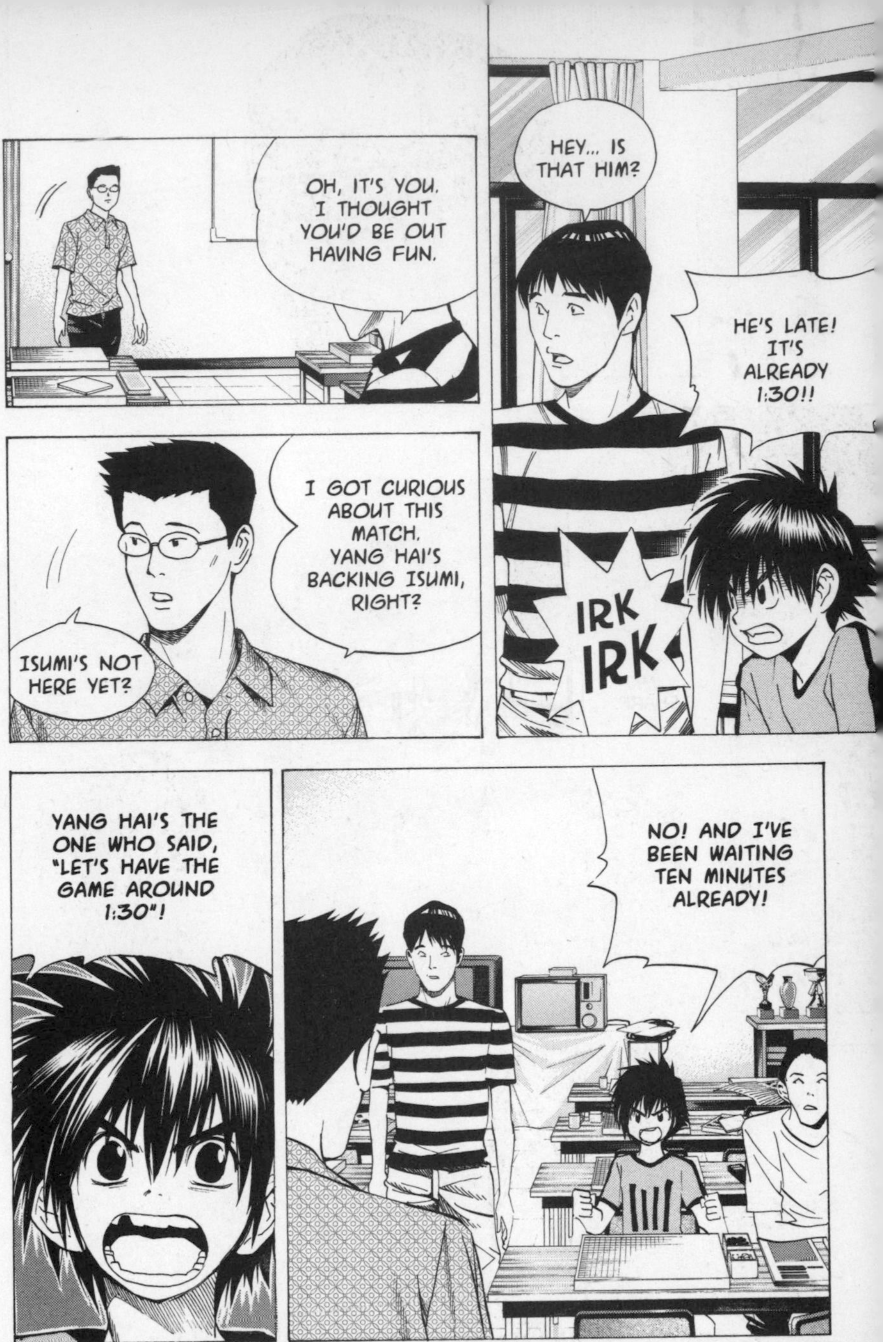
HEY... IS THAT HIM?
HE'S LATE! IT'S ALREADY 1:30!!
IRK IRK
OH, IT'S YOU. I THOUGHT YOU'D BE OUT HAVING FUN.
I GOT CURIOUS ABOUT THIS MATCH. YANG HAI'S BACKING ISUMI, RIGHT?
ISUMI'S NOT HERE YET?
NO! AND I'VE BEEN WAITING TEN MINUTES ALREADY!
YANG HAI'S THE ONE WHO SAID, "LET'S HAVE THE GAME AROUND 1:30"!

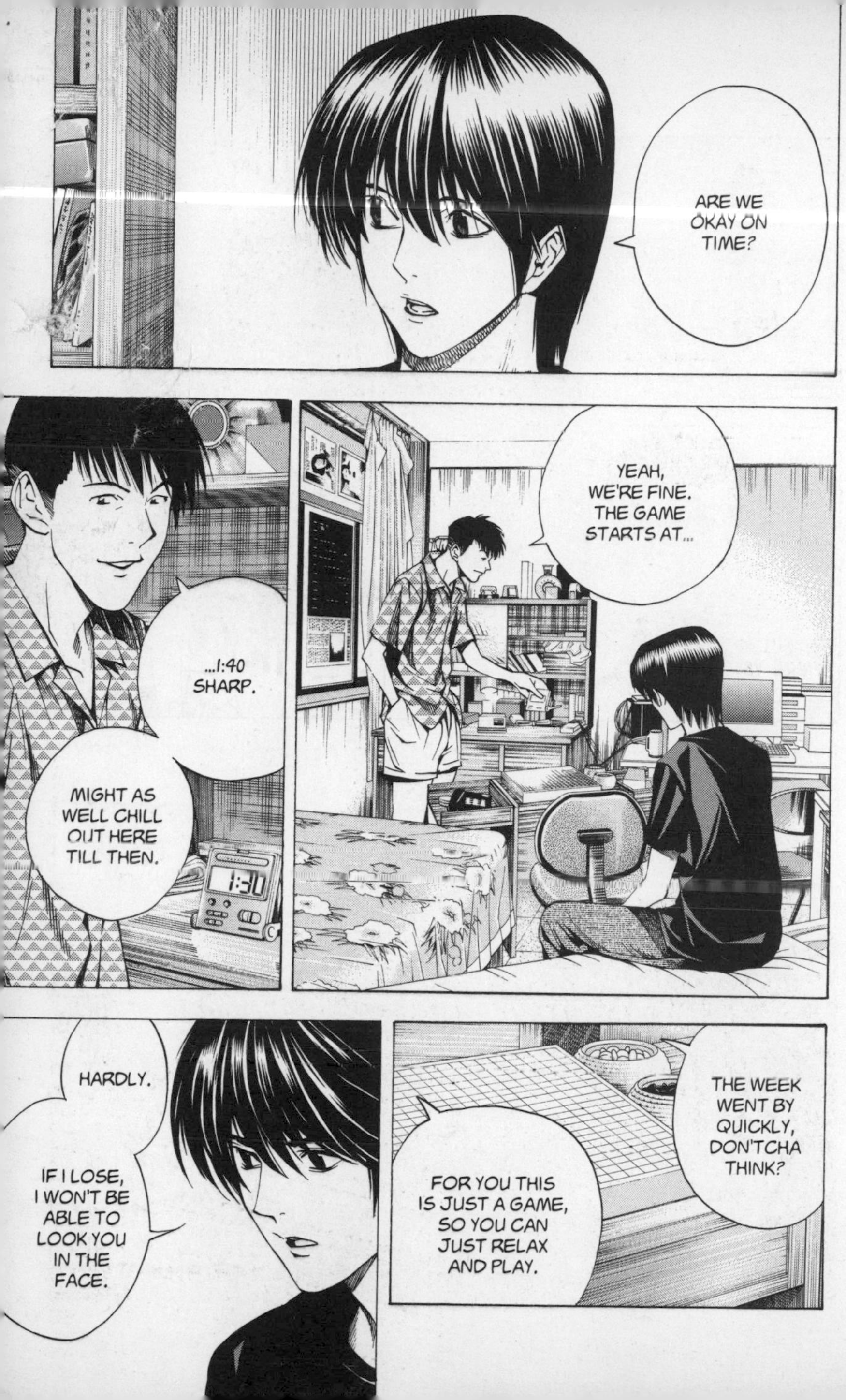
ARE WE OKAY ON TIME?
YEAH, WE'RE FINE. THE GAME STARTS AT...
...1:40 SHARP.
MIGHT AS WELL CHILL OUT HERE TILL THEN.
THE WEEK WENT BY QUICKLY, DON'TCHA THINK?
FOR YOU THIS IS JUST A GAME, SO YOU CAN JUST RELAX AND PLAY.
HARDLY.
IF I LOSE, I WON'T BE ABLE TO LOOK YOU IN THE FACE.

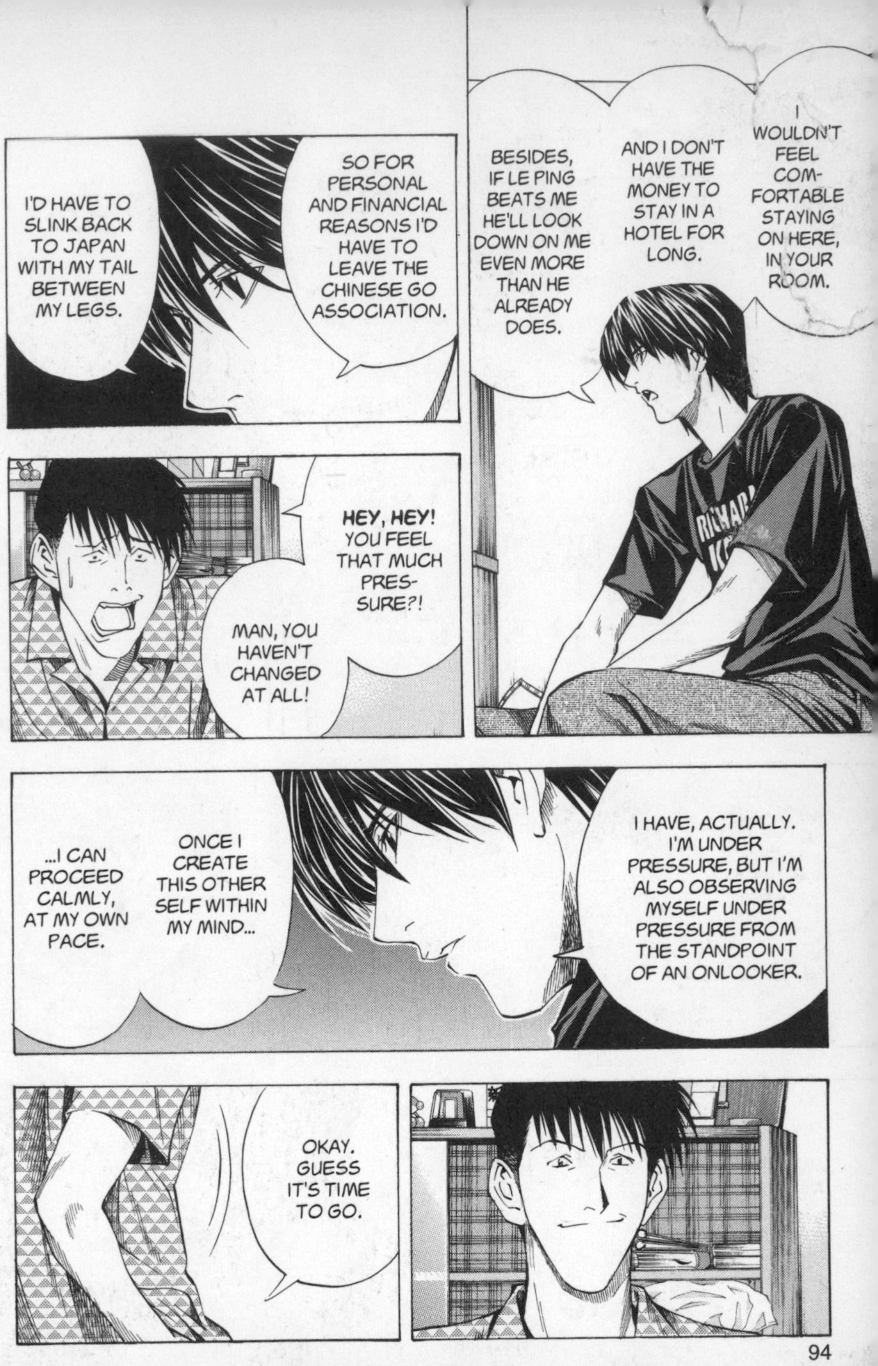
I WOULDN'T FEEL COM-FORTABLE STAYING ON HERE, IN YOUR ROOM.
AND I DON'T HAVE THE MONEY TO STAY IN A HOTEL FOR LONG.
BESIDES, IF LE PING BEATS ME HE'LL LOOK DOWN ON ME EVEN MORE THAN HE ALREADY DOES.
SO FOR PERSONAL AND FINANCIAL REASONS I'D HAVE TO LEAVE THE CHINESE GO ASSOCIATION.
I'D HAVE TO SLINK BACK TO JAPAN WITH MY TAIL BETWEEN MY LEGS.
HEY, HEY! YOU FEEL THAT MUCH PRES-SURE?!
MAN, YOU HAVEN'T CHANGED AT ALL!
I HAVE, ACTUALLY. I'M UNDER PRESSURE, BUT I'M ALSO OBSERVING MYSELF UNDER PRESSURE FROM THE STANDPOINT OF AN ONLOOKER.
ONCE I CREATE THIS OTHER SELF WITHIN MY MIND...
...I CAN PROCEED CALMLY, AT MY OWN PACE.
OKAY. GUESS IT'S TIME TO GO.

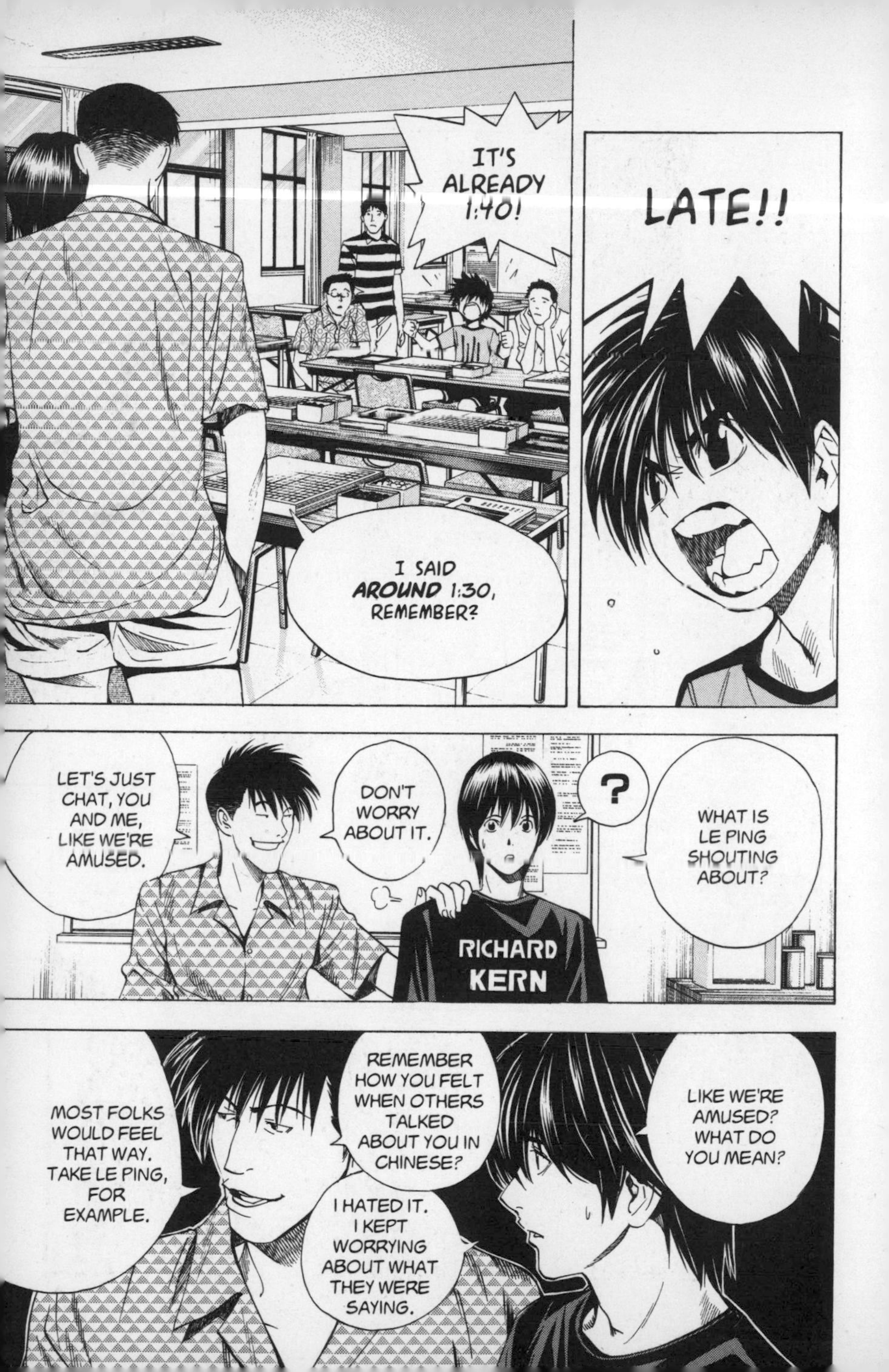
LATE!!
IT'S ALREADY 1:40!
I SAID AROUND 1:30, REMEMBER?
WHAT IS LE PING SHOUTING ABOUT?
?
DON'T WORRY ABOUT IT.
LET'S JUST CHAT, YOU AND ME, LIKE WE'RE AMUSED.
RICHARD KERN
LIKE WE'RE AMUSED? WHAT DO YOU MEAN?
REMEMBER HOW YOU FELT WHEN OTHERS TALKED ABOUT YOU IN CHINESE?
I HATED IT. I KEPT WORRYING ABOUT WHAT THEY WERE SAYING.
MOST FOLKS WOULD FEEL THAT WAY. TAKE LE PING, FOR EXAMPLE.

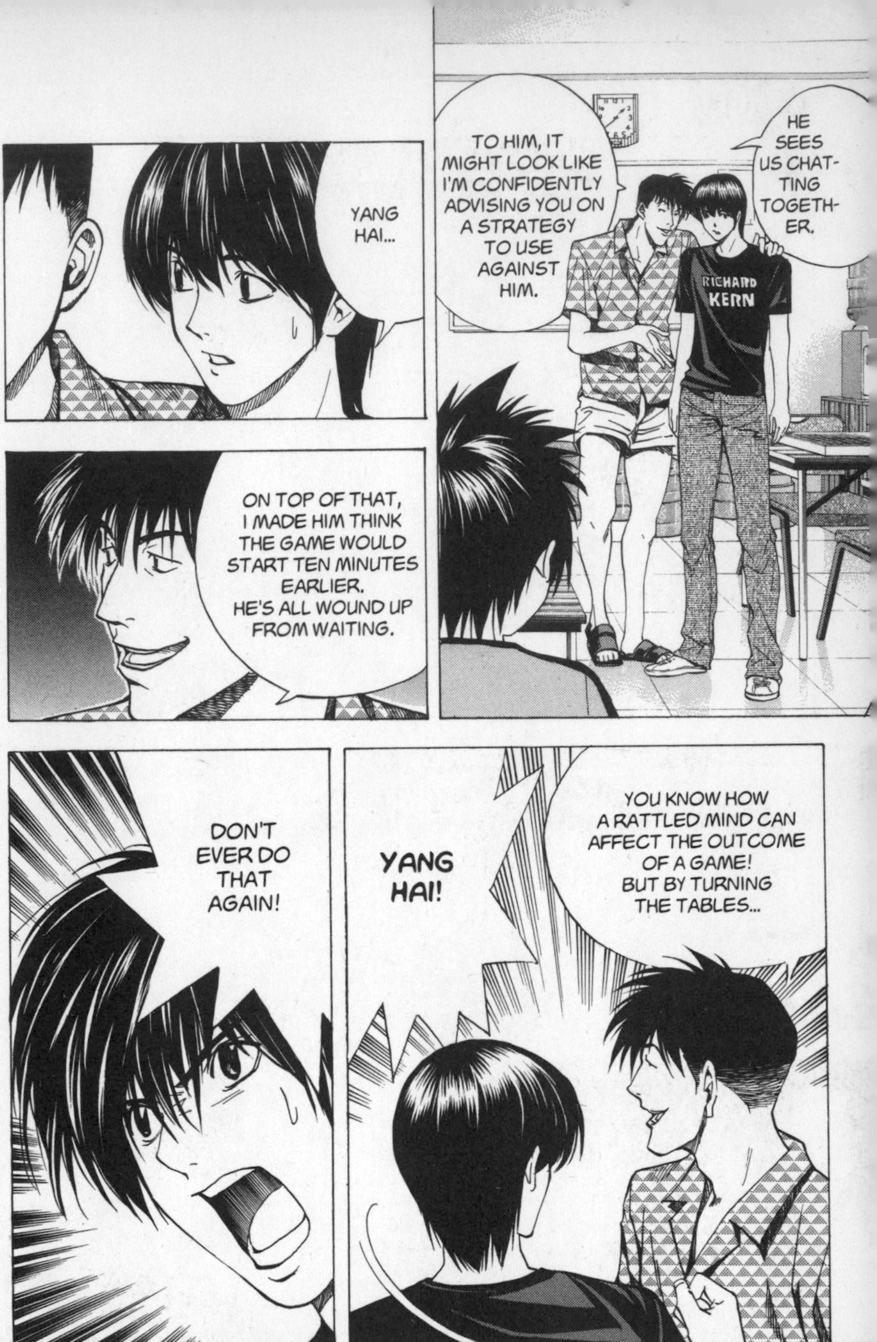
HE SEES US CHATTING TOGETHER.
TO HIM, IT MIGHT LOOK LIKE I'M CONFIDENTLY ADVISING YOU ON A STRATEGY TO USE AGAINST HIM.
RICHARD KERN
YANG HAI...
ON TOP OF THAT, I MADE HIM THINK THE GAME WOULD START TEN MINUTES EARLIER. HE'S ALL WOUND UP FROM WAITING.
YOU KNOW HOW A RATTLED MIND CAN AFFECT THE OUTCOME OF A GAME! BUT BY TURNING THE TABLES...
YANG HAI!
DON'T EVER DO THAT AGAIN!

READ THIS WAY

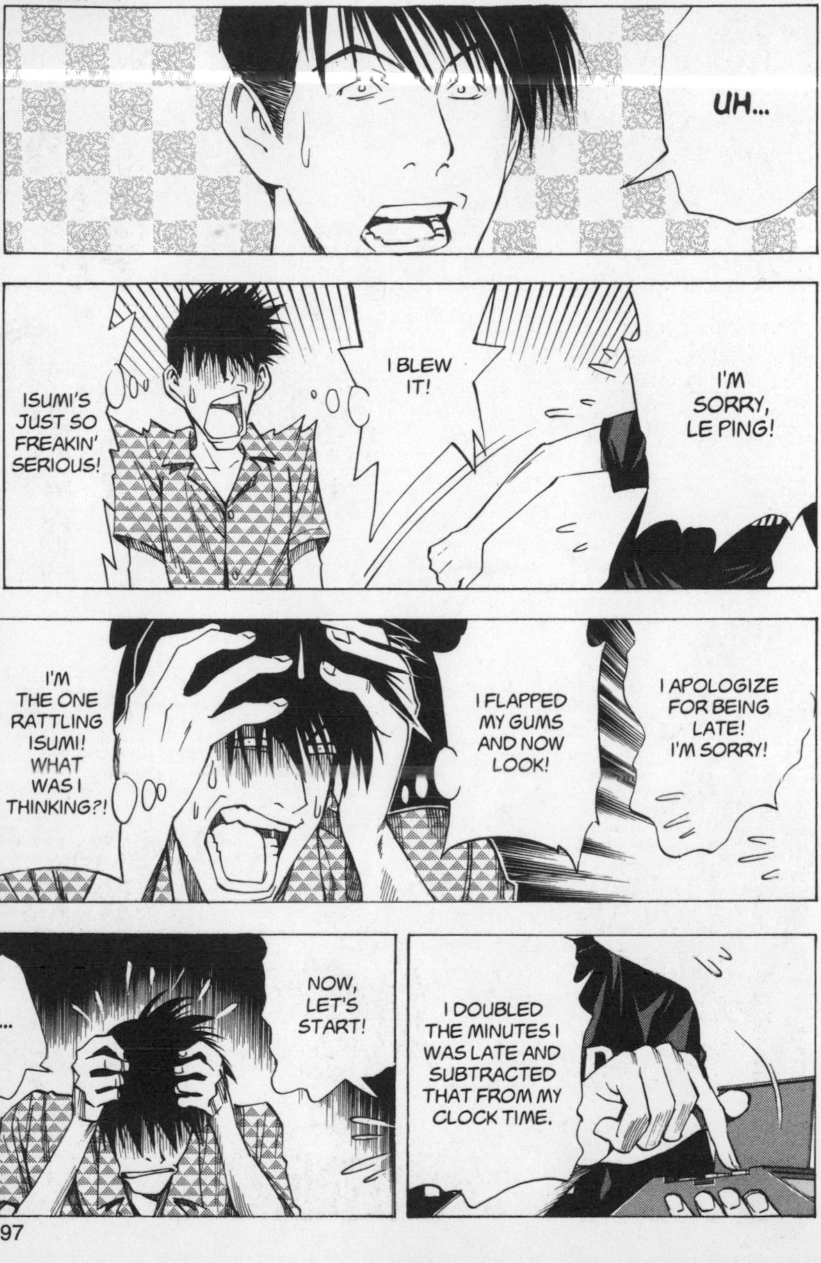
UH...
I'M SORRY, LE PING!
I BLEW IT!
ISUMI'S JUST SO FREAKIN' SERIOUS!
I APOLOGIZE FOR BEING LATE! I'M SORRY!
I FLAPPED MY GUMS AND NOW LOOK!
I'M THE ONE RATTLING ISUMI! WHAT WAS I THINKING?!
I DOUBLED THE MINUTES I WAS LATE AND SUBTRACTED THAT FROM MY CLOCK TIME.
NOW, LET'S START!
...

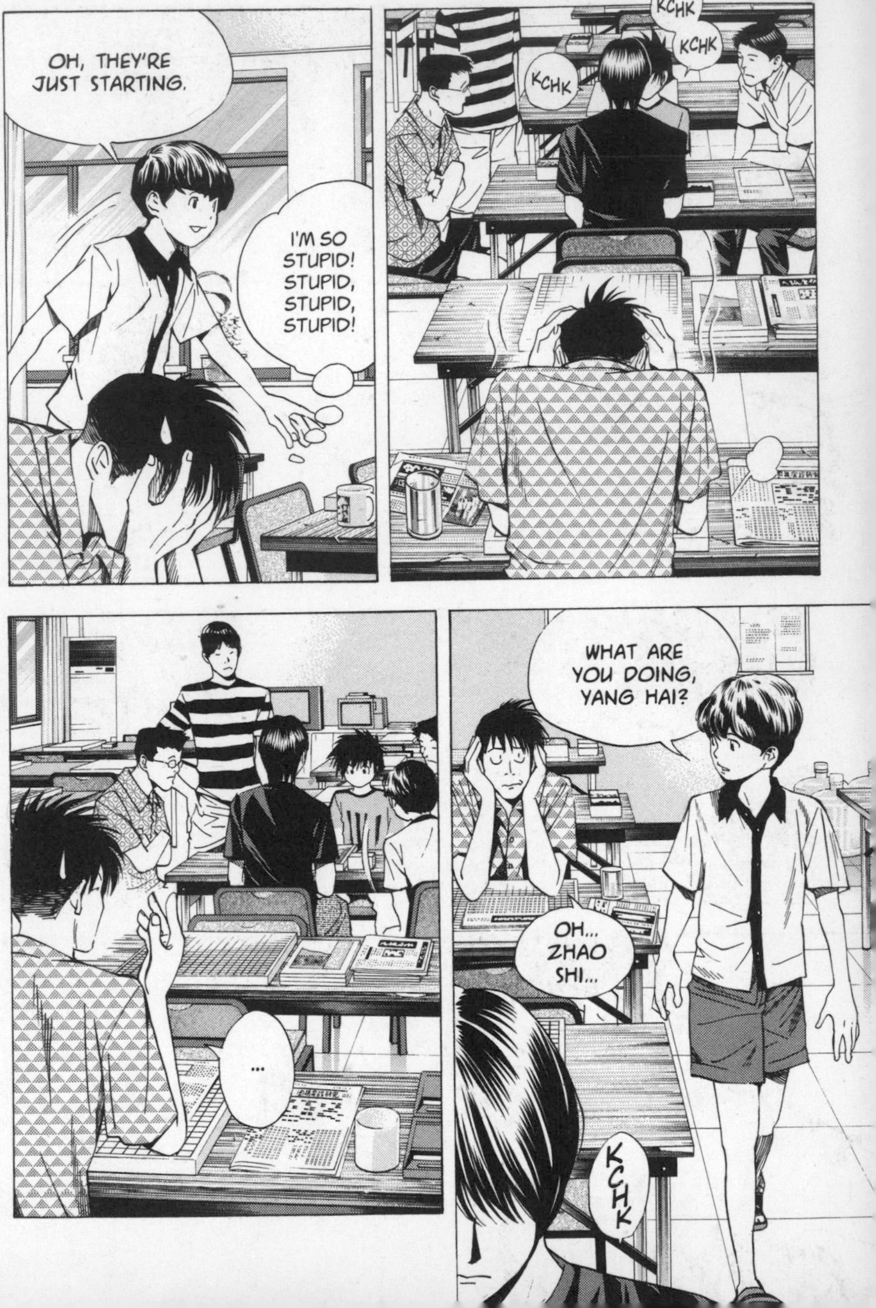
KCHK
KCHK
KCHK
OH, THEY'RE JUST STARTING.
I'M SO STUPID! STUPID, STUPID, STUPID!
WHAT ARE YOU DOING, YANG HAI?
OH... ZHAO SHI...
KCHK
...

READ THIS WAY

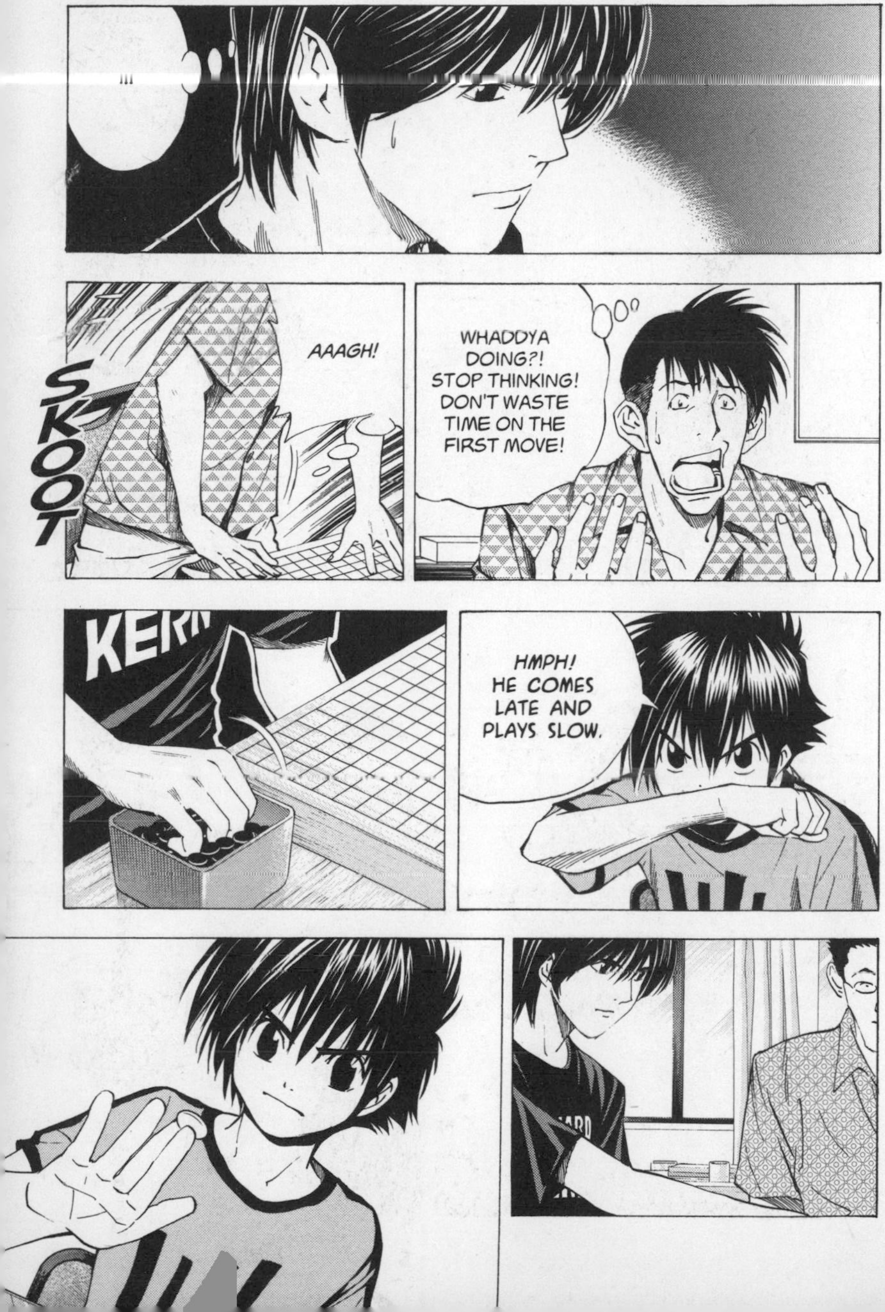
WHADDYA DOING?! STOP THINKING! DON'T WASTE TIME ON THE FIRST MOVE!
AAAGH!
SKOOT
HMPH! HE COMES LATE AND PLAYS SLOW.
KERN

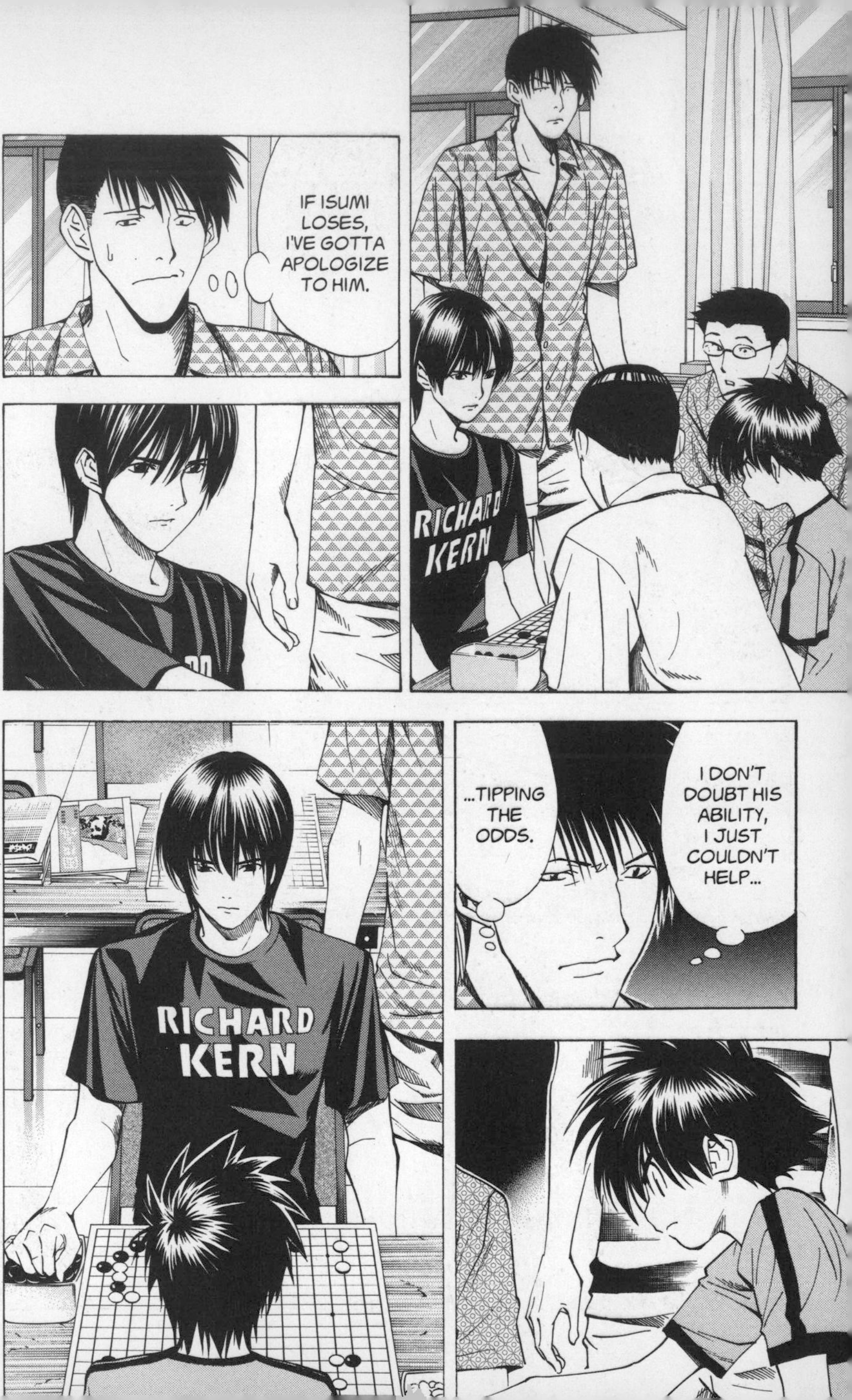
RICHARD KERN
IF ISUMI LOSES, I'VE GOTTA APOLOGIZE TO HIM.
I DON'T DOUBT HIS ABILITY, I JUST COULDN'T HELP...
...TIPPING THE ODDS.
RICHARD KERN

READ THIS WAY

...

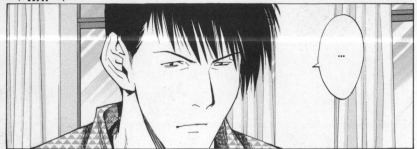

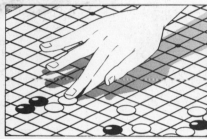

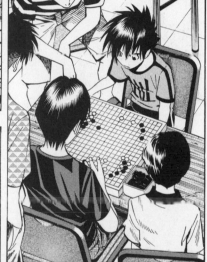

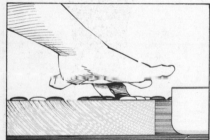

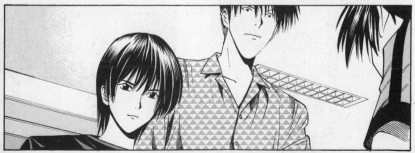

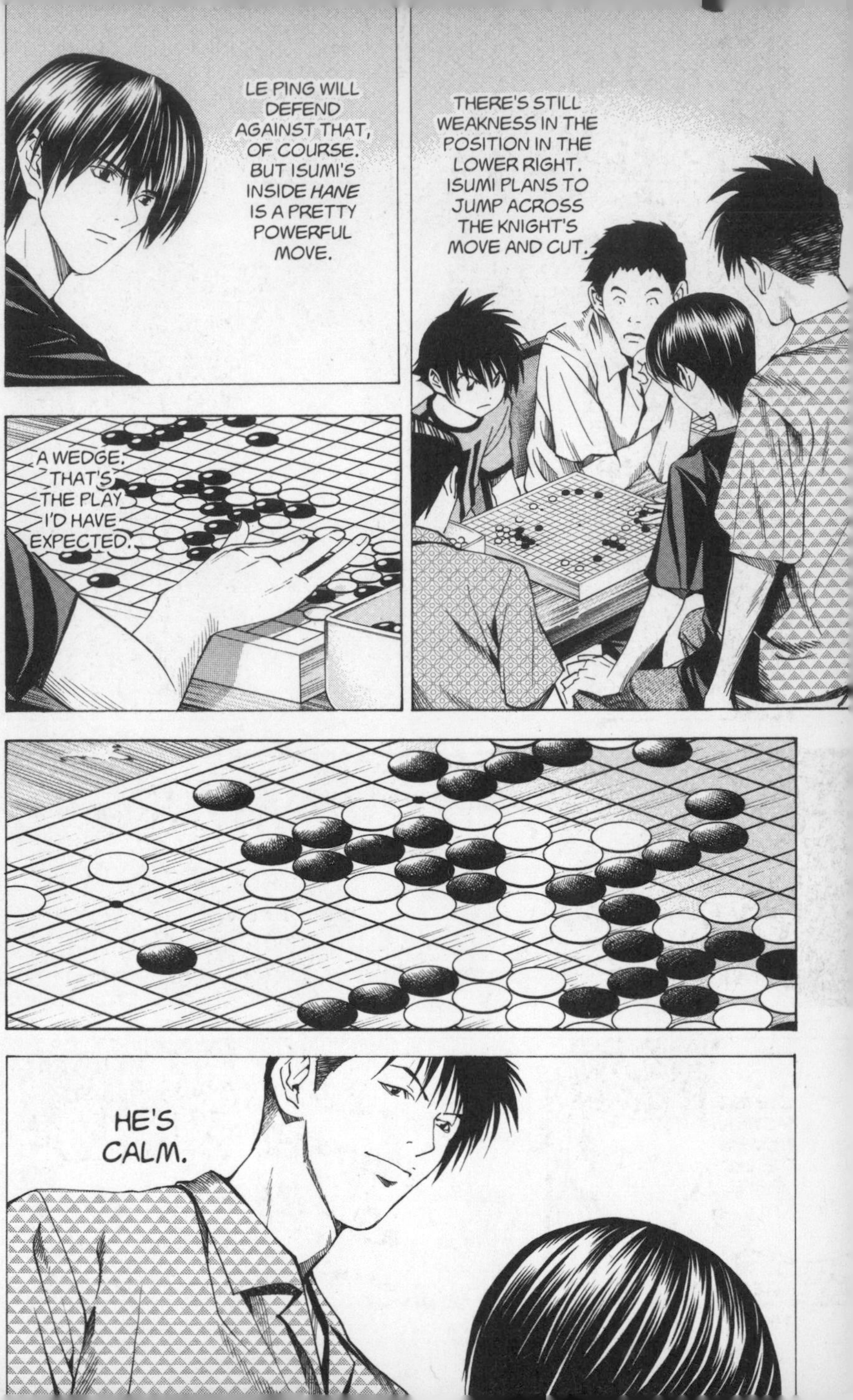
THERE'S STILL WEAKNESS IN THE POSITION IN THE LOWER RIGHT. ISUMI PLANS TO JUMP ACROSS THE KNIGHT'S MOVE AND CUT.
LE PING WILL DEFEND AGAINST THAT, OF COURSE. BUT ISUMI'S INSIDE *HANE* IS A PRETTY POWERFUL MOVE.
A WEDGE. THAT'S THE PLAY I'D HAVE EXPECTED.
HE'S CALM.

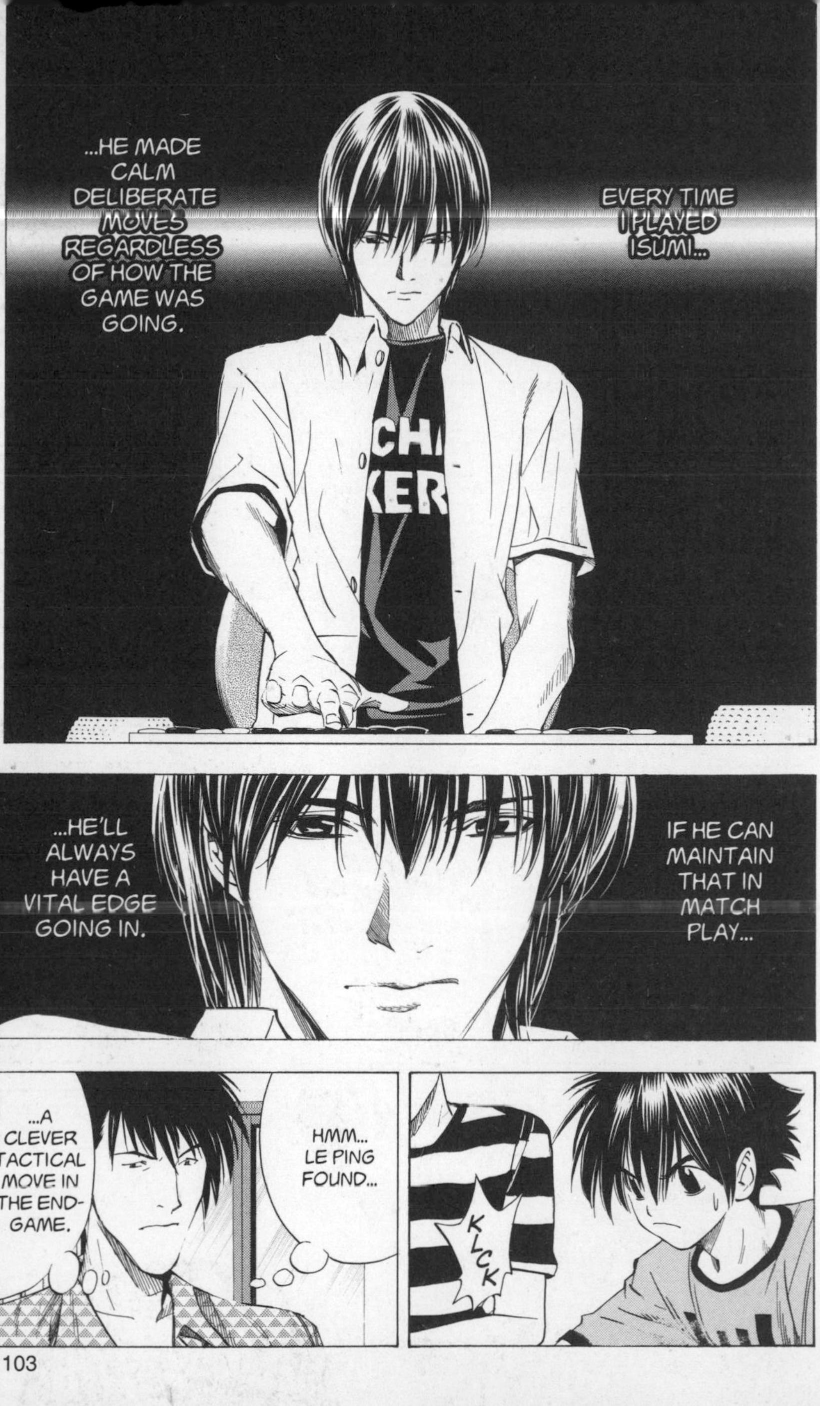
EVERY TIME I PLAYED ISUMI...
...HE MADE CALM DELIBERATE MOVES REGARDLESS OF HOW THE GAME WAS GOING.
IF HE CAN MAINTAIN THAT IN MATCH PLAY...
...HE'LL ALWAYS HAVE A VITAL EDGE GOING IN.
KLCK
HMM... LE PING FOUND...
...A CLEVER TACTICAL MOVE IN THE END-GAME.

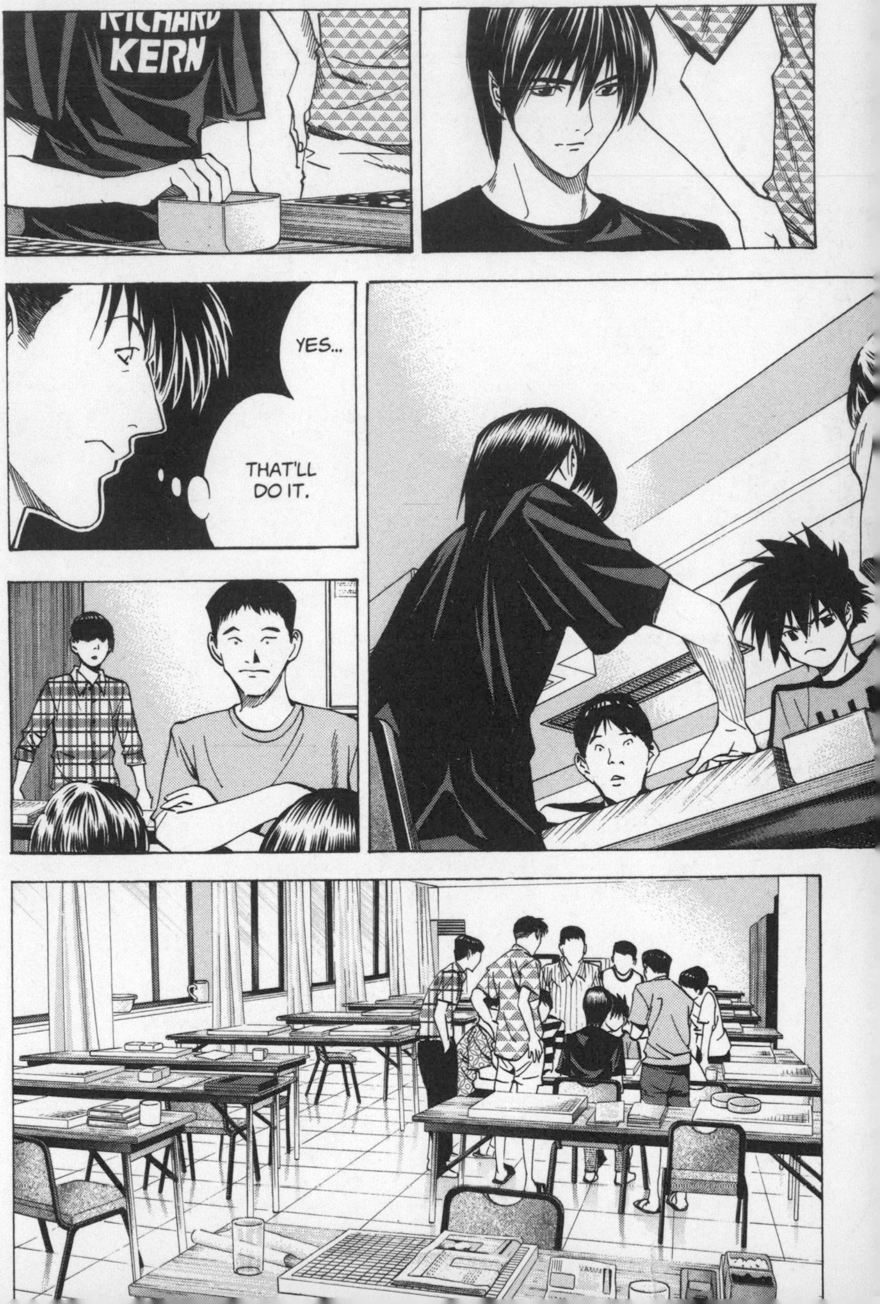
RICHARD
KERN
YES...
THAT'LL DO IT.

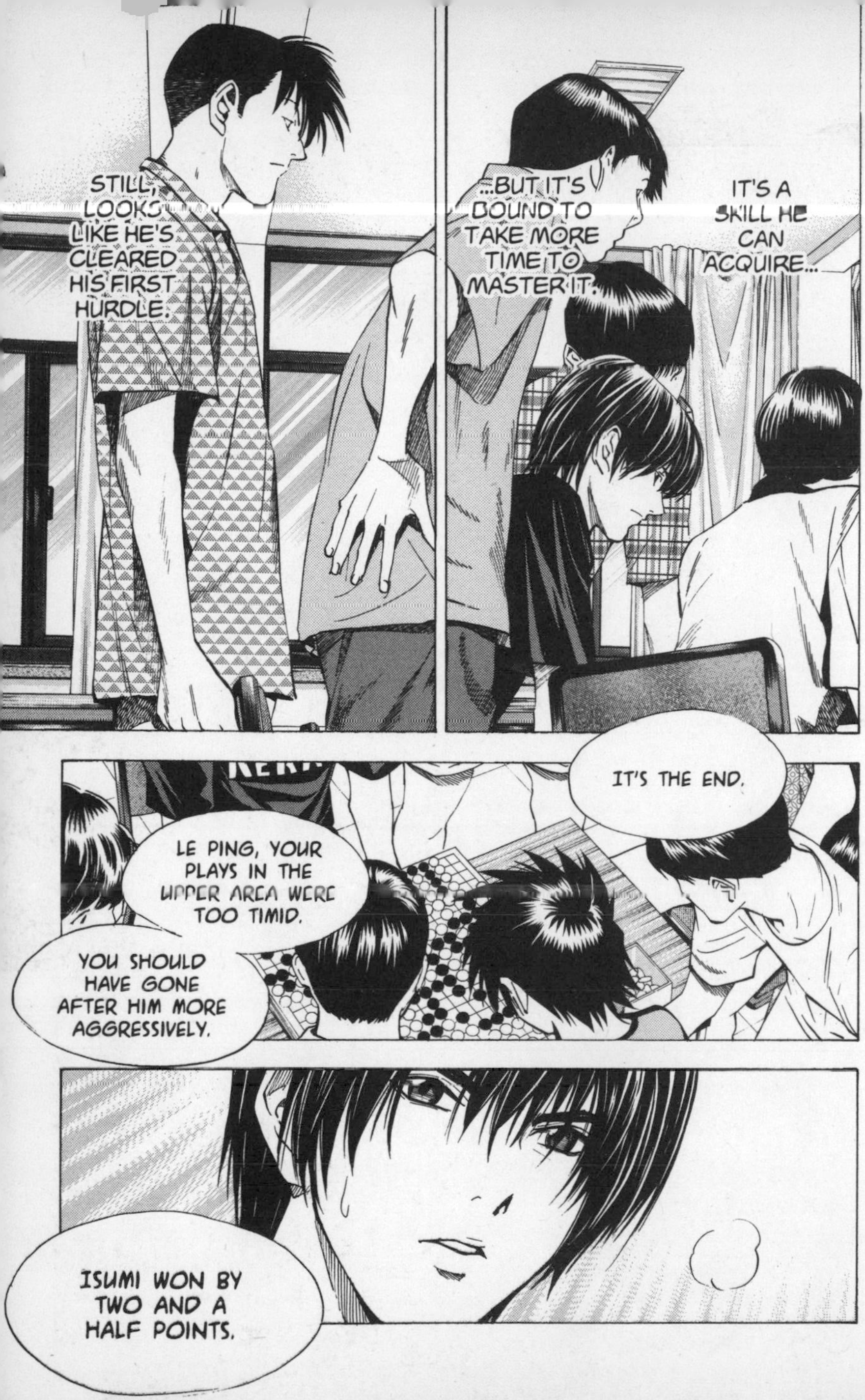
IT'S A SKILL HE CAN ACQUIRE...
...BUT IT'S BOUND TO TAKE MORE TIME TO MASTER IT.
STILL, LOOKS LIKE HE'S CLEARED HIS FIRST HURDLE.
IT'S THE END.
LE PING, YOUR PLAYS IN THE UPPER AREA WERE TOO TIMID.
YOU SHOULD HAVE GONE AFTER HIM MORE AGGRESSIVELY.
ISUMI WON BY TWO AND A HALF POINTS.

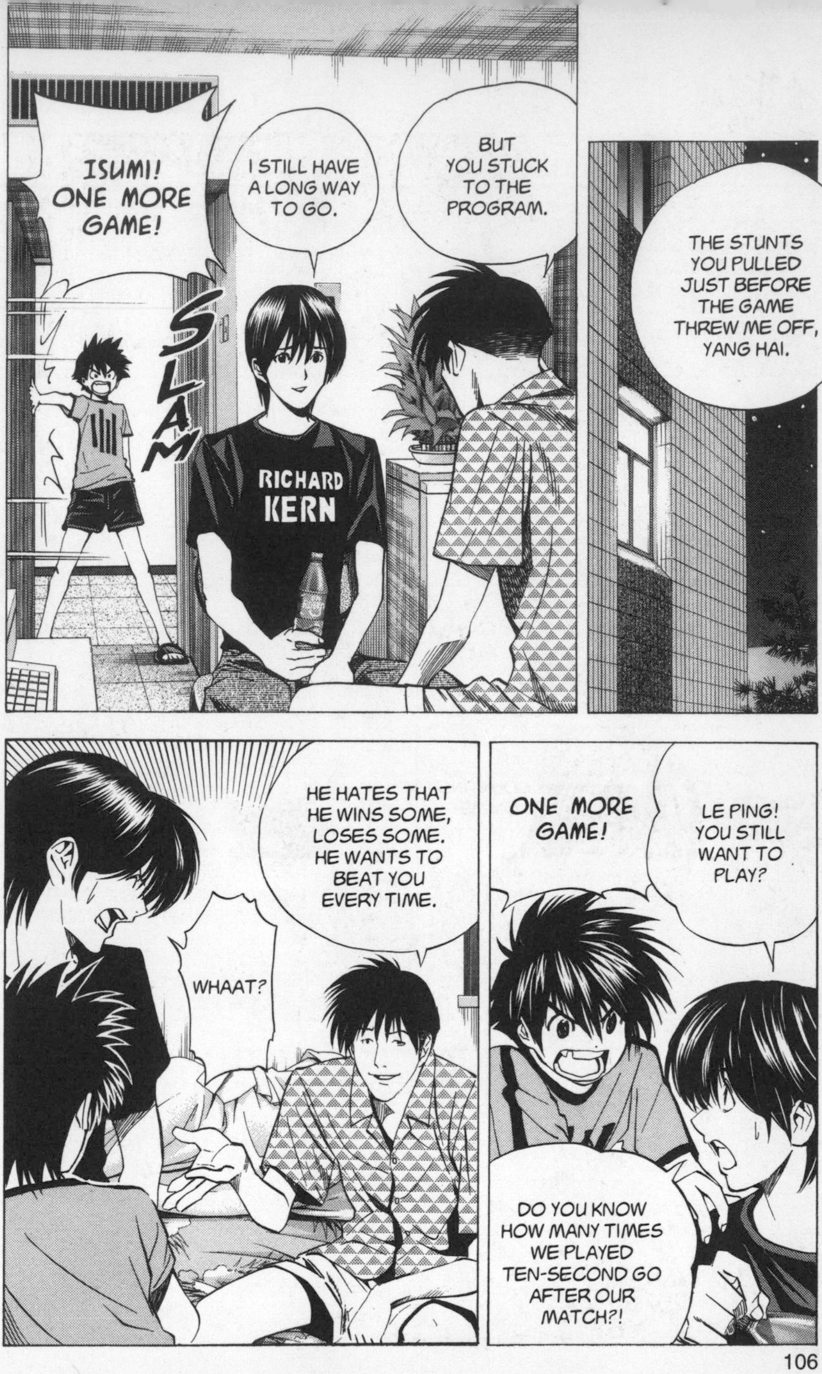
THE STUNTS YOU PULLED JUST BEFORE THE GAME THREW ME OFF, YANG HAI.
BUT YOU STUCK TO THE PROGRAM.
I STILL HAVE A LONG WAY TO GO.
ISUMI! ONE MORE GAME!
SLAM
RICHARD KERN
LE PING! YOU STILL WANT TO PLAY?
ONE MORE GAME!
DO YOU KNOW HOW MANY TIMES WE PLAYED TEN-SECOND GO AFTER OUR MATCH?!
HE HATES THAT HE WINS SOME, LOSES SOME. HE WANTS TO BEAT YOU EVERY TIME.
WHAAT?

READ THIS WAY

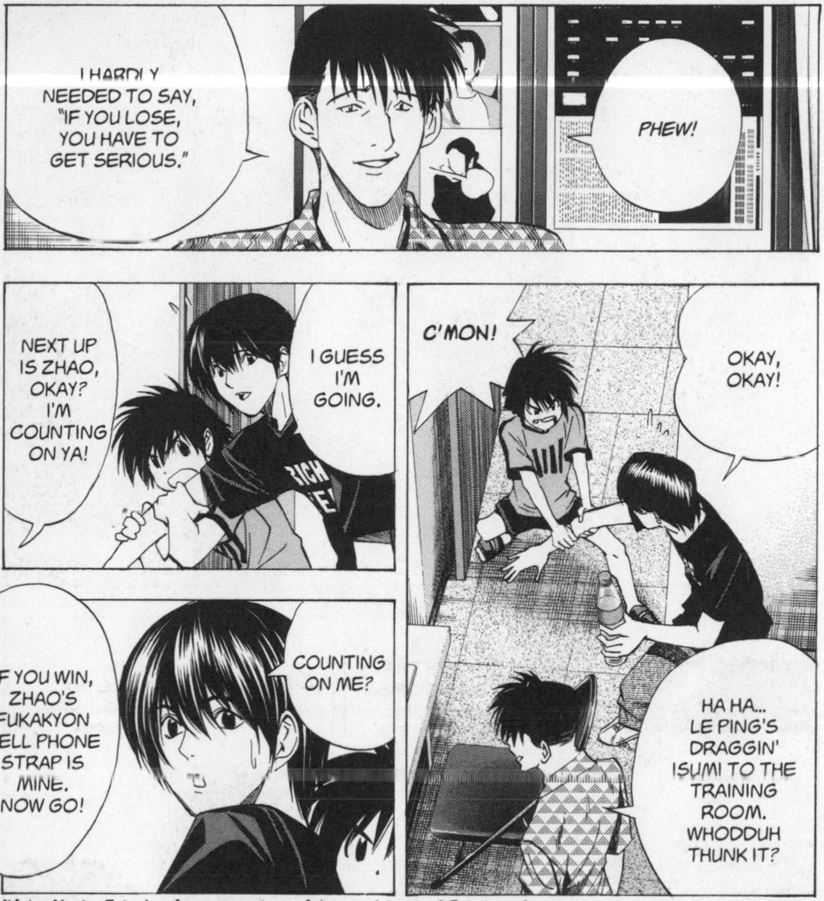
PHEW!
I HARDLY NEEDED TO SAY, "IF YOU LOSE, YOU HAVE TO GET SERIOUS."
C'MON!
OKAY, OKAY!
HA HA... LE PING'S DRAGGIN' ISUMI TO THE TRAINING ROOM. WHODDUH THUNK IT?
I GUESS I'M GOING.
NEXT UP IS ZHAO, OKAY? I'M COUNTING ON YA!
COUNTING ON ME?
IF YOU WIN, ZHAO'S FUKAKYON CELL PHONE STRAP IS MINE. NOW GO!

[Note: Kyoko Fukada = Japanese actress/singer, nicknamed Fukakyon.]

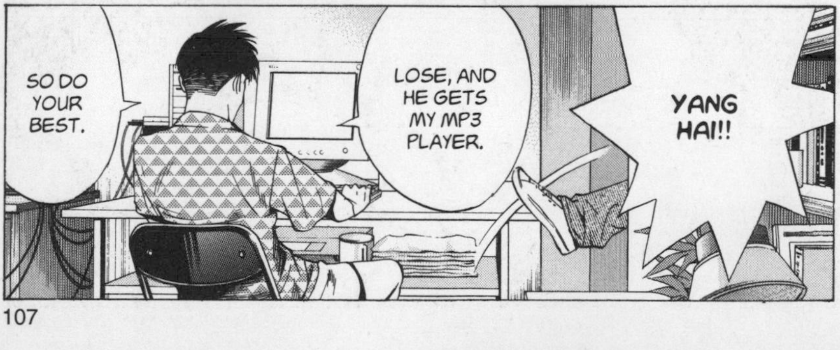
YANG HAI!!
LOSE, AND HE GETS MY MP3 PLAYER.
SO DO YOUR BEST.

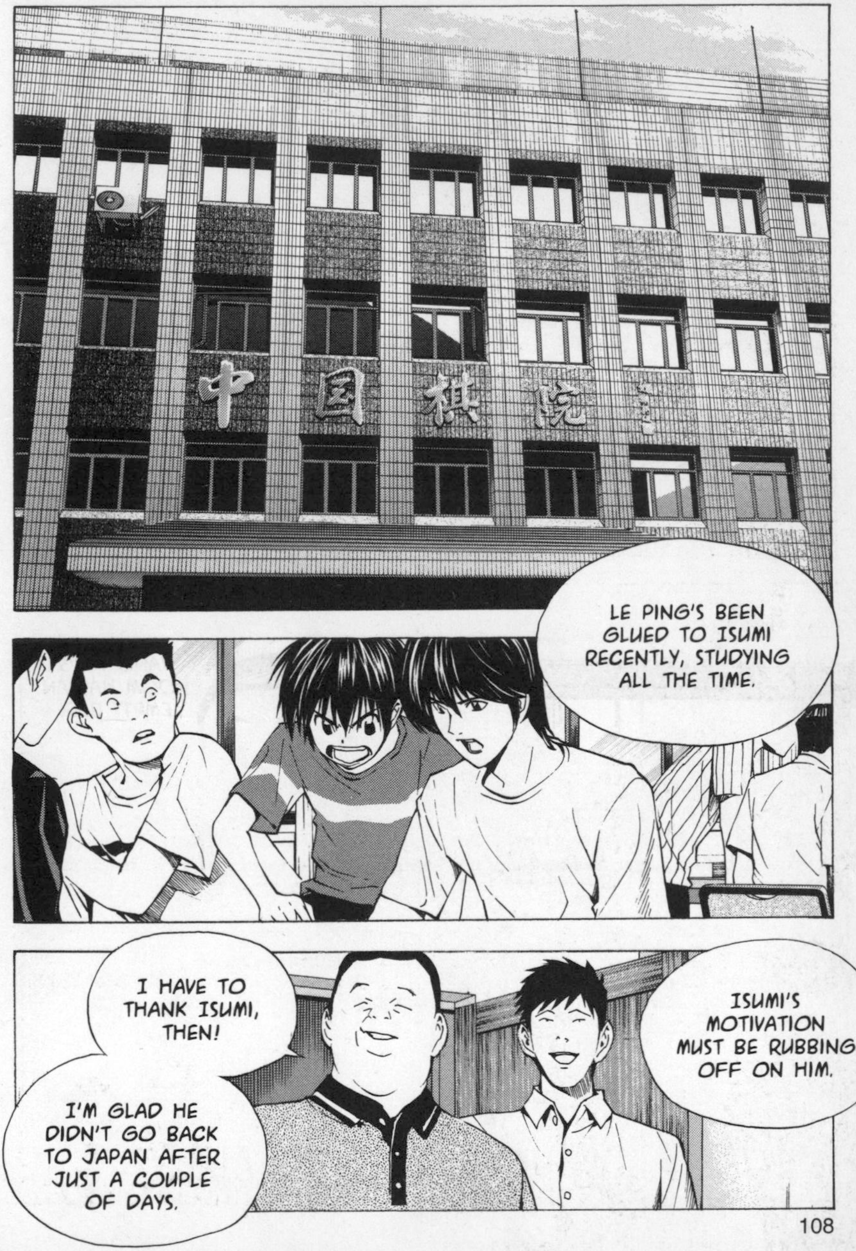
中国棋院
LE PING'S BEEN GLUED TO ISUMI RECENTLY, STUDYING ALL THE TIME.
ISUMI'S MOTIVATION MUST BE RUBBING OFF ON HIM.
I HAVE TO THANK ISUMI, THEN!
I'M GLAD HE DIDN'T GO BACK TO JAPAN AFTER JUST A COUPLE OF DAYS.

READ THIS WAY

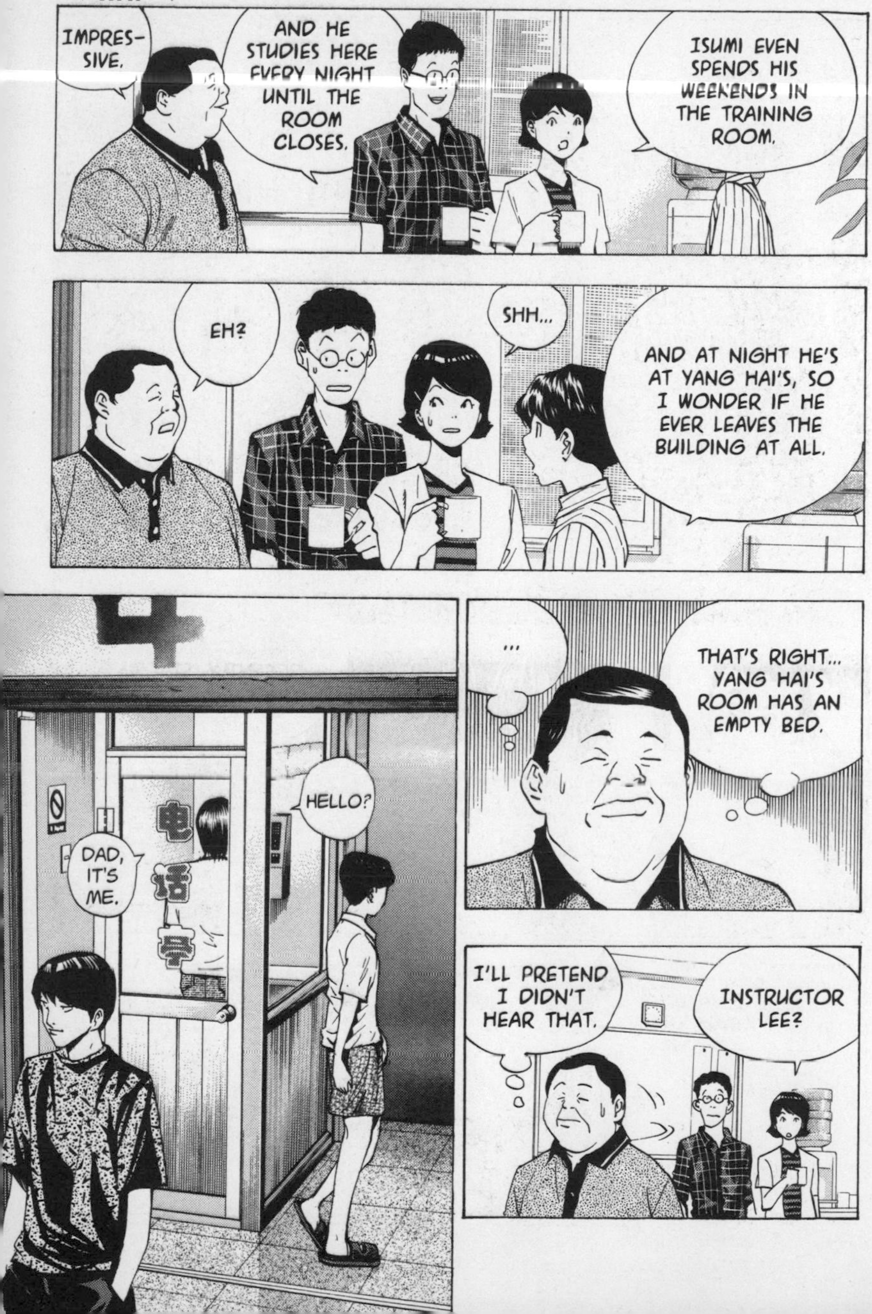
ISUMI EVEN SPENDS HIS WEEKENDS IN THE TRAINING ROOM.
AND HE STUDIES HERE EVERY NIGHT UNTIL THE ROOM CLOSES.
IMPRES-SIVE.
AND AT NIGHT HE'S AT YANG HAI'S, SO I WONDER IF HE EVER LEAVES THE BUILDING AT ALL.
SHH...
EH?
THAT'S RIGHT... YANG HAI'S ROOM HAS AN EMPTY BED.
...
INSTRUCTOR LEE?
I'LL PRETEND I DIDN'T HEAR THAT.
HELLO?
电话亭
DAD, IT'S ME.

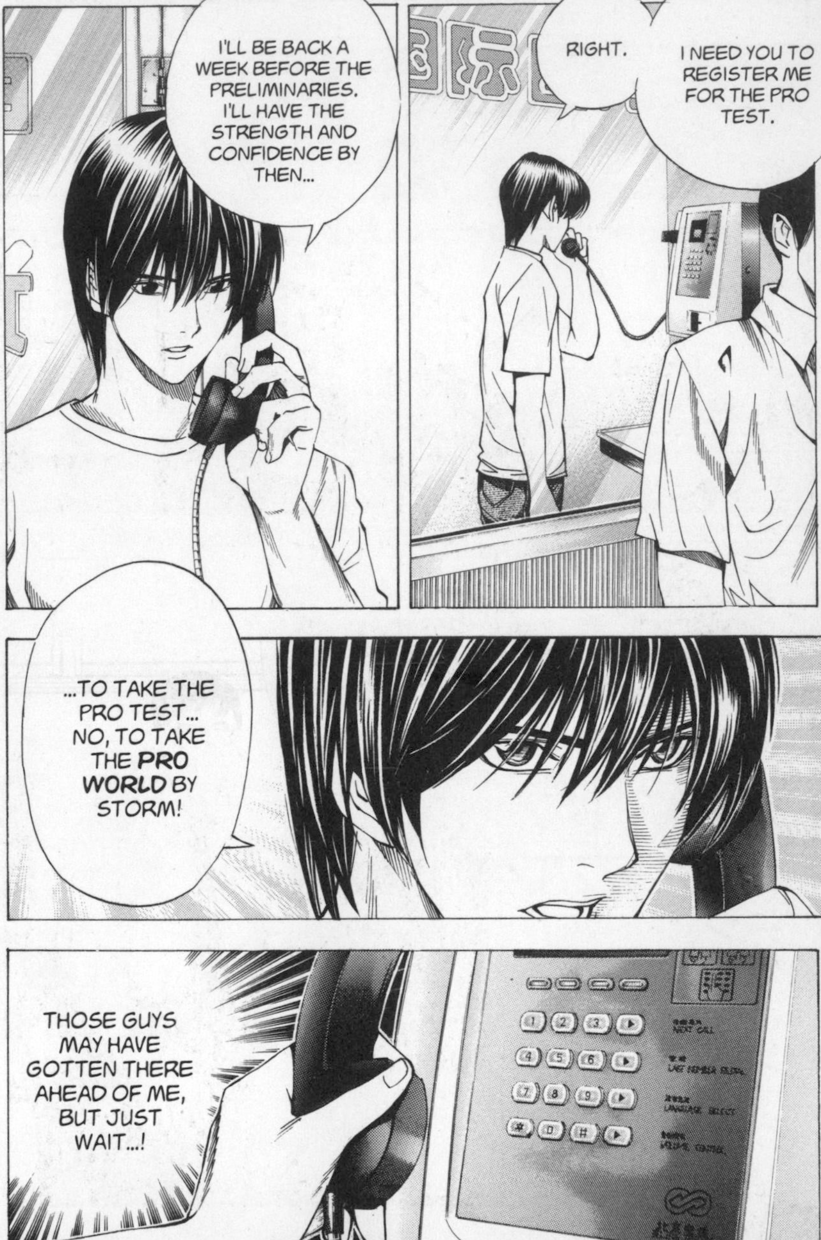
I NEED YOU TO REGISTER ME FOR THE PRO TEST.
RIGHT.
I'LL BE BACK A WEEK BEFORE THE PRELIMINARIES. I'LL HAVE THE STRENGTH AND CONFIDENCE BY THEN...
...TO TAKE THE PRO TEST... NO, TO TAKE THE **PRO WORLD** BY STORM!
THOSE GUYS MAY HAVE GOTTEN THERE AHEAD OF ME, BUT JUST WAIT...!

READ THIS WAY

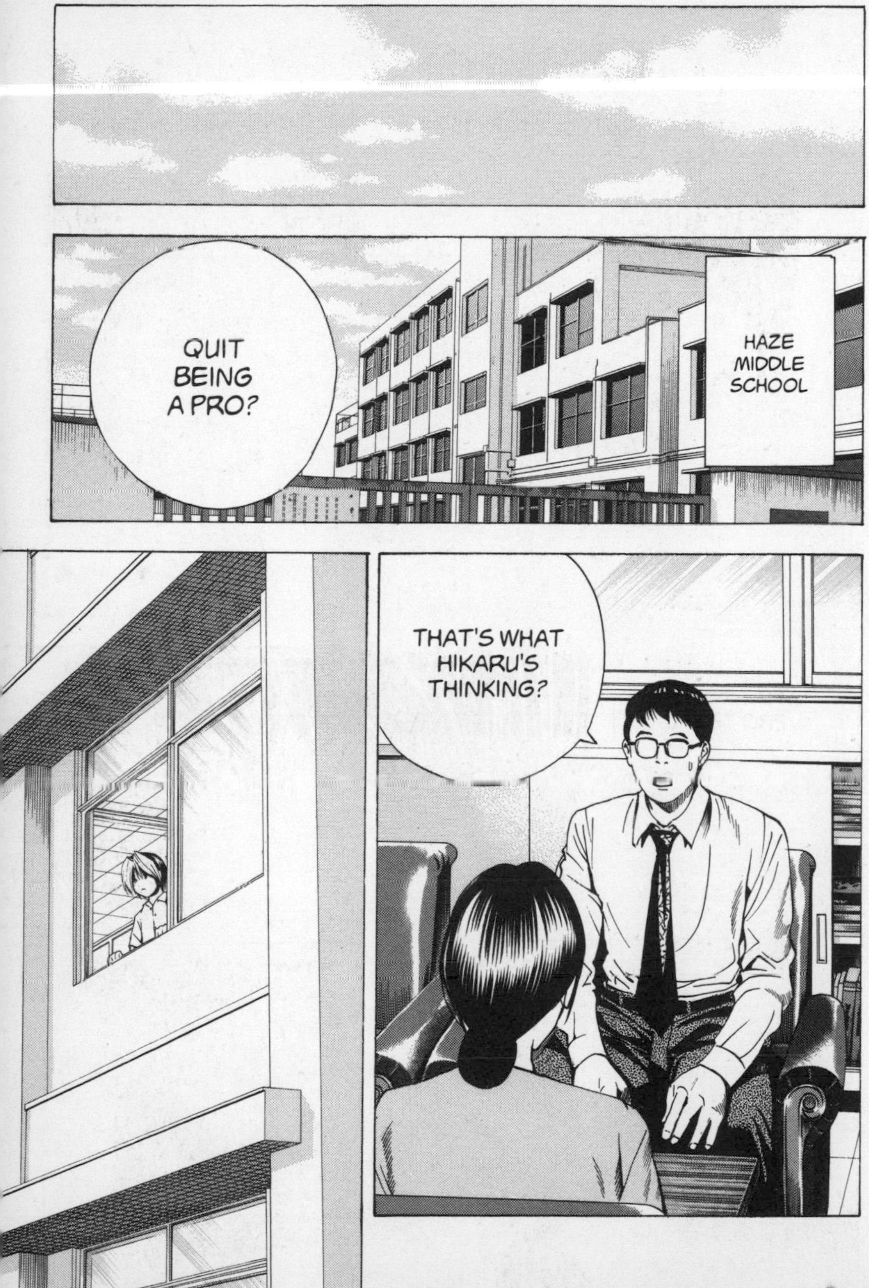
HAZE MIDDLE SCHOOL
QUIT BEING A PRO?
THAT'S WHAT HIKARU'S THINKING?

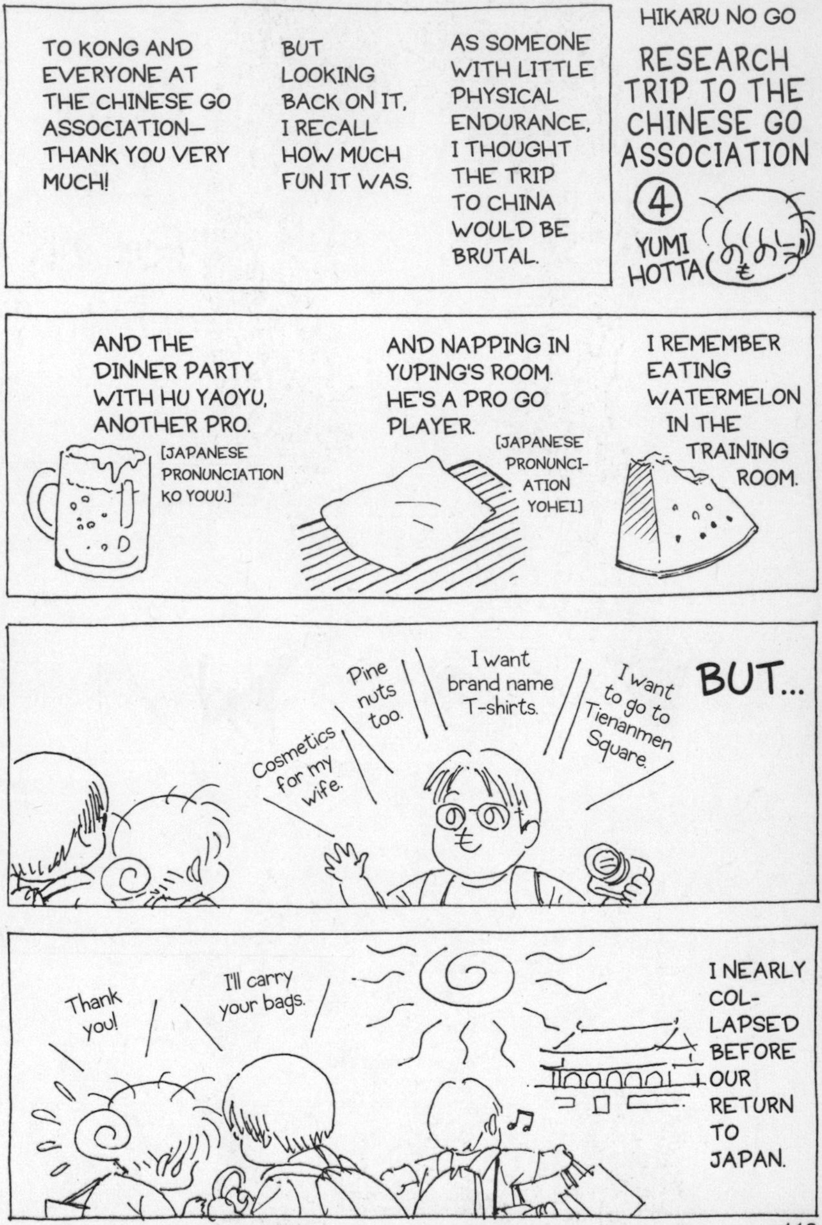
HIKARU NO GO
RESEARCH TRIP TO THE CHINESE GO ASSOCIATION
4
YUMI HOTTA
AS SOMEONE WITH LITTLE PHYSICAL ENDURANCE, I THOUGHT THE TRIP TO CHINA WOULD BE BRUTAL.
BUT LOOKING BACK ON IT, I RECALL HOW MUCH FUN IT WAS.
TO KONG AND EVERYONE AT THE CHINESE GO ASSOCIATION—THANK YOU VERY MUCH!
I REMEMBER EATING WATERMELON IN THE TRAINING ROOM.
AND NAPPING IN YUPING'S ROOM. HE'S A PRO GO PLAYER.
[JAPANESE PRONUNCIATION YOHEI.]
AND THE DINNER PARTY WITH HU YAOYU, ANOTHER PRO.
[JAPANESE PRONUNCIATION KO YOUU.]
BUT...
I want to go to Tienanmen Square.
I want brand name T-shirts.
Pine nuts too.
Cosmetics for my wife.
I NEARLY COL-LAPSED BEFORE OUR RETURN TO JAPAN.
I'll carry your bags.
Thank you!

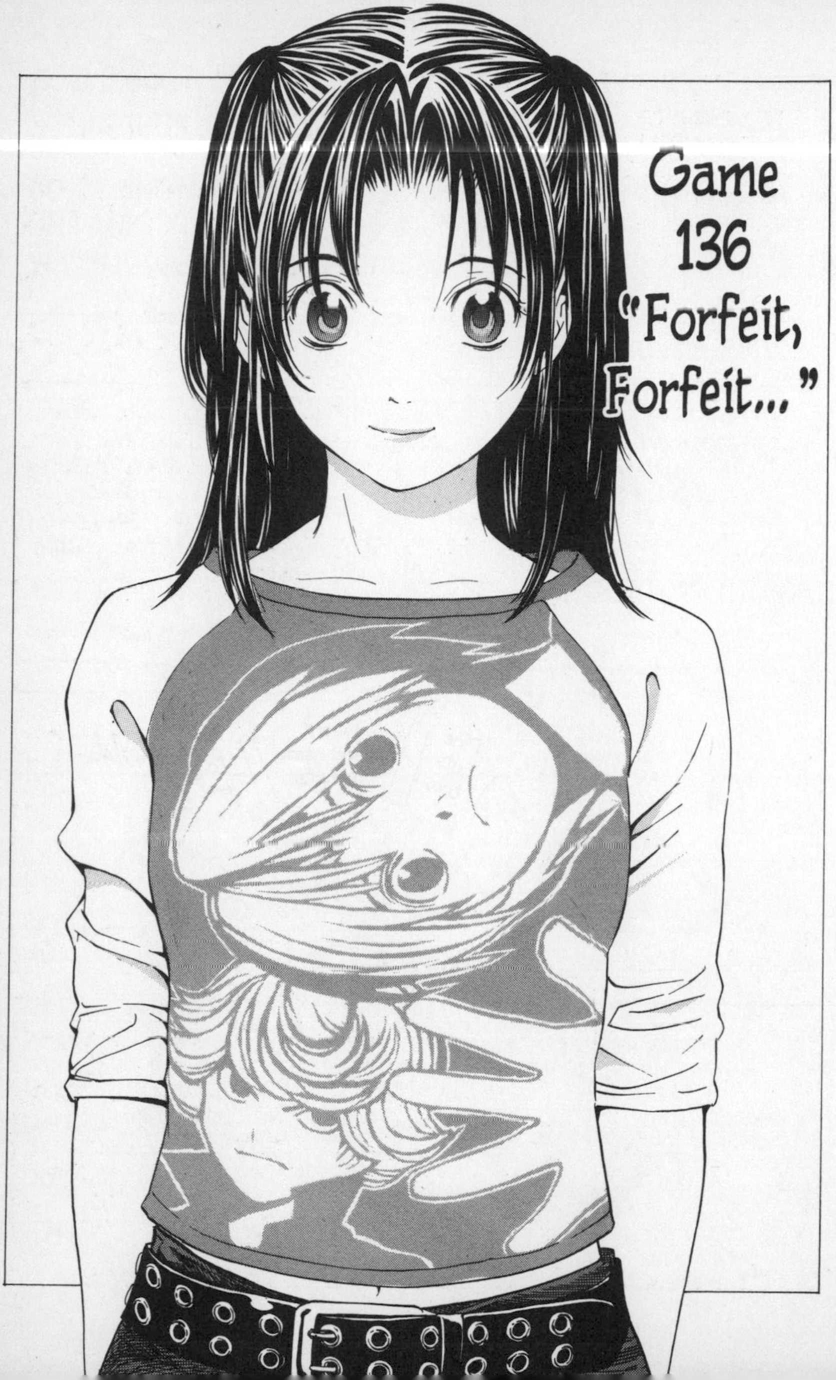
Game
136
"Forfeit,
Forfeit..."

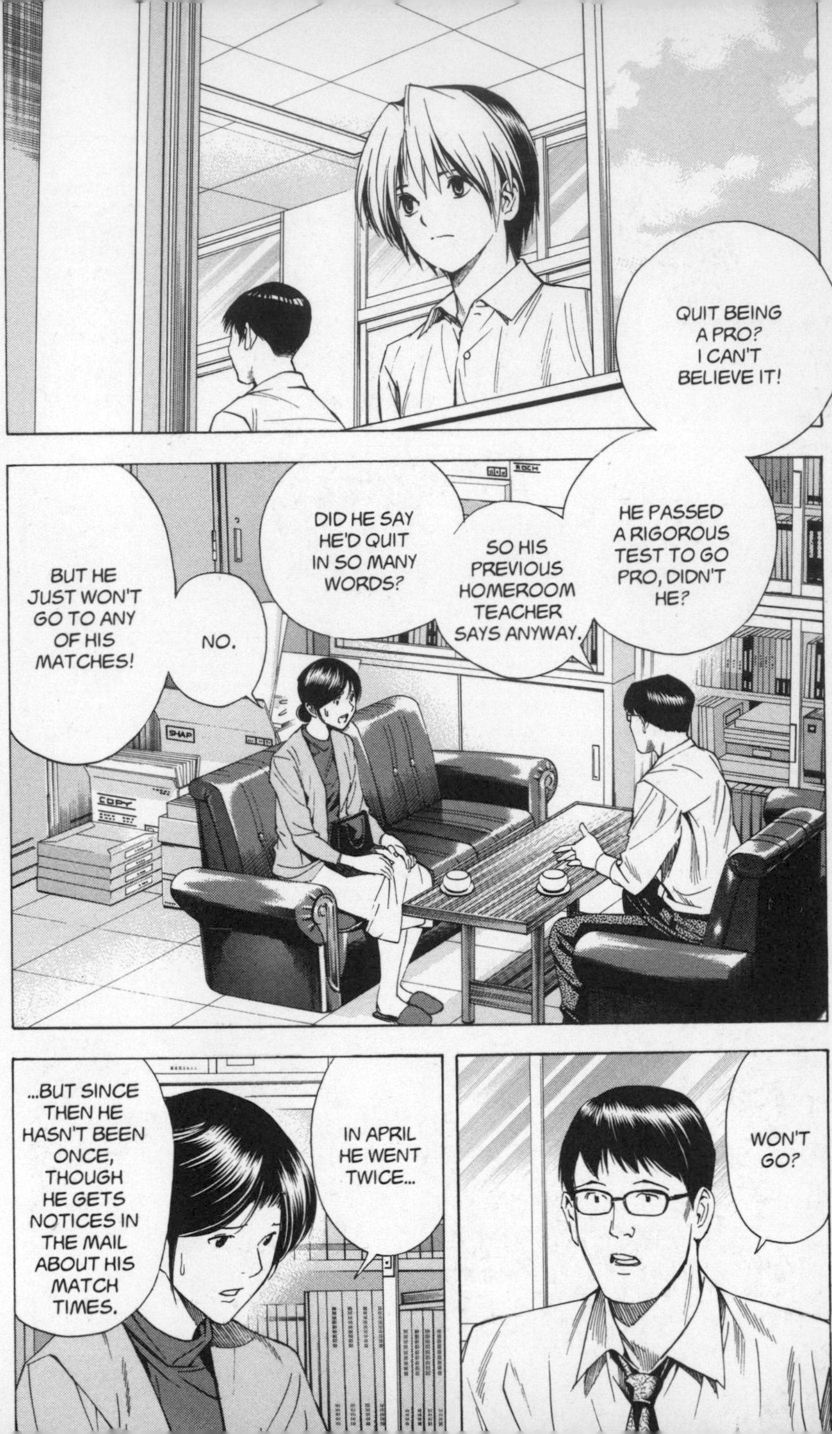
QUIT BEING A PRO? I CAN'T BELIEVE IT!
HE PASSED A RIGOROUS TEST TO GO PRO, DIDN'T HE?
SO HIS PREVIOUS HOMEROOM TEACHER SAYS ANYWAY.
DID HE SAY HE'D QUIT IN SO MANY WORDS?
NO.
BUT HE JUST WON'T GO TO ANY OF HIS MATCHES!
WON'T GO?
IN APRIL HE WENT TWICE...
...BUT SINCE THEN HE HASN'T BEEN ONCE, THOUGH HE GETS NOTICES IN THE MAIL ABOUT HIS MATCH TIMES.

READ THIS WAY

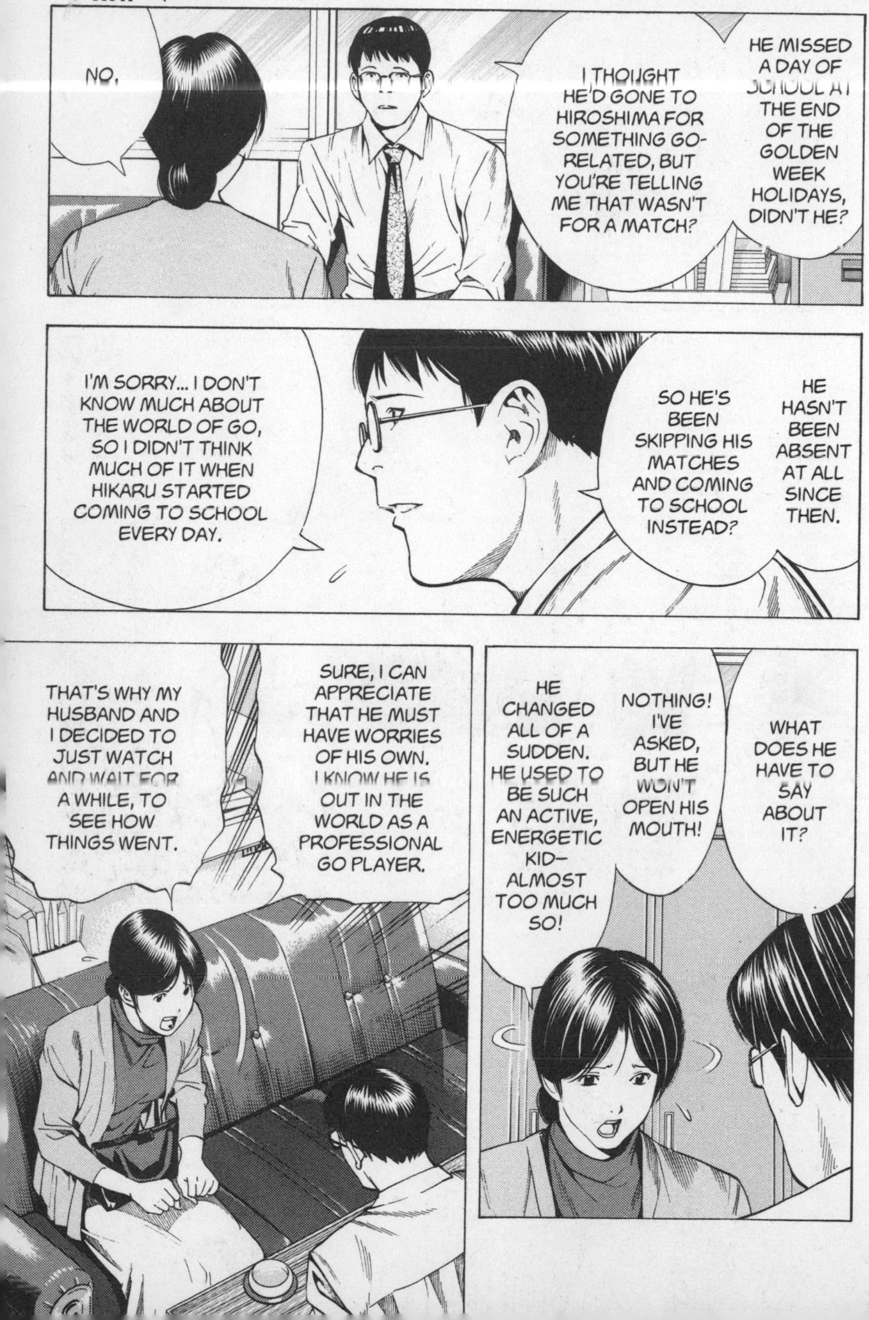
HE MISSED A DAY OF SCHOOL AT THE END OF THE GOLDEN WEEK HOLIDAYS, DIDN'T HE?
I THOUGHT HE'D GONE TO HIROSHIMA FOR SOMETHING GO-RELATED, BUT YOU'RE TELLING ME THAT WASN'T FOR A MATCH?
NO.
HE HASN'T BEEN ABSENT AT ALL SINCE THEN.
SO HE'S BEEN SKIPPING HIS MATCHES AND COMING TO SCHOOL INSTEAD?
I'M SORRY... I DON'T KNOW MUCH ABOUT THE WORLD OF GO, SO I DIDN'T THINK MUCH OF IT WHEN HIKARU STARTED COMING TO SCHOOL EVERY DAY.
WHAT DOES HE HAVE TO SAY ABOUT IT?
NOTHING! I'VE ASKED, BUT HE WON'T OPEN HIS MOUTH!
HE CHANGED ALL OF A SUDDEN. HE USED TO BE SUCH AN ACTIVE, ENERGETIC KID—ALMOST TOO MUCH SO!
SURE, I CAN APPRECIATE THAT HE MUST HAVE WORRIES OF HIS OWN. I KNOW HE IS OUT IN THE WORLD AS A PROFESSIONAL GO PLAYER.
THAT'S WHY MY HUSBAND AND I DECIDED TO JUST WATCH AND WAIT FOR A WHILE, TO SEE HOW THINGS WENT.

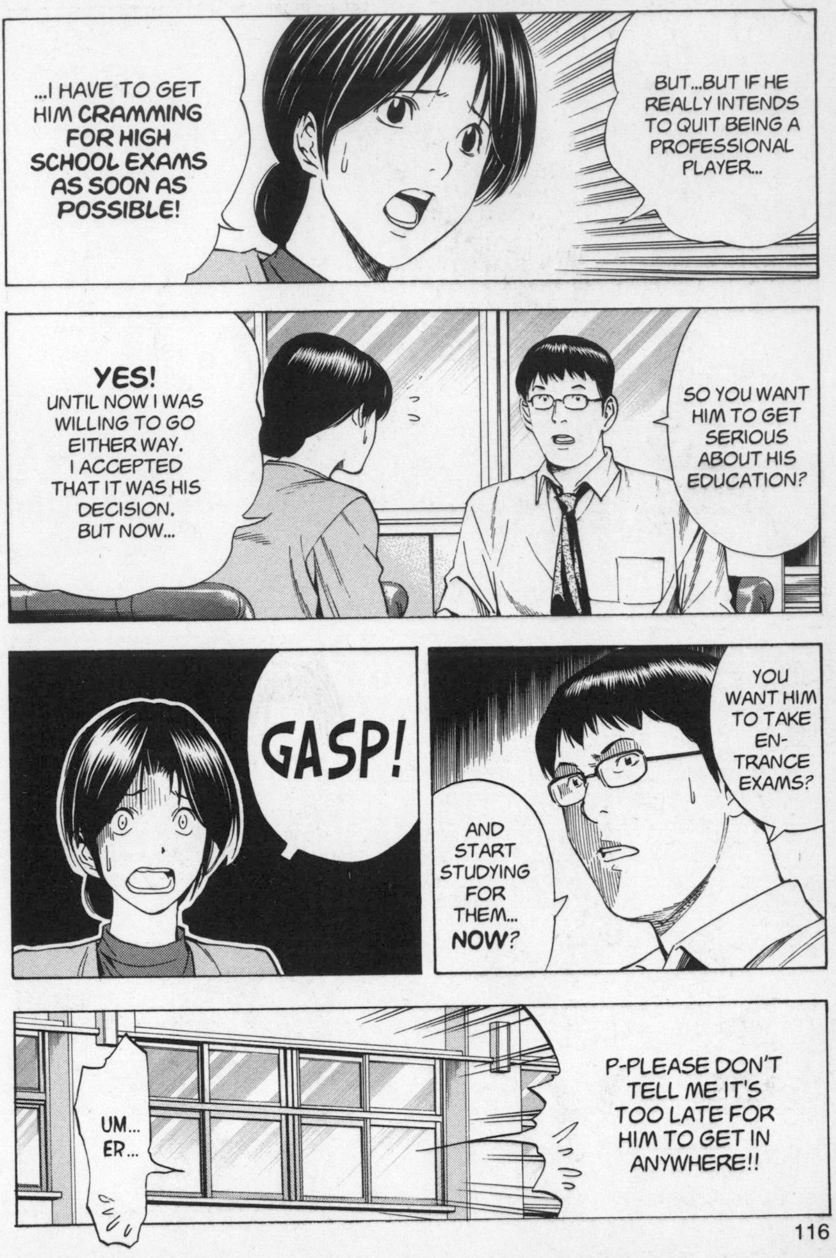
BUT...BUT IF HE REALLY INTENDS TO QUIT BEING A PROFESSIONAL PLAYER...
...I HAVE TO GET HIM CRAMMING FOR HIGH SCHOOL EXAMS AS SOON AS POSSIBLE!
SO YOU WANT HIM TO GET SERIOUS ABOUT HIS EDUCATION?
YES! UNTIL NOW I WAS WILLING TO GO EITHER WAY. I ACCEPTED THAT IT WAS HIS DECISION. BUT NOW...
YOU WANT HIM TO TAKE EN-TRANCE EXAMS?
AND START STUDYING FOR THEM... NOW?
GASP!
P-PLEASE DON'T TELL ME IT'S TOO LATE FOR HIM TO GET IN ANYWHERE!!
UM... ER...

READ THIS WAY

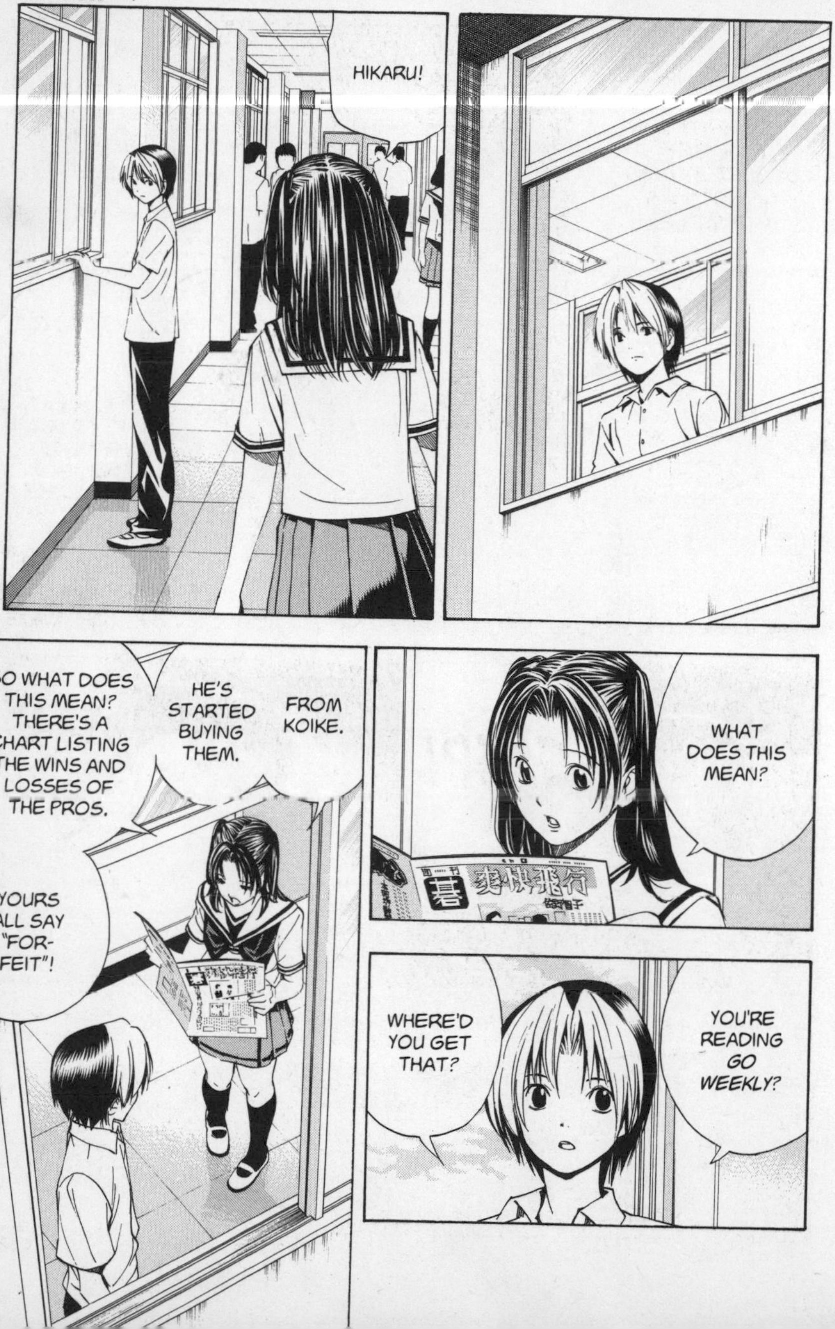
HIKARU!
WHAT DOES THIS MEAN?
YOU'RE READING GO WEEKLY?
WHERE'D YOU GET THAT?
FROM KOIKE.
HE'S STARTED BUYING THEM.
SO WHAT DOES THIS MEAN? THERE'S A CHART LISTING THE WINS AND LOSSES OF THE PROS.
YOURS ALL SAY "FOR-FEIT"!

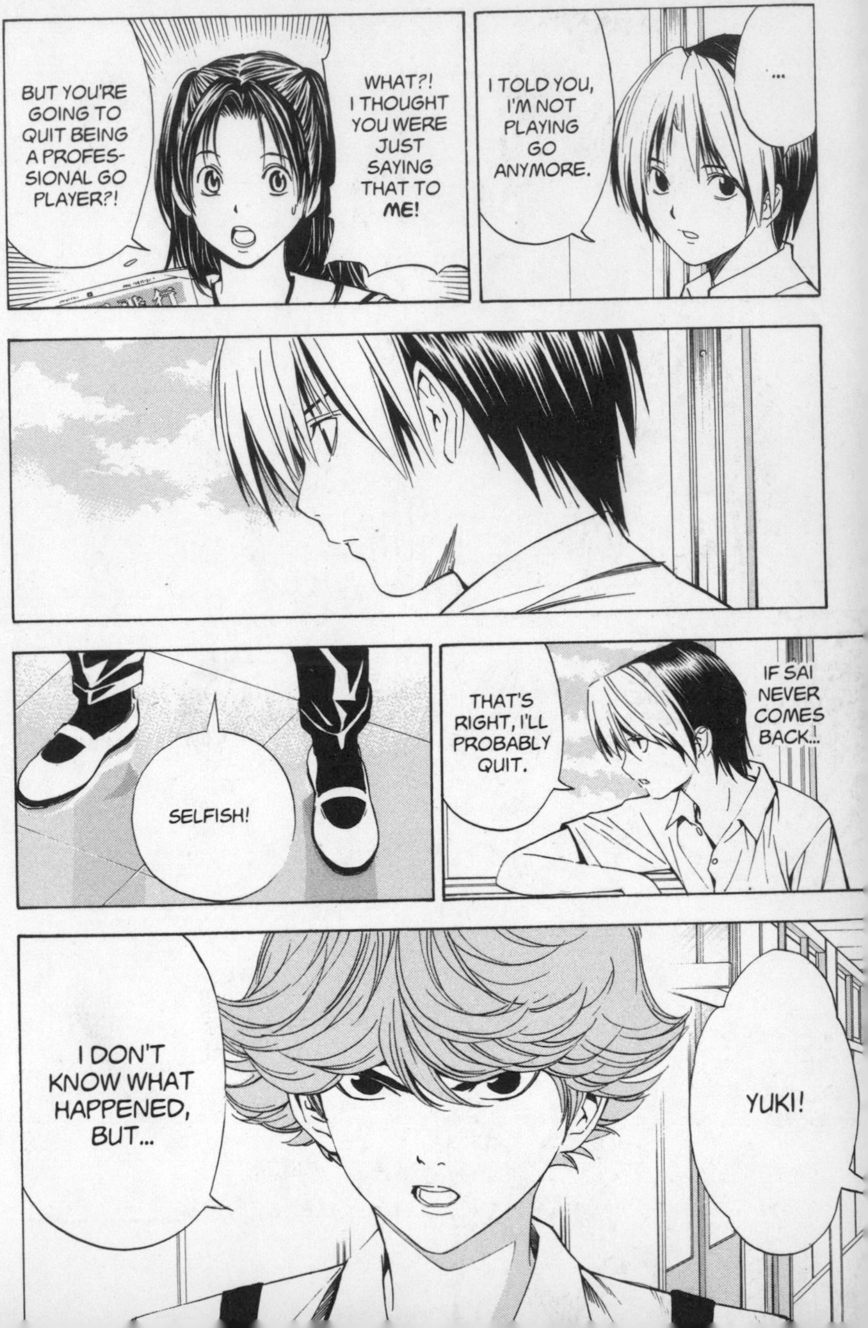
...
I TOLD YOU, I'M NOT PLAYING GO ANYMORE.
WHAT?! I THOUGHT YOU WERE JUST SAYING THAT TO **ME**!
BUT YOU'RE GOING TO QUIT BEING A PROFESSIONAL GO PLAYER?!
IF SAI NEVER COMES BACK...
THAT'S RIGHT, I'LL PROBABLY QUIT.
SELFISH!
YUKI!
I DON'T KNOW WHAT HAPPENED, BUT...

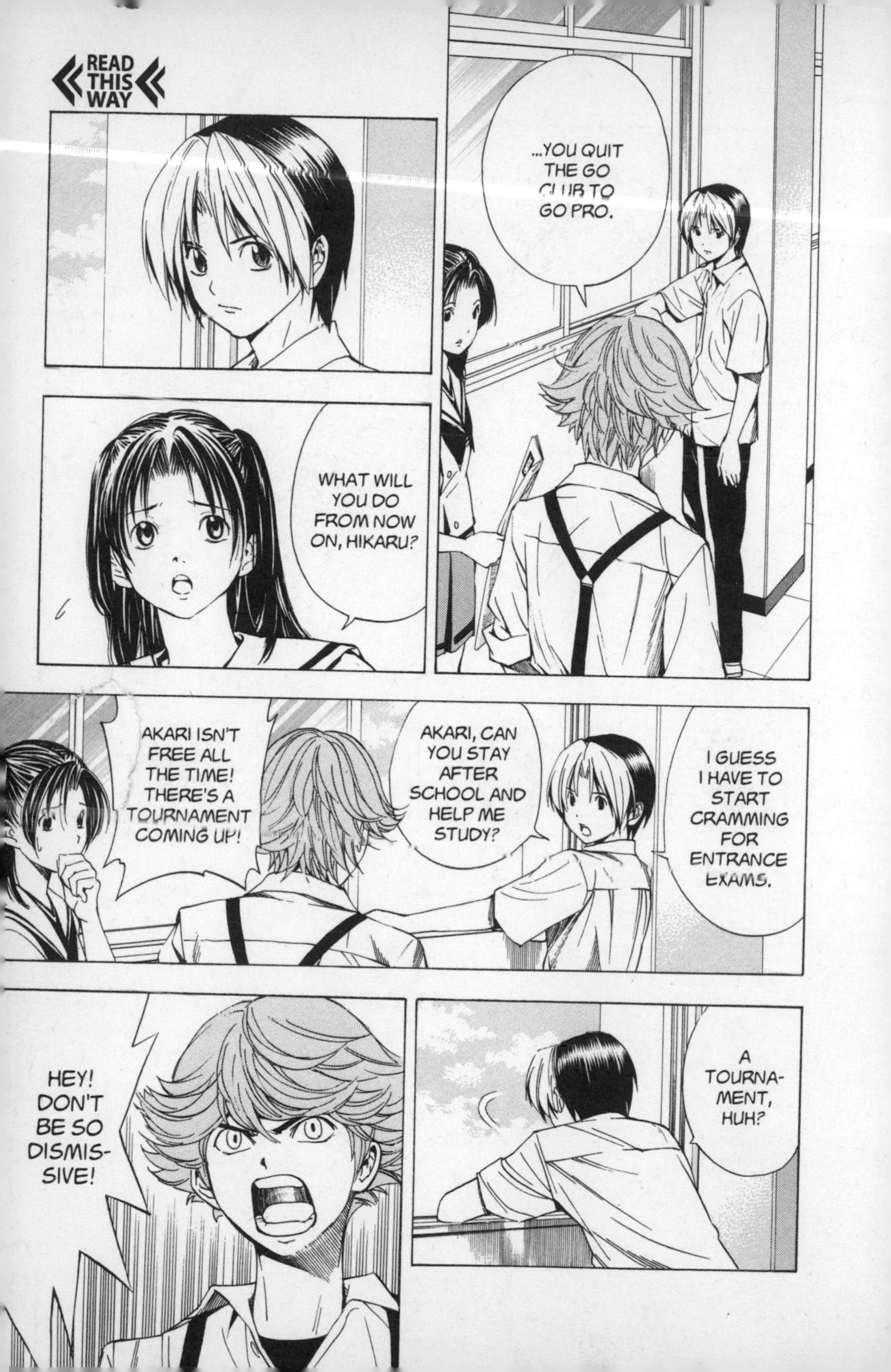
READ THIS WAY
...YOU QUIT THE GO CLUB TO GO PRO.
WHAT WILL YOU DO FROM NOW ON, HIKARU?
I GUESS I HAVE TO START CRAMMING FOR ENTRANCE EXAMS.
AKARI, CAN YOU STAY AFTER SCHOOL AND HELP ME STUDY?
AKARI ISN'T FREE ALL THE TIME! THERE'S A TOURNAMENT COMING UP!
A TOURNAMENT, HUH?
HEY! DON'T BE SO DISMISSIVE!

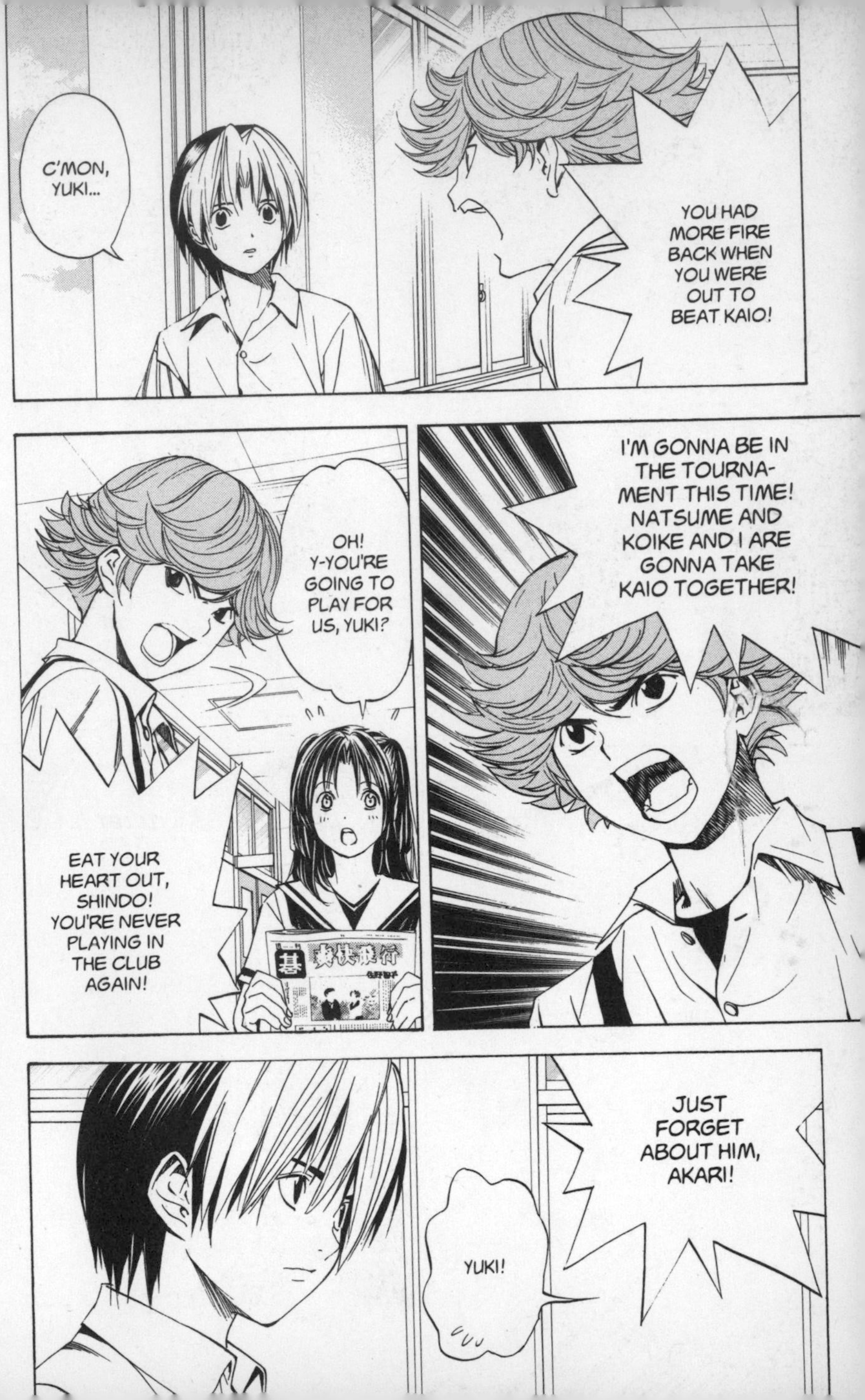
YOU HAD MORE FIRE BACK WHEN YOU WERE OUT TO BEAT KAIO!
C'MON, YUKI...
I'M GONNA BE IN THE TOURNAMENT THIS TIME! NATSUME AND KOIKE AND I ARE GONNA TAKE KAIO TOGETHER!
OH! Y-YOU'RE GOING TO PLAY FOR US, YUKI?
EAT YOUR HEART OUT, SHINDO! YOU'RE NEVER PLAYING IN THE CLUB AGAIN!
JUST FORGET ABOUT HIM, AKARI!
YUKI!

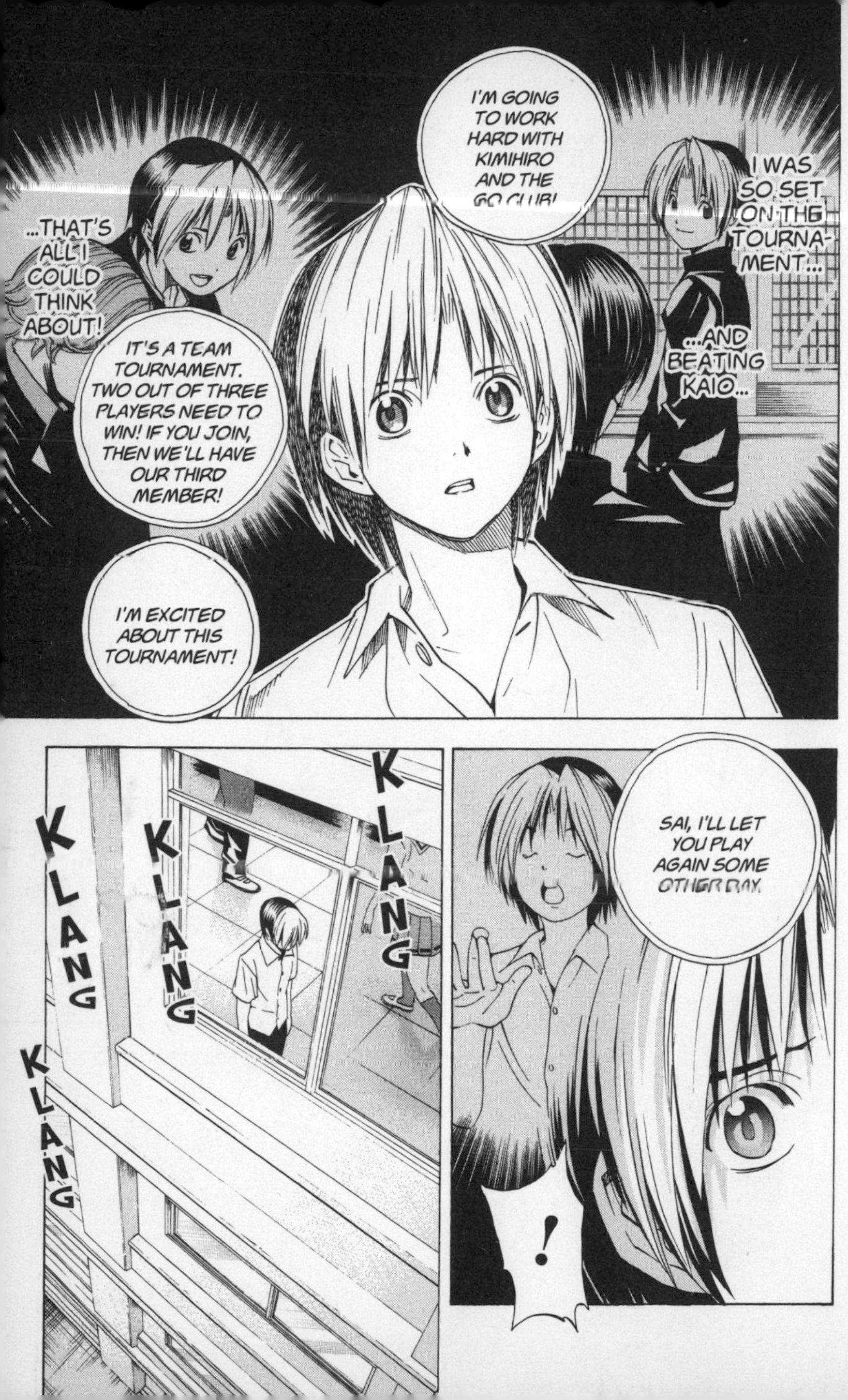
I WAS SO SET ON THE TOURNAMENT...
I'M GOING TO WORK HARD WITH KIMIHIRO AND THE GO CLUB!
...AND BEATING KAIO...
...THAT'S ALL I COULD THINK ABOUT!
IT'S A TEAM TOURNAMENT. TWO OUT OF THREE PLAYERS NEED TO WIN! IF YOU JOIN, THEN WE'LL HAVE OUR THIRD MEMBER!
I'M EXCITED ABOUT THIS TOURNAMENT!
SAI, I'LL LET YOU PLAY AGAIN SOME OTHER DAY.
!
KLANG
KLANG
KLANG
KLANG

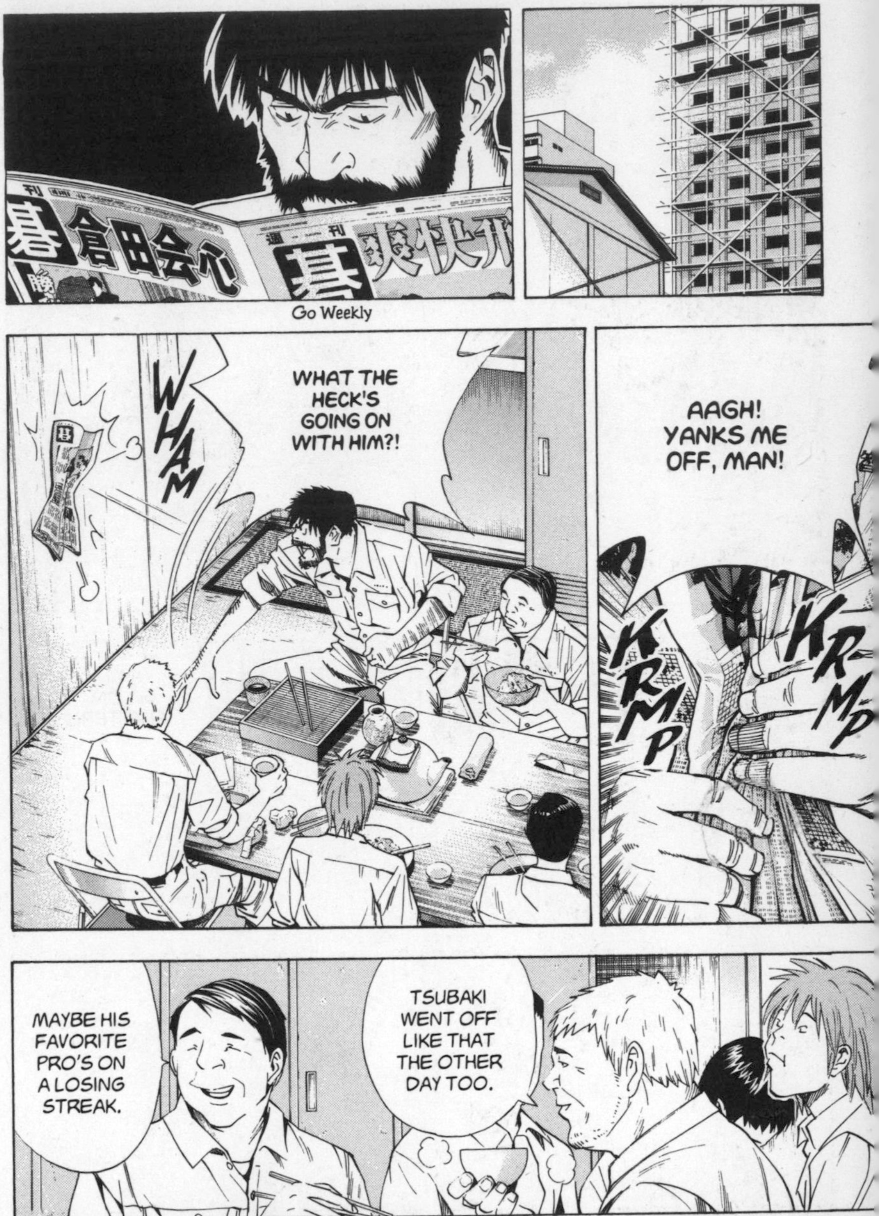
碁
倉田会心
週刊
碁
AAGH! YANKS ME OFF, MAN!
KRMP
KR-M-P
WHAT THE HECK'S GOING ON WITH HIM?!
WHAM
TSUBAKI WENT OFF LIKE THAT THE OTHER DAY TOO.
MAYBE HIS FAVORITE PRO'S ON A LOSING STREAK.
Go Weekly

READ THIS WAY

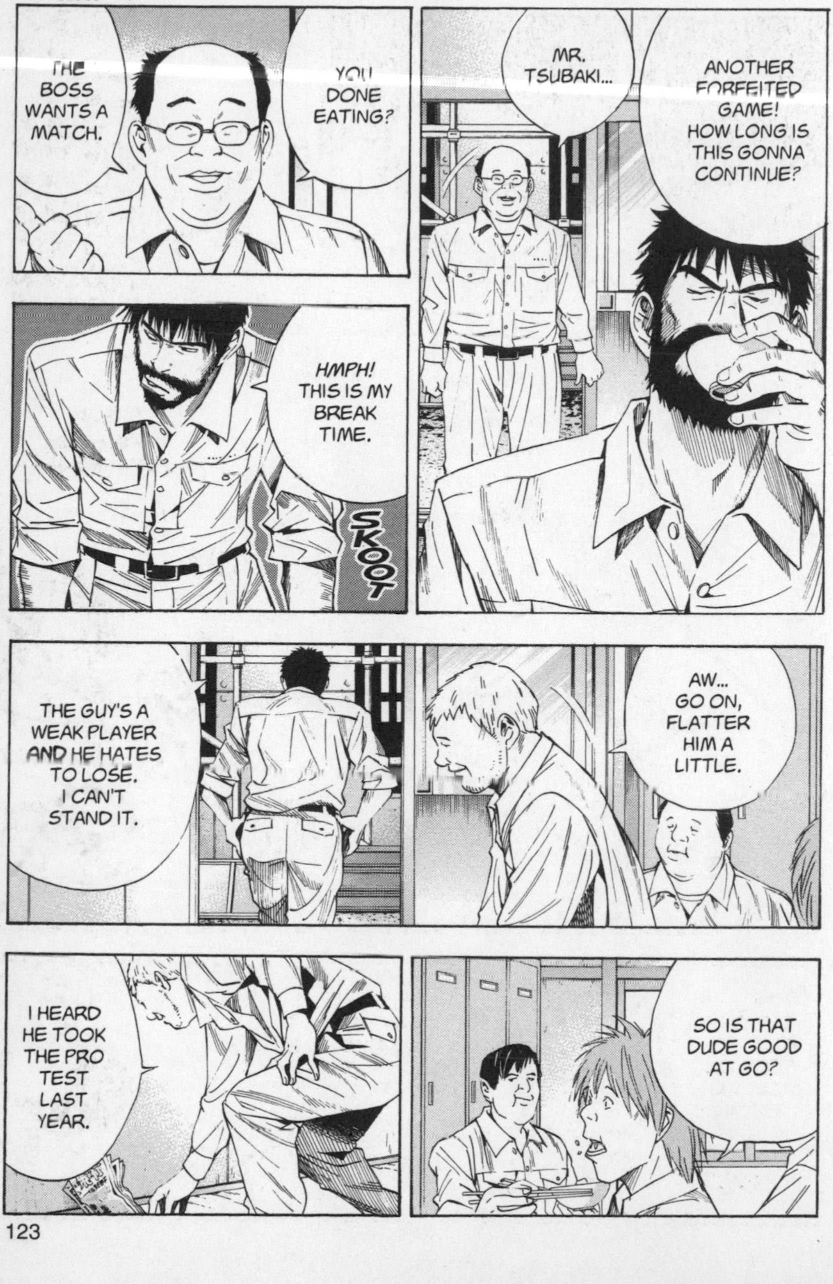
ANOTHER FORFEITED GAME! HOW LONG IS THIS GONNA CONTINUE?
MR. TSUBAKI...
YOU DONE EATING?
THE BOSS WANTS A MATCH.
HMPH! THIS IS MY BREAK TIME.
SKOOT
AW... GO ON, FLATTER HIM A LITTLE.
THE GUY'S A WEAK PLAYER AND HE HATES TO LOSE. I CAN'T STAND IT.
SO IS THAT DUDE GOOD AT GO?
I HEARD HE TOOK THE PRO TEST LAST YEAR.

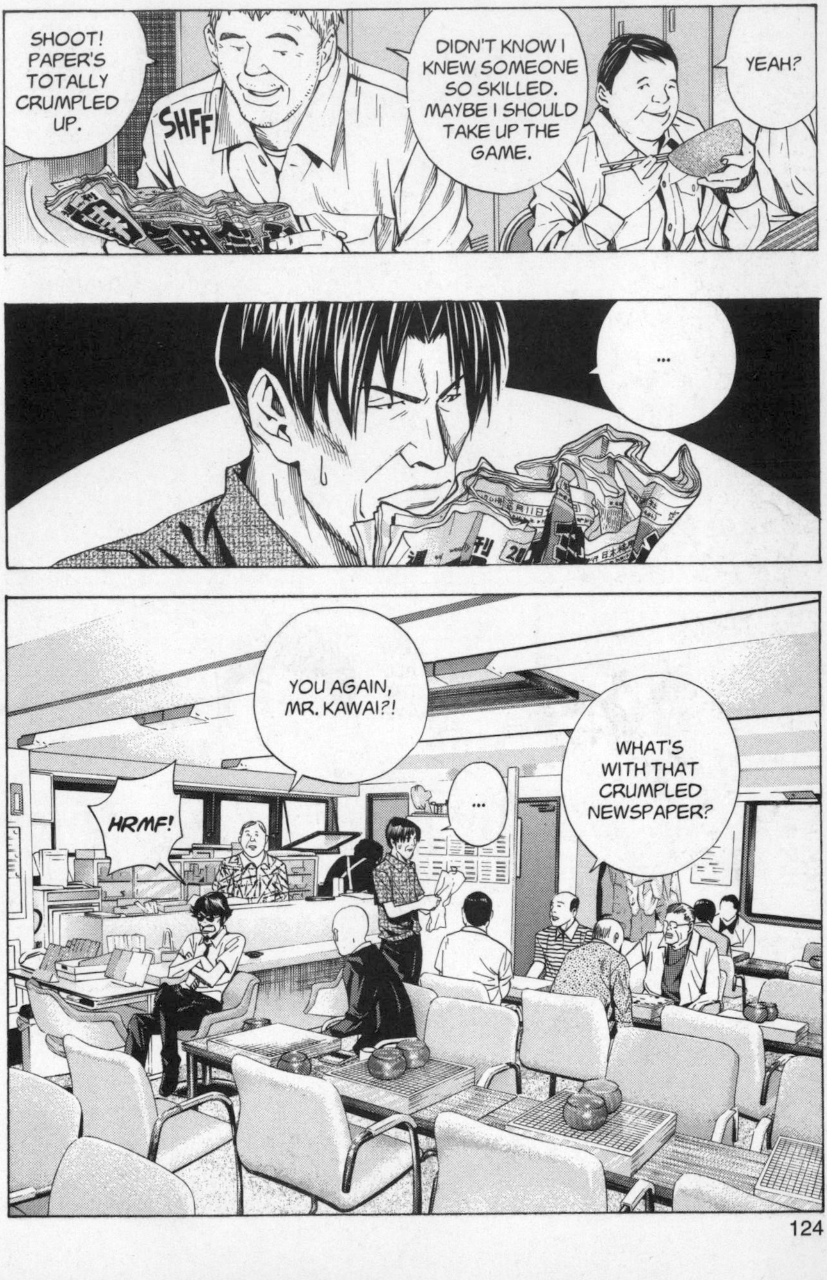
YEAH?
DIDN'T KNOW I KNEW SOMEONE SO SKILLED. MAYBE I SHOULD TAKE UP THE GAME.
SHFF
SHOOT! PAPER'S TOTALLY CRUMPLED UP.
...
WHAT'S WITH THAT CRUMPLED NEWSPAPER?
YOU AGAIN, MR. KAWAI?!
...
HRMF!

READ THIS WAY

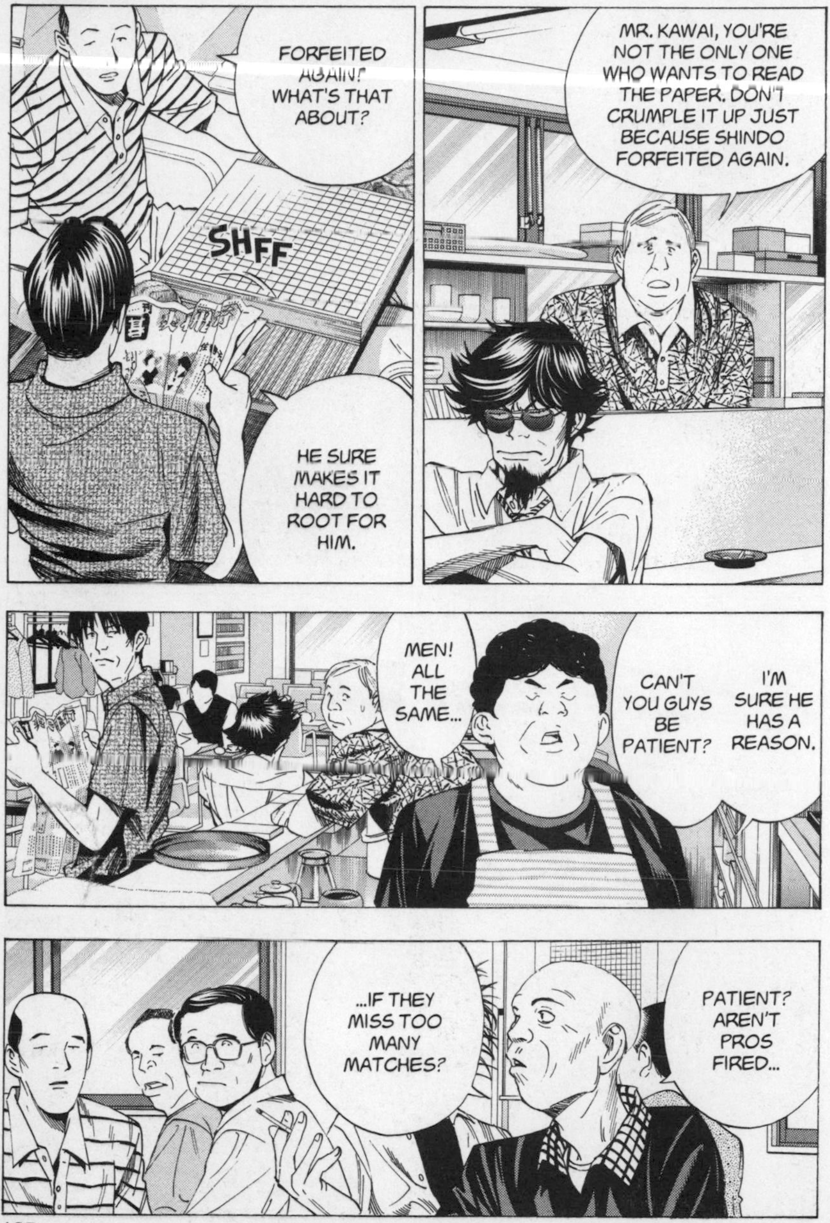
MR. KAWAI, YOU'RE NOT THE ONLY ONE WHO WANTS TO READ THE PAPER. DON'T CRUMPLE IT UP JUST BECAUSE SHINDO FORFEITED AGAIN.
FORFEITED AGAIN! WHAT'S THAT ABOUT?
SHFF
HE SURE MAKES IT HARD TO ROOT FOR HIM.
I'M SURE HE HAS A REASON.
CAN'T YOU GUYS BE PATIENT?
MEN! ALL THE SAME...
PATIENT? AREN'T PROS FIRED...
...IF THEY MISS TOO MANY MATCHES?

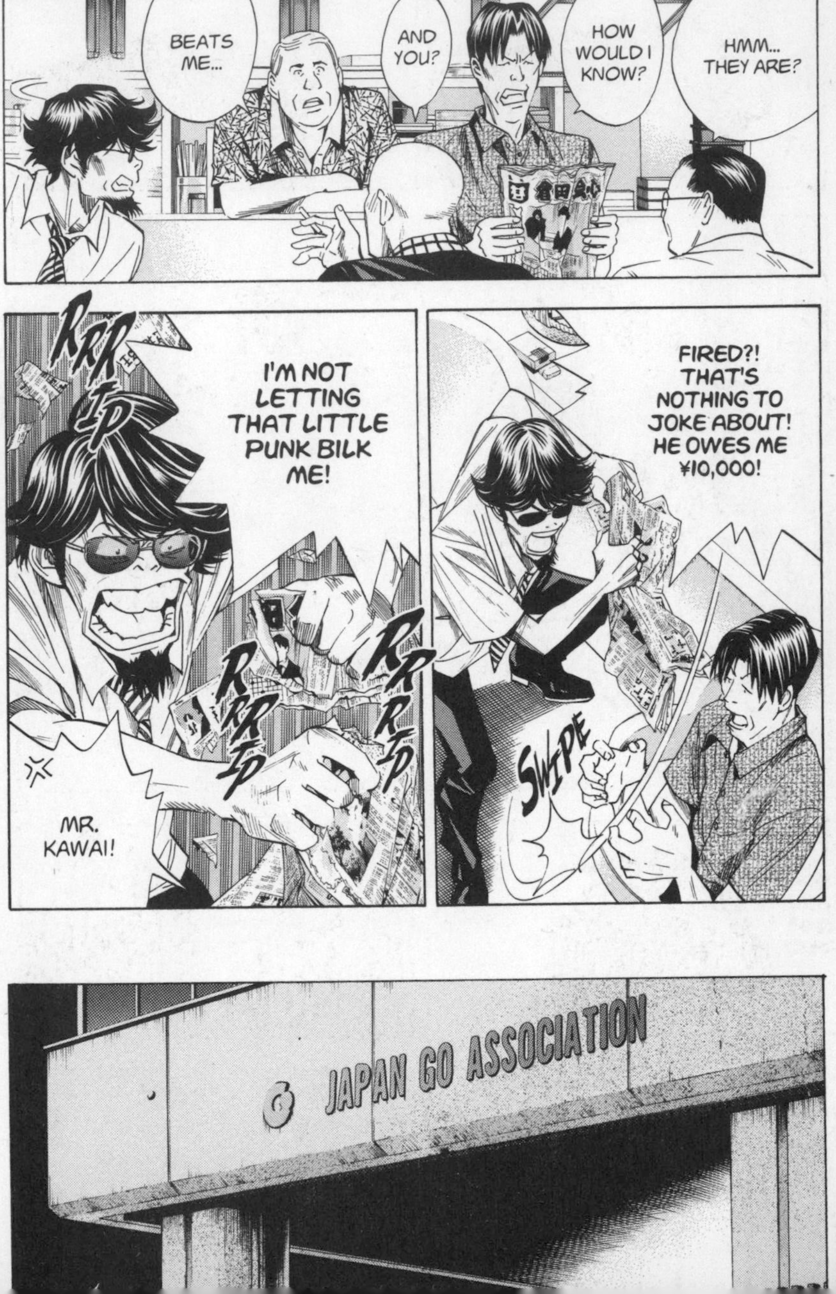
HMM... THEY ARE?
HOW WOULD I KNOW?
AND YOU?
BEATS ME...
FIRED?! THAT'S NOTHING TO JOKE ABOUT! HE OWES ME ¥10,000!
SWIPE
I'M NOT LETTING THAT LITTLE PUNK BILK ME!
RRRIP
RRRIP
RRRIP
MR. KAWAI!
JAPAN GO ASSOCIATION

READ THIS WAY

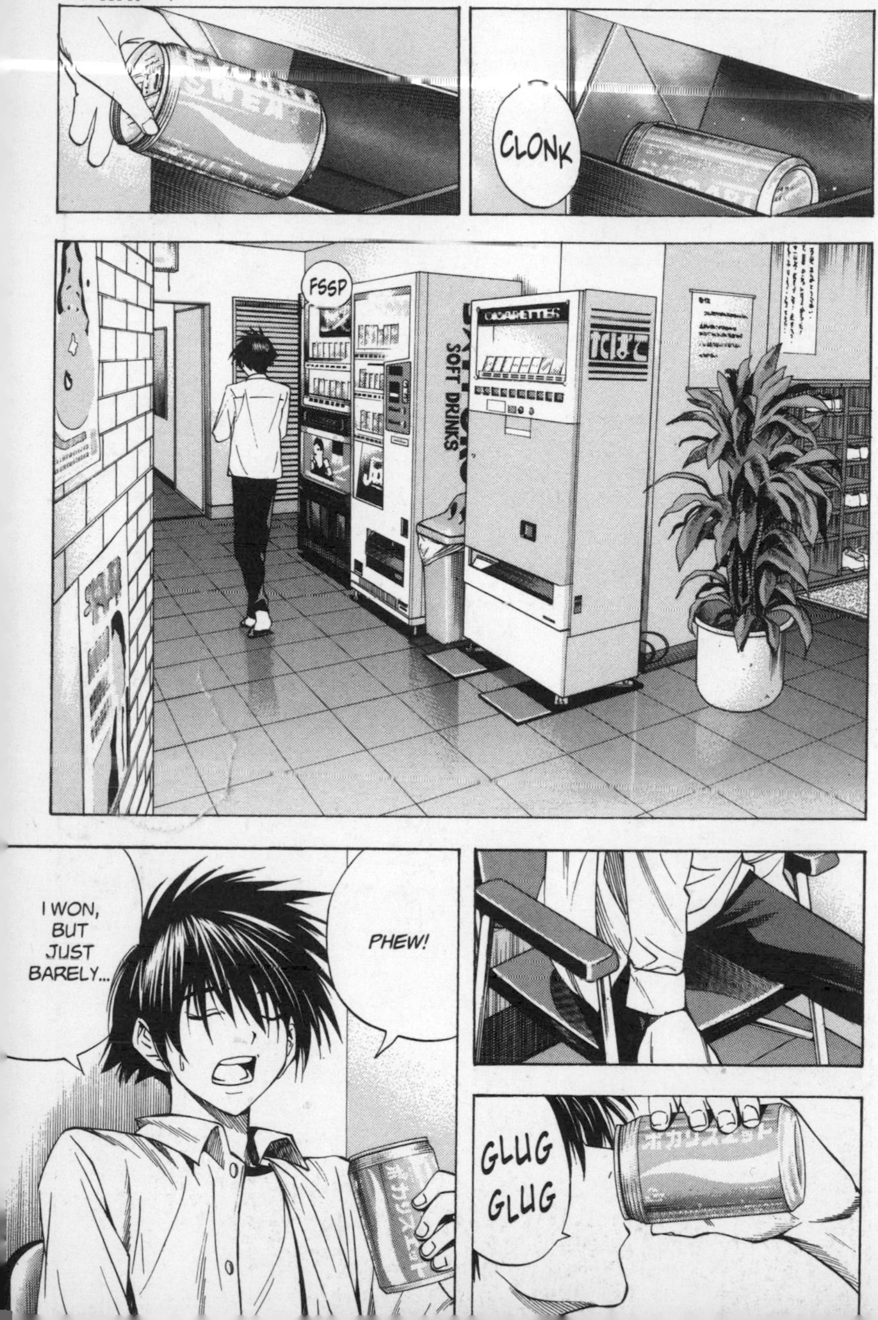
CLONK
FSSP
CIGARETTES
SOFT DRINKS
GLUG GLUG
PHEW!
I WON, BUT JUST BARELY...

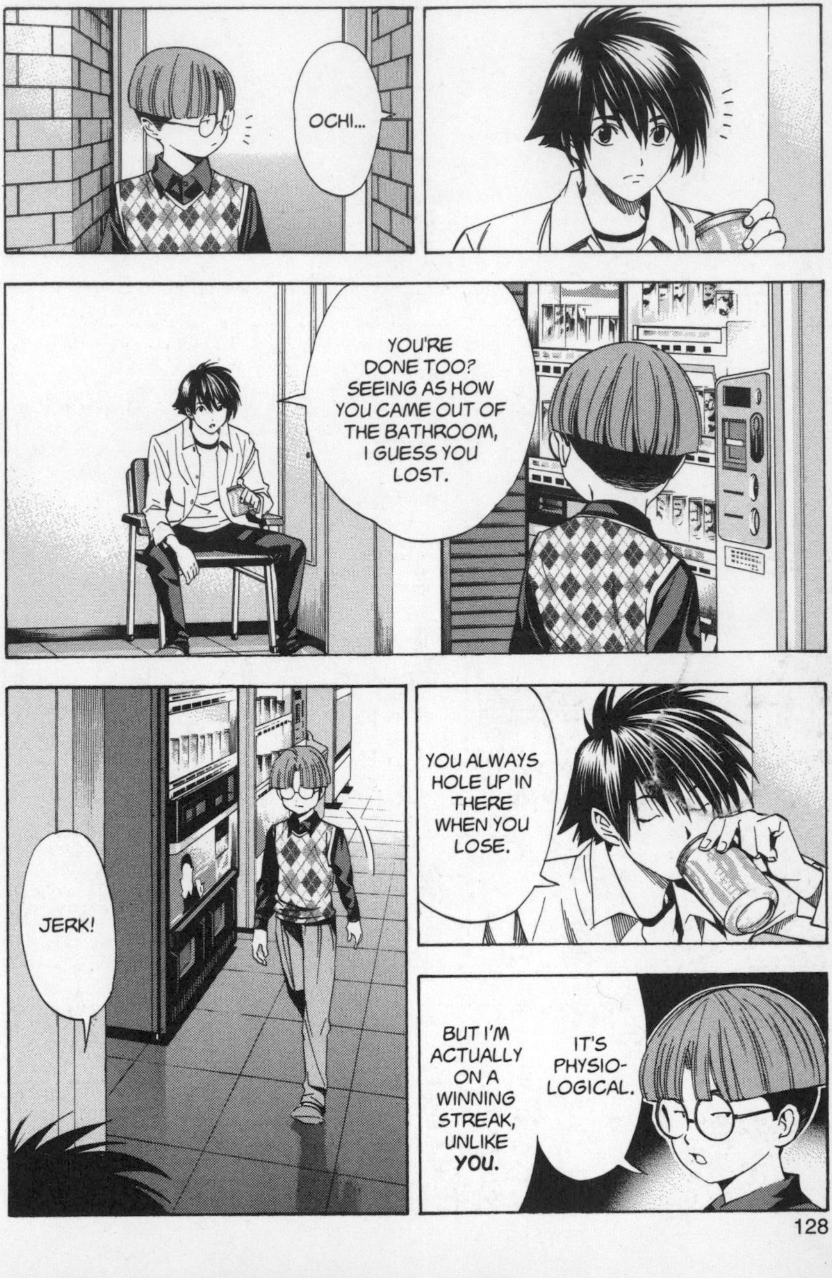
OCHI...
YOU'RE DONE TOO? SEEING AS HOW YOU CAME OUT OF THE BATHROOM, I GUESS YOU LOST.
YOU ALWAYS HOLE UP IN THERE WHEN YOU LOSE.
IT'S PHYSIO-LOGICAL.
BUT I'M ACTUALLY ON A WINNING STREAK, UNLIKE **YOU**.
JERK!

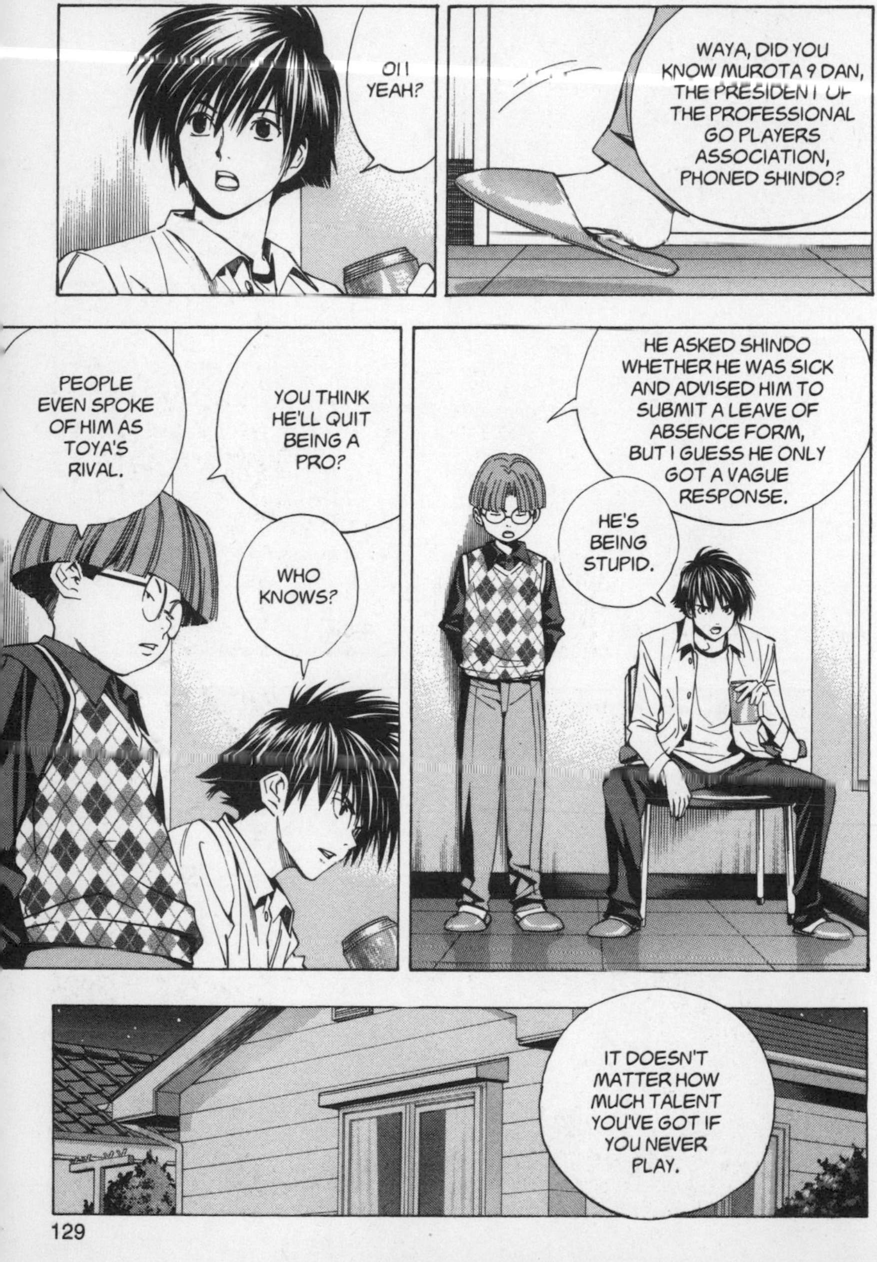
WAYA, DID YOU KNOW MUROTA 9 DAN, THE PRESIDENT OF THE PROFESSIONAL GO PLAYERS ASSOCIATION, PHONED SHINDO?
OH! YEAH?
HE ASKED SHINDO WHETHER HE WAS SICK AND ADVISED HIM TO SUBMIT A LEAVE OF ABSENCE FORM, BUT I GUESS HE ONLY GOT A VAGUE RESPONSE.
HE'S BEING STUPID.
YOU THINK HE'LL QUIT BEING A PRO?
WHO KNOWS?
PEOPLE EVEN SPOKE OF HIM AS TOYA'S RIVAL.
IT DOESN'T MATTER HOW MUCH TALENT YOU'VE GOT IF YOU NEVER PLAY.

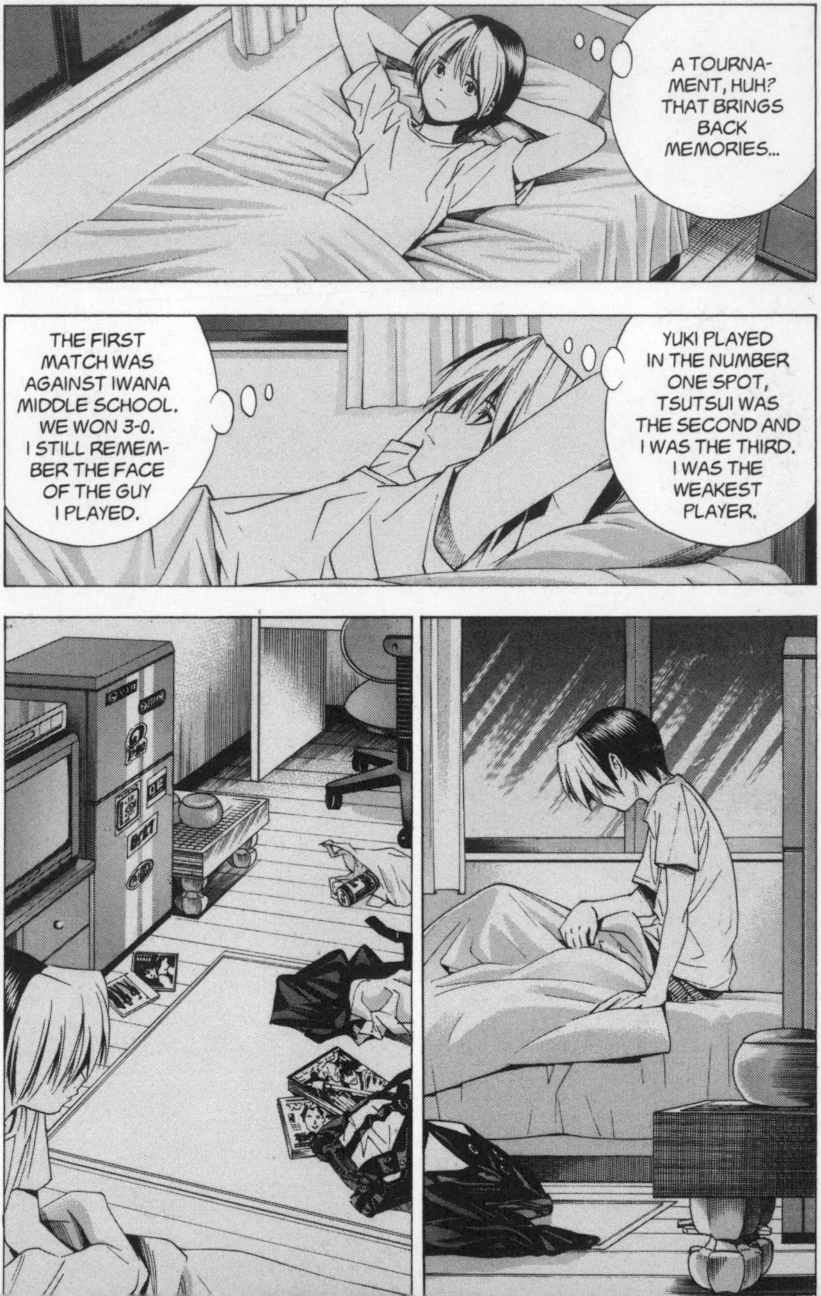
A TOURNA-MENT, HUH? THAT BRINGS BACK MEMORIES...
YUKI PLAYED IN THE NUMBER ONE SPOT, TSUTSUI WAS THE SECOND AND I WAS THE THIRD. I WAS THE WEAKEST PLAYER.
THE FIRST MATCH WAS AGAINST IWANA MIDDLE SCHOOL. WE WON 3-0. I STILL REMEMBER THE FACE OF THE GUY I PLAYED.

READ THIS WAY

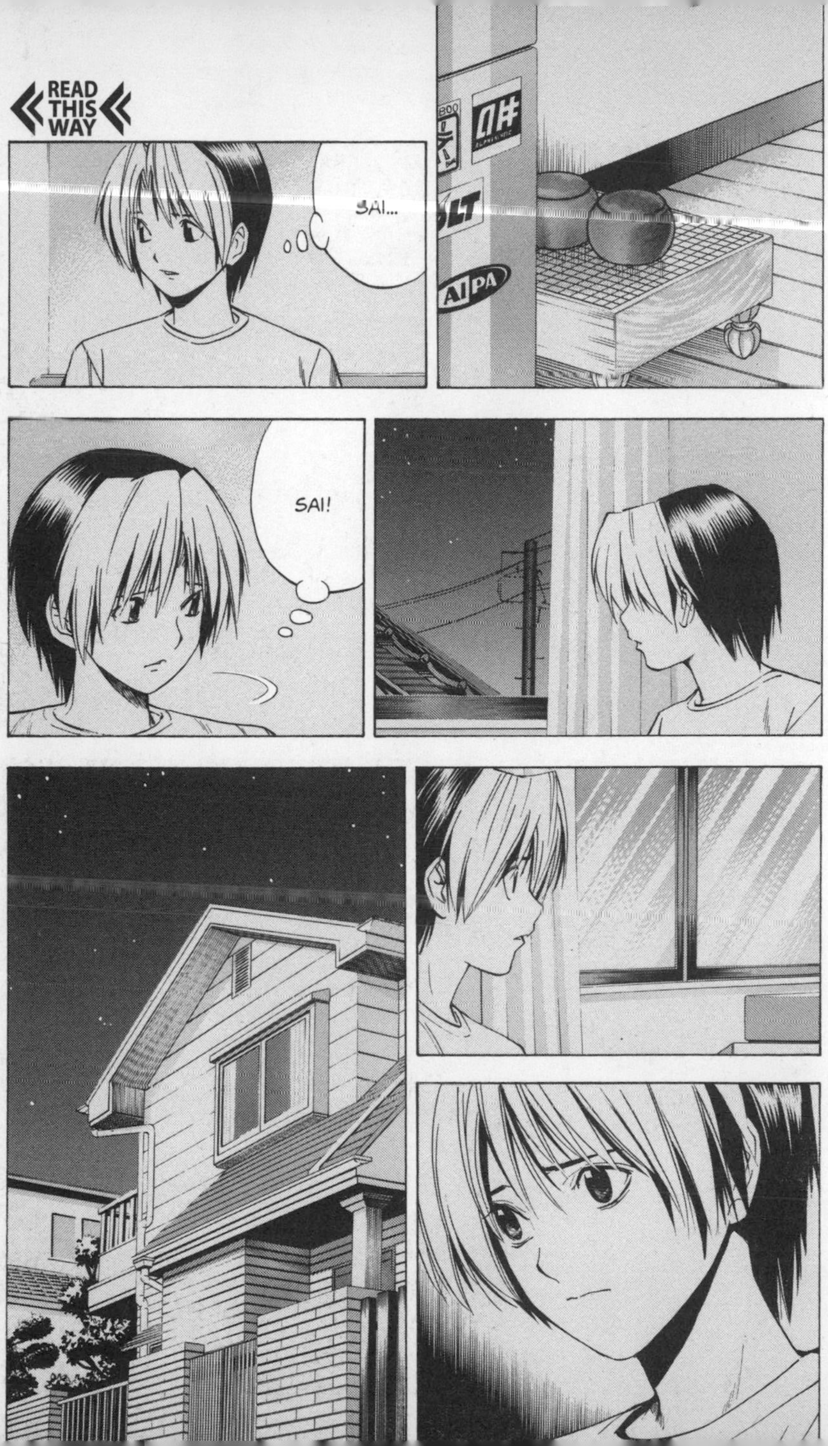
SAI...
SAI!

A WORD ABOUT HIKARU NO GO

THE CHINESE GO ASSOCIATION

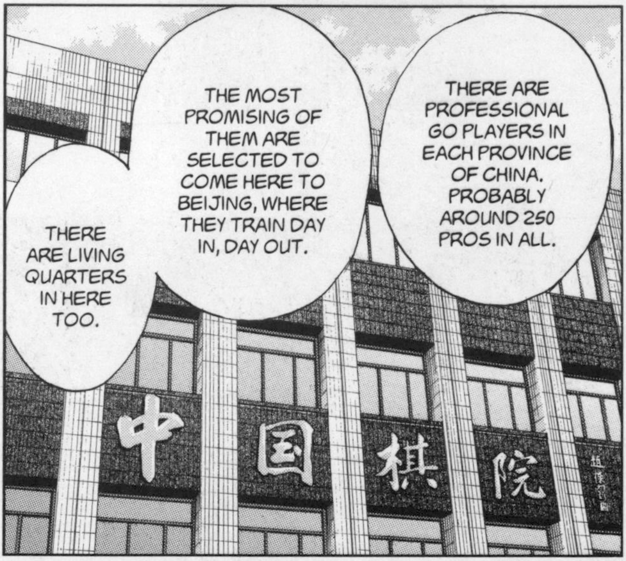
THERE ARE PROFESSIONAL GO PLAYERS IN EACH PROVINCE OF CHINA. PROBABLY AROUND 250 PROS IN ALL.
THE MOST PROMISING OF THEM ARE SELECTED TO COME HERE TO BEIJING, WHERE THEY TRAIN DAY IN, DAY OUT.
THERE ARE LIVING QUARTERS IN HERE TOO.
中国棋院

A NUMBER OF JAPANESE PROS HAVE COME HERE TO TRAIN. THE LENGTHS OF THEIR STAYS HAVE VARIED, BUT ONE PERSON STAYED FOR A WHOLE YEAR.

ARE YOU ASKING ME WHETHER ANYONE SECRETLY STAYED OVER AT THE ASSOCIATION LIKE ISUMI?

SHHH... NOT TELLING!

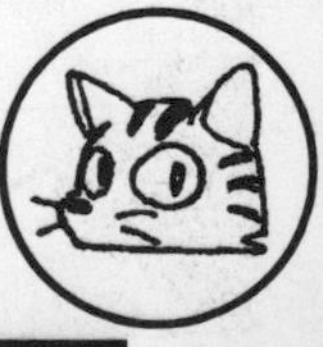

Game 137 "The Last Tournament"

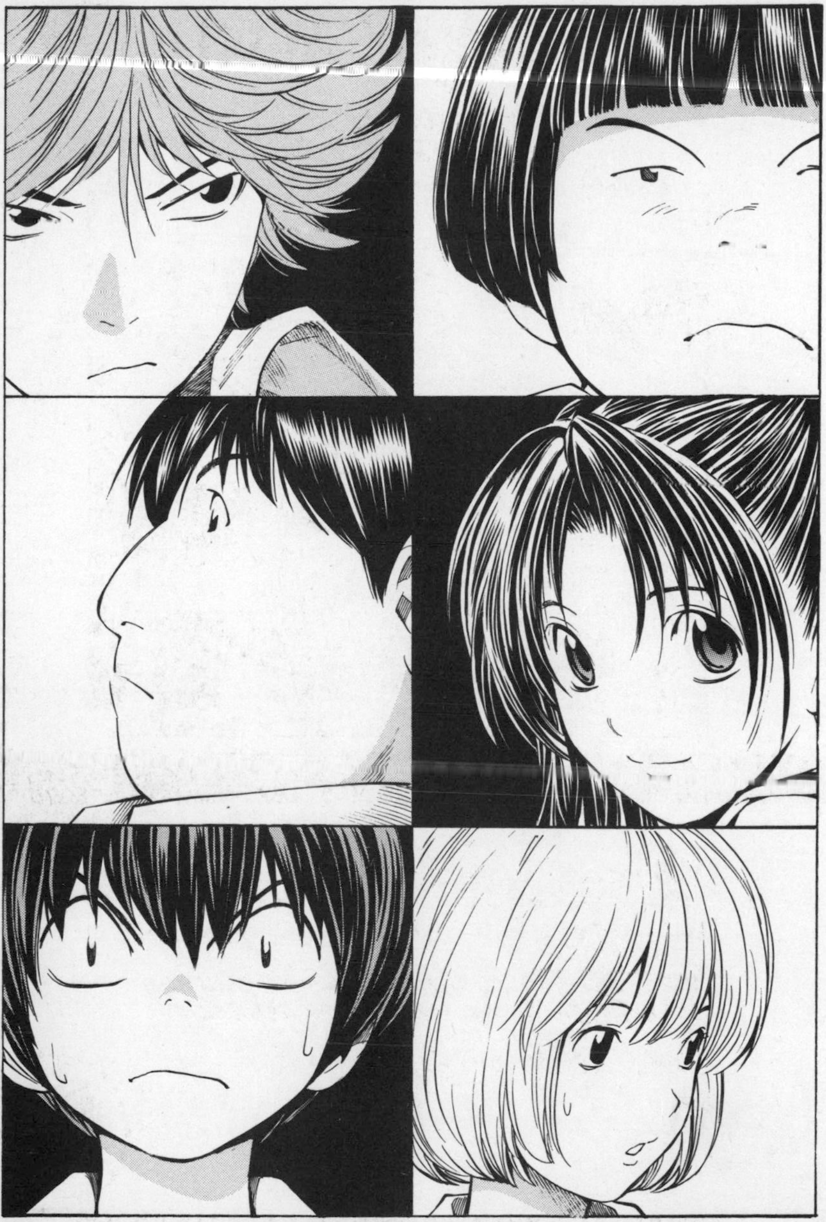

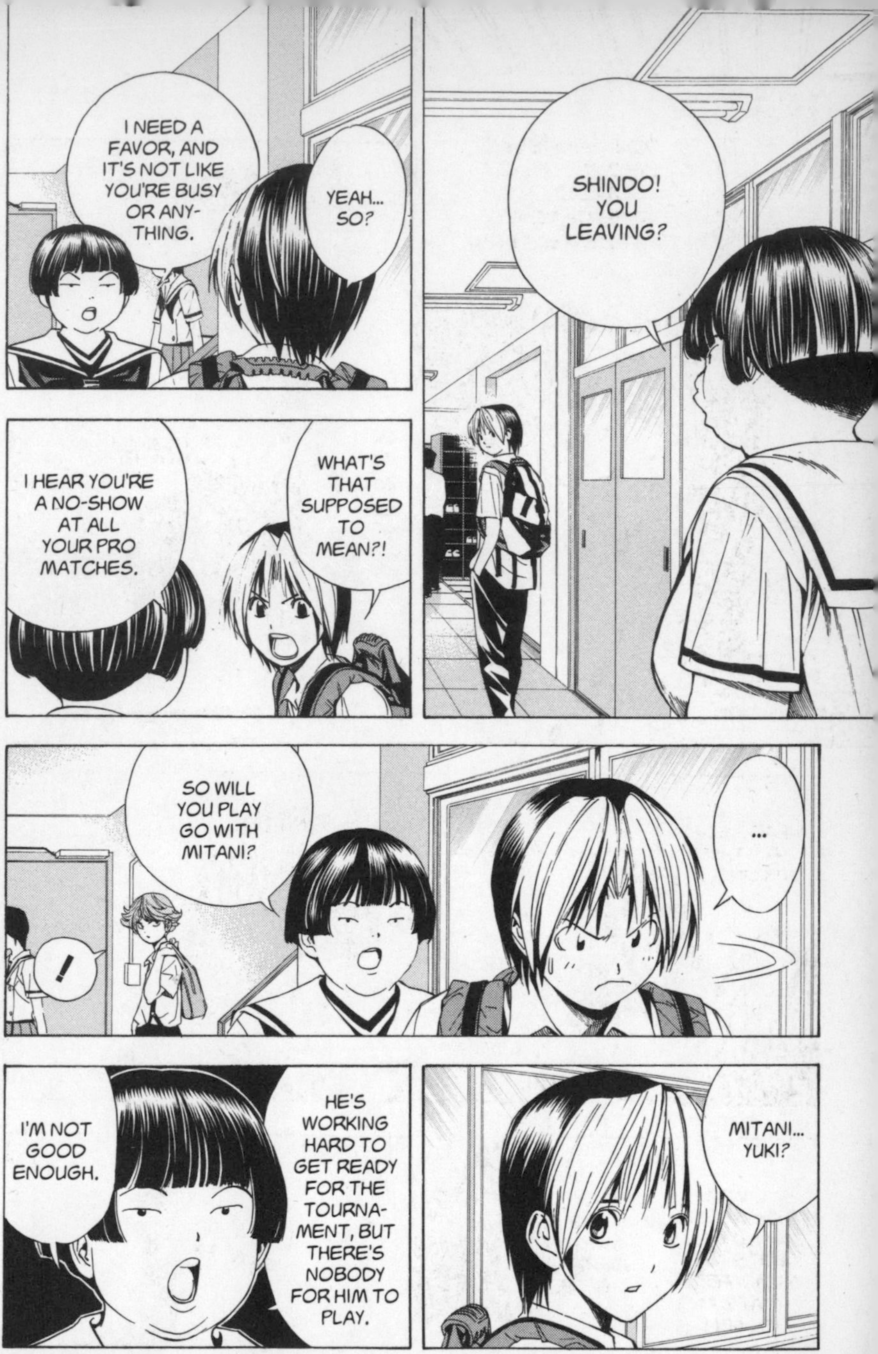
SHINDO! YOU LEAVING?
YEAH... SO?
I NEED A FAVOR, AND IT'S NOT LIKE YOU'RE BUSY OR ANY-THING.
WHAT'S THAT SUPPOSED TO MEAN?!
I HEAR YOU'RE A NO-SHOW AT ALL YOUR PRO MATCHES.
...
SO WILL YOU PLAY GO WITH MITANI?
!
MITANI... YUKI?
HE'S WORKING HARD TO GET READY FOR THE TOURNA-MENT, BUT THERE'S NOBODY FOR HIM TO PLAY.
I'M NOT GOOD ENOUGH.

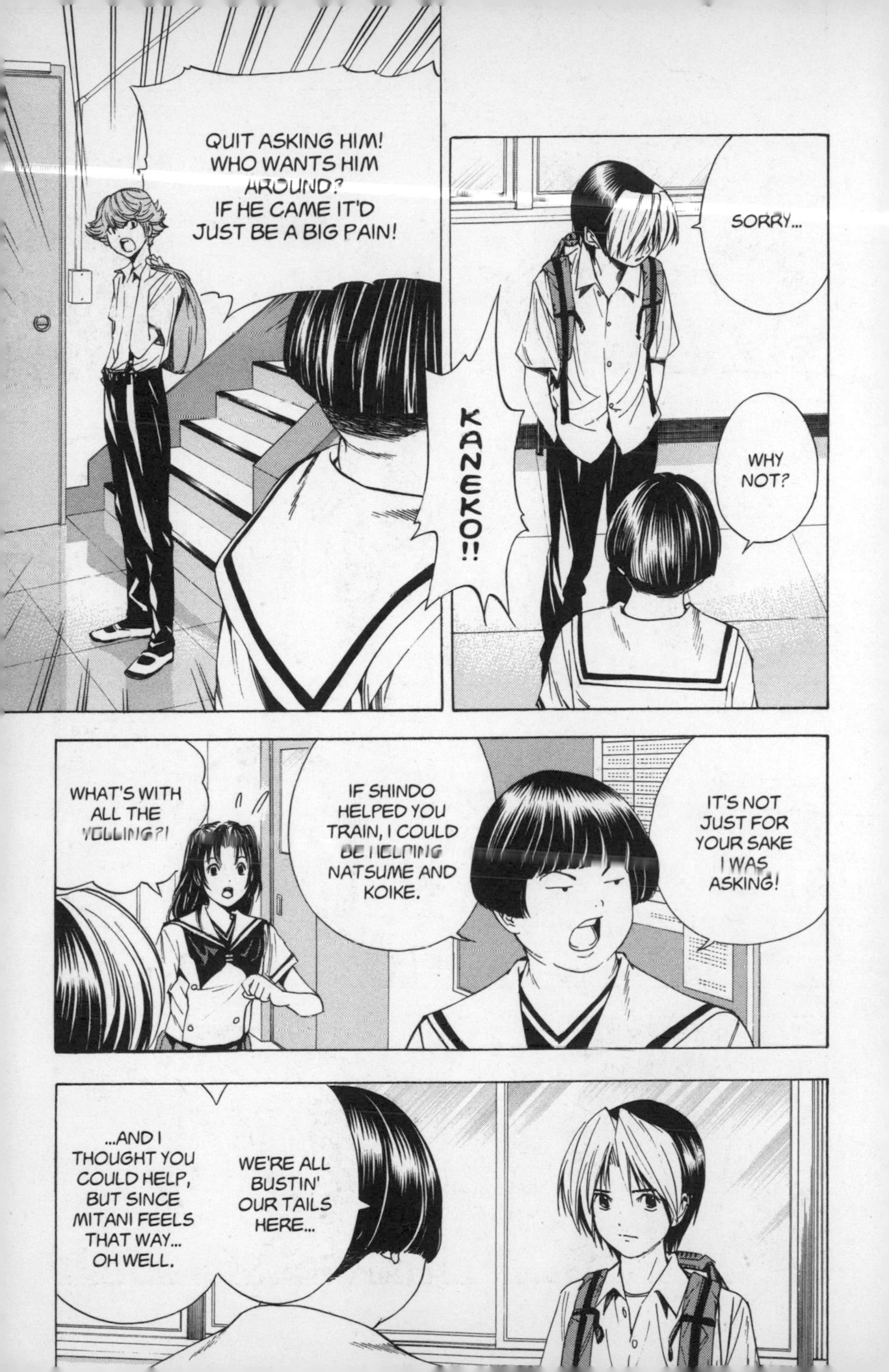
SORRY...
WHY NOT?
QUIT ASKING HIM! WHO WANTS HIM AROUND? IF HE CAME IT'D JUST BE A BIG PAIN!
KANEKO!!
IT'S NOT JUST FOR YOUR SAKE I WAS ASKING!
IF SHINDO HELPED YOU TRAIN, I COULD BE HELPING NATSUME AND KOIKE.
WHAT'S WITH ALL THE YELLING?!
WE'RE ALL BUSTIN' OUR TAILS HERE...
...AND I THOUGHT YOU COULD HELP, BUT SINCE MITANI FEELS THAT WAY... OH WELL.

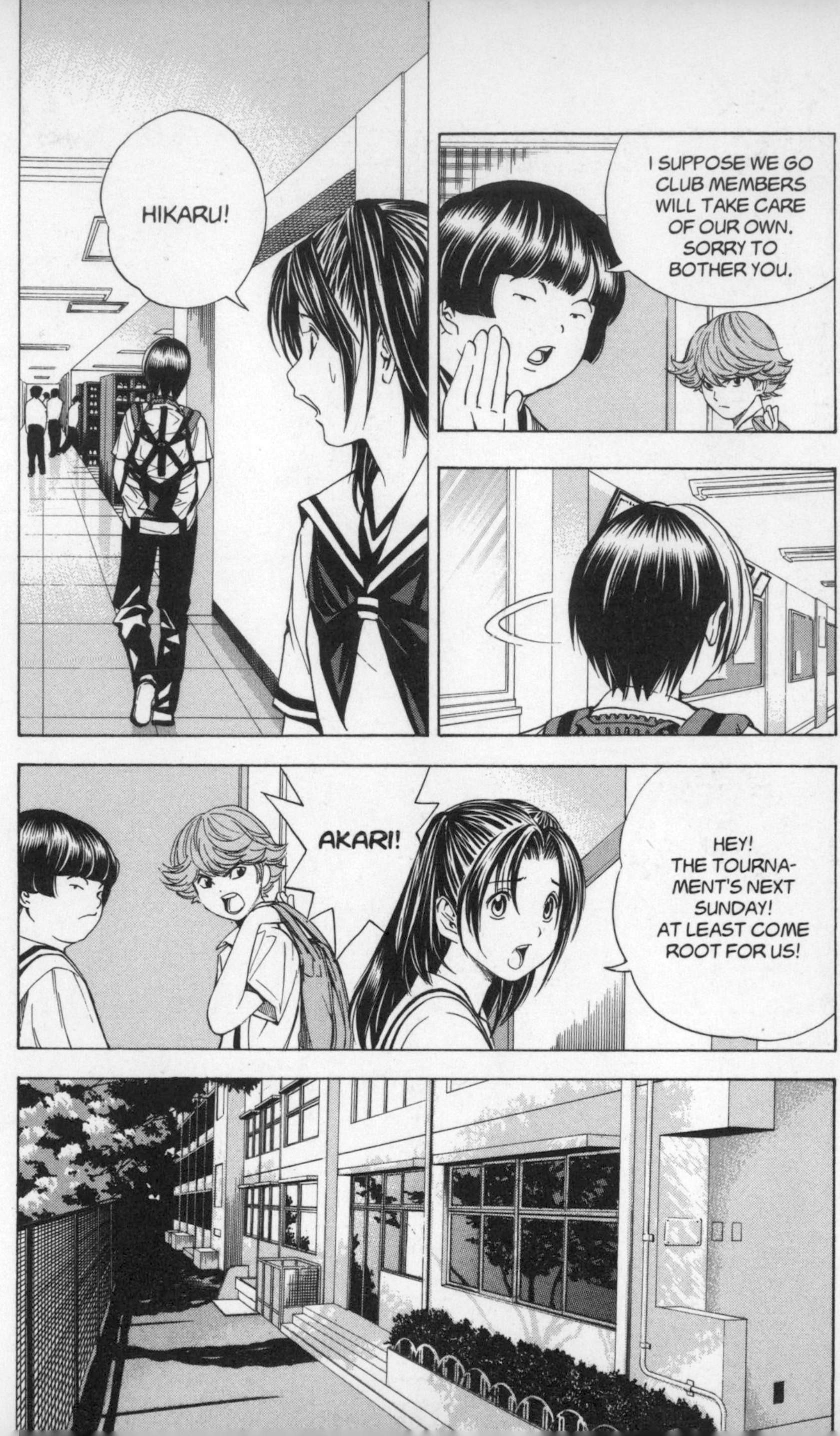
I SUPPOSE WE GO CLUB MEMBERS WILL TAKE CARE OF OUR OWN. SORRY TO BOTHER YOU.
HIKARU!
HEY! THE TOURNA-MENT'S NEXT SUNDAY! AT LEAST COME ROOT FOR US!
AKARI!

READ THIS WAY

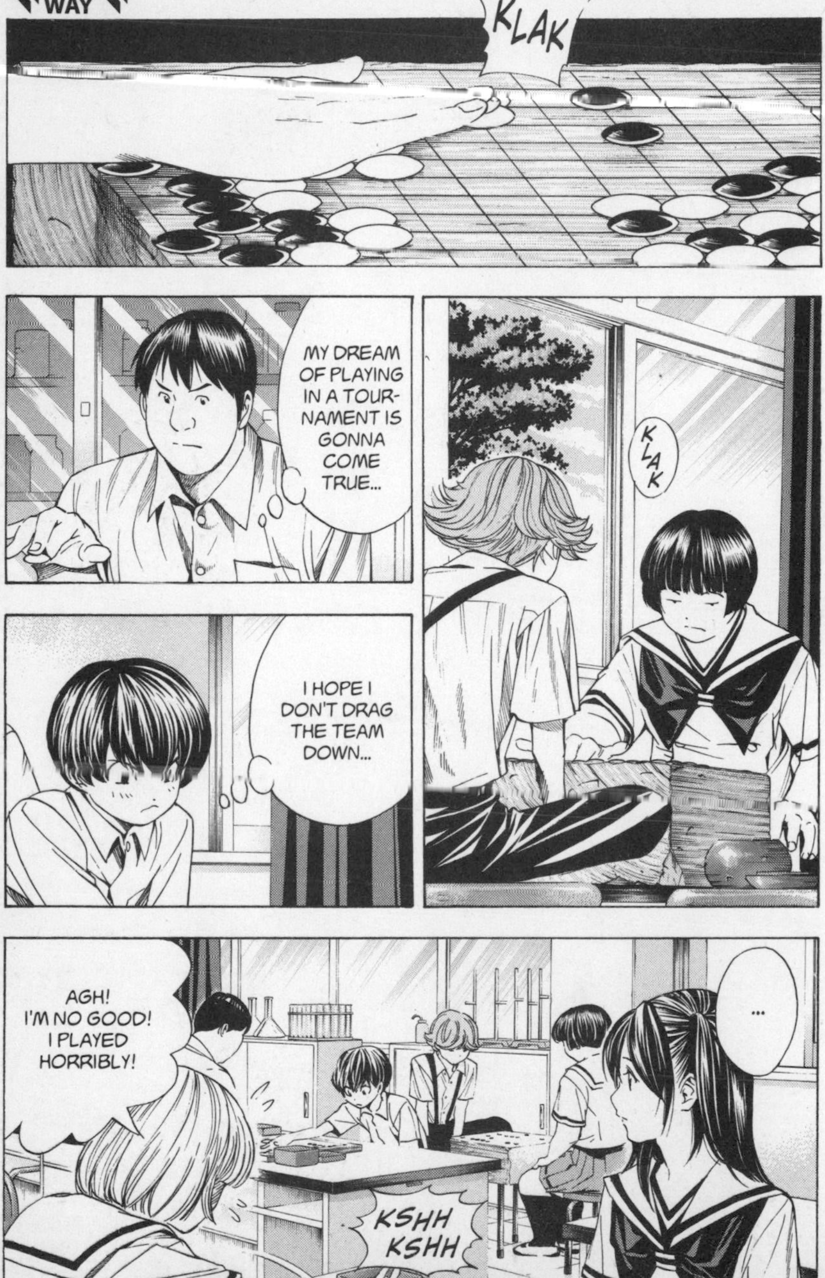
KLAK
KLAK
MY DREAM OF PLAYING IN A TOURNAMENT IS GONNA COME TRUE...
I HOPE I DON'T DRAG THE TEAM DOWN...
...
AGH! I'M NO GOOD! I PLAYED HORRIBLY!
KSHH KSHH

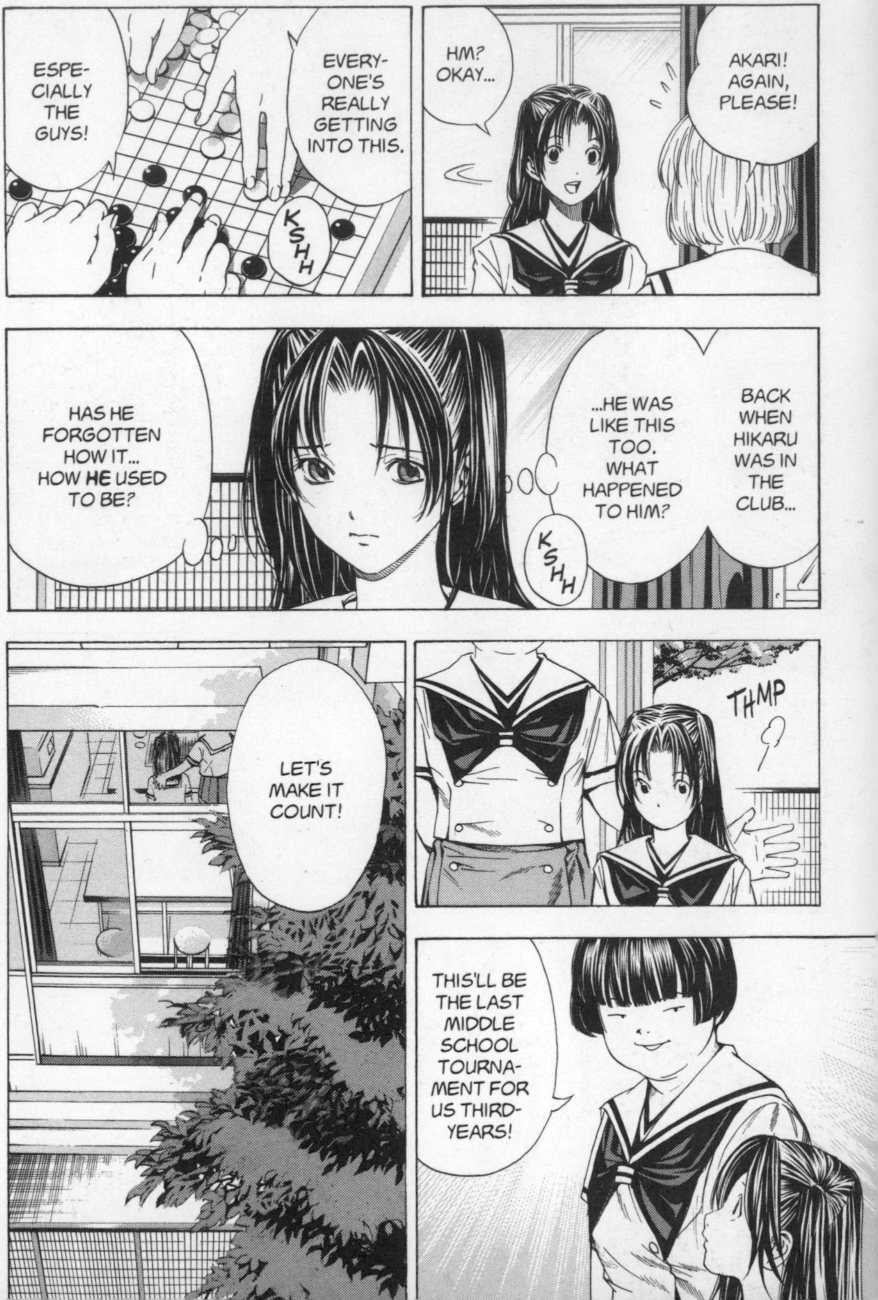
AKARI! AGAIN, PLEASE!
HM? OKAY...
EVERY-ONE'S REALLY GETTING INTO THIS.
ESPE-CIALLY THE GUYS!
KSHH
BACK WHEN HIKARU WAS IN THE CLUB...
...HE WAS LIKE THIS TOO. WHAT HAPPENED TO HIM?
KSHH
HAS HE FORGOTTEN HOW IT... HOW **HE** USED TO BE?
THMP
THIS'LL BE THE LAST MIDDLE SCHOOL TOURNA-MENT FOR US THIRD-YEARS!
LET'S MAKE IT COUNT!

READ THIS WAY

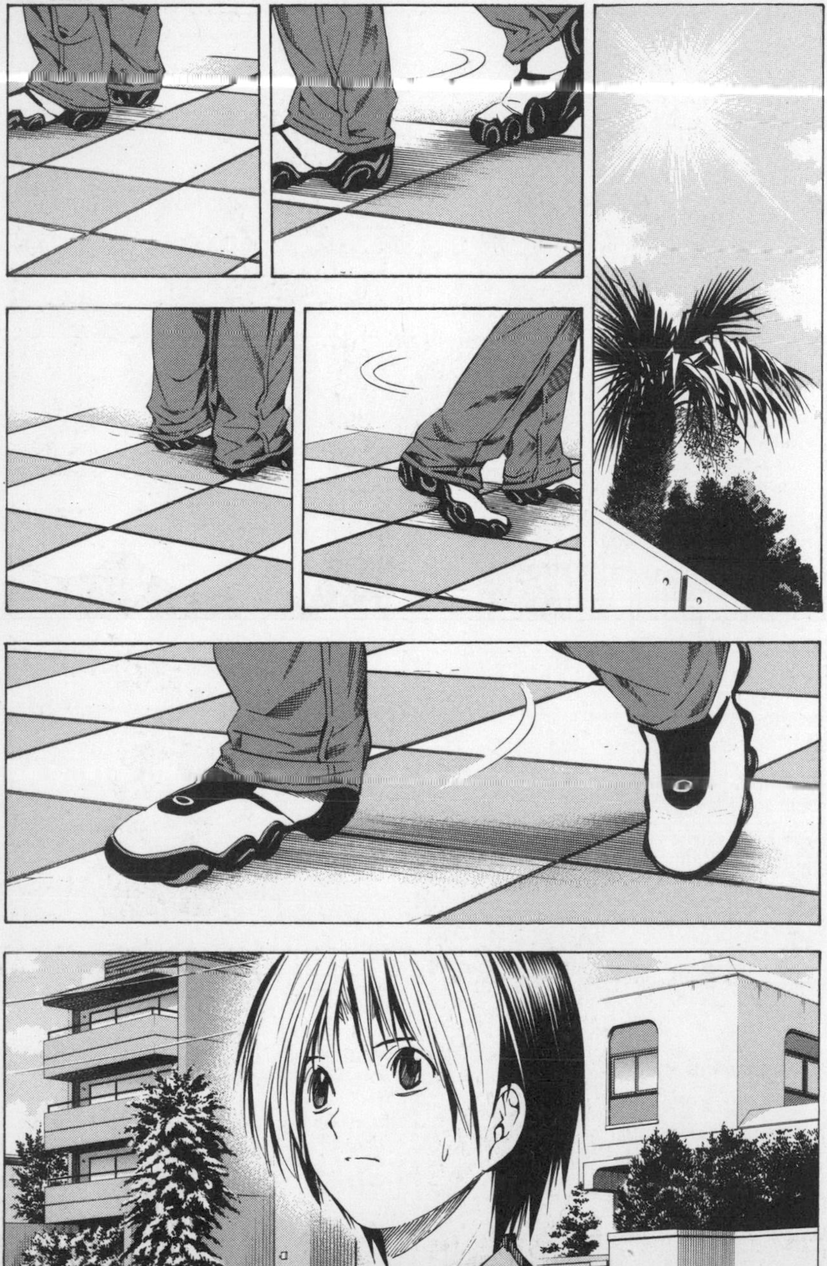

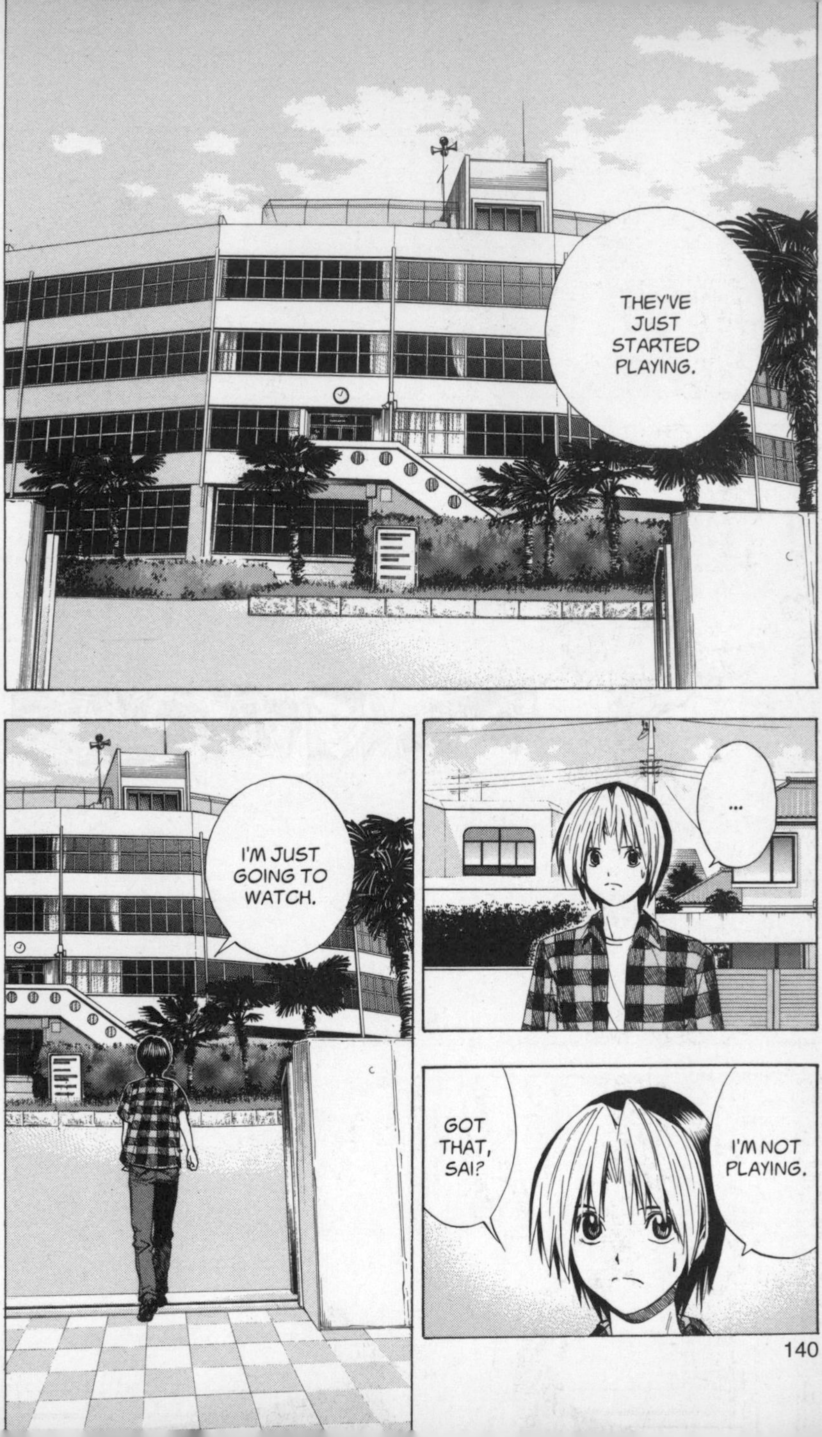
THEY'VE JUST STARTED PLAYING.
...
I'M NOT PLAYING.
GOT THAT, SAI?
I'M JUST GOING TO WATCH.

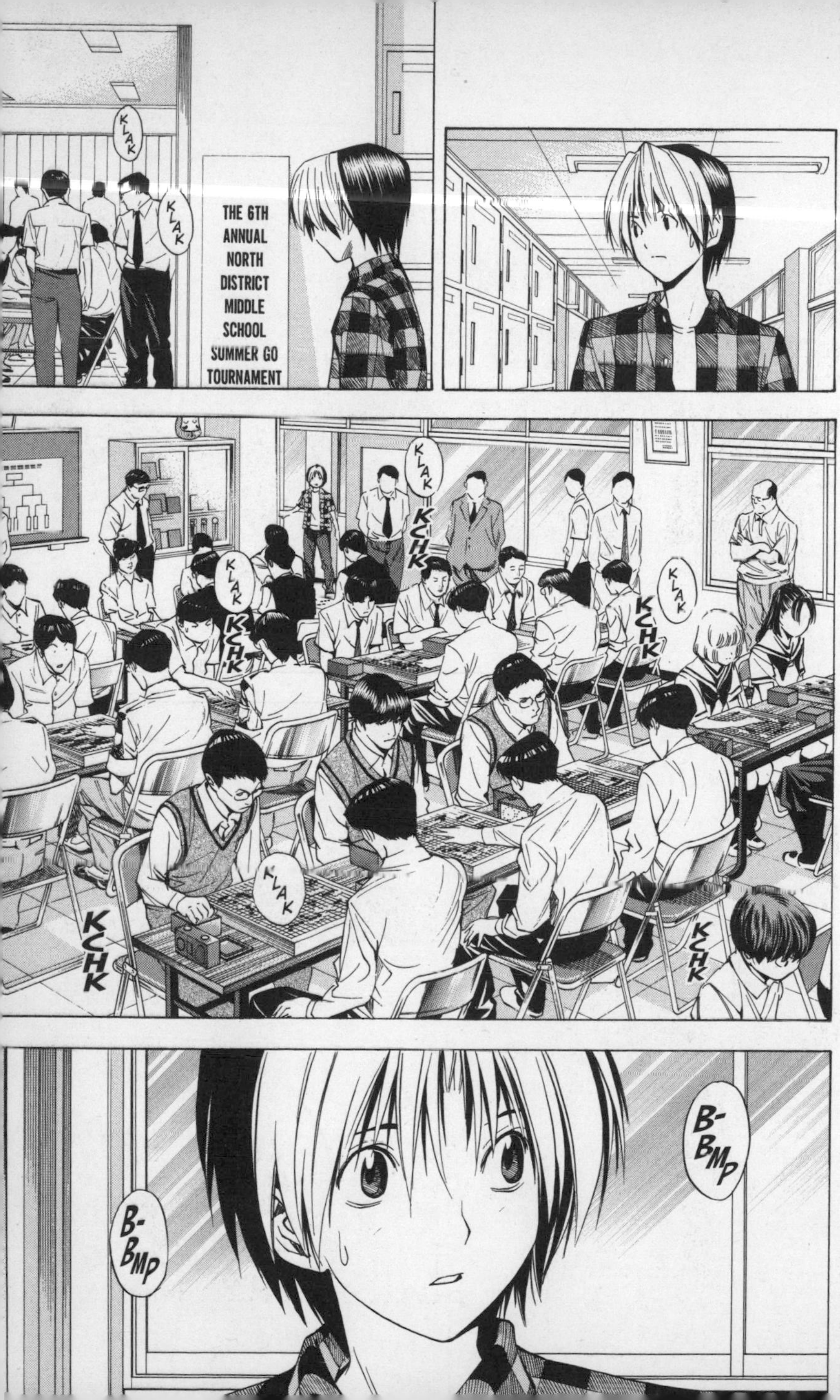
THE 6TH ANNUAL NORTH DISTRICT MIDDLE SCHOOL SUMMER GO TOURNAMENT
KLAK
KLAK
KLAK
KCHK
KLAK
KCHK
KLAK
KCHK
KCHK
KLAK
KCHK
B-BMP
B-BMP

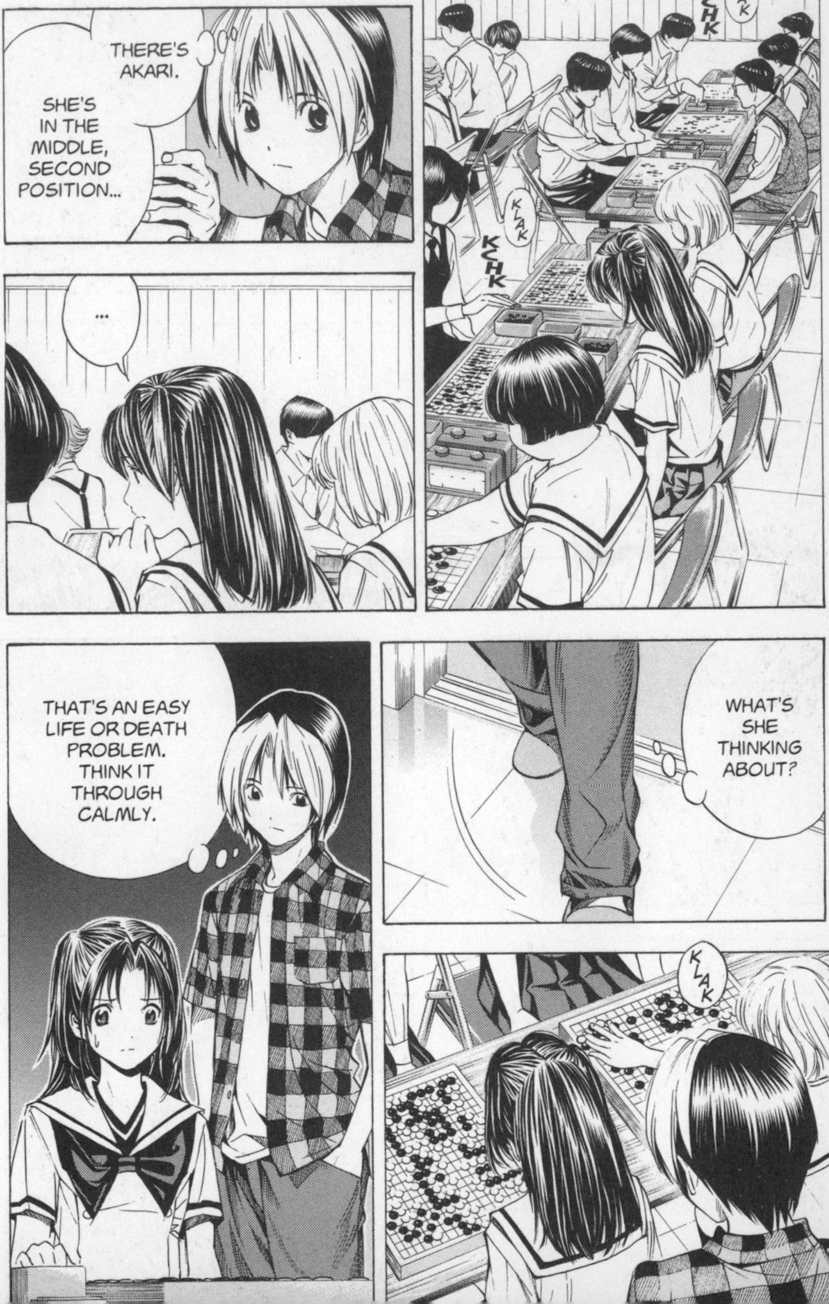
KLAK
KCHK
KLAK
KCHK
THERE'S AKARI.
SHE'S IN THE MIDDLE, SECOND POSITION...
...
WHAT'S SHE THINKING ABOUT?
KLAK
THAT'S AN EASY LIFE OR DEATH PROBLEM. THINK IT THROUGH CALMLY.

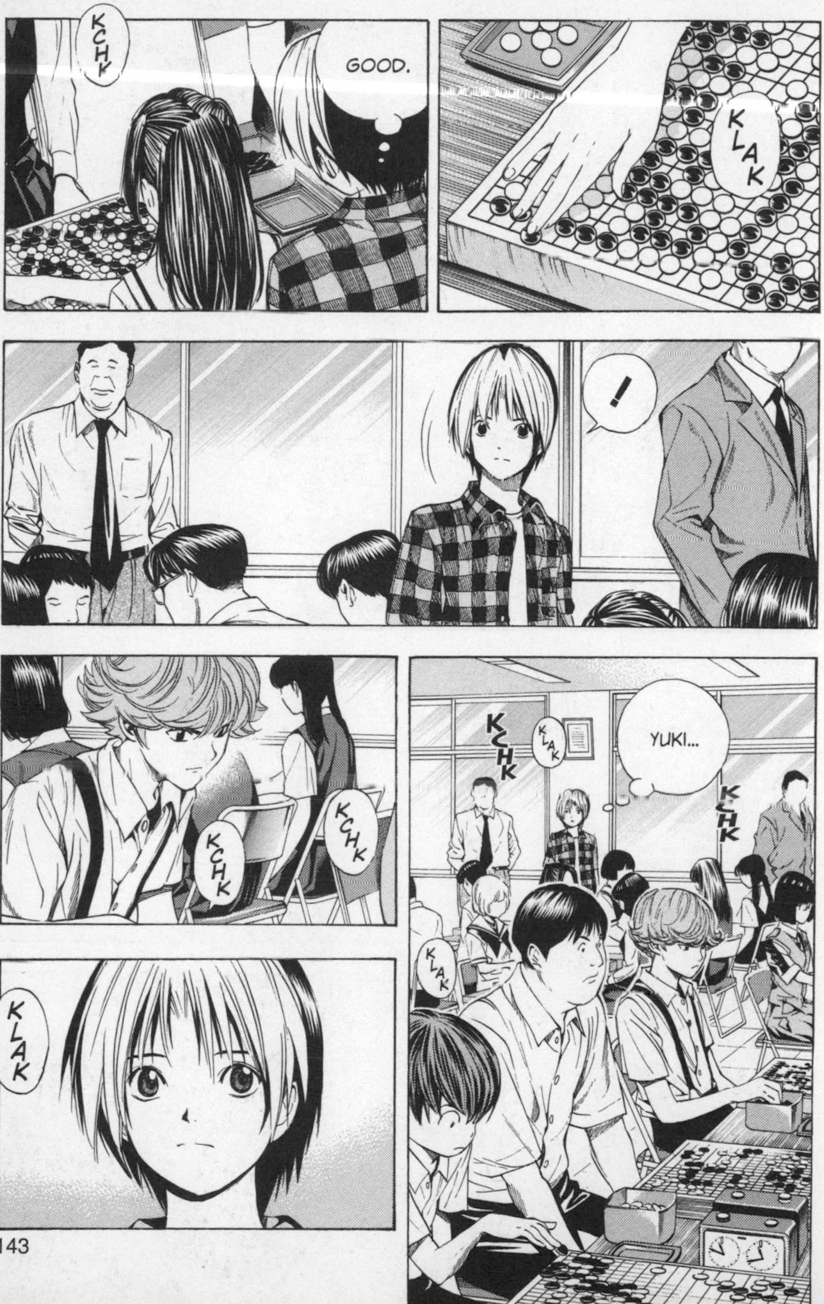
KLAK
GOOD.
KCHK
!
YUKI...
KCHK
KLAK
KCHK
KLAK
KCHK
KCHK
KLAK

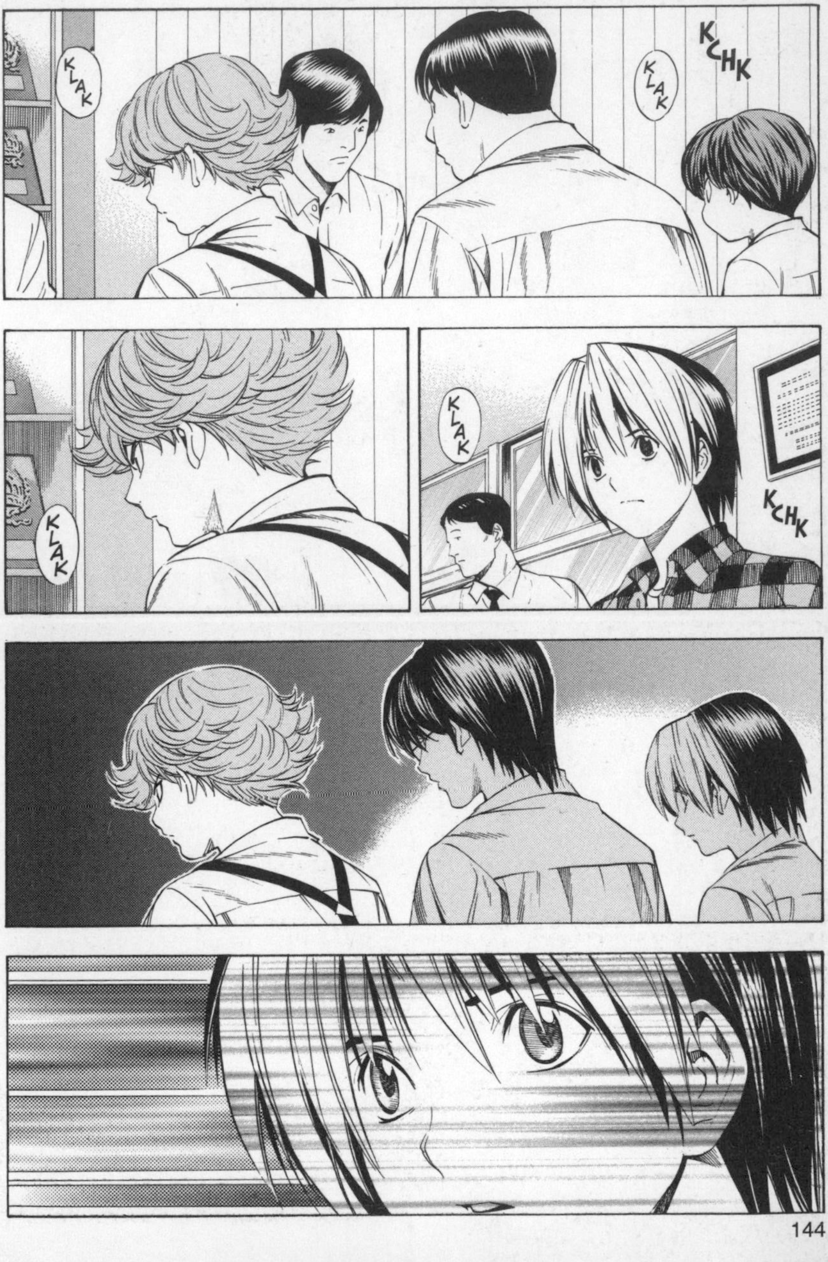
KCHK
KLAK
KLAK
KLAK
KCHK
KLAK

READ THIS WAY

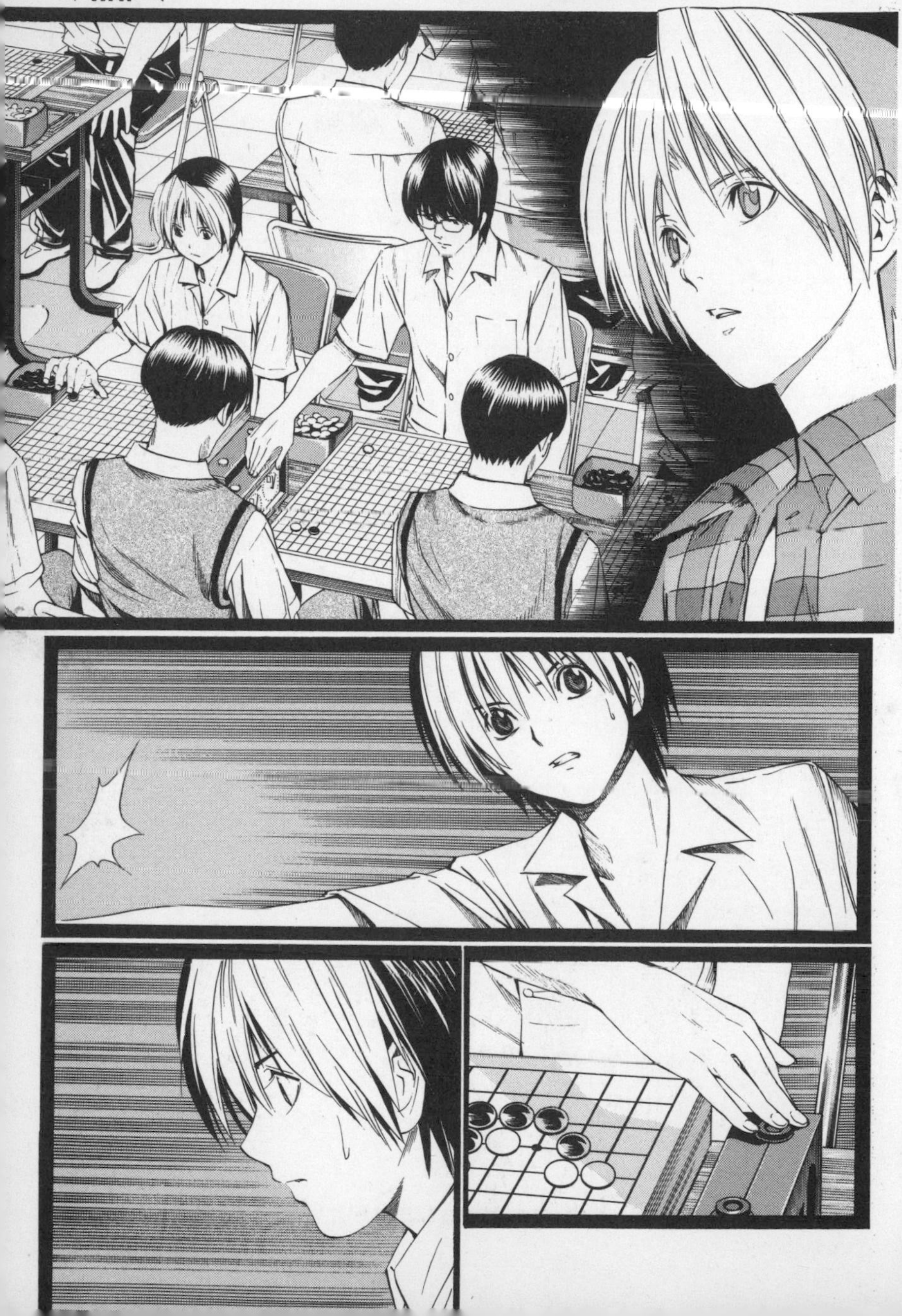

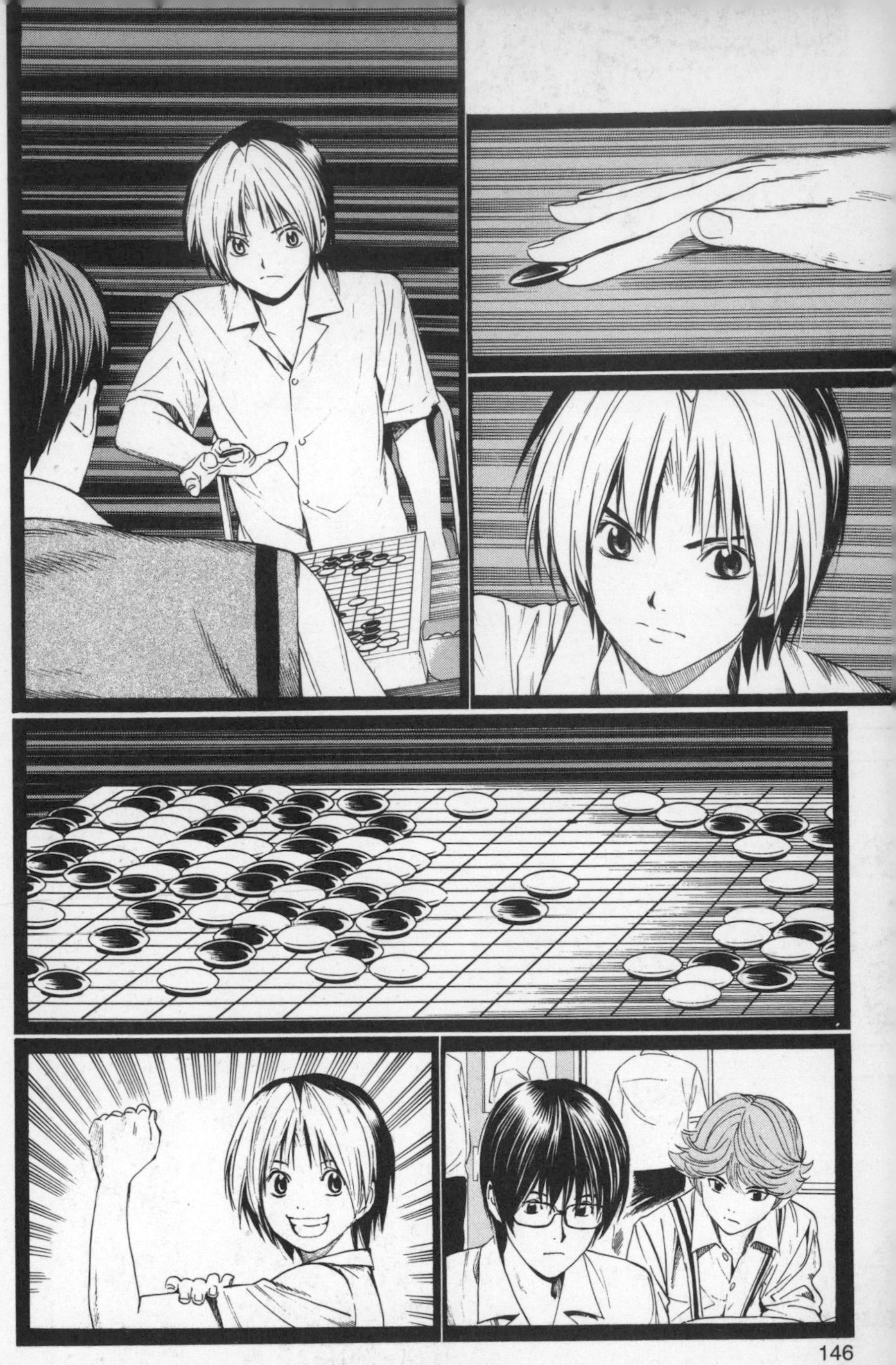

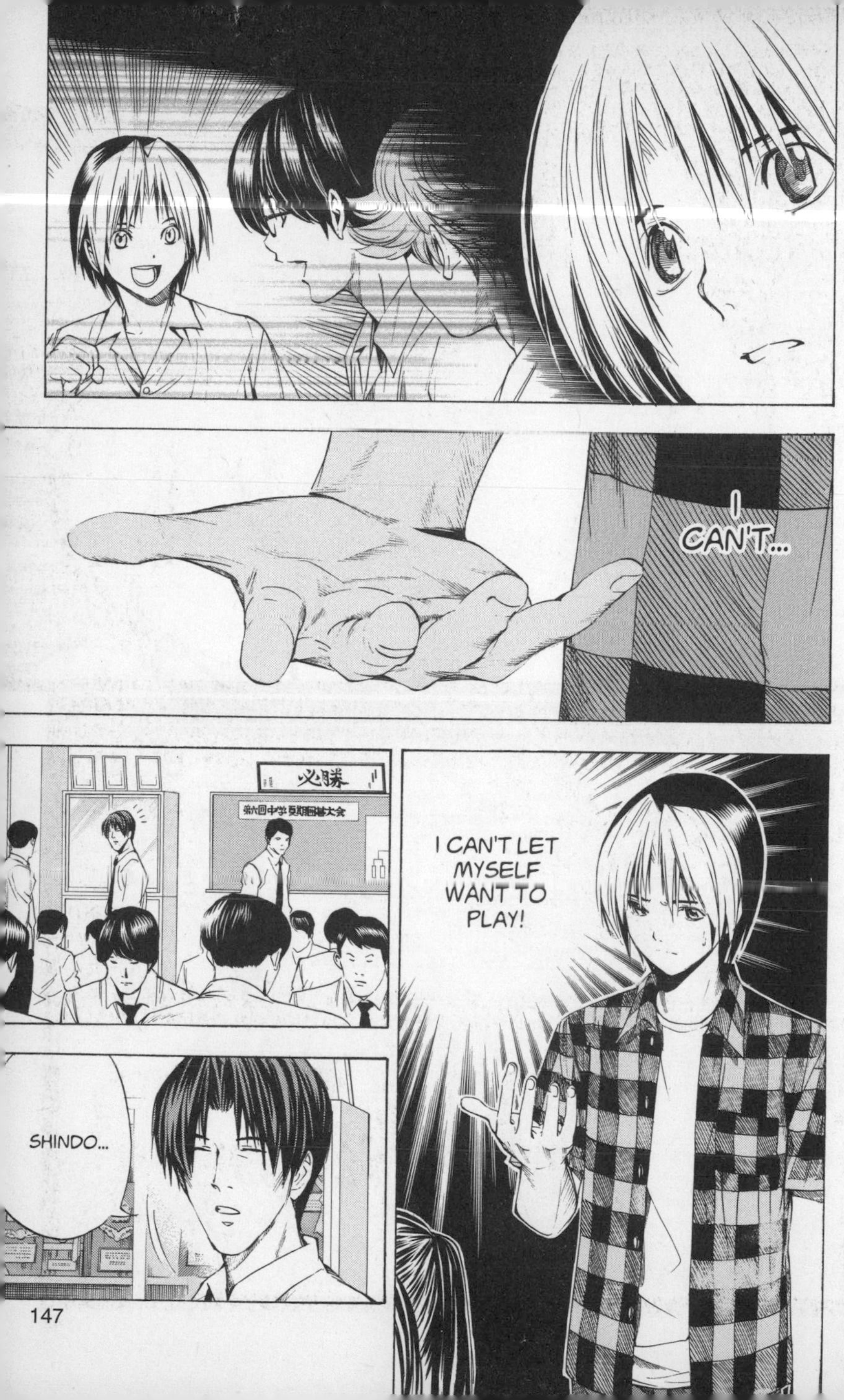
I CAN'T...
I CAN'T LET MYSELF WANT TO PLAY!
必勝
SHINDO...

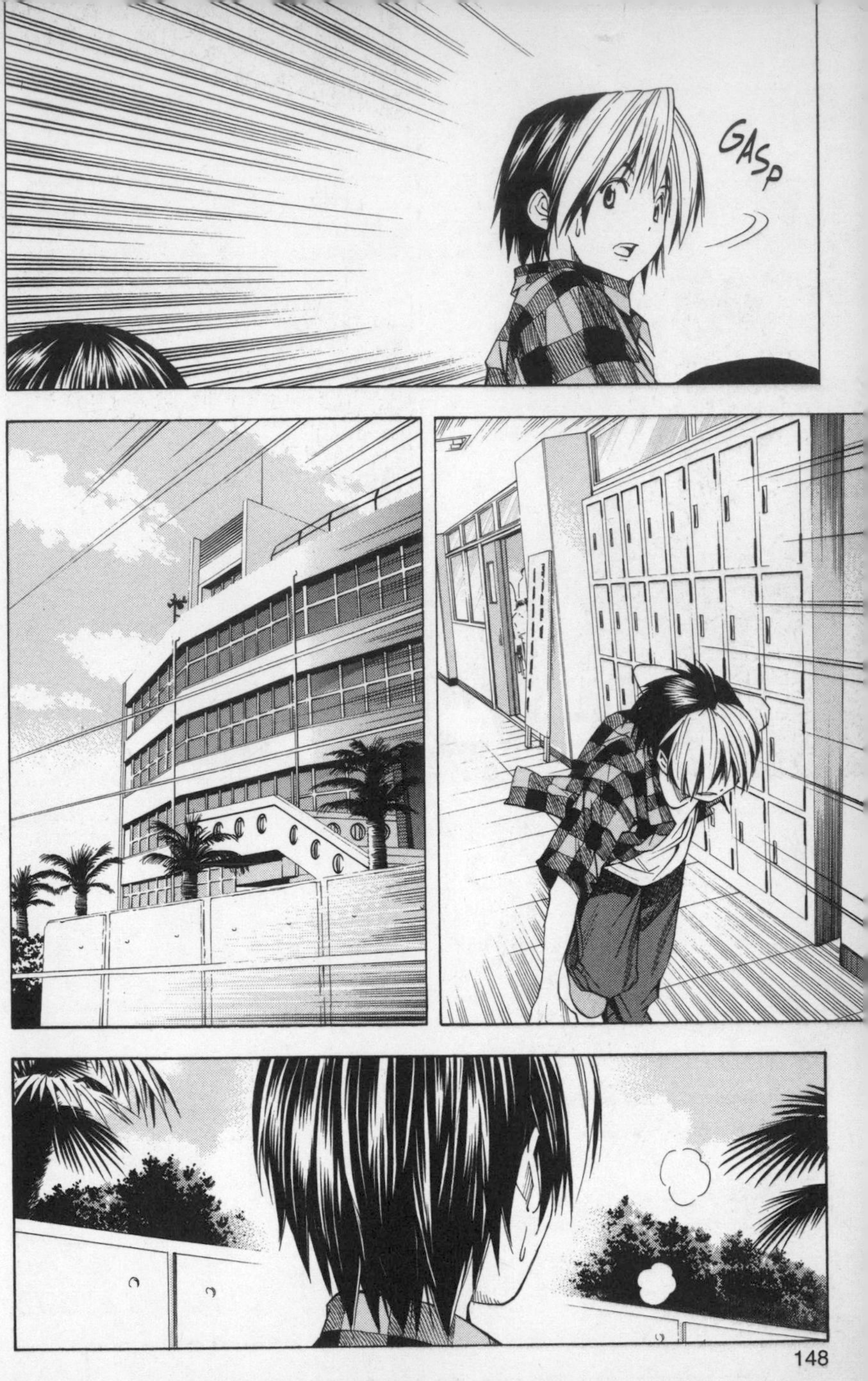
GASP

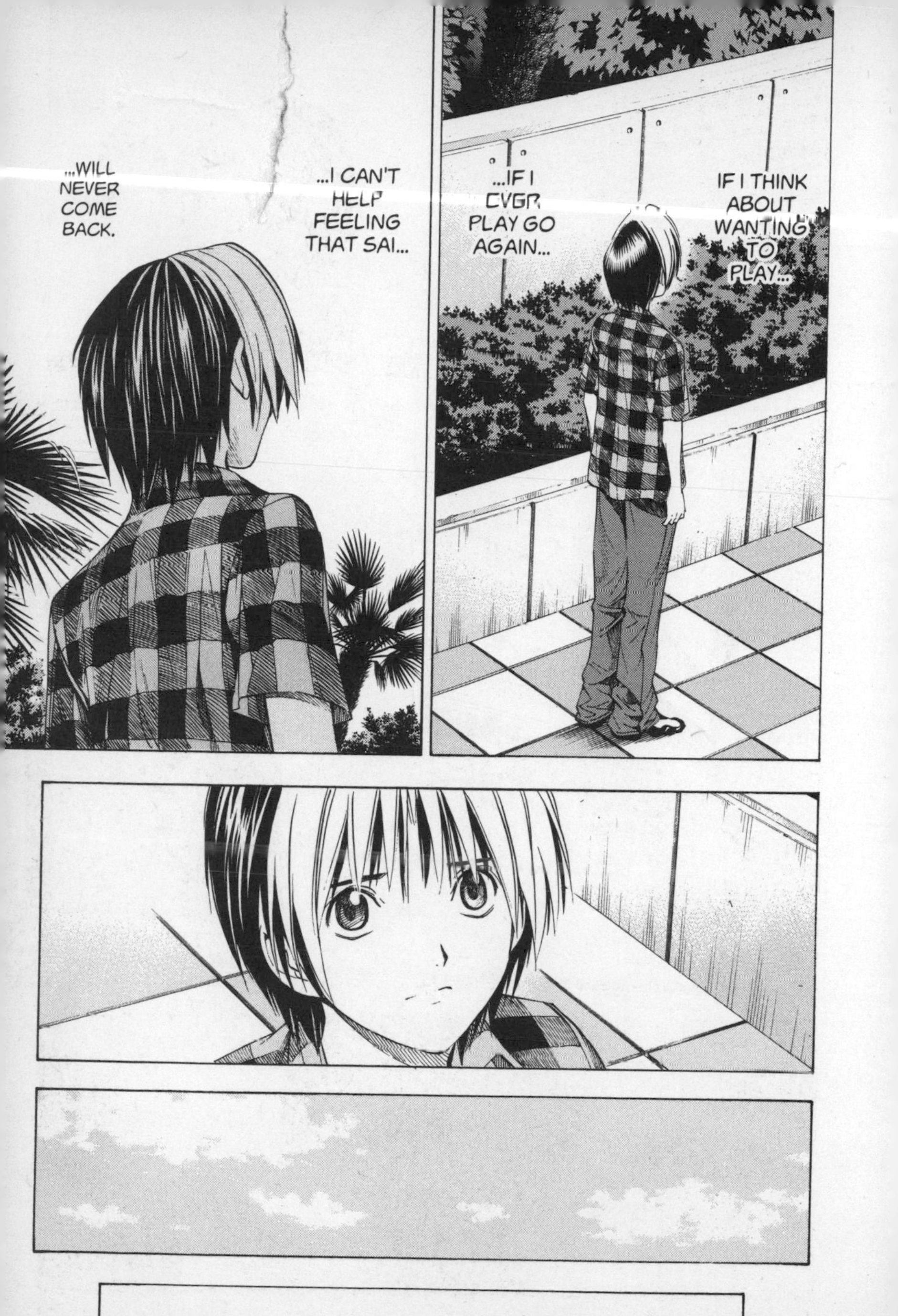
IF I THINK ABOUT WANTING TO PLAY...
...IF I EVER PLAY GO AGAIN...
...I CAN'T HELP FEELING THAT SAI...
...WILL NEVER COME BACK.

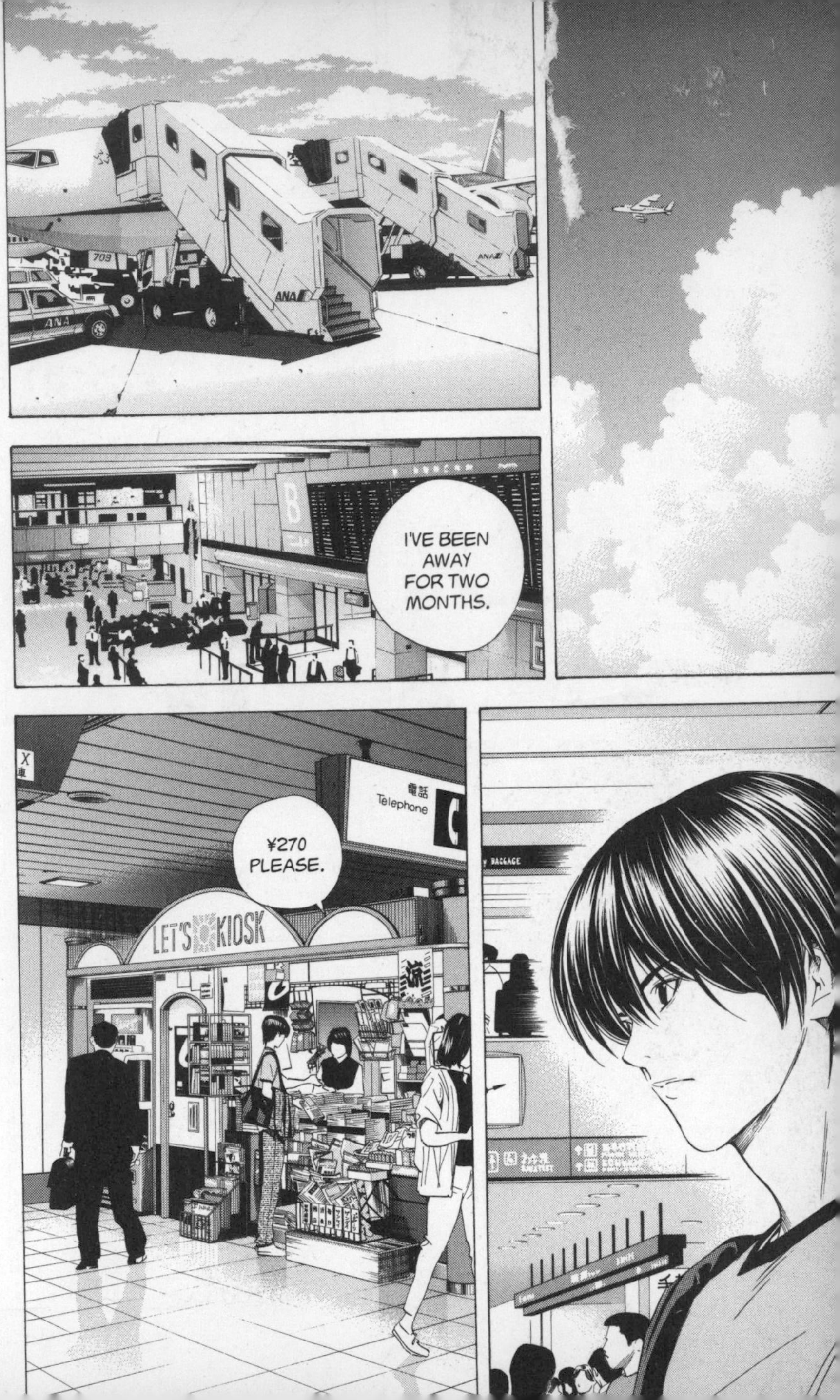
I'VE BEEN AWAY FOR TWO MONTHS.
BAGGAGE
¥270 PLEASE.
電話
Telephone
LET'S KIOSK

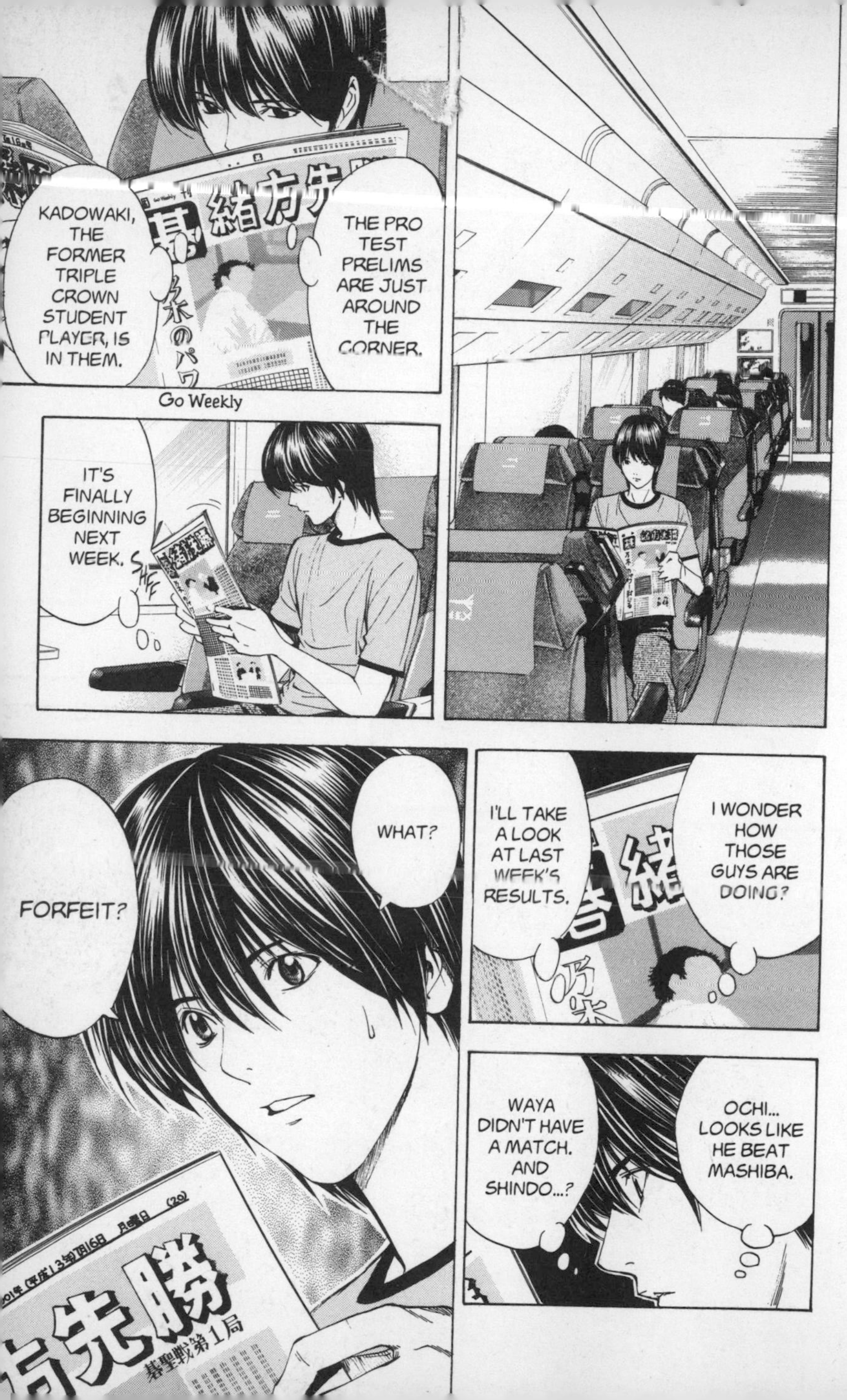
THE PRO TEST PRELIMS ARE JUST AROUND THE CORNER.
KADOWAKI, THE FORMER TRIPLE CROWN STUDENT PLAYER, IS IN THEM.
Go Weekly
IT'S FINALLY BEGINNING NEXT WEEK.
SHFF
I WONDER HOW THOSE GUYS ARE DOING?
I'LL TAKE A LOOK AT LAST WEEK'S RESULTS.
OCHI... LOOKS LIKE HE BEAT MASHIBA.
WAYA DIDN'T HAVE A MATCH. AND SHINDO...?
WHAT?
FORFEIT?

A WORD ABOUT HIKARU NO GO

THE PHONE IN THE TRAINING ROOM

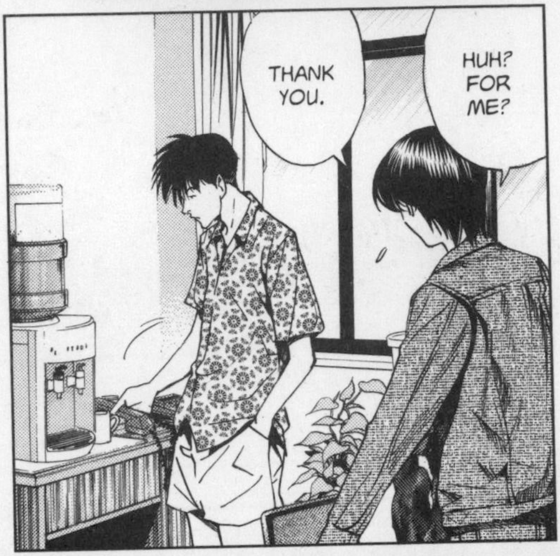
HUH? FOR ME?
THANK YOU.

THIS PHONE IS ONLY FOR INCOMING CALLS (INTERNATIONAL CALLS INCLUDED). SOMETIMES THE PLAYERS GET PHONE CALLS. THERE ARE YOUTH IN THEIR EARLY TEENS, AND THEIR PARENTS GET WORRIED AND CALL TO SAY **ARE YOU OKAY?!!**

THERE WAS A FATHER WHO CAME ON A SUNDAY TO SEE HIS KID.

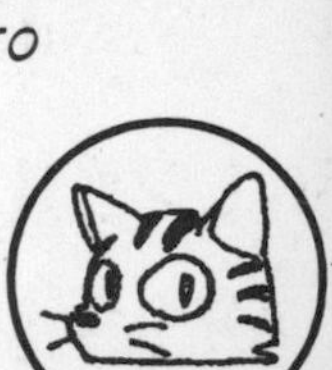

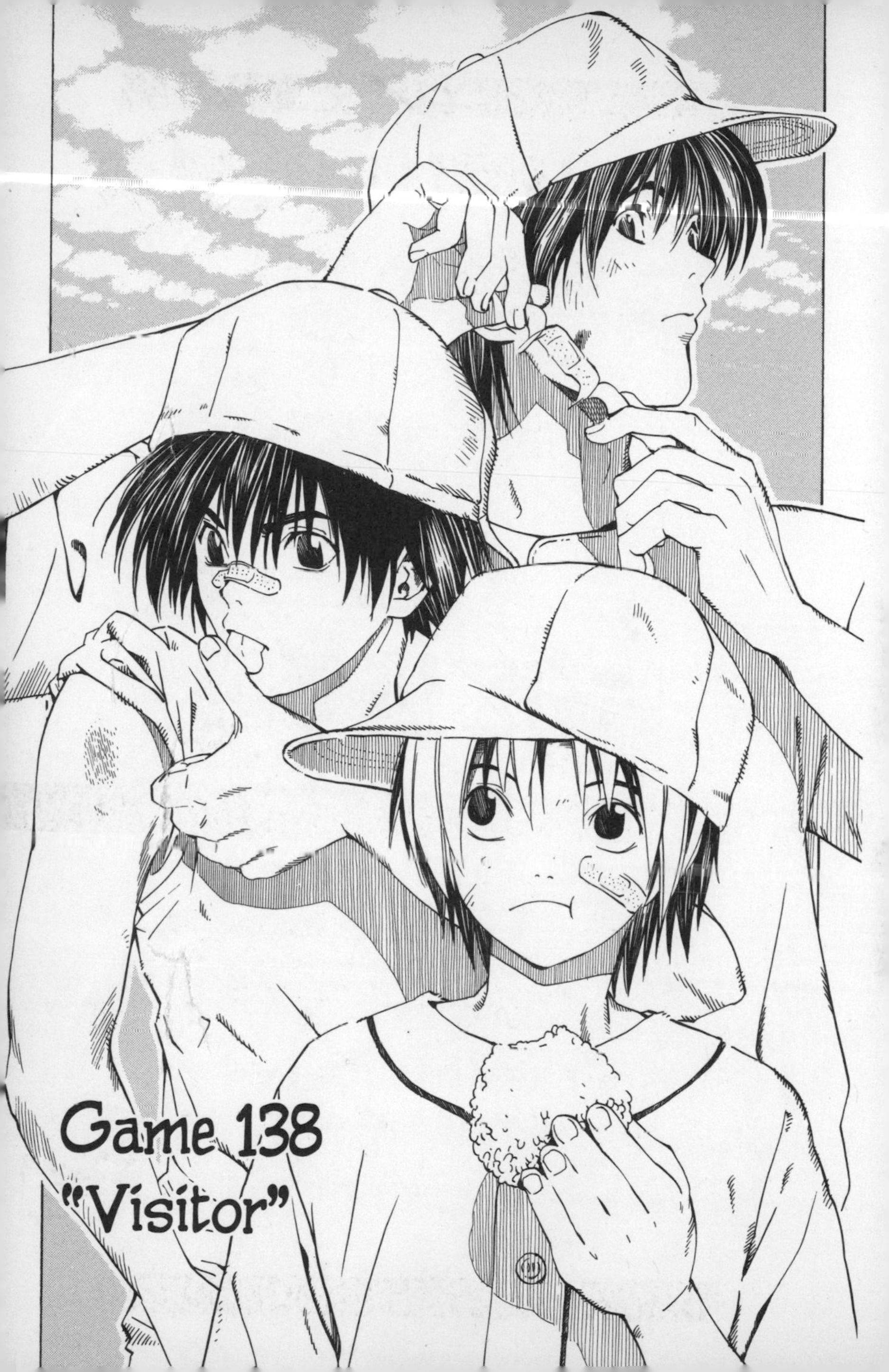
Game 138
"Visitor"

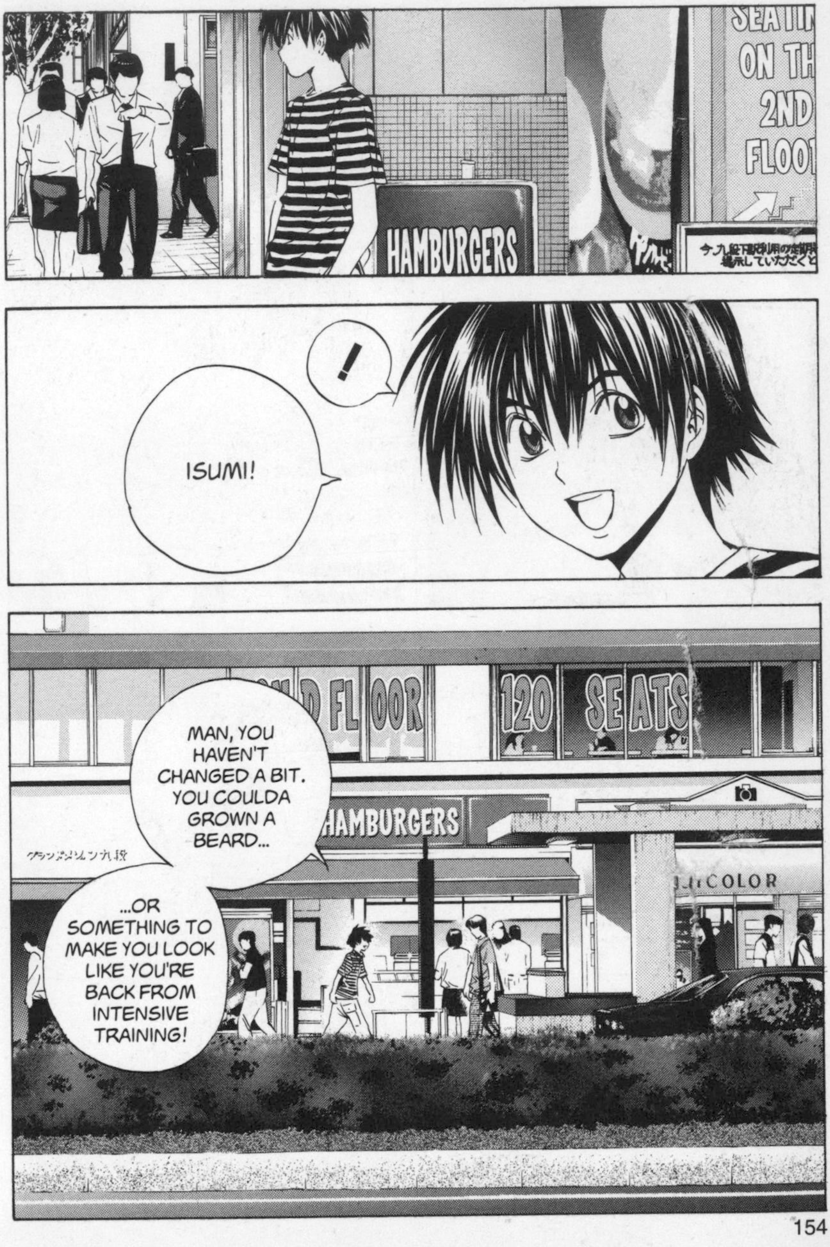
HAMBURGERS
!
ISUMI!
120 SEATS
HAMBURGERS
MAN, YOU HAVEN'T CHANGED A BIT. YOU COULDA GROWN A BEARD...
...OR SOMETHING TO MAKE YOU LOOK LIKE YOU'RE BACK FROM INTENSIVE TRAINING!

READ THIS WAY

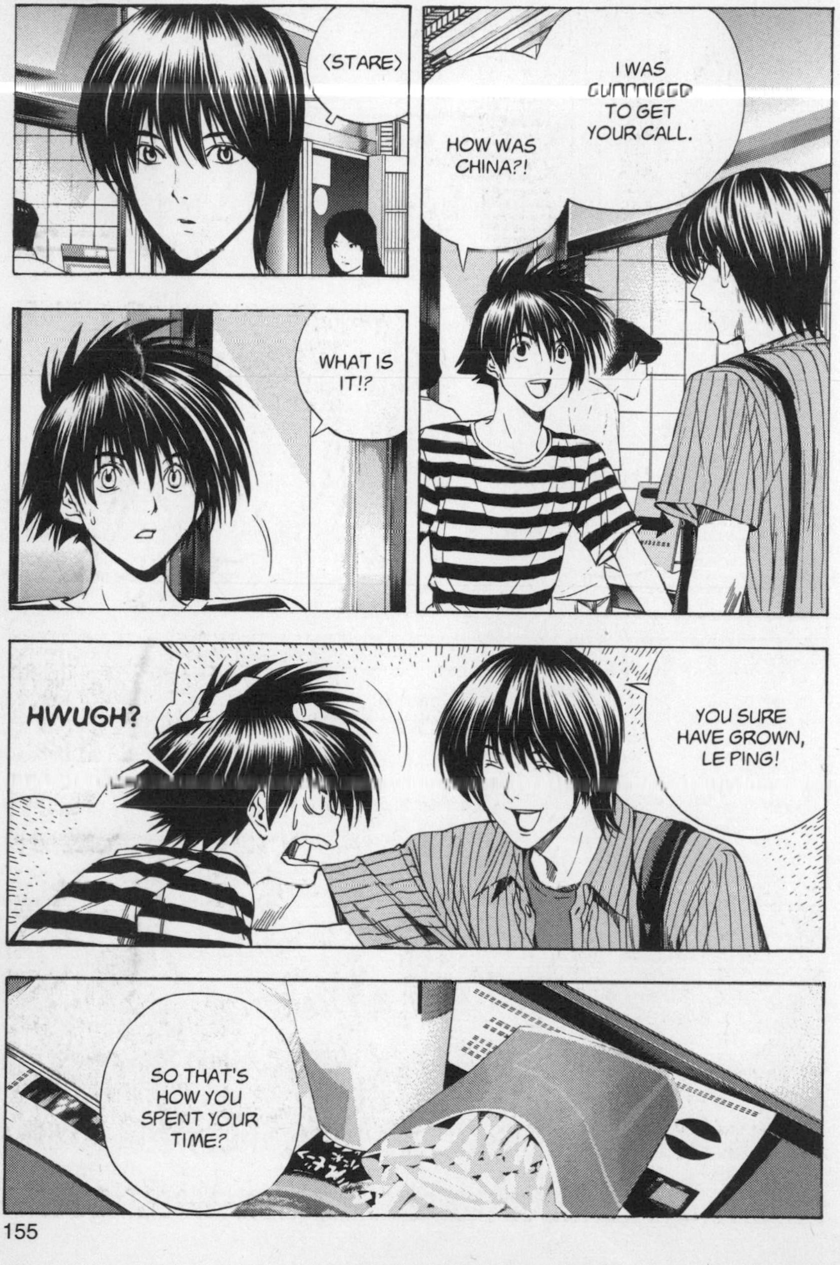

I WAS SURPRISED TO GET YOUR CALL.
HOW WAS CHINA?!
⟨STARE⟩
WHAT IS IT!?
YOU SURE HAVE GROWN, LE PING!
HWUGH?
SO THAT'S HOW YOU SPENT YOUR TIME?

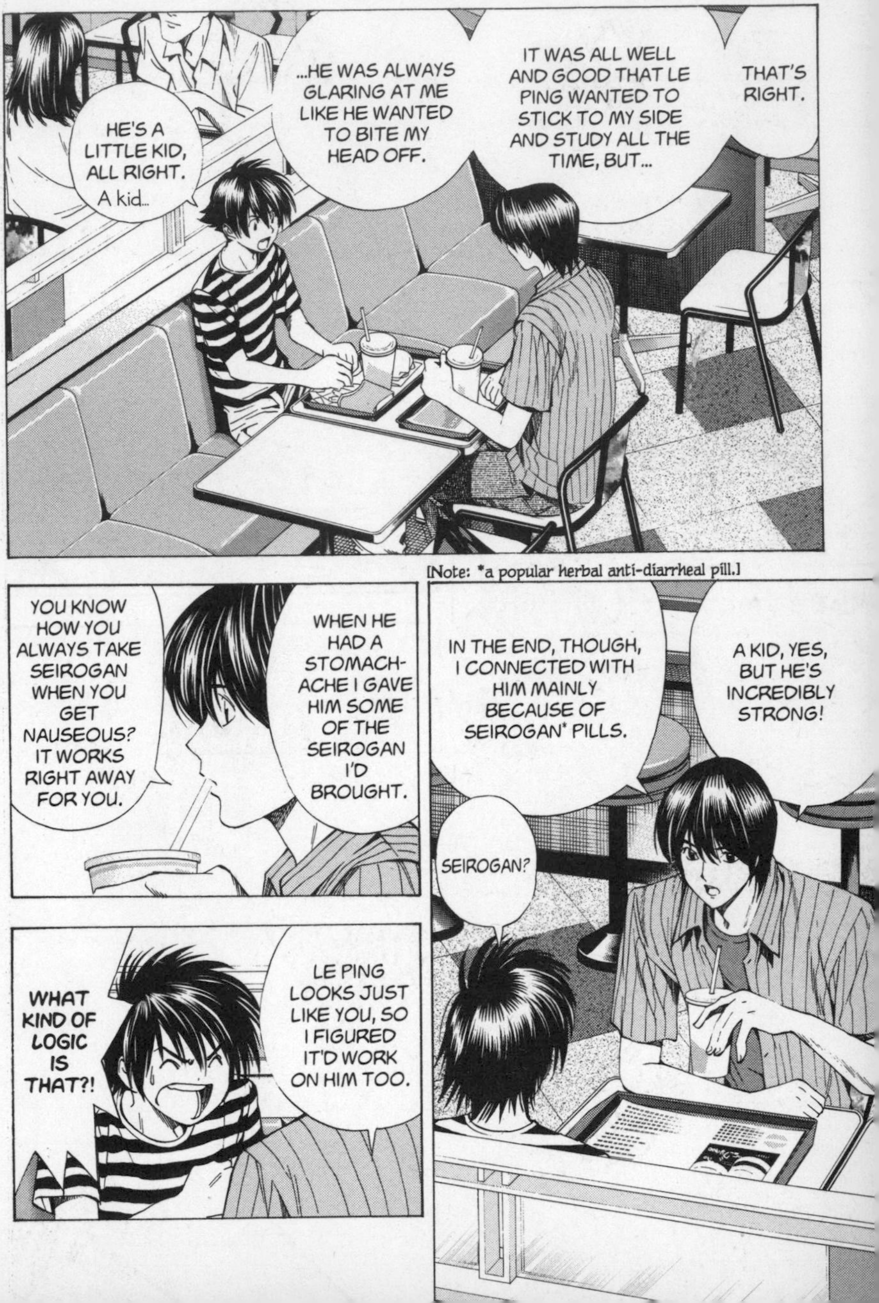
THAT'S RIGHT.
IT WAS ALL WELL AND GOOD THAT LE PING WANTED TO STICK TO MY SIDE AND STUDY ALL THE TIME, BUT...
...HE WAS ALWAYS GLARING AT ME LIKE HE WANTED TO BITE MY HEAD OFF.
HE'S A LITTLE KID, ALL RIGHT.
A kid...
[Note: *a popular herbal anti-diarrheal pill.]
A KID, YES, BUT HE'S INCREDIBLY STRONG!
IN THE END, THOUGH, I CONNECTED WITH HIM MAINLY BECAUSE OF SEIROGAN* PILLS.
SEIROGAN?
WHEN HE HAD A STOMACHACHE I GAVE HIM SOME OF THE SEIROGAN I'D BROUGHT.
YOU KNOW HOW YOU ALWAYS TAKE SEIROGAN WHEN YOU GET NAUSEOUS? IT WORKS RIGHT AWAY FOR YOU.
LE PING LOOKS JUST LIKE YOU, SO I FIGURED IT'D WORK ON HIM TOO.
WHAT KIND OF LOGIC IS THAT?!

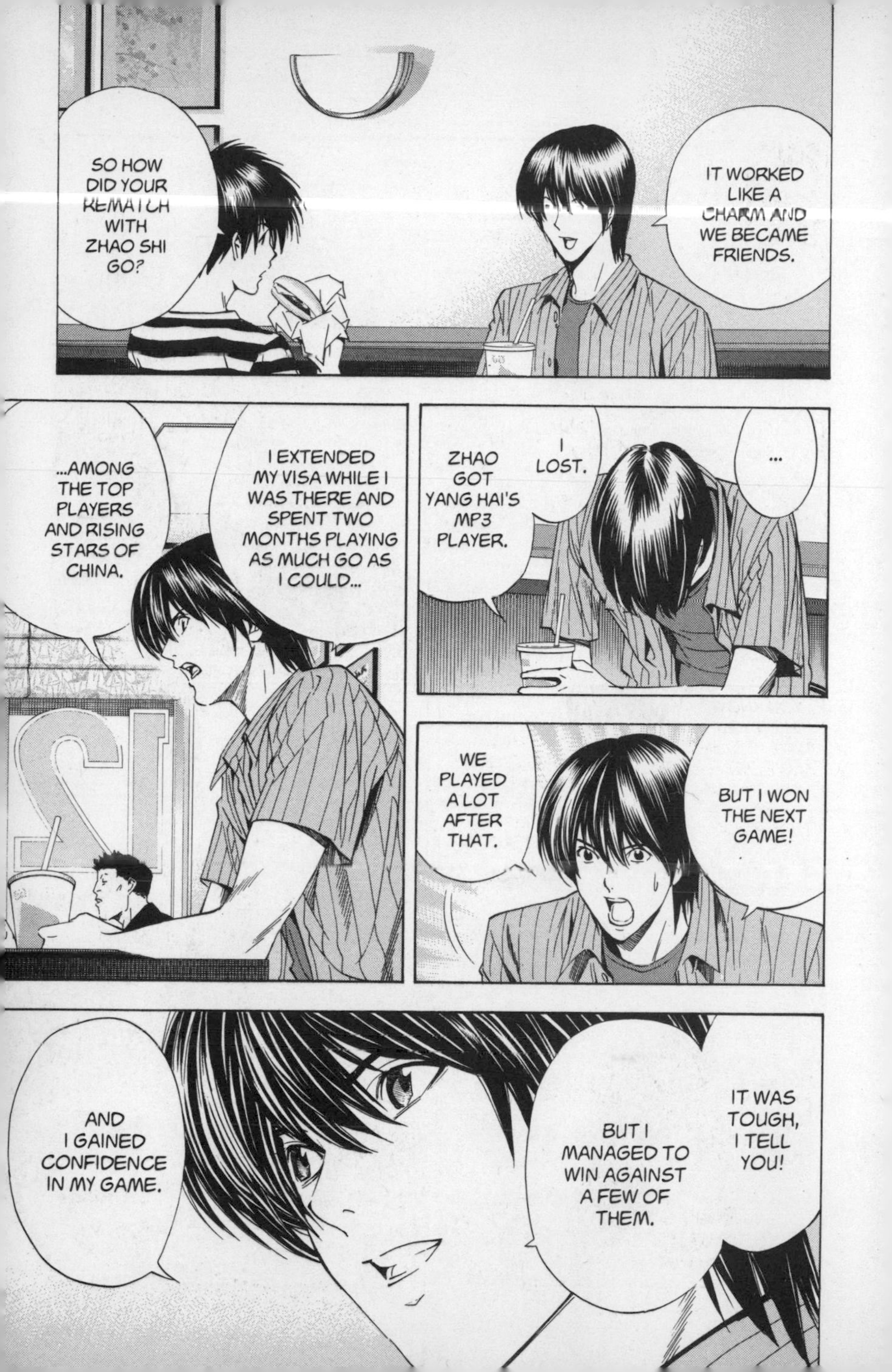
SO HOW DID YOUR REMATCH WITH ZHAO SHI GO?
IT WORKED LIKE A CHARM AND WE BECAME FRIENDS.
...
I LOST.
ZHAO GOT YANG HAI'S MP3 PLAYER.
BUT I WON THE NEXT GAME!
WE PLAYED A LOT AFTER THAT.
I EXTENDED MY VISA WHILE I WAS THERE AND SPENT TWO MONTHS PLAYING AS MUCH GO AS I COULD...
...AMONG THE TOP PLAYERS AND RISING STARS OF CHINA.
IT WAS TOUGH, I TELL YOU!
BUT I MANAGED TO WIN AGAINST A FEW OF THEM.
AND I GAINED CONFIDENCE IN MY GAME.

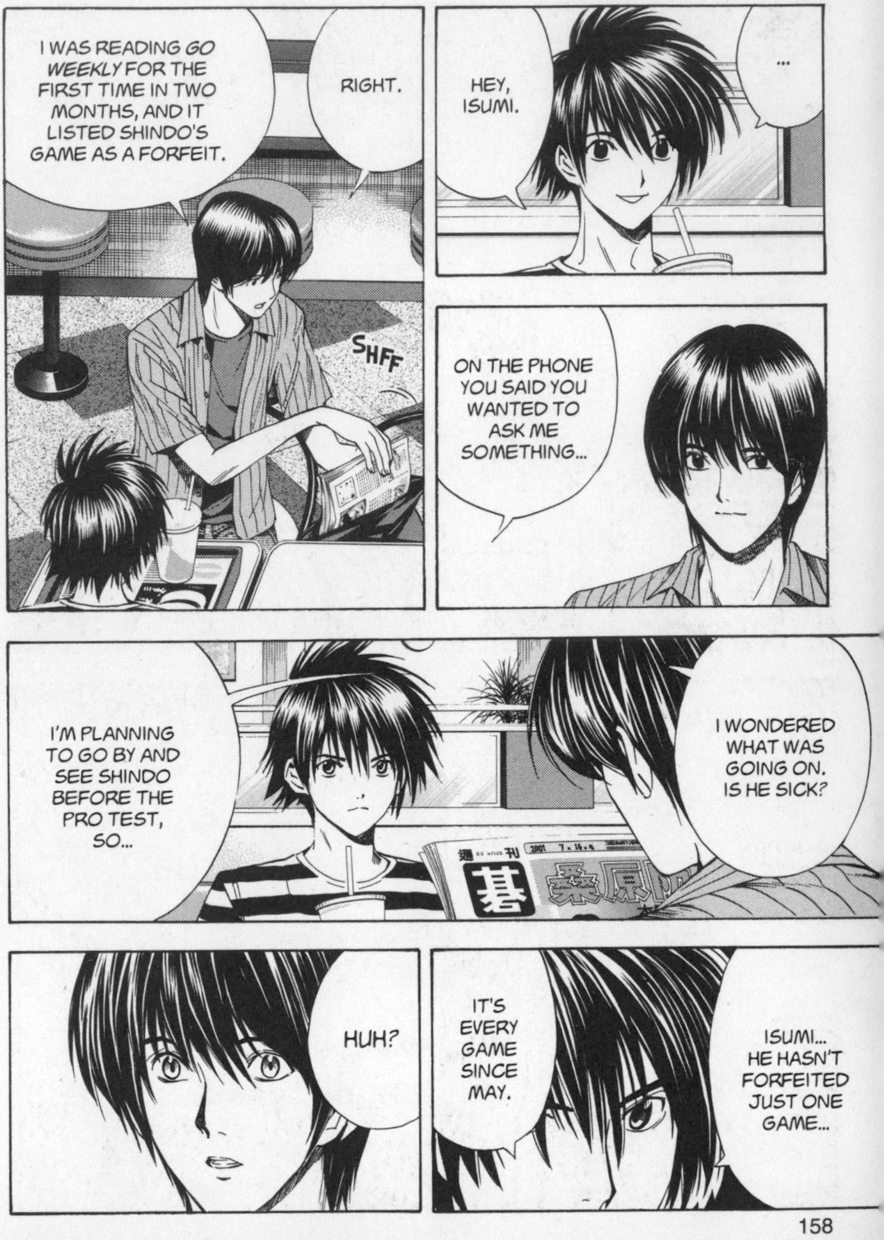
...
HEY, ISUMI.
ON THE PHONE YOU SAID YOU WANTED TO ASK ME SOMETHING...
RIGHT.
I WAS READING *GO WEEKLY* FOR THE FIRST TIME IN TWO MONTHS, AND IT LISTED SHINDO'S GAME AS A FORFEIT.
SHFF
I WONDERED WHAT WAS GOING ON. IS HE SICK?
I'M PLANNING TO GO BY AND SEE SHINDO BEFORE THE PRO TEST, SO...
ISUMI... HE HASN'T FORFEITED JUST ONE GAME...
IT'S EVERY GAME SINCE MAY.
HUH?

READ THIS WAY

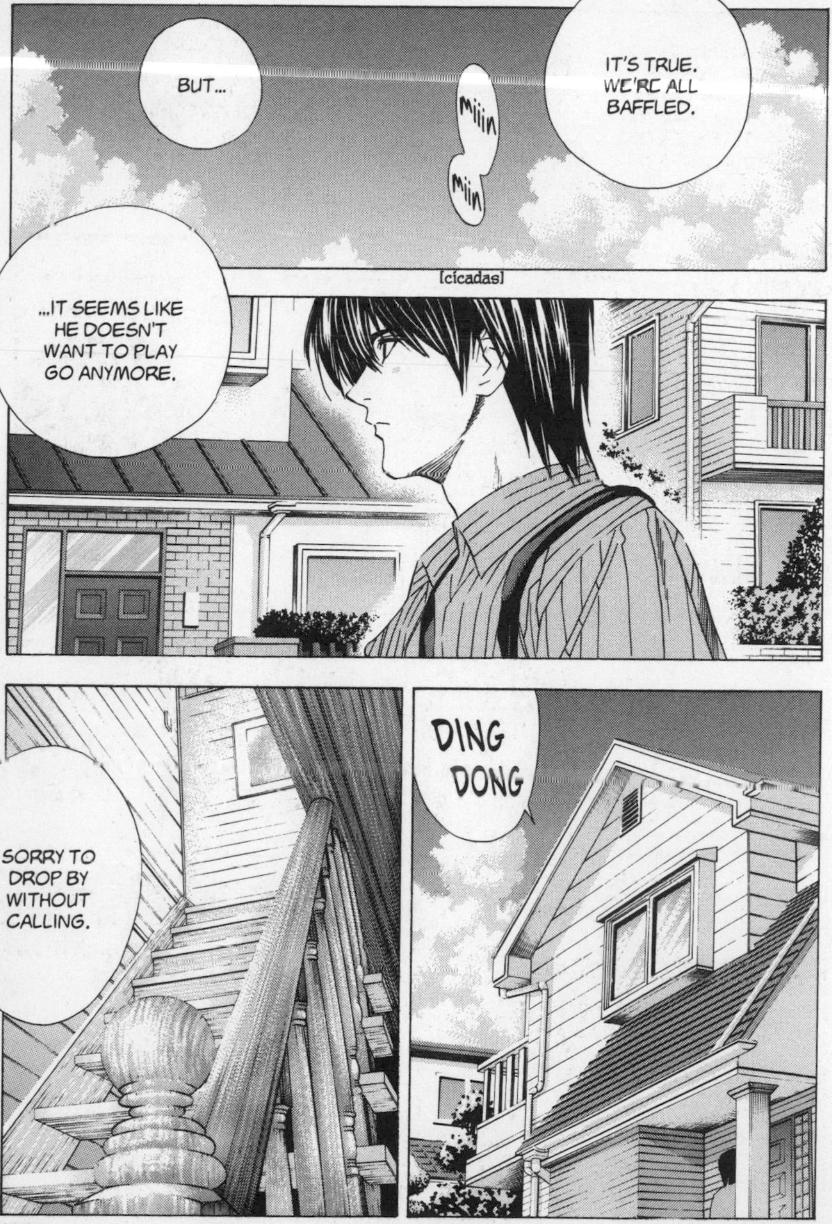
IT'S TRUE. WE'RE ALL BAFFLED.
miiin
miin
BUT...
[cícadas]
...IT SEEMS LIKE HE DOESN'T WANT TO PLAY GO ANYMORE.
DING DONG
SORRY TO DROP BY WITHOUT CALLING.

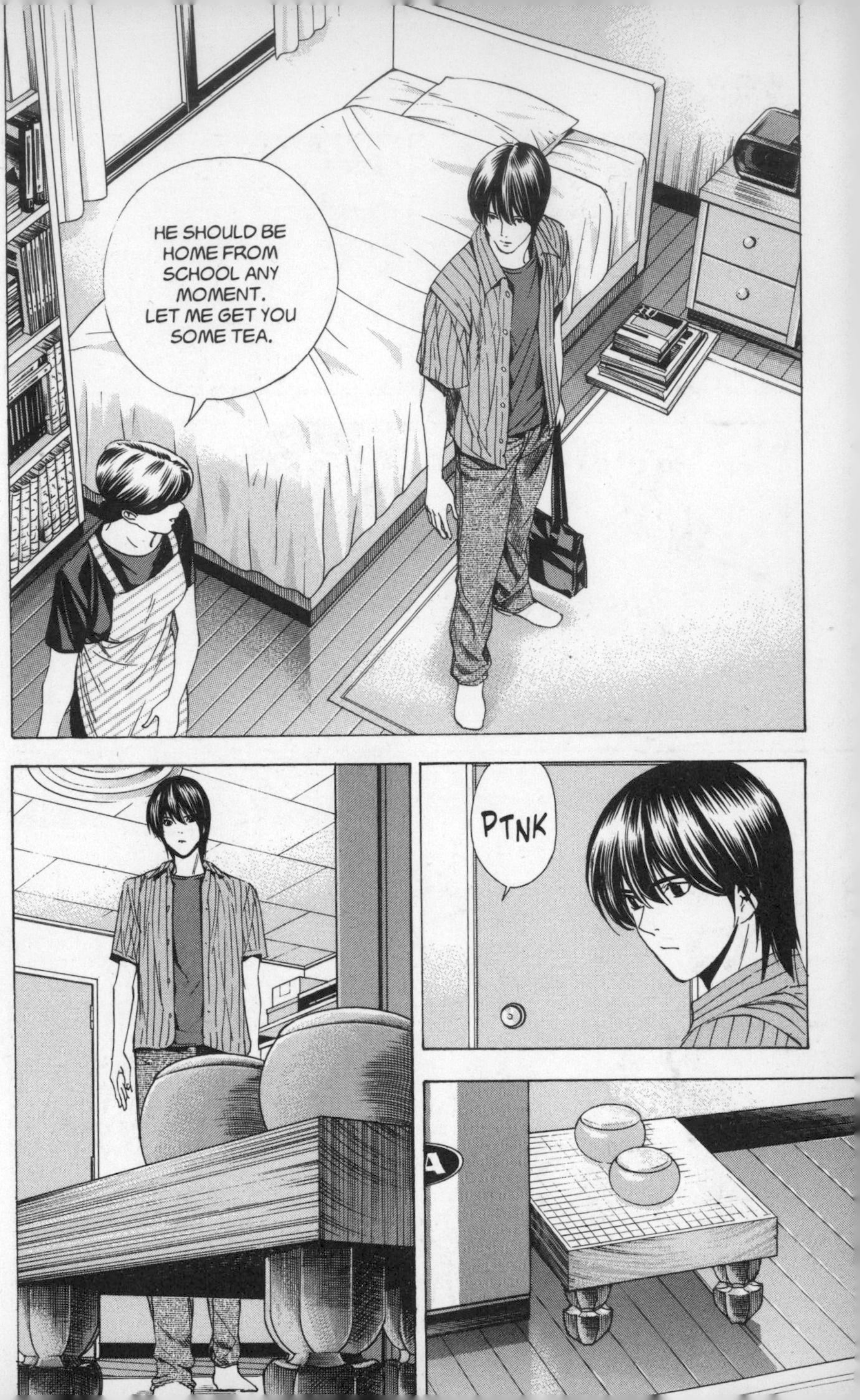
HE SHOULD BE HOME FROM SCHOOL ANY MOMENT. LET ME GET YOU SOME TEA.
PTNK

READ THIS WAY

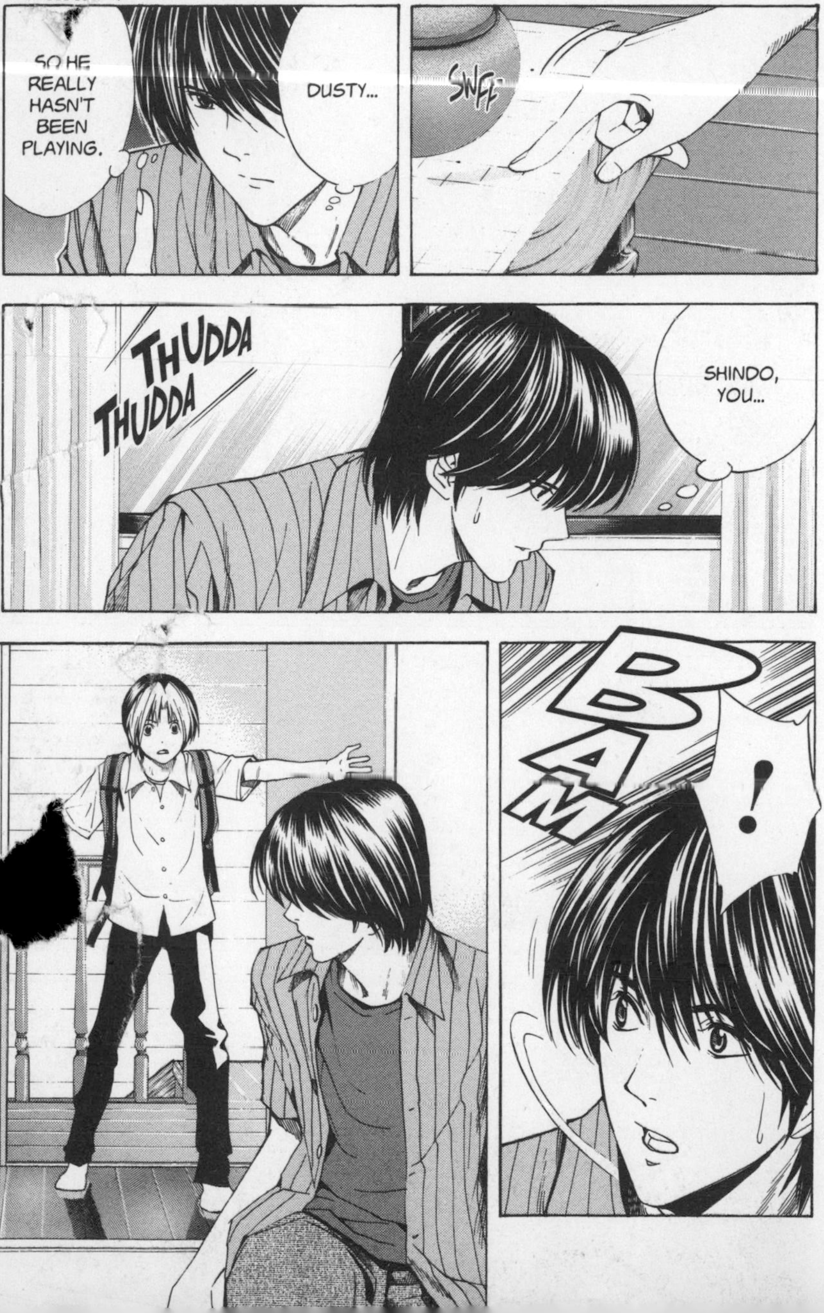
SWFF
DUSTY...
SO HE REALLY HASN'T BEEN PLAYING.
SHINDO, YOU...
THUDDA THUDDA
BAM
!

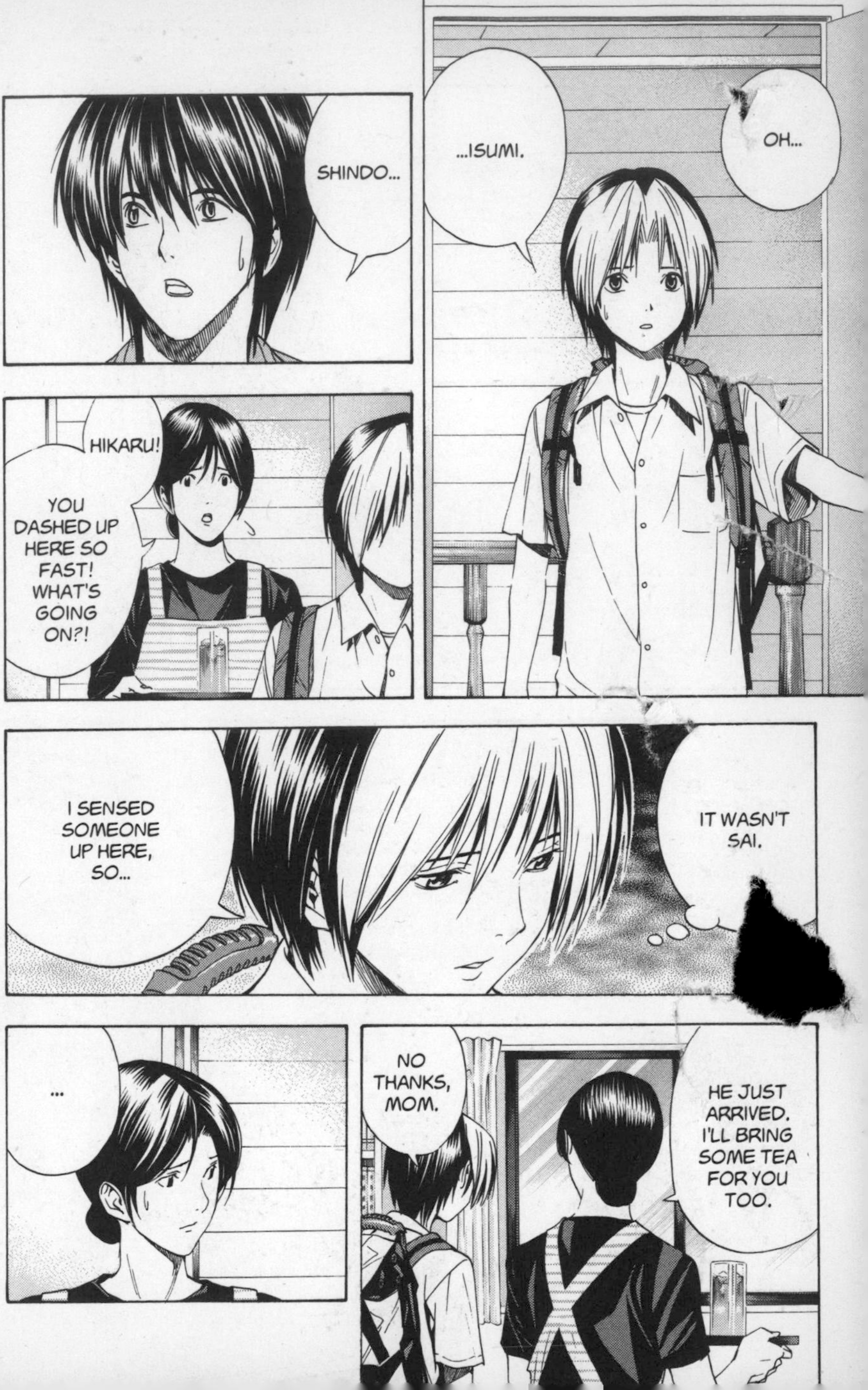
OH...
...ISUMI.
SHINDO...
HIKARU!
YOU DASHED UP HERE SO FAST! WHAT'S GOING ON?!
IT WASN'T SAI.
I SENSED SOMEONE UP HERE, SO...
HE JUST ARRIVED. I'LL BRING SOME TEA FOR YOU TOO.
NO THANKS, MOM.
...

READ THIS WAY

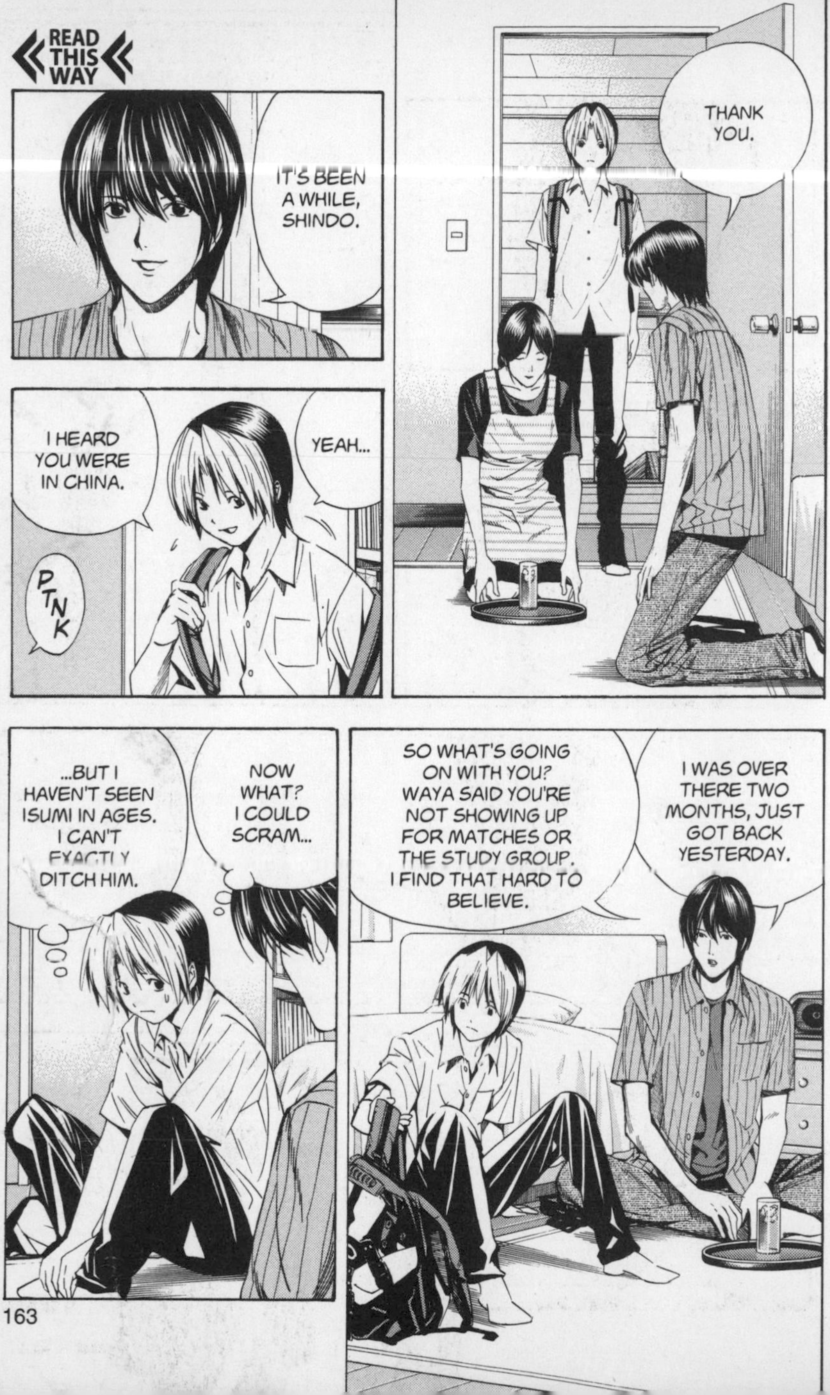
THANK YOU.
IT'S BEEN A WHILE, SHINDO.
YEAH...
I HEARD YOU WERE IN CHINA.
PTNK
I WAS OVER THERE TWO MONTHS, JUST GOT BACK YESTERDAY.
SO WHAT'S GOING ON WITH YOU? WAYA SAID YOU'RE NOT SHOWING UP FOR MATCHES OR THE STUDY GROUP. I FIND THAT HARD TO BELIEVE.
NOW WHAT? I COULD SCRAM...
...BUT I HAVEN'T SEEN ISUMI IN AGES. I CAN'T EXACTLY DITCH HIM.

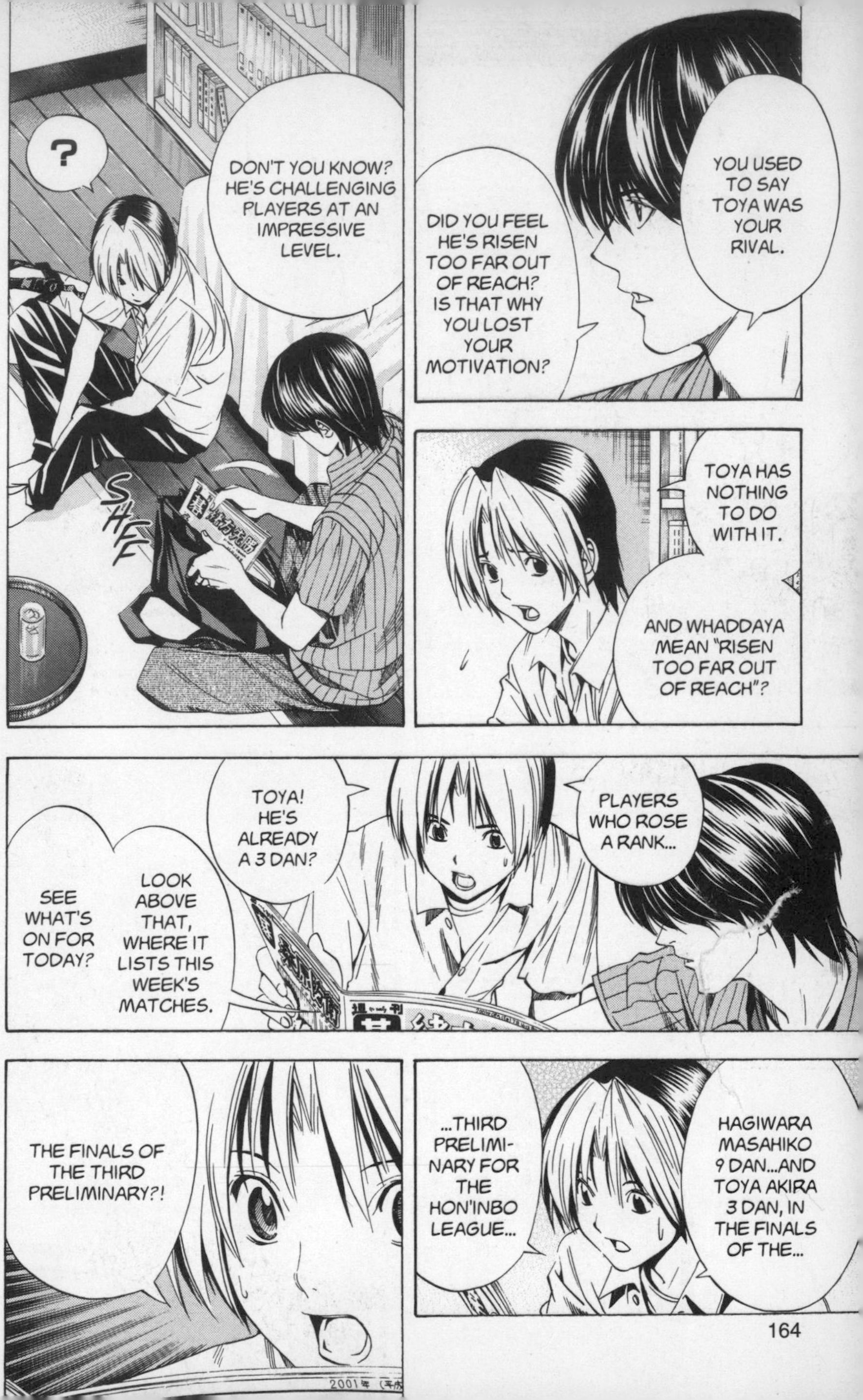
YOU USED TO SAY TOYA WAS YOUR RIVAL.
DID YOU FEEL HE'S RISEN TOO FAR OUT OF REACH? IS THAT WHY YOU LOST YOUR MOTIVATION?
TOYA HAS NOTHING TO DO WITH IT.
AND WHADDAYA MEAN "RISEN TOO FAR OUT OF REACH"?
?
DON'T YOU KNOW? HE'S CHALLENGING PLAYERS AT AN IMPRESSIVE LEVEL.
SHFF
PLAYERS WHO ROSE A RANK...
TOYA! HE'S ALREADY A 3 DAN?
LOOK ABOVE THAT, WHERE IT LISTS THIS WEEK'S MATCHES.
SEE WHAT'S ON FOR TODAY?
HAGIWARA MASAHIKO 9 DAN...AND TOYA AKIRA 3 DAN, IN THE FINALS OF THE...
...THIRD PRELIMINARY FOR THE HON'INBO LEAGUE...
THE FINALS OF THE THIRD PRELIMINARY?!

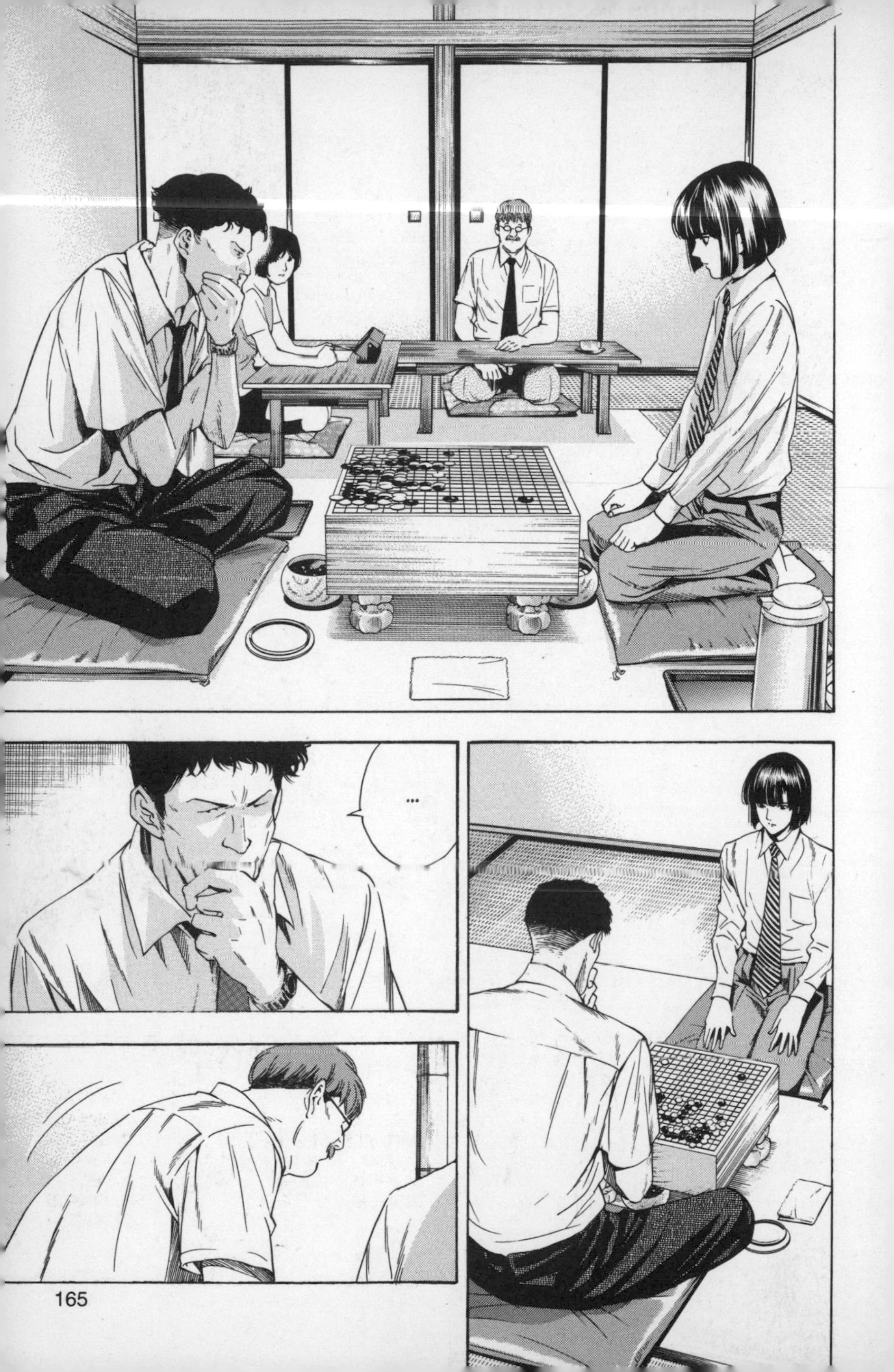
...

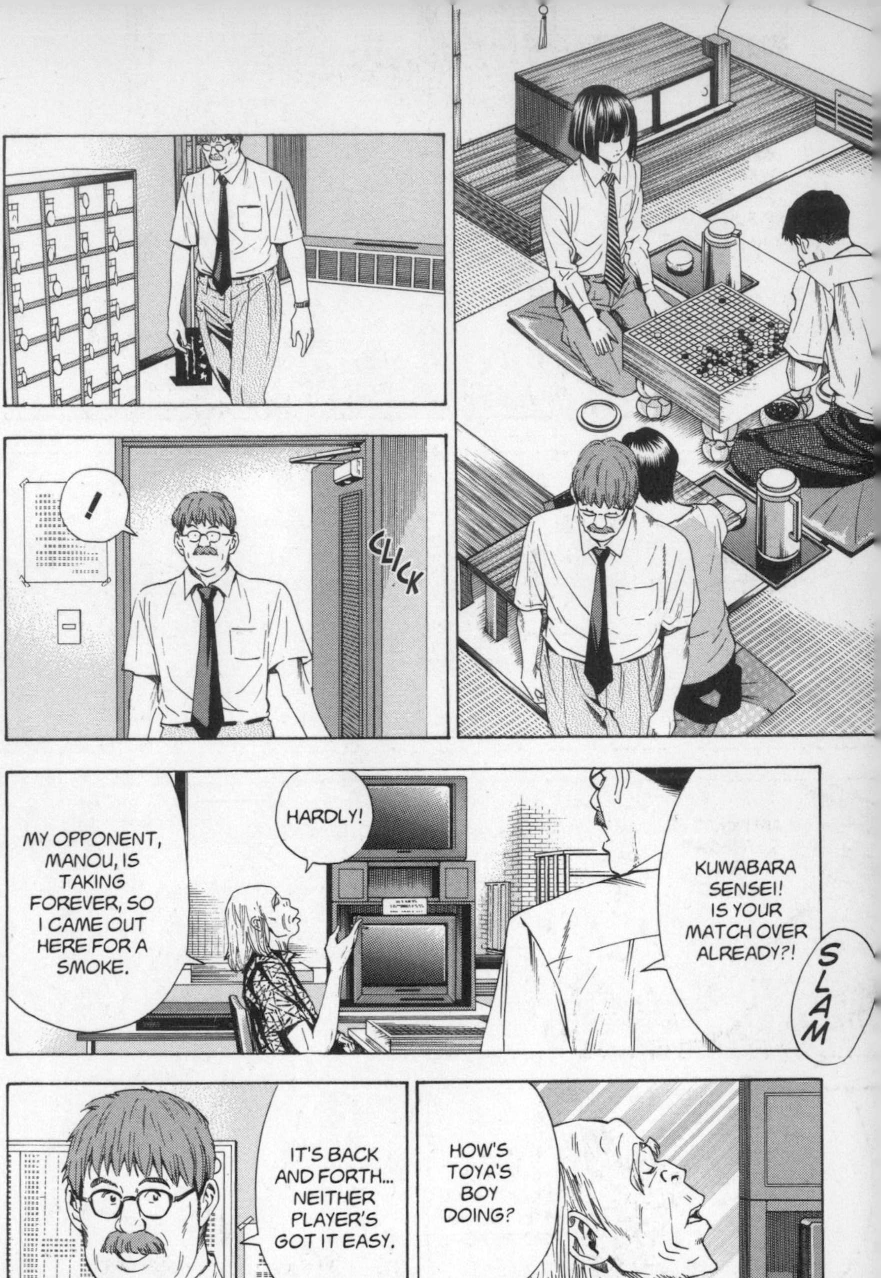
!
CLICK
SLAM
KUWABARA SENSEI! IS YOUR MATCH OVER ALREADY?!
HARDLY!
MY OPPONENT, MANOU, IS TAKING FOREVER, SO I CAME OUT HERE FOR A SMOKE.
HOW'S TOYA'S BOY DOING?
IT'S BACK AND FORTH... NEITHER PLAYER'S GOT IT EASY.

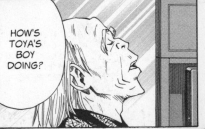

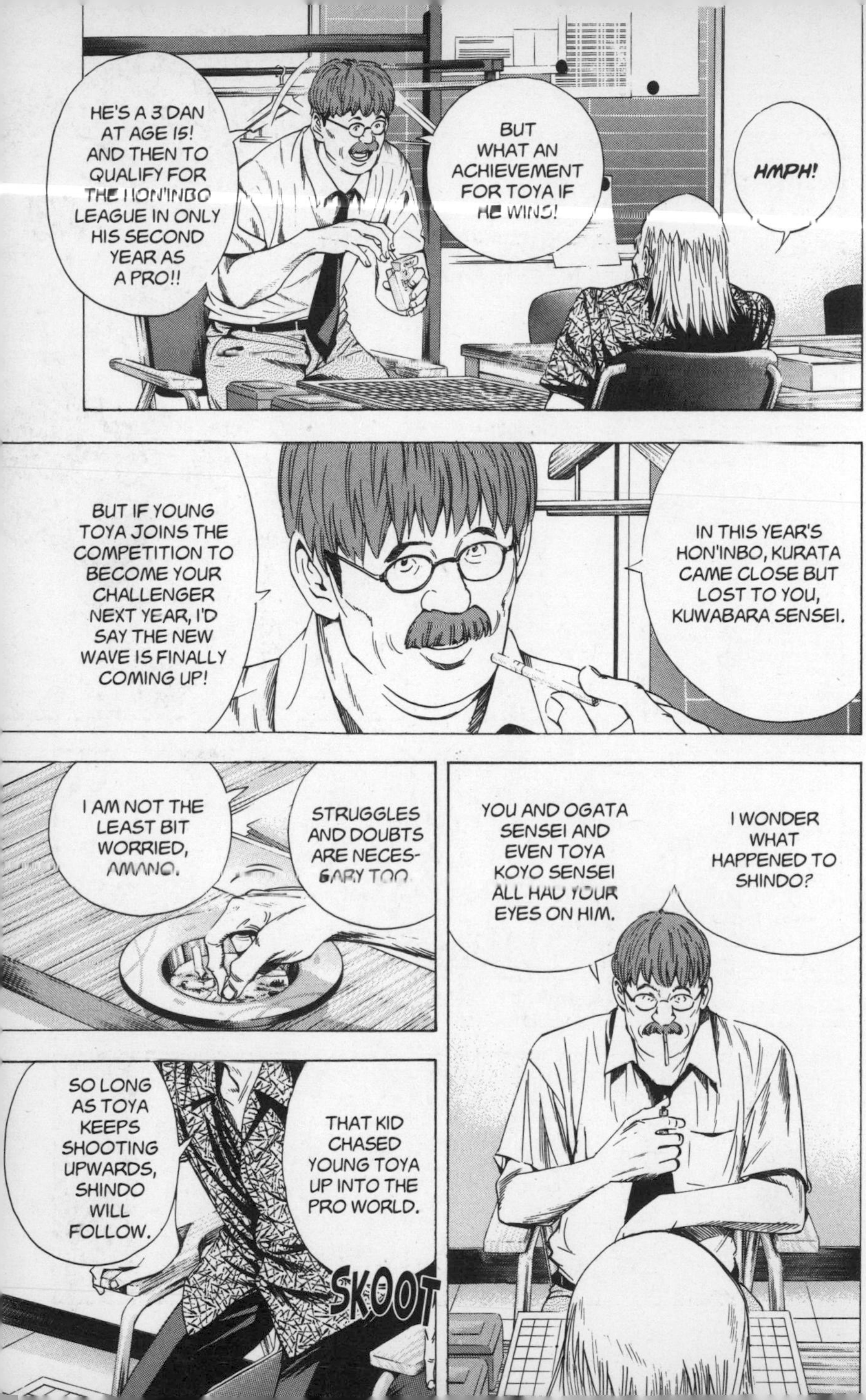
HMPH!
BUT WHAT AN ACHIEVEMENT FOR TOYA IF HE WINS!
HE'S A 3 DAN AT AGE 15! AND THEN TO QUALIFY FOR THE HON'INBO LEAGUE IN ONLY HIS SECOND YEAR AS A PRO!!
IN THIS YEAR'S HON'INBO, KURATA CAME CLOSE BUT LOST TO YOU, KUWABARA SENSEI.
BUT IF YOUNG TOYA JOINS THE COMPETITION TO BECOME YOUR CHALLENGER NEXT YEAR, I'D SAY THE NEW WAVE IS FINALLY COMING UP!
I WONDER WHAT HAPPENED TO SHINDO?
YOU AND OGATA SENSEI AND EVEN TOYA KOYO SENSEI ALL HAD YOUR EYES ON HIM.
STRUGGLES AND DOUBTS ARE NECES-SARY TOO.
I AM NOT THE LEAST BIT WORRIED, AMANO.
THAT KID CHASED YOUNG TOYA UP INTO THE PRO WORLD.
SO LONG AS TOYA KEEPS SHOOTING UPWARDS, SHINDO WILL FOLLOW.
SKOOT

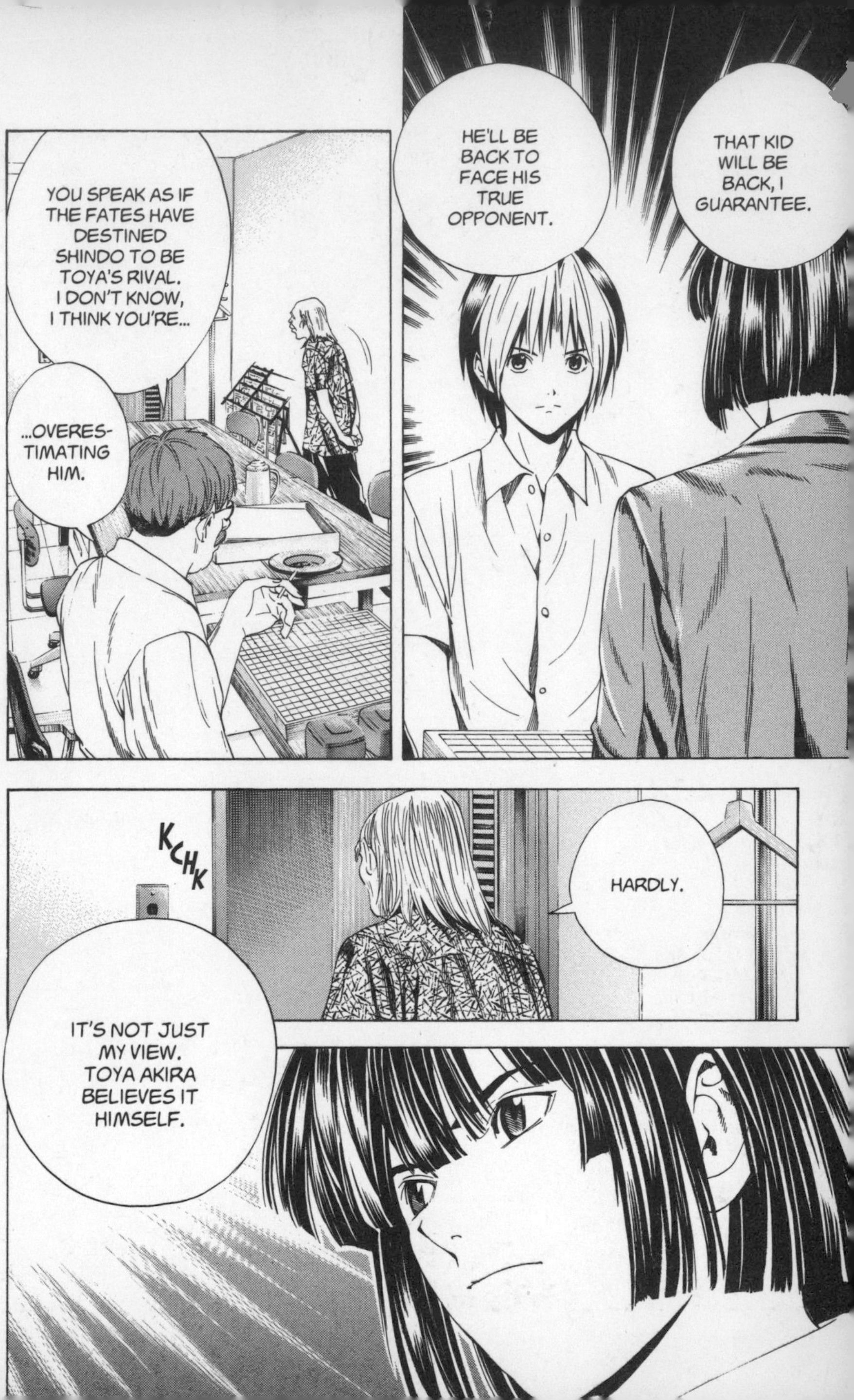
THAT KID WILL BE BACK, I GUARANTEE.
HE'LL BE BACK TO FACE HIS TRUE OPPONENT.
YOU SPEAK AS IF THE FATES HAVE DESTINED SHINDO TO BE TOYA'S RIVAL. I DON'T KNOW, I THINK YOU'RE...
...OVERES-TIMATING HIM.
HARDLY.
KCHK
IT'S NOT JUST MY VIEW. TOYA AKIRA BELIEVES IT HIMSELF.

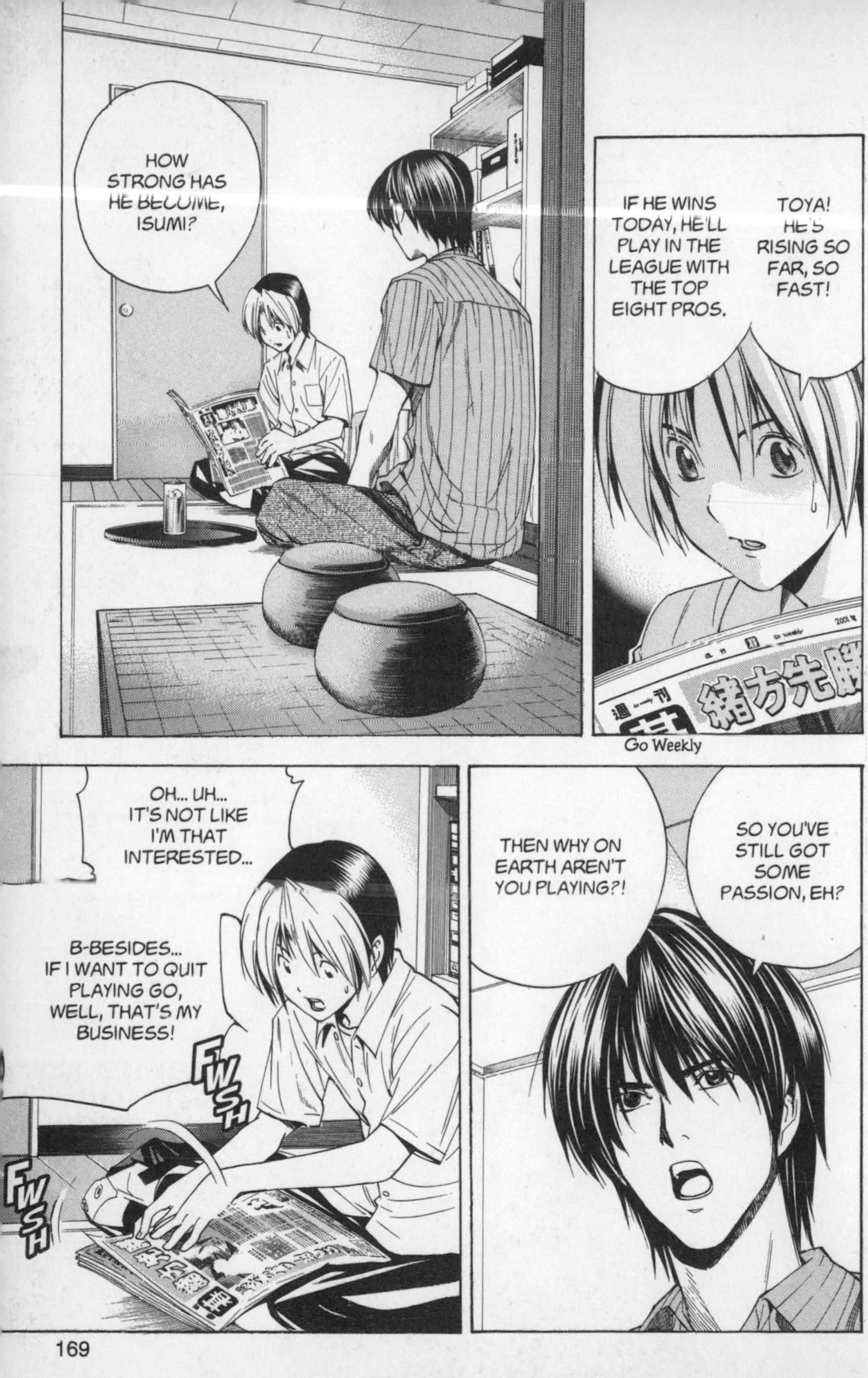
TOYA! HE'S RISING SO FAR, SO FAST!
IF HE WINS TODAY, HE'LL PLAY IN THE LEAGUE WITH THE TOP EIGHT PROS.
Go Weekly
HOW STRONG HAS HE BECOME, ISUMI?
SO YOU'VE STILL GOT SOME PASSION, EH?
THEN WHY ON EARTH AREN'T YOU PLAYING?!
OH... UH... IT'S NOT LIKE I'M THAT INTERESTED...
B-BESIDES... IF I WANT TO QUIT PLAYING GO, WELL, THAT'S MY BUSINESS!
FWSH
FWSH

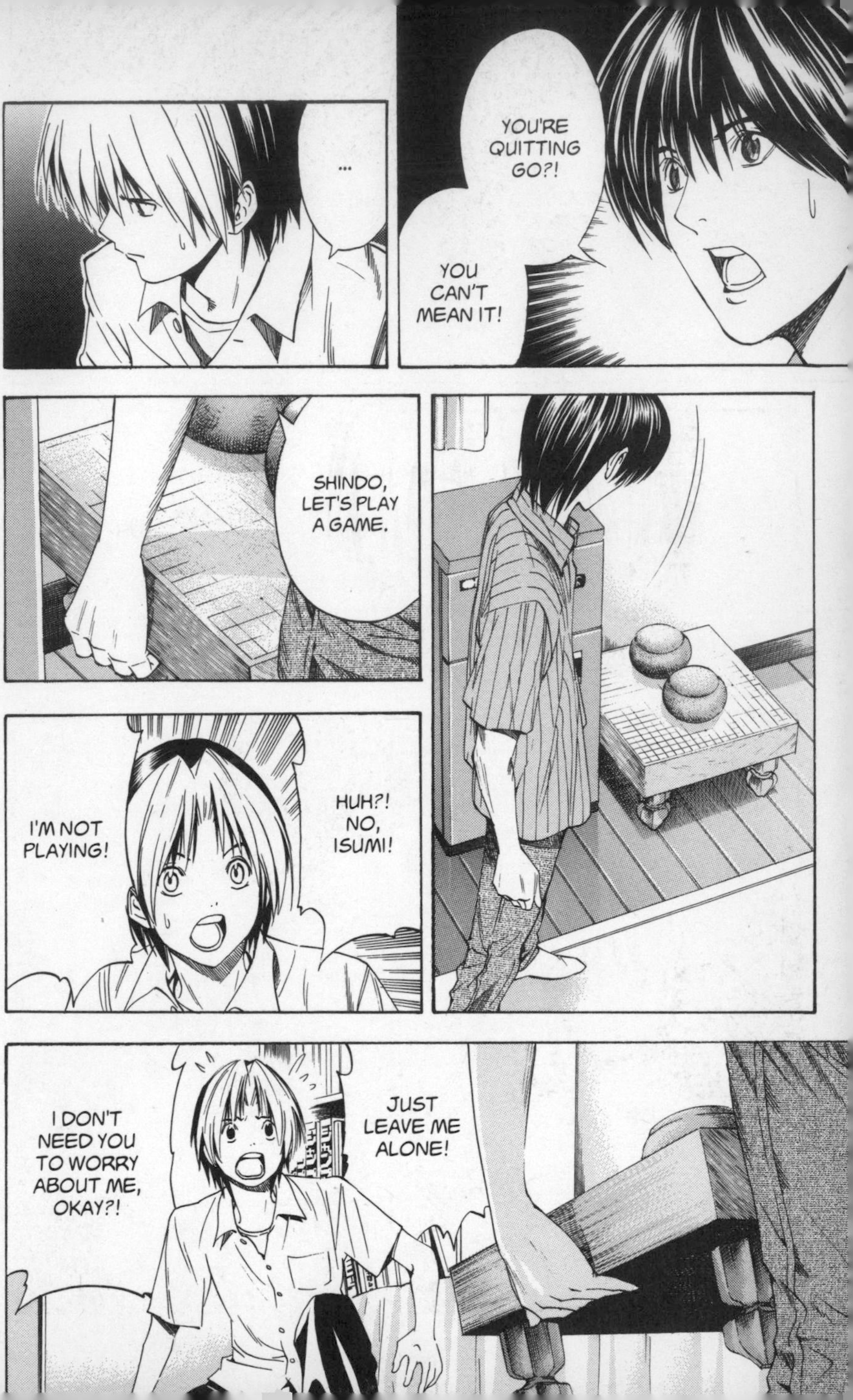
YOU'RE QUITTING GO?!
YOU CAN'T MEAN IT!
...
SHINDO, LET'S PLAY A GAME.
HUH?! NO, ISUMI!
I'M NOT PLAYING!
JUST LEAVE ME ALONE!
I DON'T NEED YOU TO WORRY ABOUT ME, OKAY?!

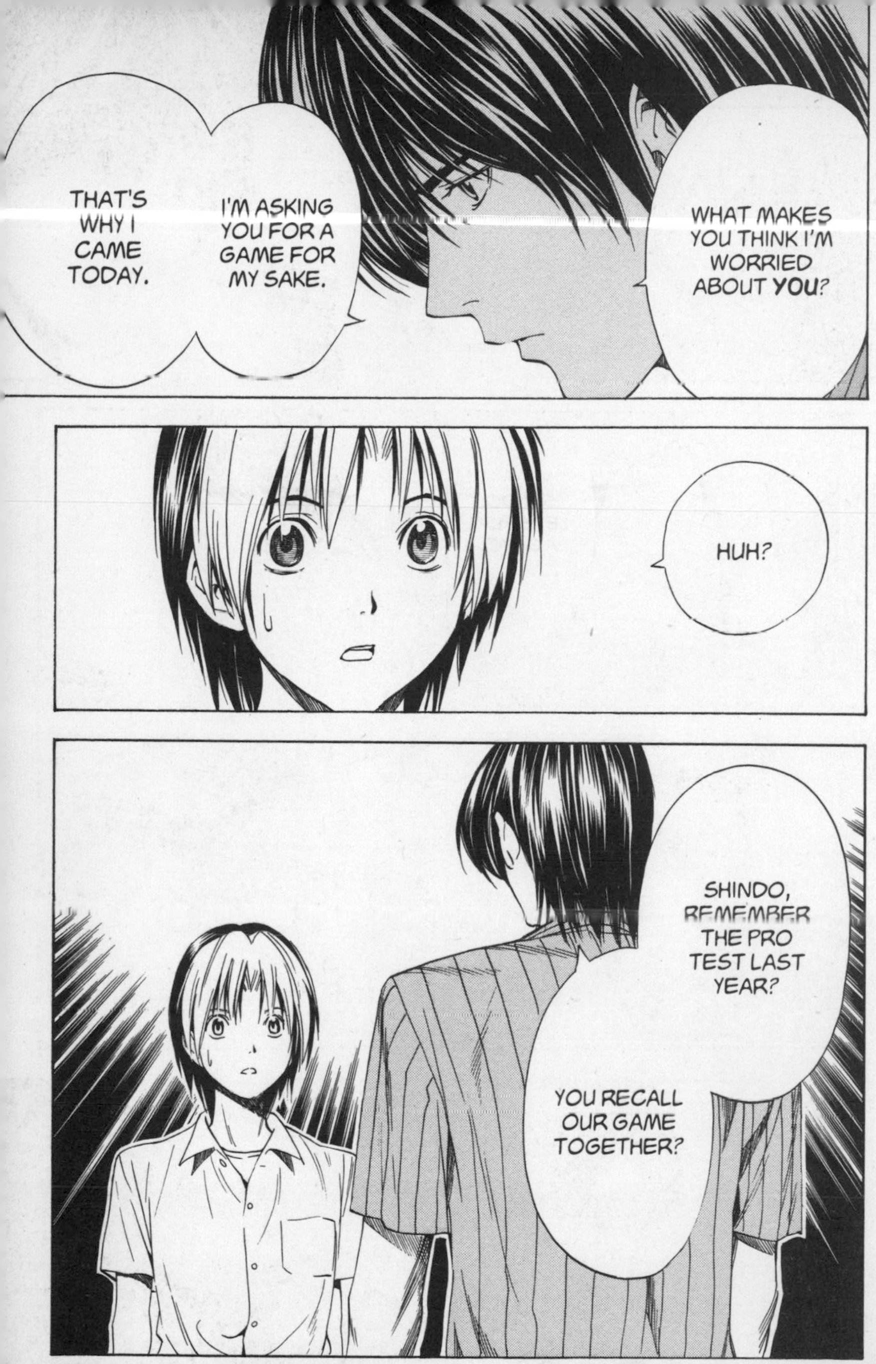
WHAT MAKES YOU THINK I'M WORRIED ABOUT **YOU**?
I'M ASKING YOU FOR A GAME FOR MY SAKE.
THAT'S WHY I CAME TODAY.
HUH?
SHINDO, REMEMBER THE PRO TEST LAST YEAR?
YOU RECALL OUR GAME TOGETHER?

A WORD ABOUT HIKARU NO GO

CHINESE GO STONES

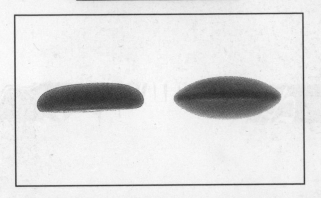

THE GO STONE ON THE RIGHT IS A JAPANESE STONE AS SEEN FROM THE SIDE. IT IS ROUNDED BOTH ON THE TOP AND BOTTOM.

TO THE LEFT IS A CHINESE GO STONE.
ONE SIDE IS FLAT. THE CLACK OF THE STONE HITTING THE BOARD IS DIFFERENT THAN WITH JAPANESE STONES.

AND WHILE I'M ON THE TOPIC, KOREAN STONES ARE THE SAME AS JAPANESE STONES.

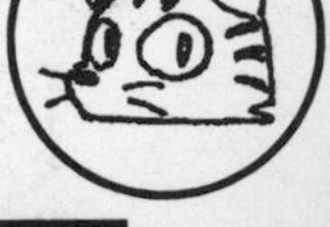

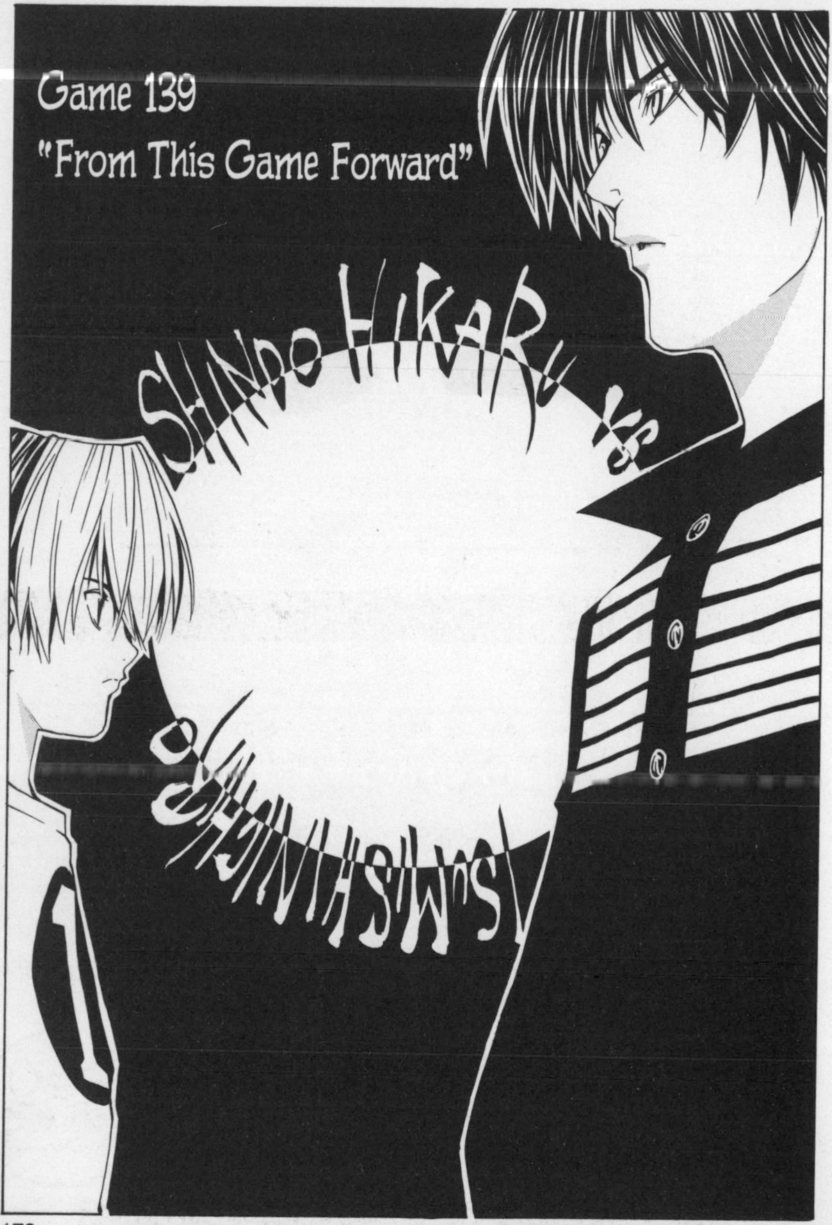
Game 139
"From This Game Forward"
SHINDO HIKARU VS
ISUMI SHINICHIRO

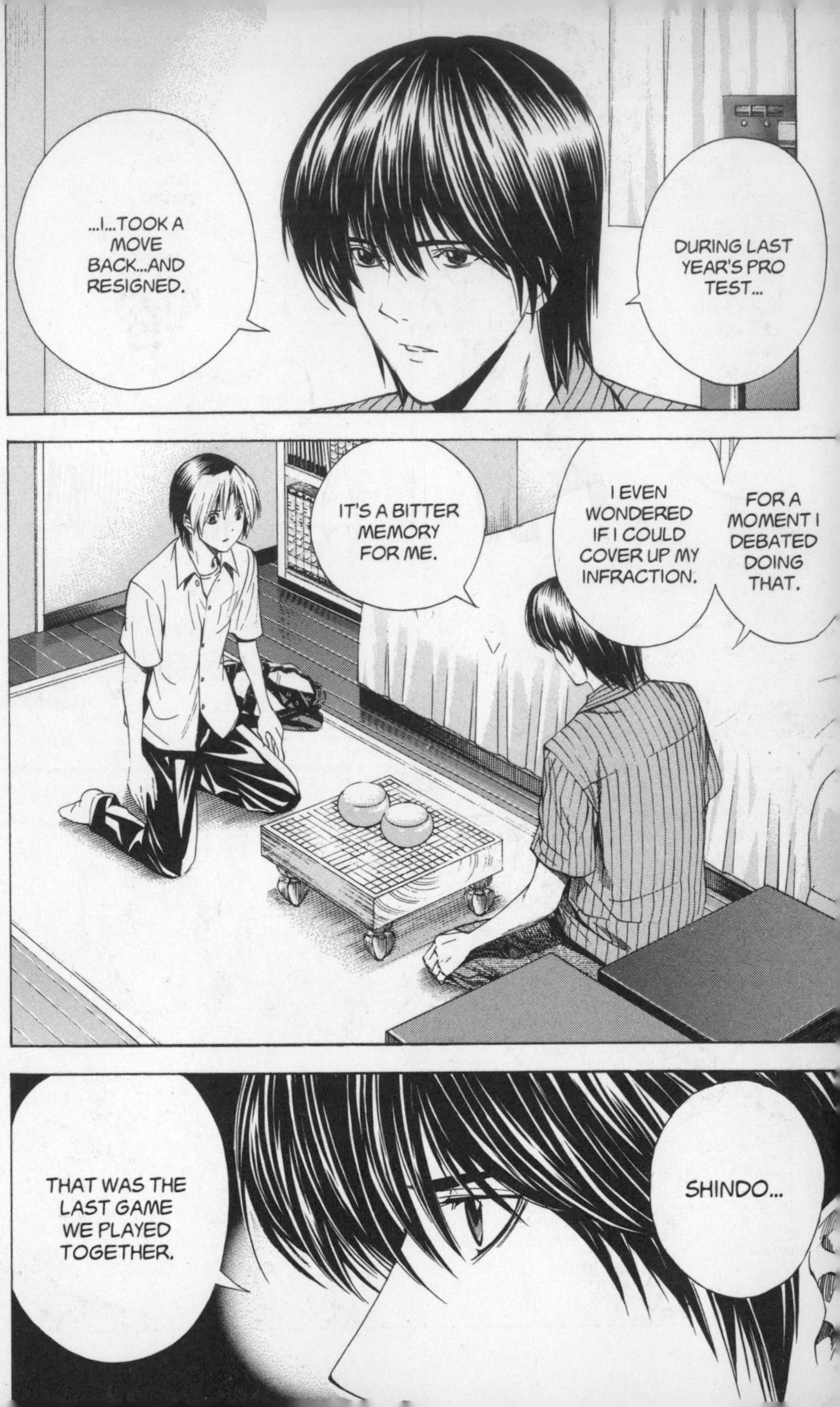
DURING LAST YEAR'S PRO TEST...
...I...TOOK A MOVE BACK...AND RESIGNED.
FOR A MOMENT I DEBATED DOING THAT.
I EVEN WONDERED IF I COULD COVER UP MY INFRACTION.
IT'S A BITTER MEMORY FOR ME.
SHINDO...
THAT WAS THE LAST GAME WE PLAYED TOGETHER.

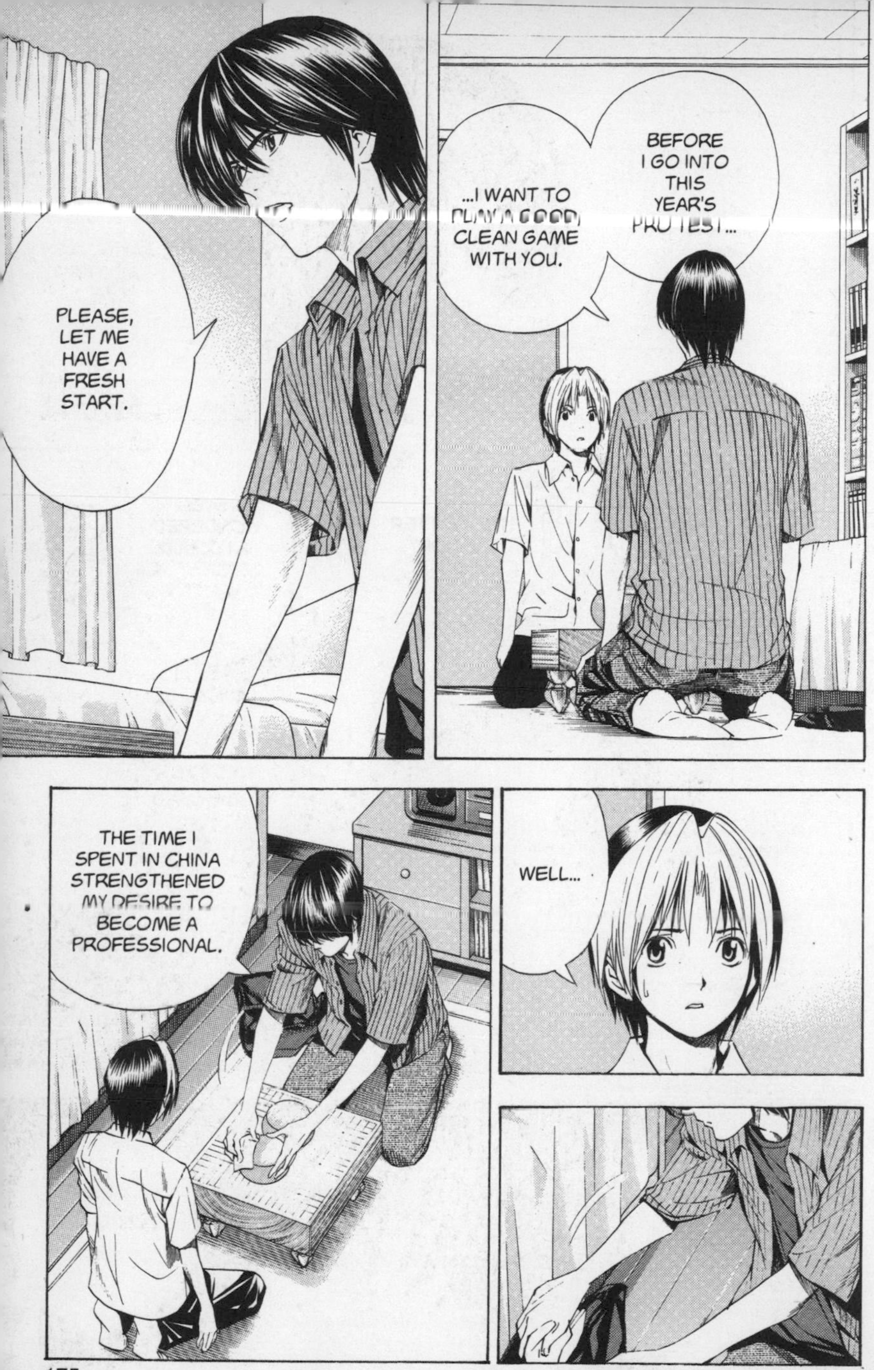
BEFORE I GO INTO THIS YEAR'S PRO TEST...
...I WANT TO PLAY A GOOD, CLEAN GAME WITH YOU.
PLEASE, LET ME HAVE A FRESH START.
WELL...
THE TIME I SPENT IN CHINA STRENGTHENED MY DESIRE TO BECOME A PROFESSIONAL.

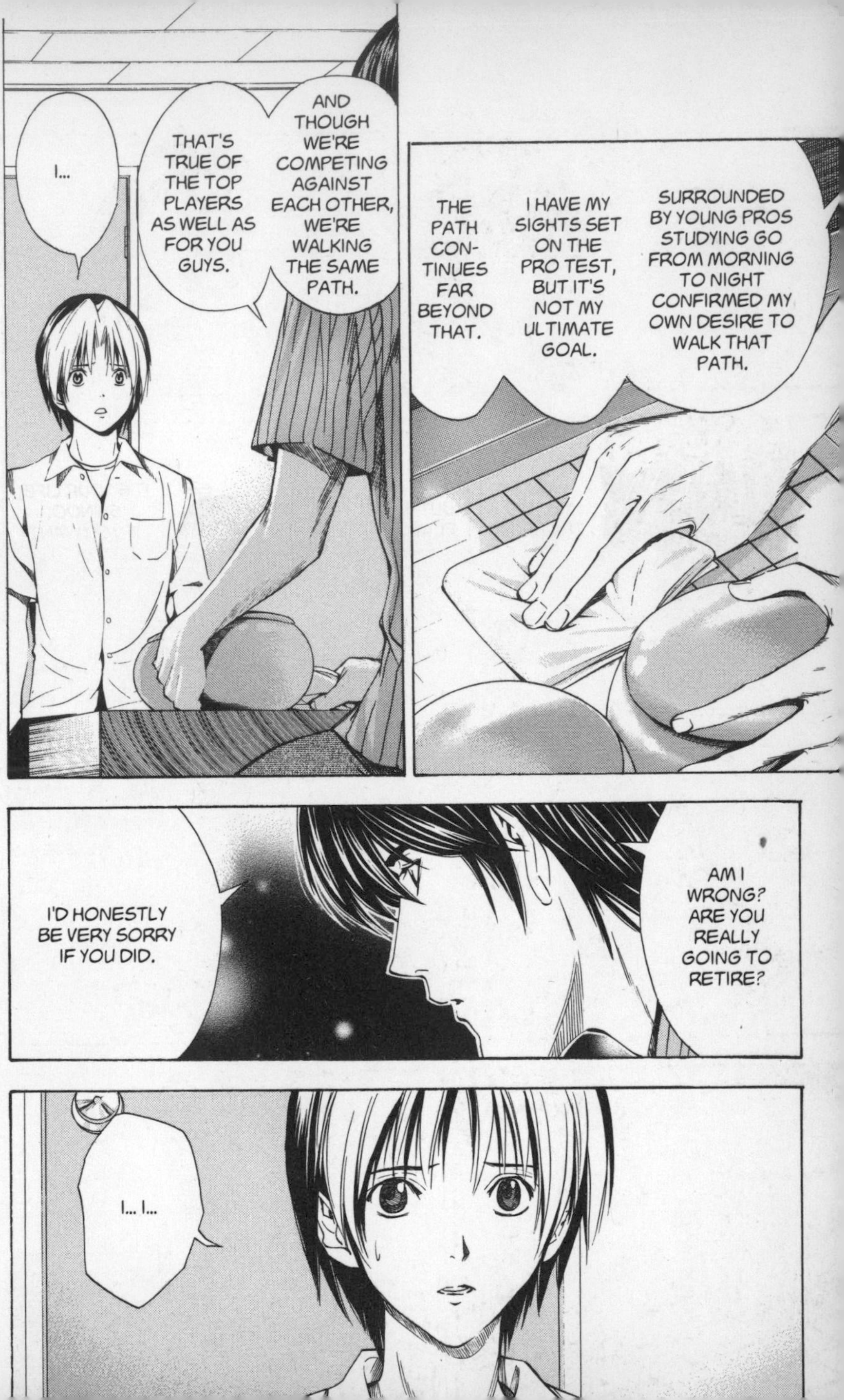
SURROUNDED BY YOUNG PROS STUDYING GO FROM MORNING TO NIGHT CONFIRMED MY OWN DESIRE TO WALK THAT PATH.
I HAVE MY SIGHTS SET ON THE PRO TEST, BUT IT'S NOT MY ULTIMATE GOAL.
THE PATH CON-TINUES FAR BEYOND THAT.
THAT'S TRUE OF THE TOP PLAYERS AS WELL AS FOR YOU GUYS.
AND THOUGH WE'RE COMPETING AGAINST EACH OTHER, WE'RE WALKING THE SAME PATH.
I...
AM I WRONG? ARE YOU REALLY GOING TO RETIRE?
I'D HONESTLY BE VERY SORRY IF YOU DID.
I... I...

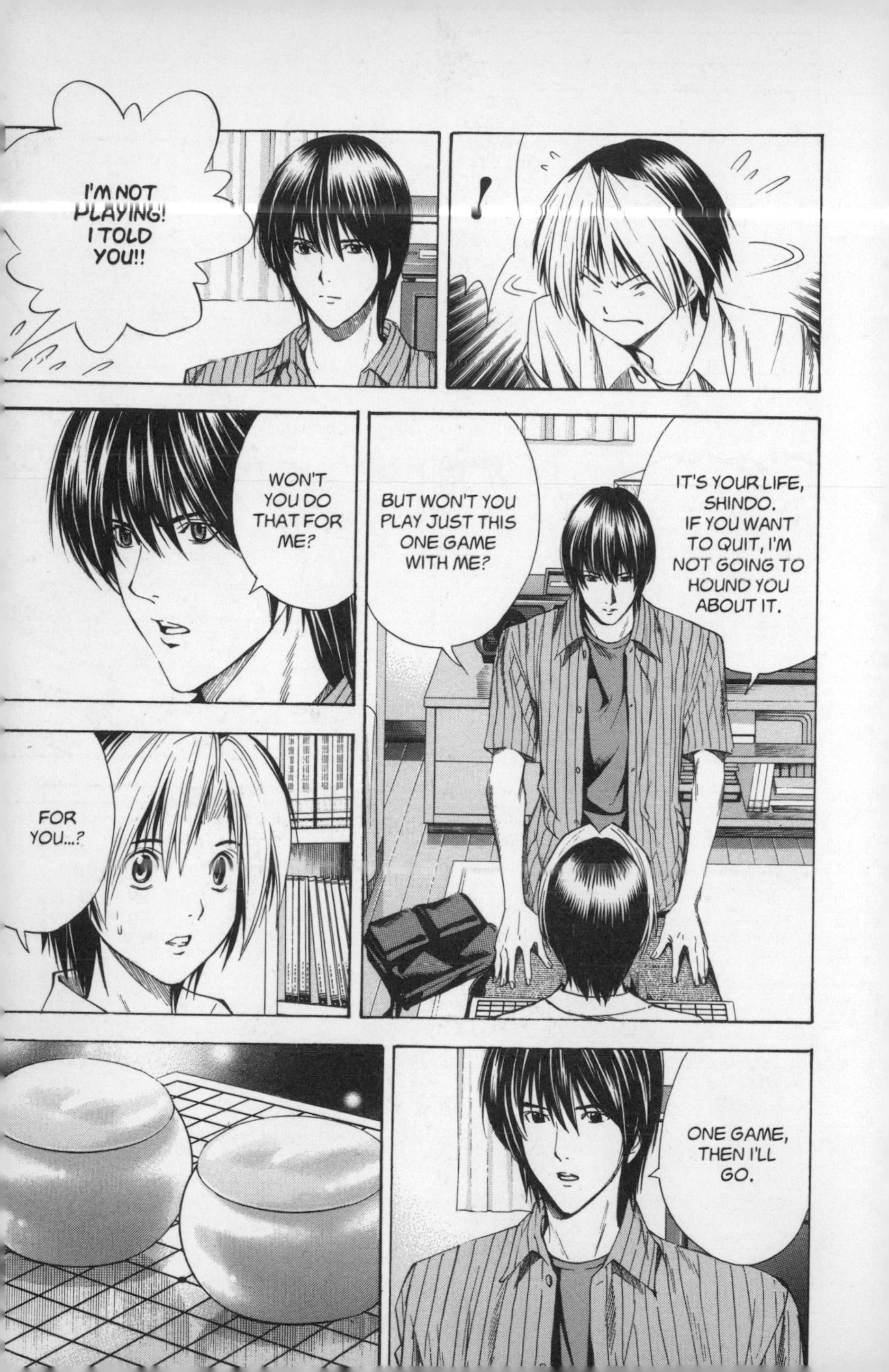
!
I'M NOT PLAYING! I TOLD YOU!!
IT'S YOUR LIFE, SHINDO. IF YOU WANT TO QUIT, I'M NOT GOING TO HOUND YOU ABOUT IT.
BUT WON'T YOU PLAY JUST THIS ONE GAME WITH ME?
WON'T YOU DO THAT FOR ME?
FOR YOU...?
ONE GAME, THEN I'LL GO.

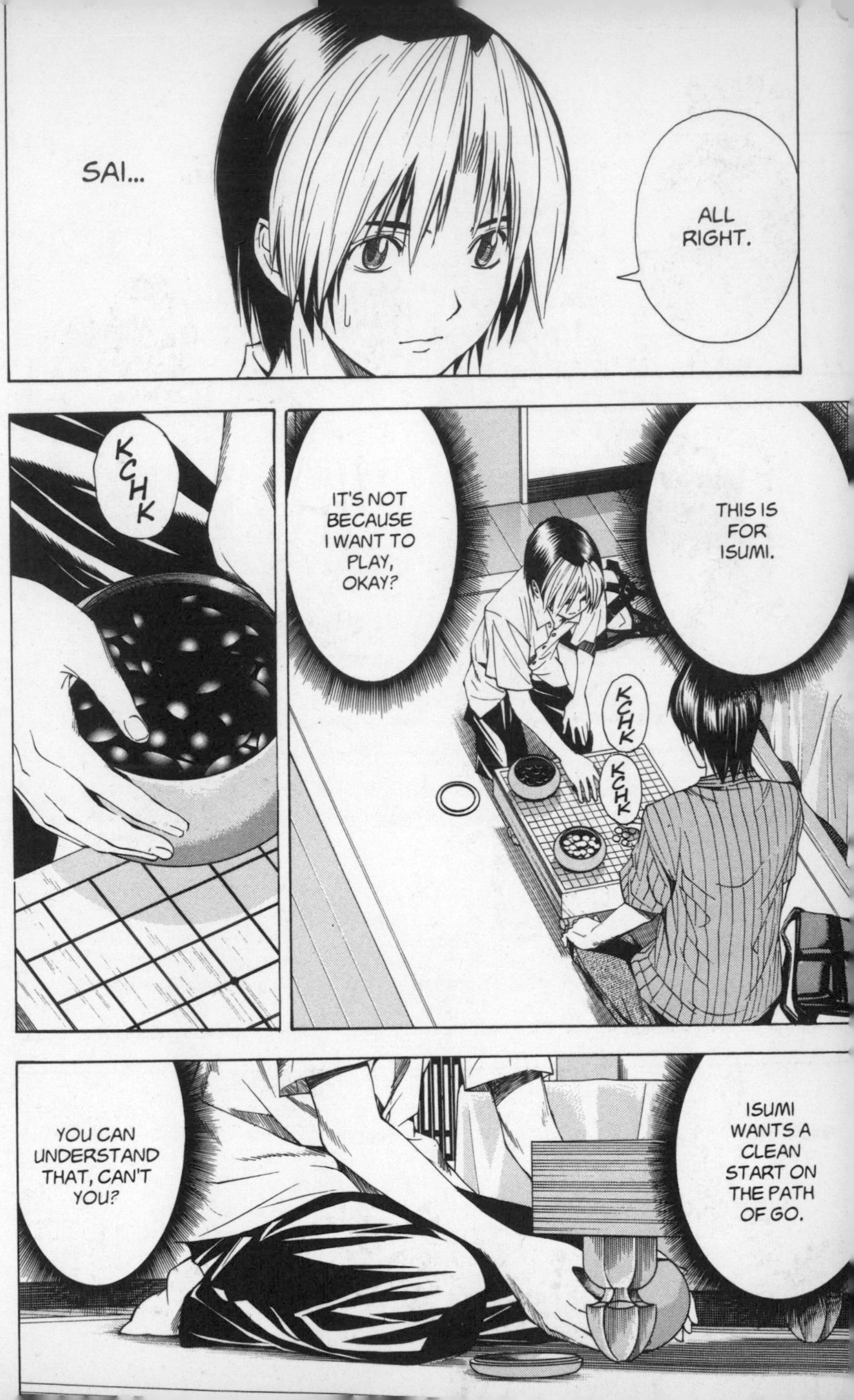
ALL RIGHT.
SAI...
THIS IS FOR ISUMI.
IT'S NOT BECAUSE I WANT TO PLAY, OKAY?
KCHK
KCHK
KCHK
ISUMI WANTS A CLEAN START ON THE PATH OF GO.
YOU CAN UNDERSTAND THAT, CAN'T YOU?

READ THIS WAY

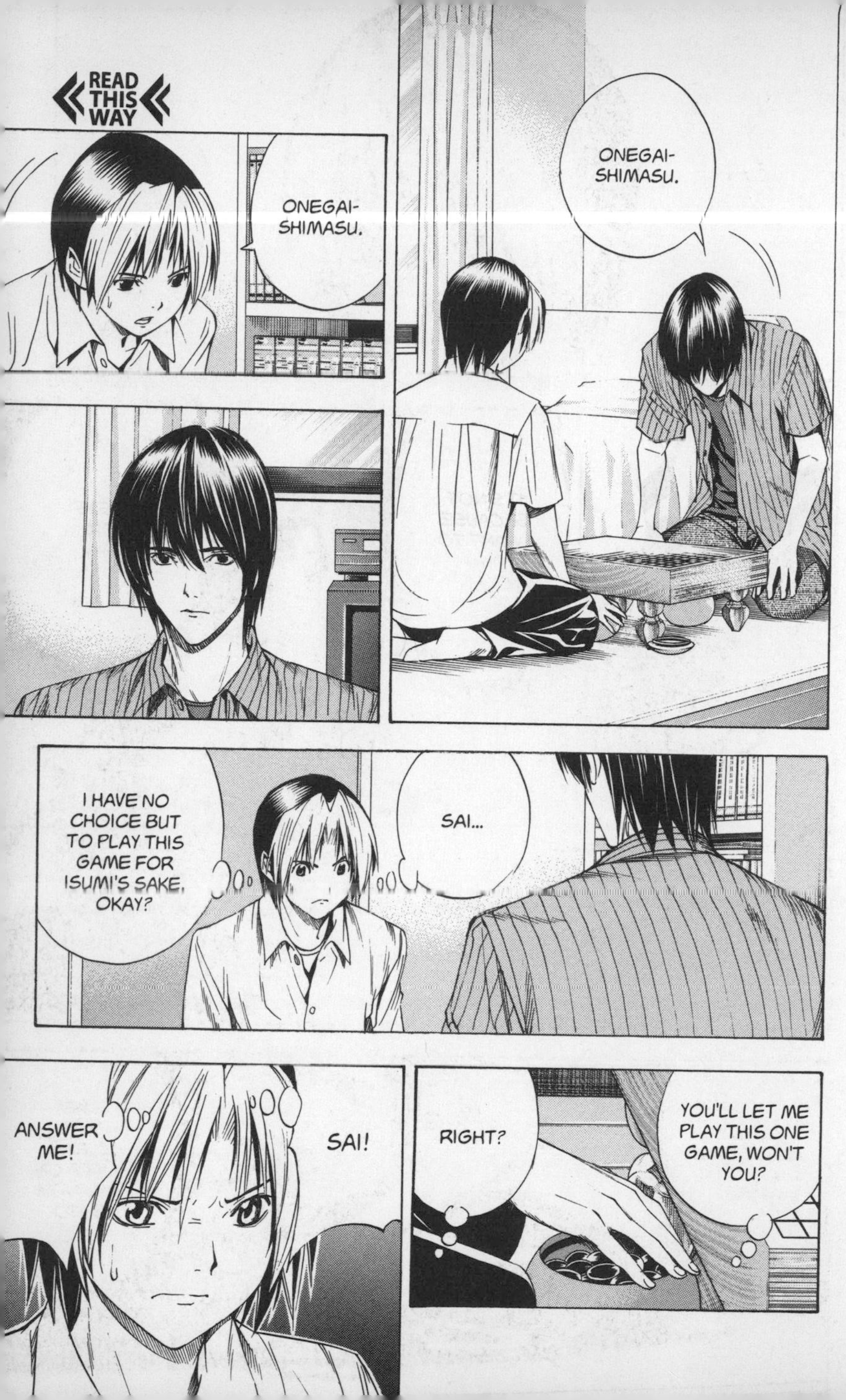

ONEGAI-SHIMASU.
ONEGAI-SHIMASU.
SAI...
I HAVE NO CHOICE BUT TO PLAY THIS GAME FOR ISUMI'S SAKE, OKAY?
YOU'LL LET ME PLAY THIS ONE GAME, WON'T YOU?
RIGHT?
SAI!
ANSWER ME!

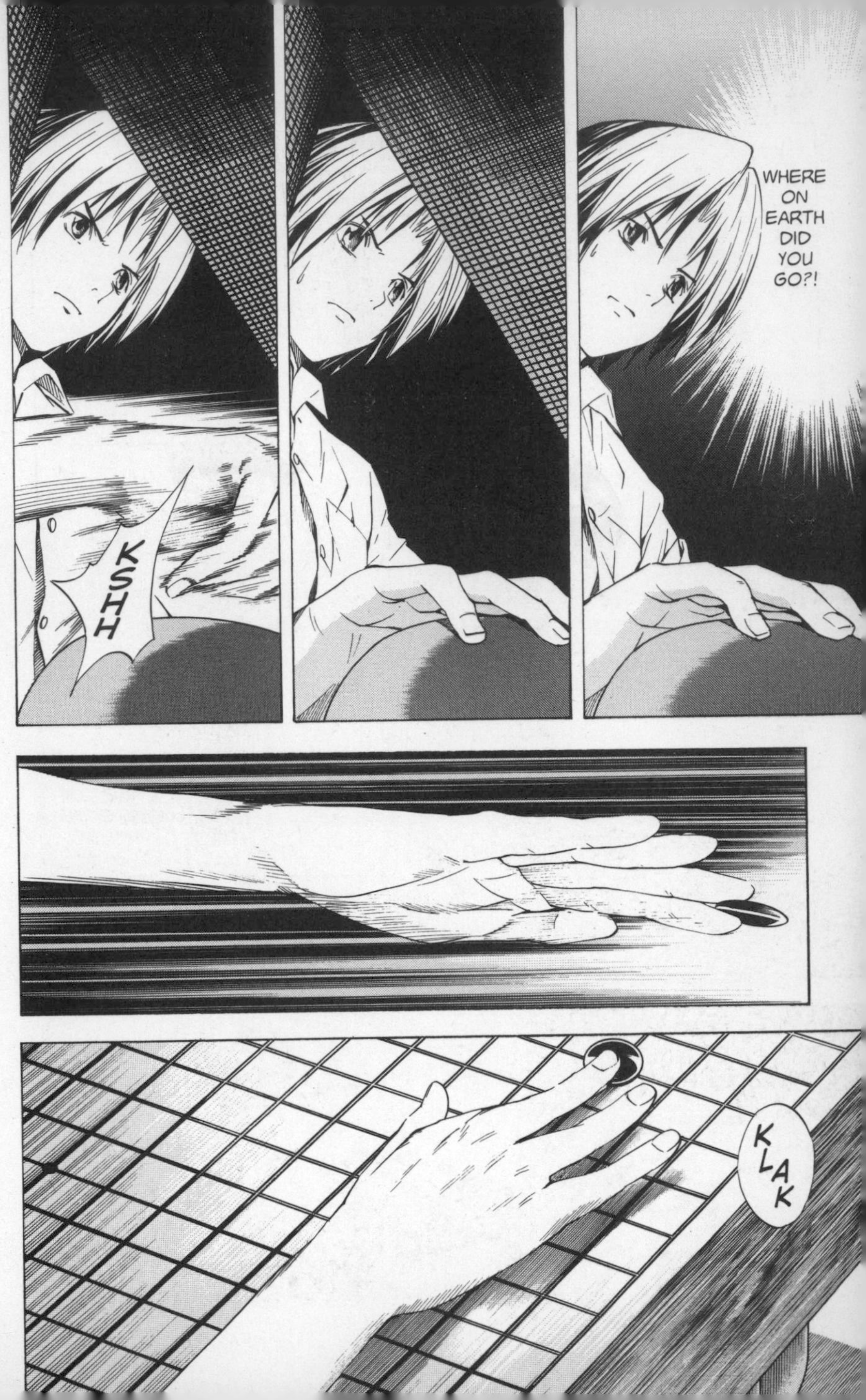
WHERE ON EARTH DID YOU GO?!
KSHH
KLAK

READ THIS WAY

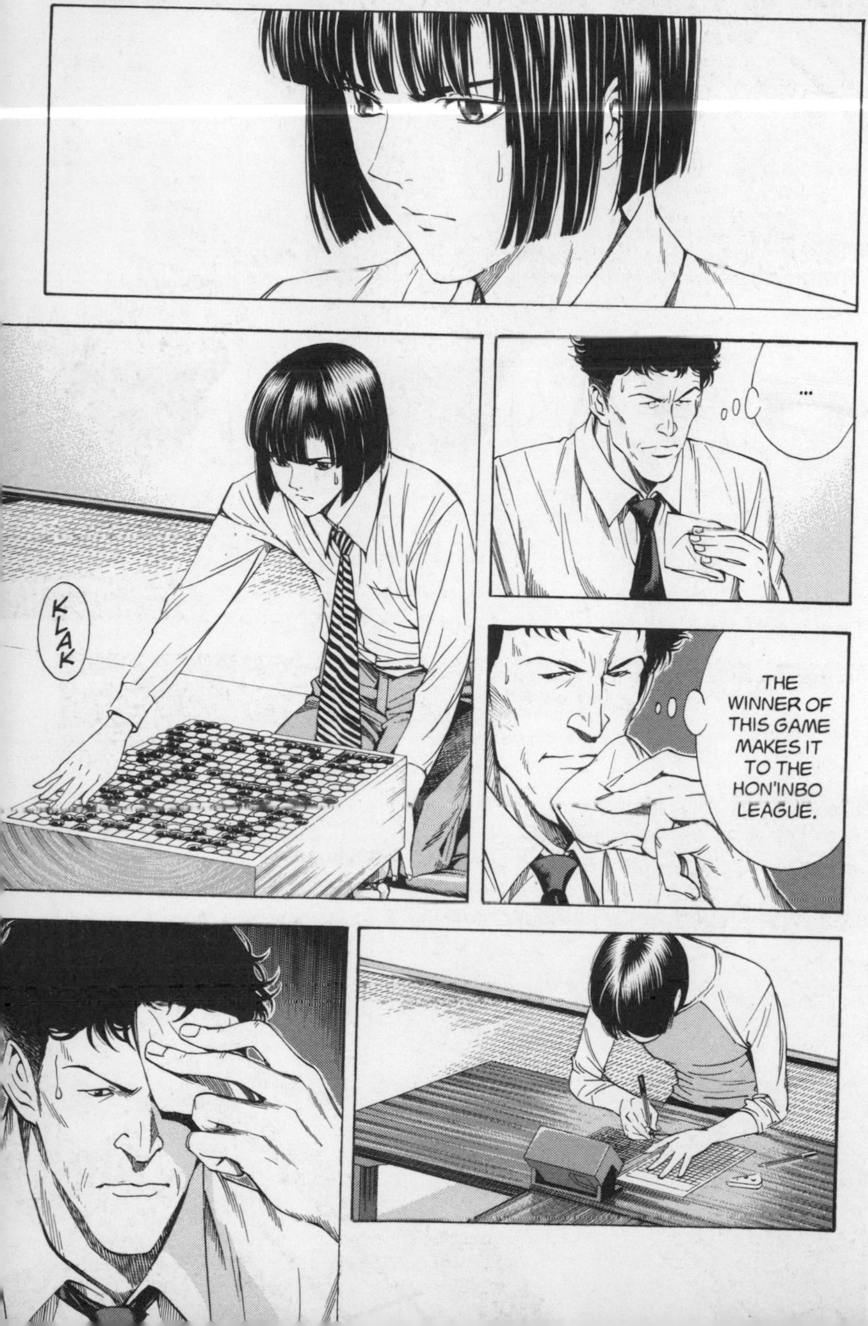
...
THE WINNER OF THIS GAME MAKES IT TO THE HON'INBO LEAGUE.
KLAK

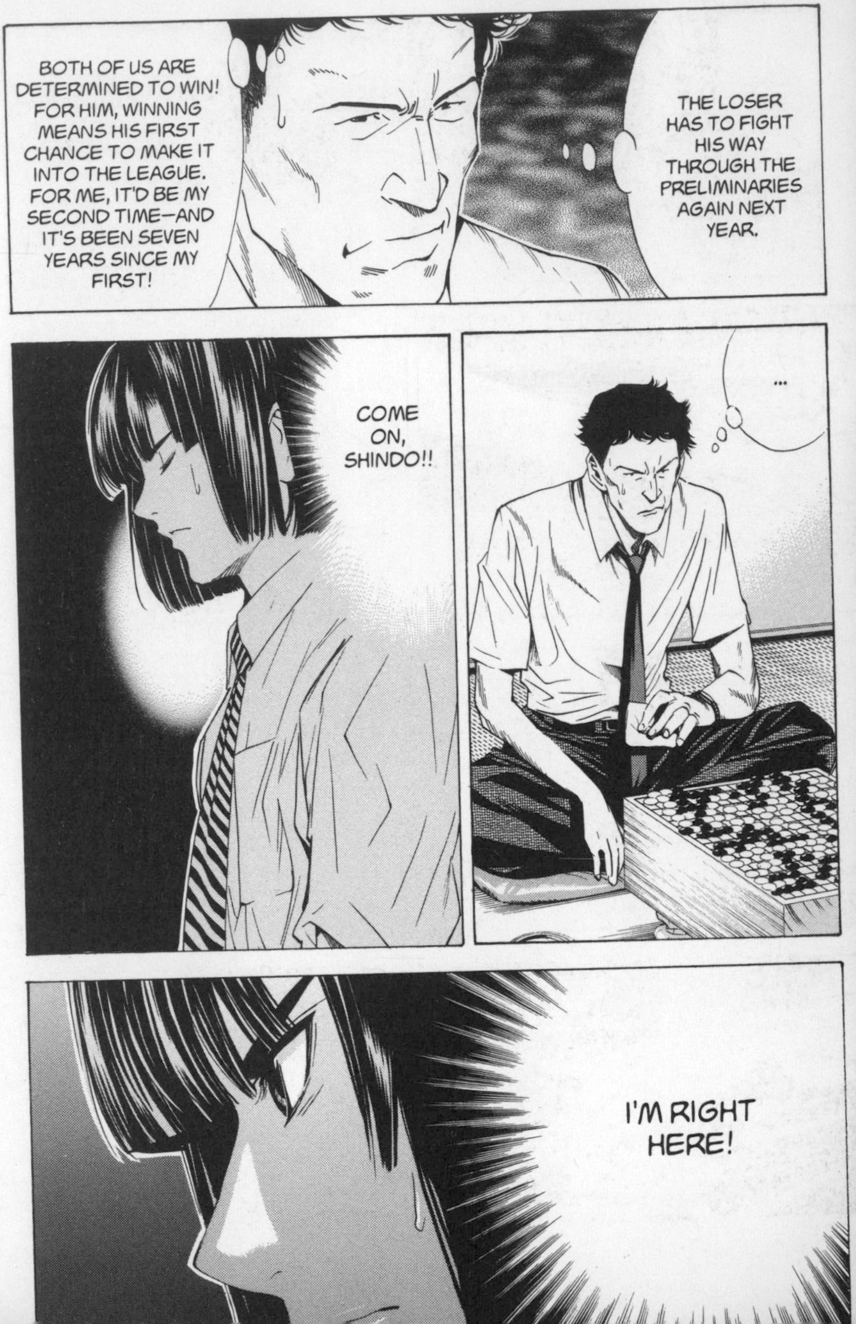
THE LOSER HAS TO FIGHT HIS WAY THROUGH THE PRELIMINARIES AGAIN NEXT YEAR.
BOTH OF US ARE DETERMINED TO WIN! FOR HIM, WINNING MEANS HIS FIRST CHANCE TO MAKE IT INTO THE LEAGUE. FOR ME, IT'D BE MY SECOND TIME—AND IT'S BEEN SEVEN YEARS SINCE MY FIRST!
...
COME ON, SHINDO!!
I'M RIGHT HERE!

...

KLAK

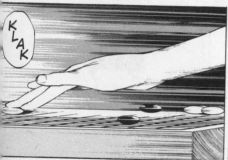

KLAK

I MUSTN'T GET EXCITED!

WATCH IT...

KLAK

BUT...

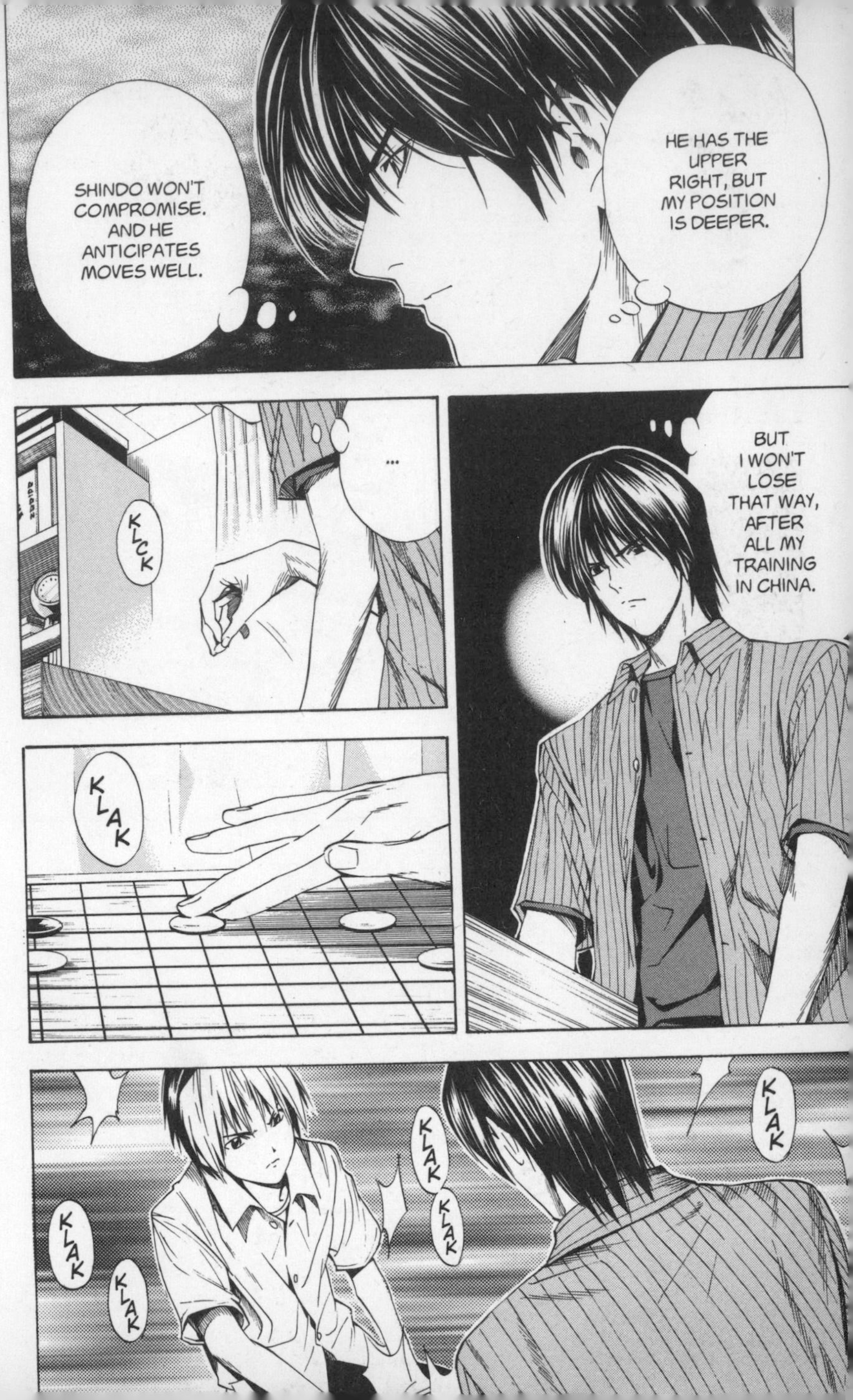
HE HAS THE UPPER RIGHT, BUT MY POSITION IS DEEPER.
SHINDO WON'T COMPROMISE. AND HE ANTICIPATES MOVES WELL.
BUT I WON'T LOSE THAT WAY, AFTER ALL MY TRAINING IN CHINA.
...
KLCK
KLAK
KLAK
KLAK
KLAK
KLAK
KLAK

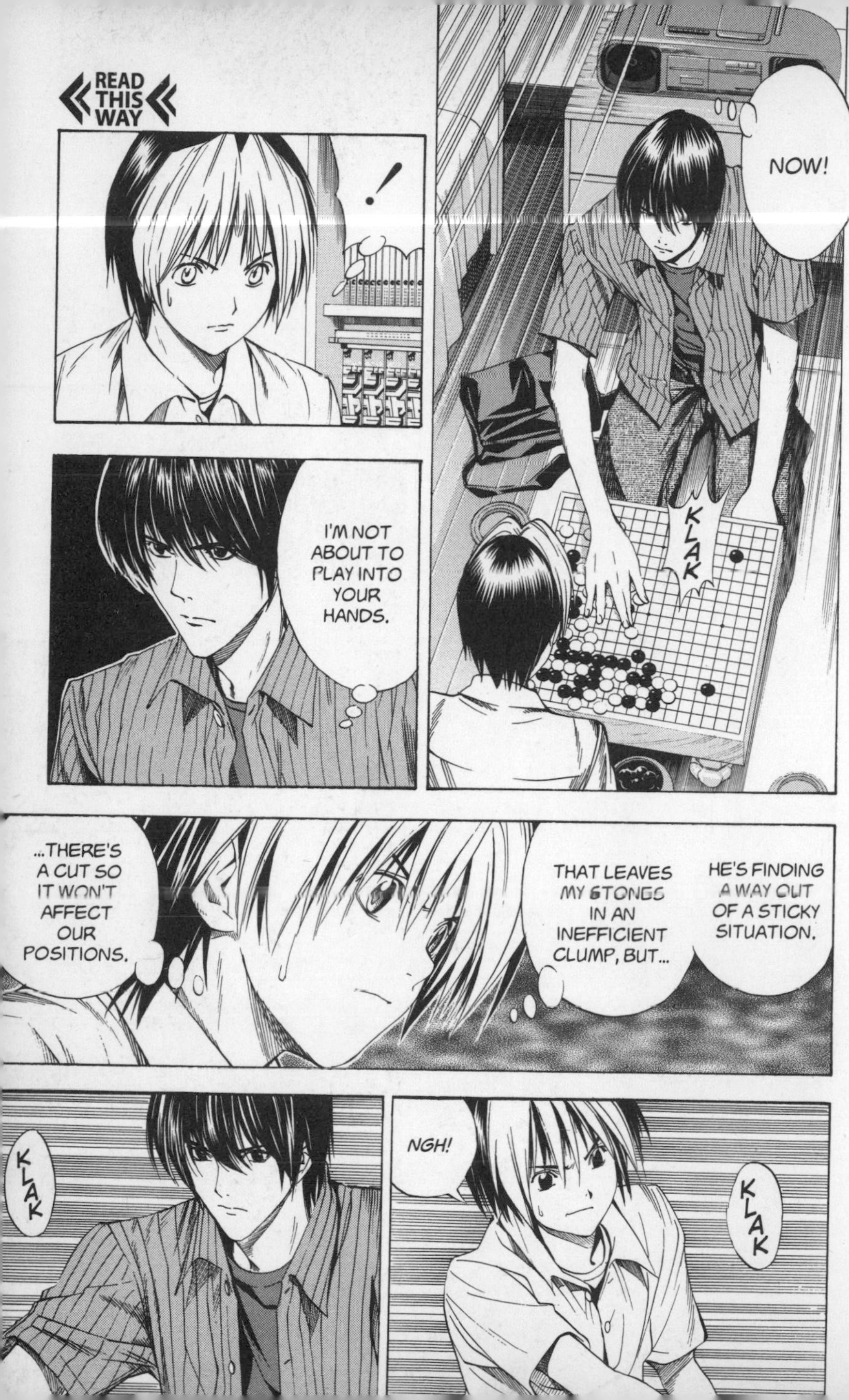
READ THIS WAY
NOW!
KLAK
!
I'M NOT ABOUT TO PLAY INTO YOUR HANDS.
HE'S FINDING A WAY OUT OF A STICKY SITUATION.
THAT LEAVES MY STONES IN AN INEFFICIENT CLUMP, BUT...
...THERE'S A CUT SO IT WON'T AFFECT OUR POSITIONS.
NGH!
KLAK
KLAK

KLAK
ANOTHER FORCING MOVE.
I CAN'T SPEND TIME RE-SPONDING TO THAT.
I CAN'T AFFORD TO GET BEHIND IN TERRITORY.
KLAK
KLAK
KLAK
ISUMI'S STONE IS FLOATING!
IF I RIP THROUGH WHITE'S POSITION WHILE ATTACKING HERE...
KLAK

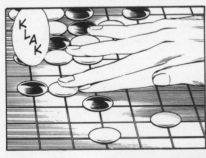

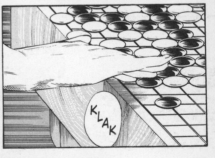

IF I
CONNECT
HERE...

...I'LL HAVE
MORE
TERRITORY!

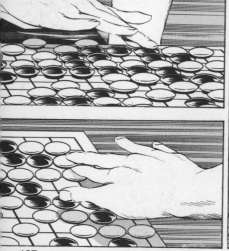

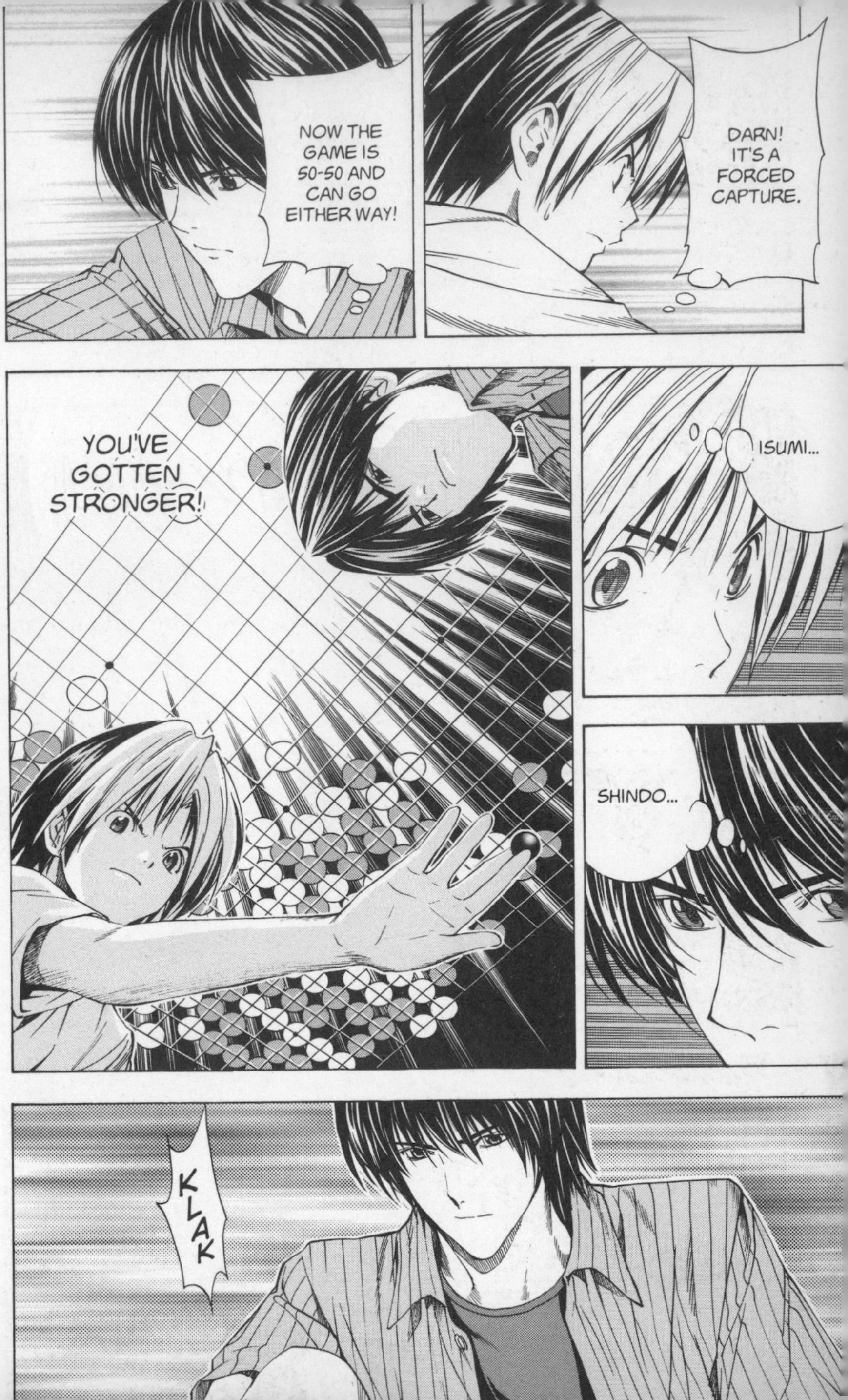
DARN! IT'S A FORCED CAPTURE.
NOW THE GAME IS 50-50 AND CAN GO EITHER WAY!
ISUMI...
SHINDO...
YOU'VE GOTTEN STRONGER!
KLAK

IF I CAN THREATEN THE WHITE STONES IN THE UPPER AREA...

KLAK

UNGH...

GASP!

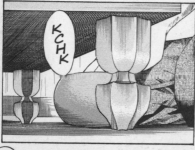

KCHK

...

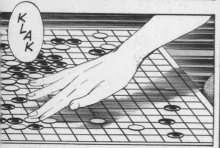

KLAK

189

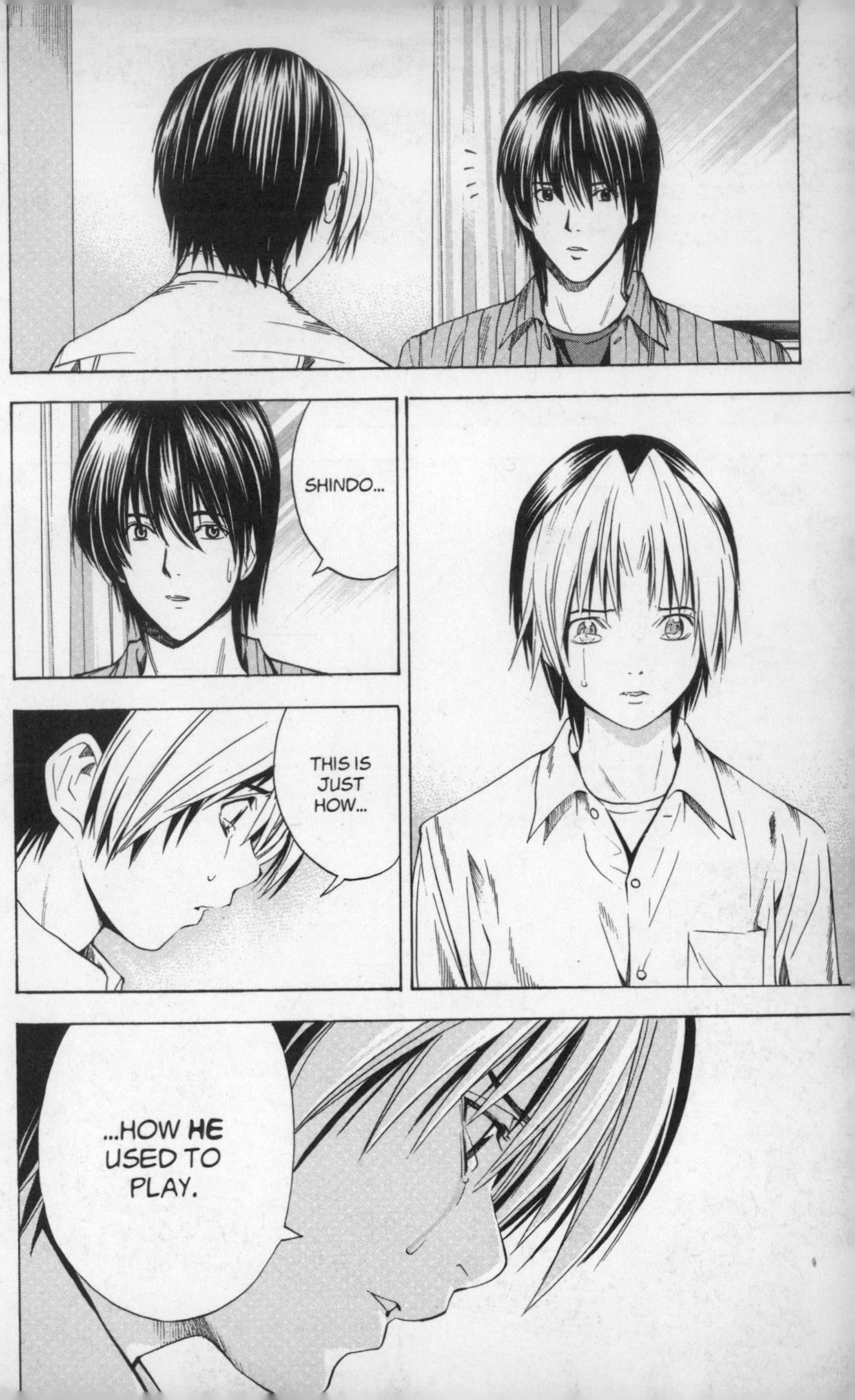
SHINDO...
THIS IS JUST HOW...
...HOW HE USED TO PLAY.

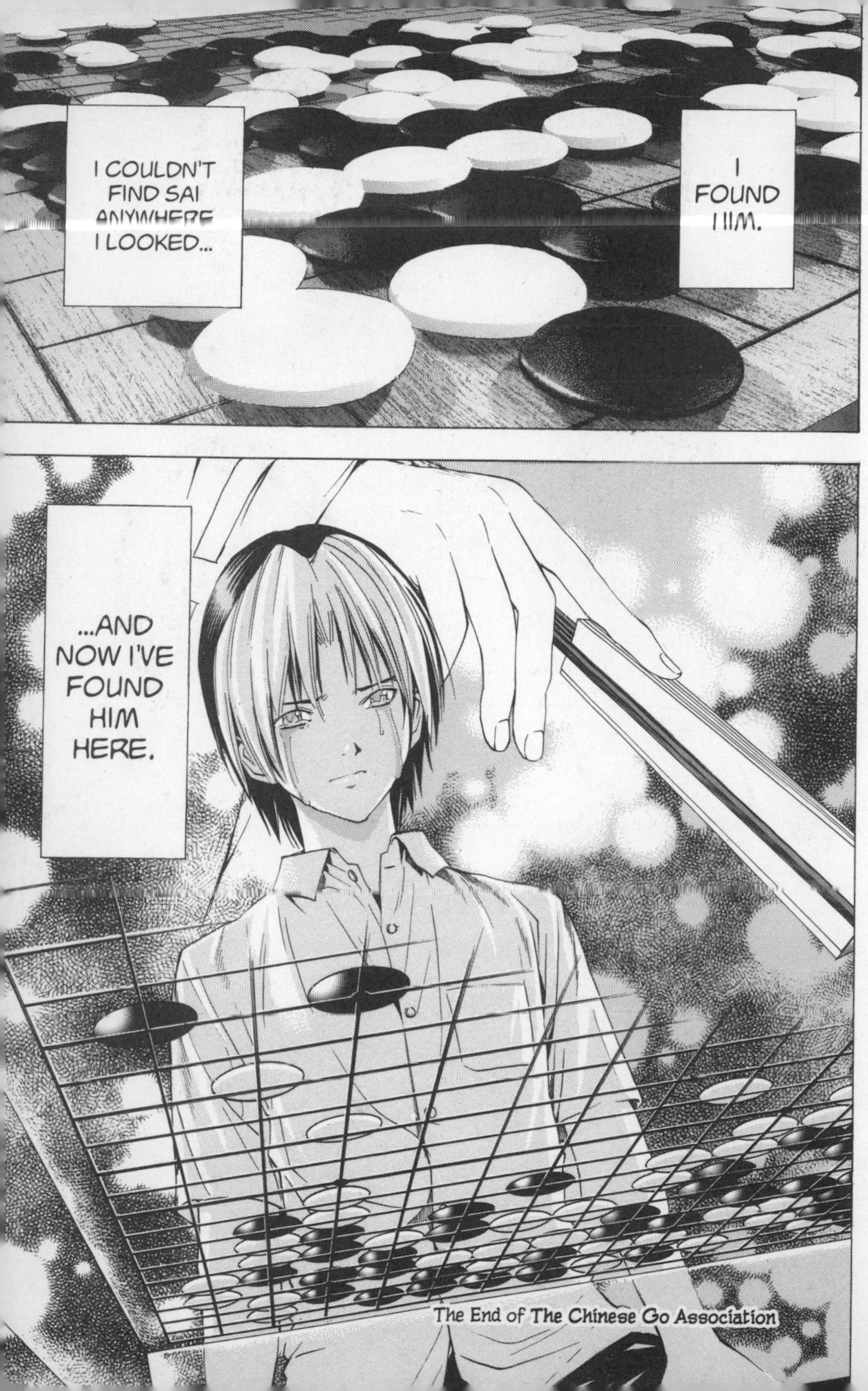
I FOUND HIM.
I COULDN'T FIND SAI ANYWHERE I LOOKED...
...AND NOW I'VE FOUND HIM HERE.
The End of The Chinese Go Association

Next Volume Preview

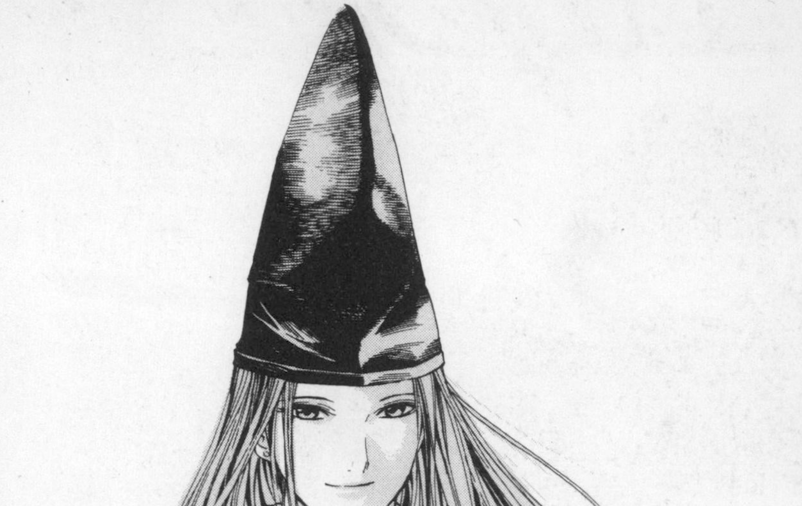

From the moment he began playing go, Hikaru has relied on Sai's supernatural support. Now that his mentor has vanished into thin air, will he be able to handle the demands of life as a pro on his own? Meanwhile, Hikaru's archrival Akira is playing so well even veteran players tremble at the mention of his name. And now, at long last, the two boys will face each other across a go board...

COMING OCTOBER 2009

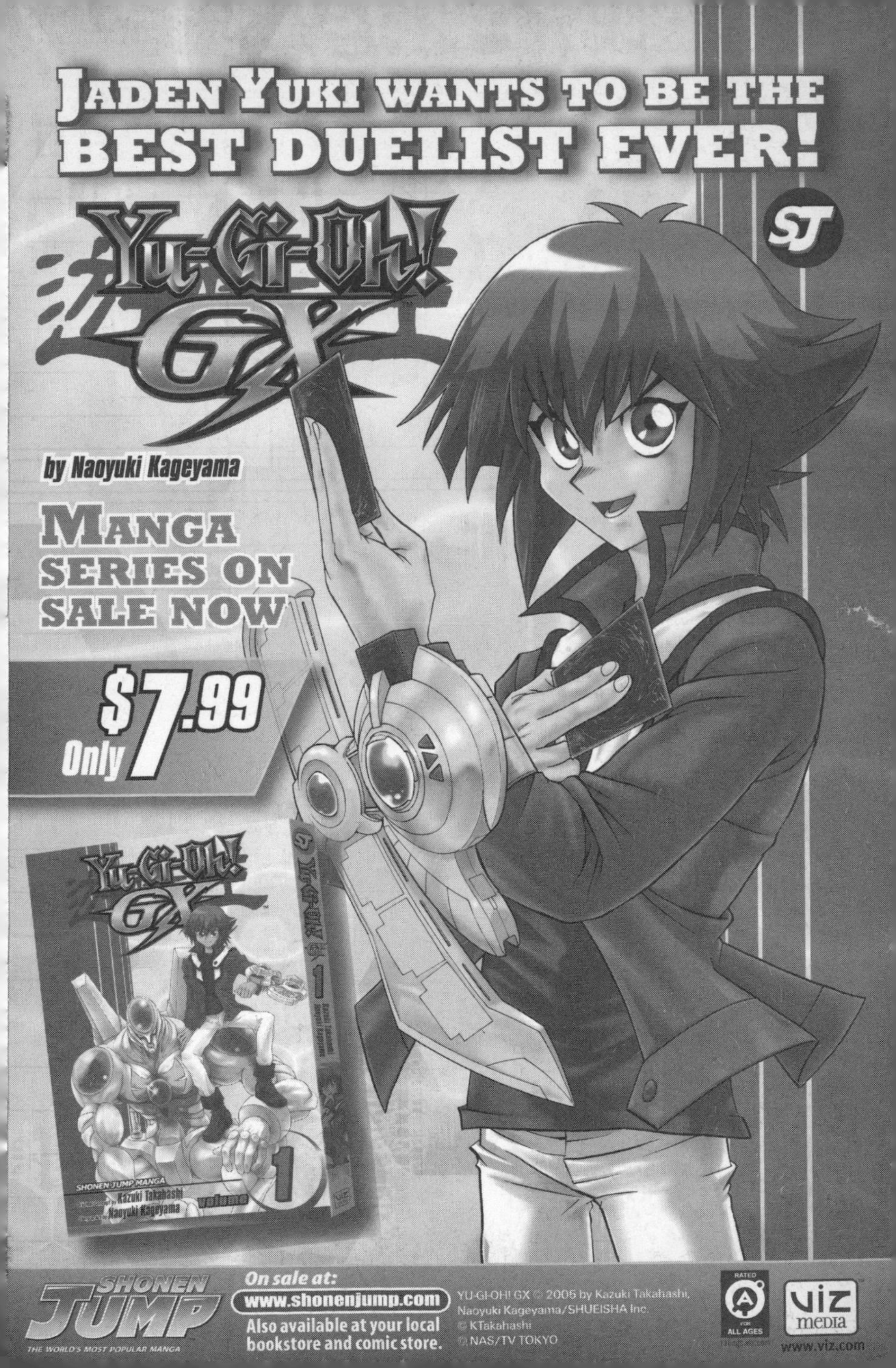

JADEN YUKI WANTS TO BE THE
BEST DUELIST EVER!
SJ
YU-GI-OH! GX
by Naoyuki Kageyama
MANGA
SERIES ON
SALE NOW
Only $7.99
YU-GI-OH! GX
SHONEN JUMP MANGA
Kazuki Takahashi
Naoyuki Kageyama
volume
1
SHONEN JUMP
THE WORLD'S MOST POPULAR MANGA
On sale at:
www.shonenjump.com
Also available at your local
bookstore and comic store.
YU-GI-OH! GX © 2005 by Kazuki Takahashi,
Naoyuki Kageyama/SHUEISHA Inc.
© KTakahashi
© NAS/TV TOKYO
RATED
A
FOR
ALL AGES
VIZ
media
www.viz.com

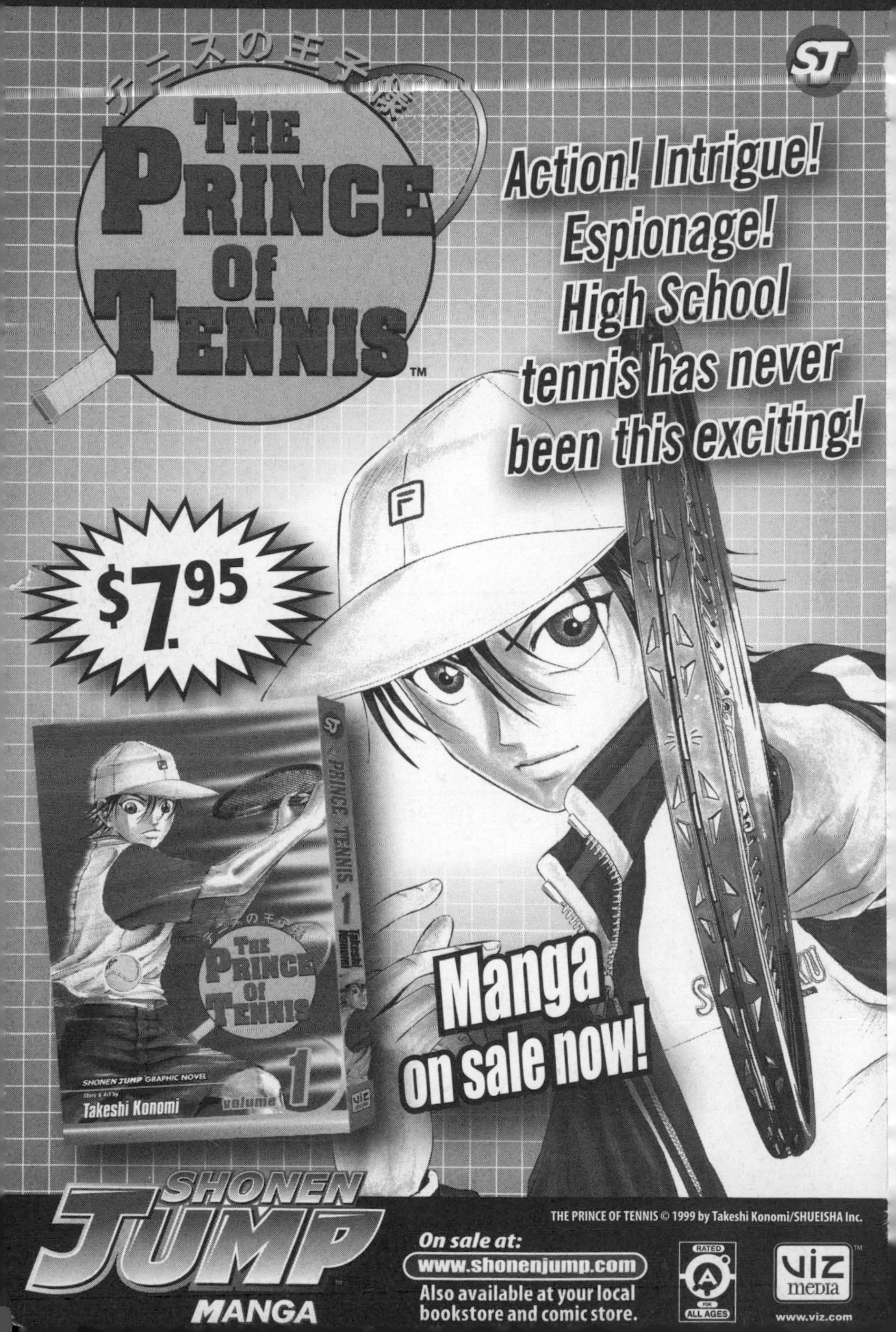

SJ
THE PRINCE OF TENNIS™
Action! Intrigue! Espionage! High School tennis has never been this exciting!
$7.95
SHONEN JUMP GRAPHIC NOVEL
Story & Art by
Takeshi Konomi
volume 1
Manga on sale now!
SHONEN JUMP MANGA
THE PRINCE OF TENNIS © 1999 by Takeshi Konomi/SHUEISHA Inc.
On sale at:
www.shonenjump.com
Also available at your local bookstore and comic store.
RATED A FOR ALL AGES
VIZ media
www.viz.com

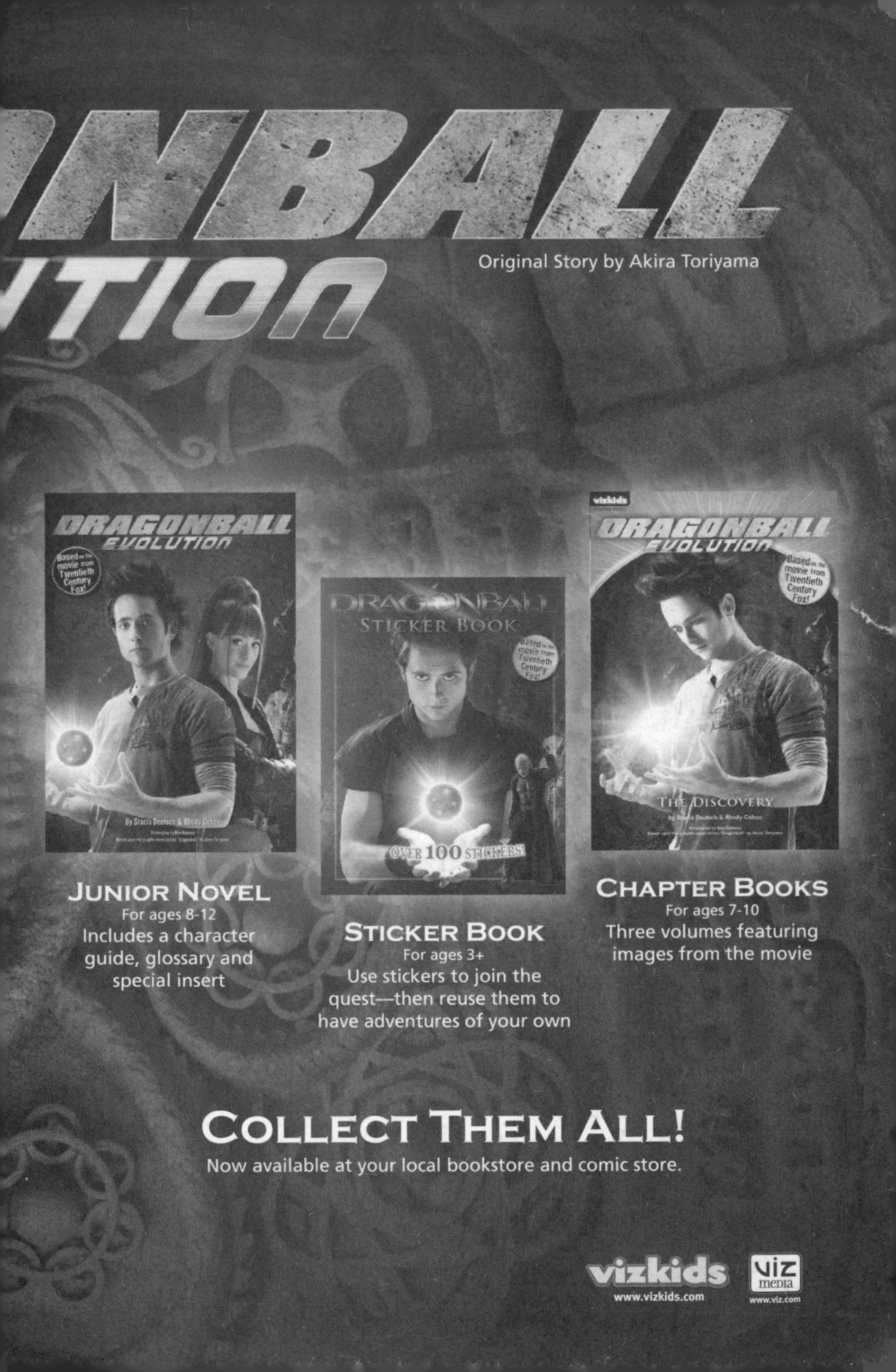

NBALL
TION
Original Story by Akira Toriyama
DRAGONBALL EVOLUTION
Based on the movie from Twentieth Century Fox!
By Stacia Deutsch & Rhody Cohon
DRAGONBALL STICKER BOOK
Based on the movie from Twentieth Century Fox!
OVER 100 STICKERS!
vizkids
DRAGONBALL EVOLUTION
Based on the movie from Twentieth Century Fox!
THE DISCOVERY
by Stacia Deutsch & Rhody Cohon
JUNIOR NOVEL
For ages 8-12
Includes a character guide, glossary and special insert
STICKER BOOK
For ages 3+
Use stickers to join the quest—then reuse them to have adventures of your own
CHAPTER BOOKS
For ages 7-10
Three volumes featuring images from the movie
COLLECT THEM ALL!
Now available at your local bookstore and comic store.
vizkids
www.vizkids.com
VIZ media
www.viz.com

DRAGO
EVOL

Goku and his friends must save the world from evil Lord Piccolo!

Tell us what you think about SHONEN JUMP manga!

Our survey is now available online.
Go to: www.SHONENJUMP.com/mangasurvey

Help us make our product offering better!